# THE EMPTY SEASHELL

# THE EMPTY SEASHELL

## WITCHCRAFT AND DOUBT ON AN INDONESIAN ISLAND

## NILS BUBANDT

Cornell University Press
Ithaca and London

First published 2014 by Cornell University Press
First printing, Cornell Paperbacks, 2014

Printed in the United States of America

Library of Congress Cataloging-in-Publication Data

Bubandt, Nils, author.
    The empty seashell : witchcraft and doubt on an Indonesian island /
Nils Bubandt.
        pages cm
    Includes bibliographical references and index.
    ISBN 978-0-8014-5295-6 (cloth : alk. paper)
    ISBN 978-0-8014-7945-8 (pbk. : alk. paper)
    1. Witchcraft—Indonesia—Halmahera. 2. Halmahera (Indonesia)—
Religion. 3. Ethnology—Indonesia—Halmahera. 4. Belief and doubt.
I. Title.
    BF1584.I5B83    2014
    133.4'30959856—dc23          2014025811

Cornell University Press strives to use environmentally responsible
suppliers and materials to the fullest extent possible in the publishing
of its books. Such materials include vegetable-based, low-VOC inks
and acid-free papers that are recycled, totally chlorine-free, or partly
composed of nonwood fibers. For further information, visit our website at
www.cornellpress.cornell.edu.

Cloth printing          10 9 8 7 6 5 4 3 2 1
Paperback printing      10 9 8 7 6 5 4 3 2 1

For L.—my adopted father in Buli—
who taught me everything he didn't know about witches

And for Asta—my daughter in Denmark—
the only child in kindergarten who knew exactly what her father did at work:
wrote a book about witches

# CONTENTS

# PREFACE

## The Dog That Wasn't

I have never seen a cannibal witch. The closest I have ever come to seeing one was in June 1992. I had been doing fieldwork for four months in Buli, a coastal and predominantly Christian village on the island of Halmahera in eastern Indonesia, and for reasons that I hope will become apparent, the experience of *not* seeing a witch goes to the heart of the topic of this ethnography—namely, the presence and absence of witchcraft in Buli.

It was well past midnight. Still, I could not fall asleep. I had been suffering from a cold for a few days, but I had nevertheless arranged to go on a fishing trip with Kenari and his son-in-law, Anton, the next day.[1] We were supposed to leave when the morning star (*siwséwil ca*) rose over the bay—at around four o'clock in the morning—in order to catch the offshore breeze (*latan wagaf*) that would bring us to the distant reefs before the sun grew enough in strength to make the coral fish less "lazy" and therefore harder to spear. Unable to find rest, I fetched my shortwave radio and clambered under the mosquito net. I was fine-tuning the radio to the news on BBC World when I heard something outside the house, right outside the corner post next to my bed. It sounded like a dog gnawing on a juicy bone. In itself, this was not unusual. Dogs and cats were a constant nuisance to me. They would sneak into the kitchen, breaching the barricade I had set up at the door, and steal any food that was not securely locked up. However, there was something out of the ordinary about the sound of this particular dog. The sound of chewing did not come from the ground. Rather, it appeared to emanate from the top of the house, as if the dog had somehow climbed the house post and was now masticating on top of the roof. This was impossible. Dogs cannot climb vertical slopes. Besides, the house had a sago-leaf roof, and a dog would fall straight through it, even if it managed to climb up there. I listened for a while. But apart from the background chirping of crickets, the occasional chewing sounds were all I heard. It would take too long to light up the petroleum pressure lamp, I decided. Instead, feeling slightly unsettled, I grabbed a flashlight in one hand and a machete in the other and went outside. I found nothing suspicious. So I went back inside and climbed into bed. There was definitely something strange, even eerie, about this dog that I could not find.

I had heard many stories about the *gua*—cannibal witches who attack people to eat their liver—but I had always shrugged them off. They were ethnographically interesting but not directly relevant to my existence or the conditions of my fieldwork. When I was caught in the dark, however, these stories of the *gua* and the anxiety they provoke in Buli were suddenly all too real. *Gua*, also referred to in the regional dialect of Indonesian as *suanggi*, are human beings—fellow villagers, neighbors, family, or friends—whose greed has forced them into an alliance with a *gua* spirit. They appear to be ordinary humans, but sometimes, especially at night, they turn into *gua*: witches, cannibals, shape-shifters. Essentially, the *gua* spirit possesses its human host and enables the host to fly around at night to prey on other people against whom the host holds a grudge. Some say that it is merely the head of the human host that goes on these nocturnal jaunts, its entrails dangling from its neck. I had heard that cannibal witches would often congregate on the edge of the village where my house was located, and from time to time one could indeed hear the high-pitched calls of the *ngangá*, the *kokók*, and the *cokaíko*—bird forms that the *gua* can assume—from the nearby sago swamp. I had also been told that the *gua* preferred to perch in the rafters of houses and hide there until the inhabitants had fallen asleep before jumping onto the chest of their victim to eat his or her liver. Only a few weeks earlier I had been to a funeral wake, where whispers that the deceased had been attacked by a *gua* in precisely this manner had alternated with Christian psalms and prayer for his salvation. Finally, I was also aware that *gua* witches preferred to attack people who were alone, and that they frequently disguised themselves as ordinary animals just before they attacked. Dogs and wild pigs were animal shapes that the cannibal witches often assumed. In fact, I recalled in the darkness, the *gua*'s favorite animal double was the hunting dog—the most human of all animals.

Perhaps I should have installed electricity in the house after all, as people had advised me to do. Perhaps I should have listened to those who had warned me not to live alone: especially not here, so close to the sago swamps and coconut groves that line both sides of the river that runs through the village of Waiflí. During the first few weeks after my then girlfriend—plagued by asthma and recurring tropical ulcers—had left, and I had insisted on remaining alone in the house in Waiflí, a small group of children would turn up every evening, as if by prior arrangement, and pick a spot to sleep in the house. They were insistent, albeit clearly not enthusiastic about staying, and I suspected they had been told to do so by Kenari, my adopted father in the village, in order to keep me company. Everybody knows that *gua* witches rarely attack people in groups. Therefore there is safety in numbers when guarding against witchcraft, also for adults in the company of children. After a while, however, the children had stopped coming. Presumably, their disinclination had won out over adult insistence. Now, alone in the dark with the gnawing sounds of the invisible dog, I was beginning to regret my elective solitude. But I told myself I was just being silly. I tucked the mosquito net tight around the mattress and turned up the volume on the radio.

BBC World News reported that Denmark had scored a surprise win over Germany to take the European Cup in soccer. The news broadcast also featured a report from Israel on the election campaign that would secure Yitzhak Rabin a second term in office as prime minister, followed by an analysis of the joint memorandum of understanding signed by superpower leaders Bush and Yeltsin to continue the reduction of nuclear arms. The radio program was barely audible above the static. That night in the dark, this added to my feeling that even the soccer triumph of my own native country, the rekindled prospects for peace in the Middle East, and a significant decrease in the threat of nuclear war were a world away. Cameos from a world I missed, but from which I also felt detached. It took more than a decade, and a long analytical detour, for me to realize that the two worlds of uncertainty—global insecurity in a post–Cold War era, and the uncertainty and absence that traverse all aspects of witchcraft in Buli—were, in fact, similar; that far from being a phenomenon that epitomizes the quintessentially exotic, witchcraft for people in Buli was characterized by the same aporias and (im)possibilities that haunt Western concerns about global security (Burke 2002). Witchcraft is similar to the risk of nuclear war, of global warming, or, perhaps most aptly, of contemporary terrorism: they all constitute an overriding but indeterminable threat, a threat that is both real and yet often absents itself from daily experience. Just as I have never seen a cannibal witch, I have never had firsthand experience of nuclear war or seen a terrorist in the flesh. "World risks" like nuclear war and terrorism, to use Ulrich Beck's (2002) term, may be driven by a different epistemological logic than the localized danger of witchcraft, but experientially the terrorist and the witch are similar in at least three ways. Both, firstly, are seemingly everywhere and nowhere at the same time. The witch, like the terrorist, is a radical other, simultaneously real and unimaginable (Baudrillard 1993; 2003:62). It is the uncertain reality of such absence and impossibility that interests me in this book. Not-seeing the dog was in many ways as real as seeing it, its absence somehow potent testimony to its reality. And yet this reality was continuously in question, uncertain. Secondly, like terrorism, witchcraft is particularly pernicious when it recruits its evildoers from inside one's own trusted ranks (Geschiere 2013); when the radical other may in fact be like oneself. Under such conditions, a frightening duality of presence and absence, an impossible "other" at the heart of the self, characterizes both terrorism and, as this book will try to show, witchcraft. Thirdly, as in the War on Terror where counterterrorism often seems to breed and reinvigorate terrorism, the attempts to deny, combat, and eradicate the radical other of witchcraft in Buli appear to reproduce, historically and socially, the very problem they seek to banish. This, too, is a theme that runs through the chapters of this book.

A few minutes after I had cranked up the volume on the radio the chewing sound was back. This time, it was even closer, louder. In the darkness, panic set in. "Maybe the dog is inside the house!" I remember thinking. I snatched up the flashlight and leaned over the edge of my mattress to peer under the bed. Nothing. Now I was sure the dog had to be just outside. I darted outside, this time forgetting my sarong. Again, nothing. By this point, I was torn. Even as I mustered all my critical reason, I could not deny the tingling sensation on my spine. The invisible *gua* was bodily real in a way that all my doubts about its reality could not dispel. And yet I wanted to stand my ground, in and with this house—physically and epistemologically. A few months into fieldwork the house had become my comfort zone, my bastion of privacy in the social sea of village life. It was a place to which I could withdraw to write notes, listen to the radio, and escape for a few precious hours from the pressure of people speaking to me in Buli and taking pleasure in my halting answers. This house, I felt, was where I could be an anthropologist—of the proper kind who writes (Geertz 1973:19).

I had borrowed the house from Alena, one of my adopted sisters, during her pregnancy. Alena and her husband, Anton, had moved temporarily to Kenari's house. Alena—so I learned much later—had repeatedly encountered spirits near the house and was afraid that a *gua* or a *puntiana* (a female spirit that is said to eat or steal the fetus from the mother's womb) was trying to claim her unborn baby. So it was through an ironic set of circumstances—which, unbeknownst to me, had seen Anton and Alena flee the house in fear of witches and other spirits to a safe haven in the company of family closer to the center of the village—that their house had, foolishly in the eyes of most people in Buli, become my sanctuary, and the place where I could maintain some semblance of personal privacy and professional identity. No witch, or at least so I felt, was going to chase me out of it. The chewing did not return. Still, I got no sleep the rest of that night. Maybe it was my cold that made me restless; maybe it was the absent dog that continued to make its presence felt.

The next morning, well before dawn, I went fishing with Kenari and Anton as planned. Standing in the darkness of the lean-to that served as their kitchen, preparing our spear guns and fishing tackle before we set off, I told Kenari and Selena, his wife, about the previous night. I told them about not being able to sleep and about hearing a dog. I stopped midsentence in my account, racking my brain for the local word for "chewing," when Kenari finished the sentence for me: ". . . a dog eating?" Surprised that Kenari could guess what I wanted to say, I confirmed it, perhaps a little too enthusiastically. Hearing this, Selena turned her head sharply and launched into one of the tirades for which she was notorious:

> It was a *gua*. That is what they do! They sit and watch us, to prey on us (*tantano it*). Now do you understand? You were lucky you didn't fall asleep. Otherwise, it would have "sat on you" (*tontonga au*) for sure. Don't you realize that the area back there is full of *gua*, including . . . I do not care, Kenari, I am telling him . . . "The Bald One"!

Kenari took his wife's apparent defiance stoically; the time for concealment had clearly passed. At the same time, he still seemed less sure that it was a *gua*. Or rather, he emphasized how knowledge about the whys and wherefores of witchcraft was itself a complicated matter:

> Maybe it was a *gua* and maybe it wasn't. You Westerners have the idea that there are no *gua* and therefore you aren't afraid of them. I agree completely with this. It is a very good system, and you are right. But you have to be careful, Nils. You should not be too foolhardy. Don't walk around alone without aim or purpose (*sebarang*). And don't announce that you do not believe in *gua*! After all, there might be a *gua* present hearing this who wants to prove you wrong! You have to be careful not to act as if you are too "high" (*puiso*), but also do not act too "lowly" (*papo*). Don't act like a big boss, ordering people around while remaining tight with your money. On the other hand, don't give your heart [literally, "your liver"] to everyone indiscriminately. A person with "a soft liver" [*hati lombo*, in Malukan Malay] also easily becomes the victim of a *gua*.

In the village of Buli, he continued, one had to be circumspect:

> As our ancestors used to say, "You must be cautious, my friend (*Mpake istiár, watau*). When you wade through the river, look out for barnacles (*sisiám*) in the water." If you don't, you will cut your feet! It is the same with

the *gua*, Nils. Don't frolic in the water without looking down to see where you step. You have to take care (*mjaga*)!

Clearly, the reality of witches required caution in Buli. This need for caution was only heightened by the epistemological uncertainties of witchcraft. The very fact that the reality of witchcraft hides itself from human beings—like the barnacles in the tidal mouth of the river—means that one has to be extra careful. For almost a century, Dutch missionaries and local ministers had preached that there were no witches, and being a good Christian himself, Kenari had to agree. At the same time, announcing this could, in itself, be dangerous if a witch heard it. The contradiction embodied in this statement is painfully clear to people in Buli, and it is by no means a sign of failed or inconsistent logic. Nor is it proof that they have no abstract theoretical interest in the matter, as E. E. Evans-Pritchard (1937) famously claimed about the Azande. Rather, it is a contradiction, patent to all in Buli, that grows by necessity from the ontology and epistemology of witchcraft itself. Ontologically, witches are real, but this reality itself has an ambiguous status because it is expressed in absence as much as in presence. This means that the epistemology of witchcraft, the conditions of knowing anything about witches, is always fraught at best and riddled with contradiction. Witchcraft entails an exceedingly corporeal experience (being straddled and having your liver eaten), but at the same time the reality of the *gua* absents itself from, and is in practice inaccessible to, human experience, human senses, and human understanding. This (ir)reality paradoxically serves only to exacerbate its menace. In that sense, the fact that I did not see a *gua* that night was pretty much as close to the reality of witchcraft as anyone ever comes in Buli. The corporeal and experiential reality of witchcraft is intimated more truthfully by an account of its absence and the necessary doubts about it than by an account of beliefs about its presence. Witchcraft is not an object of belief but an experiential aporia. It is an intractable problem, an experience that has no meaningful culmination. The *gua*'s presence is as real as it is impossible. Its absence, meanwhile, is as frustratingly unnerving as it is eagerly anticipated. When it comes to witchcraft, nothing is certain. And while it could have been "The Bald One," an older man and a former church leader (I. *majelis*), who in his *gua* form had been gnawing outside my house the night before, it might also have been something else. Even Selena had to admit this. When it comes to witchcraft, humans can only "guess" (*fatailo*). The following week or so, I slept in Kenari and Selena's already packed house. This arrangement—as we all agreed—was "better" (*mancapá*).

A skeptical anthropologist who does not quite see a witch in the shape of a dog: this is as close a match to the uncertainties that characterize Buli witchcraft as I can think of. For my uneasy skepticism of a witch I could not see was not at all the privileged symptom of a Western "disbelief" that was radically different from "native beliefs" in witchcraft. Rather, as this book will seek to show, my doubts intimately reflected the doubt and skepticism that run through all aspects of witchcraft for Buli people. The absent dog is in that sense my "arrival story" (Pratt 1986), my literary device to introduce the impossible experience that witchcraft constitutes in Buli. The truly unsettling truth about witchcraft in Buli is that it is always unsettled. As a consequence, the reality of witchcraft can never be stabilized into belief. Rather, it is continuously left in suspension, in doubt. Witchcraft is most present, in all manner of ways, through its absence; its reality constituted by its impossibility. The epistemological and ontological concerns associated with these aporias, and their consequences for the way we think anthropologically about witchcraft in particular and about doubt in general, are the subject of this book.

*[handwritten annotations:]*

literary devices to illustrate ye idea of witchcraft

Scot – yes, of course there are witches, it is implore to think otherwise, but in true case here is no witchcraft, doubt triumphs...

doubt & change / becoming

perfect metaphor for a flux of very [?] totally destructive + self-contradictory nation / deconstruction

Witchcraft is like Brexit...?

Derrida – the moment we understand text undermines or deconstructs itself

ye fact that it is impossible makes it more real?

we want to believe...

Julian Wolfreys calls trauma a kind of aporia, from which there is no recovery, no end

aporia – "an irresolvable internal contradiction or logical disjunction in a text, argument or theory" Rhetorically – "where the speaker expresses a doubt – possibly feigned – + asks the audience how to proceed" (dubitatio)

# Acknowledgments

M ore than two decades in the making, this book has had plenty of time to incur more debts than I will ever be able to repay. It began its life with nineteen months of fieldwork in North Maluku between 1991 and 1993, supplemented incrementally by an additional twenty-six months between 1995 and 2012. This latter period happened to witness the emergence of new and incredibly exciting theoretical literature on witchcraft within both anthropology and history. This literature rebelled against the idea that witchcraft was a "traditional" phenomenon, and highlighted instead how the contradictions and injustices inherent in global modernity were incorporated into the perpetually malleable beliefs about witchcraft. This book is a contribution to these recent studies of the close links between witchcraft and modernity. It also differs, I think, from much of this literature by beginning and ending not with belief but with doubt. Staying ethnographically close to doubt has meant that this book cannot follow the now-popular path of describing how witchcraft beliefs change in the acid bath of an uncertain modernity. Rather, it follows how people have historically sought to harness the assumed certainties of modernity in an unsuccessful attempt to grapple with the doubts of witchcraft. The book proposes the need to rethink not only the relationship between witchcraft and modernity but also modernity's alleged monopoly on doubt.

Over the years, many people have directed me toward this conclusion. Each of the following has in his or her own way contributed to making this book possible, without any of them being responsible for its flaws: Douglas Lewis, James Fox, Michael Young, Penny Graham, June Carey, Rohan Bastin, Bob Tonkinson, Borut

Telban, Don Gardner, Ward Keeler, Philip Taylor, Thomas Reuter, Gary Kildea, Chris Duncan, Jos Platenkamp, Knut Rio, Annelin Eriksen, Bruce Kapferer, Don Kulick, Mark Graham, Rane Willerslev, Poul Pedersen, Lotte Meinert, Morten Axel Pedersen, Rikke Gotfredsen, Joel Robbins, Niels Barfoed, James Scott, Keir Martin, Thomas Wentzer, Rasmus Dyring, Morten Nielsen, Patsy Spyer, Nina Vohnsen, Ton Otto. Many thanks also to Anne Skjelborg, still my close friend, for the years she managed to put up with me talking about this book, as well as to the Bubandt "clan," Ellis, Ole, Anne, Helle, and Find, for relentlessly teasing me about "this book you say you are writing."

I owe a particular thank you to the staff and guests at Klitgaarden, an academic retreat in the windswept north of Denmark where I did much of the actual writing. Klitgaarden, it turned out, was the perfect place to think about the power of absence. And Sanne Krogh Groth: thank you for being there, too, and for being there in general. Anna Tsing and Peter Geschiere took a keen and kind interest in this project and have both been fantastic throughout. I want to thank Anna for our Klitgaarden "brainstorm walks," which always made me think differently about my material. Peter earned my complete admiration and eternal gratitude for his generous and incredibly intelligent comments on an earlier draft of the manuscript. Thanks are also owed to the second and anonymous reviewer for Cornell University Press for an immensely astute reading and a thought-provoking set of comments. I hope I have answered at least some of the queries and objections raised by Peter and this reviewer, and I accept that all remaining errors are my own. Heidi Flegal from Fluency read the entire manuscript and provided innumerable and invaluable suggestions for change that vastly improved the quality and consistency of its language and presentation. Louise Hilmar from Moesgaard Museum drew the diagrams and maps. Ingeborg Eggink from the Tropenmuseum in Amsterdam provided kind and efficient permission to reproduce archival photographs. Thanks, finally, to Peter Potter, Susan Specter, and Marian Rogers at Cornell University Press for agreeing to publish this and for all their work on its production.

Initial fieldwork research in Indonesia between 1991 and 1994 was financed by an Australian National University scholarship and undertaken under the auspices of LIPI (Lembaga Ilmu Pengetahuan Indonesia) under the sponsorship of Pattimura University in Ambon. Mus Huliselan, Nelles Janwarin, Bupati Bahar Andili, Lucky Sondakh, and Sinyo Harry Sarundajang were helpful at various stages with administrative affairs and permits. The dozen or so periods of fieldwork in Buli between 1995 and 2012 were generously financed by the Danish Research Council for the Humanities (SHF), the Crown Prince Frederik and Crown Princess Mary Foundation, the Carlsberg Foundation, the Danish Council for Strategic Research, and the Danish Research Council for Independent

Research on the Humanities (FKK). This book was made possible by a kind grant from the Aarhus University Research Fund.

There is no word for "thank you" in the Buli language. Gifts are reciprocated in kind and not in words. A lot, then, continues to be owed to a lot of people in Buli and North Maluku who decided to include me in their lives and who passionately shared my interest in trying to puzzle out what the hell the *gua* and the *suanggi* were up to: Sandara Guslaw and Lingoro Veplun and their children, Lazarus, Afrina, Afrida, Lukas, Lamek, Yulin, Atalina, Alte, Lisna, and Yance, all of whom have families of their own now; Sefe, Ipsan, and Annie Raja; Wadaka Batawi, Kaibi Raja, and Wilhelm; Tangkea Guslaw and his family; Om Siang; Om Bulia Raja and family; Om Ponco Batawi and Samadar Batawi; Serikat Guslaw and Maria Rorano, as well as their children, Marlinus, Sarni, Hermince, Goliat, and Erik, all of whom have families of their own; Yehuda Guslaw and family; Mengapa Barabakem and family; Dirikus Ibis and family; Merdeka Tayawi and Tako Bauronga, Mapíng Gogó Tayawi, and Sepnat Bauronga; Kandati Raja and Baima Tomalou; Moki Wararag and family. Thanks also to Nulzuludin Sjah and family; Firman Sjah and family; Abdullah Sjah and family; Anghany Tanjung and family; Assegaf Yahya and family; Tetti Herawati and family; Chi Meydi and Pak Reymon and Pak Siong. It is my hope that this book does not disappoint or embarrass anyone, and that one day the *gua* will be gone from Buli (and the *suanggi* from North Maluku) without the shadow of a doubt.

Back in Denmark, Asta accepted my frequent absences stoically against the promise that we would one day go to Buli together. I vow to honor that promise.

# THE EMPTY SEASHELL

# THE SHELL OF THE NAUTILUS

Convention in Buli has it that if you find a live nautilus cephalopod (*benga-benga*), you are a witch, a *gua*. No one knows—or admits to knowing—exactly what the strange creature that occupies the distinctive nautilus shells looks like, and I have never heard anyone claim they had actually found a living nautilus. And yet it is common knowledge that the nautilus shells can have an occupant, a disturbing "content" (*ni loló*).

Empty shells of the chambered nautilus (a primitive relative of the octopus), called *Nautilus pompilius* in the scientific literature, regularly drift ashore on the tidal atolls and coral reefs that form an arc around Buli village on the central eastern coast of the island of Halmahera. Coveted by international shell traders for their enigmatic beauty and symmetry, in Buli these empty shells are like traces of a crime, indices of a dreaded possibility. The absent cephalopod is one of the many signs of the hidden yet undeniable reality of witchcraft. The empty shells are also a troubling reminder that the witch or *gua* might be none other than yourself. They are evidence of the absent presence of the *gua*, the irrefutable but fundamentally inaccessible reality of witchcraft that hovers on the edge of human understanding, human language, and the human senses, but which nevertheless remains a constant visceral and emotional concern in everyday life. The *gua* is a reality "under erasure" (Derrida 1976), its meaning and reality both confirmed and undermined by its own nature. It is simultaneously an irrepressible physical reality and an inaccessible metaphysicality. The *gua* is on the one hand eminently corporeal: it beats people up, possesses them, eats their liver, molests and kills them. On the other

hand, it is a shadowy figure that can only ever be glimpsed through one's periph-
eral vision, never gazed upon directly. In truth, nothing about the *gua* is certain;
it is a master of deception, playing tricks on human consciousness, knowledge,
memory, and senses. A *gua* witch can take any form—human or nonhuman, animal or mechanical. It can become invisible, steal your shadow, and occupy your
body without detection. It may use the face of a friend, distort the memory of both
its victims and its hosts, and disguise the effects of its attacks as "ordinary" forms
of illness. Where the *gua* is concerned, as people in Buli say, "We can only guess"
(*itet rai be*). The possibility that the nautilus shell may have "something in it" (*ni
loló*) when you find it on the beach therefore intimates a reality that remains by necessity "undecidable." When someone discovers a nautilus shell he or she is in the
presence of an existential possibility with which all people in Buli live: that anyone
could be a witch without knowing it. Upon first seeing the shell from afar, floating in the shallow water, the lone fisherman or shellfish collector is faced with the
possibility that the shell could have an occupant, and that he or she, too, could have
a hidden "content," a *gua* spirit. This inescapable yet undecidable possibility of
witchcraft—its suffusion of all aspects of Buli subjectivity and sociality as well as
its relevance for a different approach to the study of witchcraft more generally—is
the topic of this book.

People in Buli make a sharp distinction between the *gua* and its frequently fatal
illness (*ungan*)—which I will call "witchcraft"—on the one hand, and *payao* or
*bodiga*—which I will call "sorcery"—on the other.[1] In close—and for me personally uncanny—conformity with the description of witchcraft and sorcery given
by E. E. Evans-Pritchard (1937) in his classic work on the Azande in Southern
Sudan, sorcery in Buli is an acquired or learned technique associated with spells
and the manipulation of objects, while witchcraft has a corporeal and "psychic"
component. For Buli people, as for the Azande, witchcraft is associated with a
kernel or seed, nocturnal flight, the ability to turn into animal form, and the cannibalistic consumption of the victim's organs. I use Evans-Pritchard's distinction
between sorcery and witchcraft not only because it fits Buli categories so well,
but also for comparative reasons.[2] Southeast Asia is thus characterized by a curious feature: sorcery and magic are extremely widespread in the region (e.g., Endicott 1970; Kendall 2010; Lieban 1967; Klima 2002; Skeats 2010; Siegel 2006;
Watson and Ellen 1993). Witchcraft however, in the narrow sense employed by
Evans-Pritchard, is extremely rare (Ellen 1993b:8; Winzeler 2008:180).[3] Indeed,
the few studies of witchcraft from Southeast Asia all come from the eastern part
of Indonesia, and are essay-like in length. The analyses are from Bali (Belo 1949;

*homo floresiensis "hobbits"*

Covarrubias 1937:321–357), from Flores (Forth 1989), from Maluku (Bubandt 1998b), and from Papua (Miedema et al. 1998; Stasch 2001). This account of witchcraft, the first monograph to focus on witchcraft "in the narrow sense" in Southeast Asia, deals in other words with an understudied and still poorly understood regional phenomenon.

Despite the fact that accusations of sorcery and witchcraft in Buli surround deaths with roughly equal frequency,[4] witchcraft in Buli is shot through with uncertainty to an extent that sorcery is not. Witchcraft in Buli is about embodied subjectivity in the most profound sense of eating and being eaten (Bataille 1992); it is, as Peter Geschiere (1997) aptly puts it in the original French title to his great monograph on witchcraft in postcolonial West Africa, about "the flesh of others" (*la viande des autres*). But at the same time as cannibal witchcraft is radically corporeal, it also stubbornly remains existentially opaque. The inaccessibility of witchcraft is thereby continuously belied by its viscerality, in the same way that its innate nature is belied by its unknowability.

The proclivity to become a *gua* (*mahagua*) derives from a bodily entity or "seed" (*geo*).[5] Some patrilines (I. *fam*) are associated with witchcraft in particular— some say this is because their animal spirit (*suang*), upon which they ritually rely to provide them with fighting magic and to protect them against the *gua*, had in fact revealed itself to be a *gua*. The seed can also be inherited ambi-lineally from one's mother or one's father or be deliberately fed to someone.[6] The seed only becomes active, however, if one's "inside" (*uló*) is disposed toward greed, envy, jealousy, or lechery. Such people will eventually be approached by a *gua* spirit in their dreams and offered fresh fruit or raw cuts of meats. Sometimes, it is said, such a person will laugh in their sleep with excitement at the offering from the witch spirit (*gua ca nlal i*). Actually, though, the fruit or meat is human liver (*yatai*), and once human liver has been tasted, the cannibalistic desire for more is so strong that the *gua* spirit is able to evict and replace the shadow-consciousness (*gurumin*) of the person. Once possessed in this way, the person becomes the "outrigger" (*pelang*) of the *gua* spirit and acquires the ability to fly (*soro*) and to change shape, but is continuously haunted by an insatiable hunger for human liver, which it tries to satisfy by attacking other people in the village.[7] The attacks are vicious and visceral, demeaning and unpredictable, and both men and women, adults and children, fall prey to them.[8]

The illness that follows a *gua* attack is called *ungan. Ungan* can be divined and cured by a healer (*sowsów*) through the application of herbs and spells. While many people know some specific curing technique for *ungan*, there are some healers who are said to be especially knowledgeable and who are sought out to treat serious cases, but they are not specialists in the sense that they make an exclusive living as a healer. In former times healers conducted nightly, shamanistic rituals called *famamá* and *famtúlo*, in which ancestral and animal spirits were enlisted in the healing process, but these ceremonies have not been performed in Waiflí since the 1950s, when Christianity took hold in the village. Finally, a cure—the most effective of all—can be worked by the witch. For this reason, the family of a severely afflicted victim often seeks to entice village authorities, church ministers, and police officers to coerce the suspected *gua* into offering a cure, something the suspected *gua* usually tries to avoid by fleeing the village because agreeing to such a cure is seen as an admission of guilt.

If the attack is an incomprehensible tragedy for the victim, it is equally traumatizing for the accused *gua*. Witchcraft (*mahagua*) is always bad (*mayai*). It is never associated with success or any accepted form of power, and no one freely admits to being a *gua*, although the nature of witchcraft being what it is, one can never know whether one is a *gua*, or not. People accused of witchcraft never acquiesce when confronted with the accusation, but they are nevertheless tormented by uncertainty about the possibility that they might be witches without knowing it. Consequently, there are potentially many *gua* in Buli. Both men and women can become witches—and do so with roughly equal frequency. Even children can be witches. I have knowledge of eighty-three witchcraft attacks since the 1930s, in which a specific *gua* was suspected. Some two dozen named, suspected *gua* have been associated with these attacks. Of this group, eleven were men, and thirteen were women. But there are many other suspected *gua* who may not yet have killed anyone or who have given up trying to do so. It was common knowledge, for instance, that at least six possible *gua* lived within fifty meters of the house I occupied in the 1990s. Apart from "The Bald One," whom we met in the preface, there was the married couple two houses inland who were suspected of eating Selena, my adopted mother, in 1996. There was also the teenage girl in the neighboring house, and the old man in the house across the street from where I lived who had been a *gua* in the 1960s but had since been cured, as well as the young mother two houses toward the sea. I expect that most individuals in Buli would be able to point to at least a handful of possible *gua* at any given time.

Witchcraft, finally, appears to be somehow unique to Buli. Attacks happen—incomprehensibly—only within each village: neighbors attack neighbors; kin attack kin; friends attack friends—without any predictability. While sorcery is regional, and sorcery techniques are often bought or obtained from other parts of the province of North Maluku (Bubandt 2006, 2011), witchcraft is stubbornly local. People in Buli have a strong sense that witchcraft is particularly virulent in their community; that it is fixed in space to them, in spite of the fact that similar versions of witchcraft exist in most other communities in North Maluku, and versions of it—associated with the Malay concept of *suanggi*—can be found throughout eastern Indonesia.

The distinction between sorcery and witchcraft in Buli and North Maluku is comparatively interesting because the ontology and epistemology—and therefore also the politics—of the sorcery and witchcraft in the region are so markedly different. The *gua* is thus a more primordial being than a sorcerer (see fig. 1). "All the *gua* knows is to eat" (*gua nto be seli*), as the saying goes. The sorcerer is a craftier figure, available for hire to fulfill various purposes. For this reason, sorcery is an instrument in North Malukan regional politics in ways that witchcraft, so far, has never been (Bubandt 2011). While sorcery in eastern Indonesia, like the Taiwanese ghost cults or African witchcraft phenomena examined by Peter Geschiere and others, can be harnessed by political elites for their own purposes, there is no "power of indeterminate meaning," to use Geschiere's apt phrase, associated with witchcraft on Halmahera: no royal courts, no professional healers, no accused witches derive authority, wealth, or social power from witchcraft (I. *suanggi*). Without a clear political function or social role, witchcraft, I suggest, is adrift socially and politically. But witchcraft is also adrift epistemologically, because it is unmoored from any clear causal link to human meaning and knowledge. Witchcraft in Buli happens without the full knowledge of the *gua* himself or herself, and even victims are often unaware that they have been corporeally attacked until they (sometimes) regain memories of the attack just before they die. The actions and effects of witchcraft are both invisible and unknowable; anybody can be a witch, and any body can become its victim. A form of indeterminacy that has no clear meaning and comes with no evident social power, witchcraft in Buli is always in doubt.

## Toward an Anthropology of Doubt

Doubt and skepticism, long-established themes in theology and philosophy (Broughton 2002; Hecht 2010; Whitman 2008), have recently begun to also stir the interest of anthropologists (Bandak and Jørgensen 2012; Gable 2002; Pelkmans 2011b; Taussig 2003). Doubt, as Mathijs Pelkmans (2011b:16) has convincingly argued, is ephemeral and unstable, inherently contradictory, and active. Doubt is never passive, because once "the dubious object is caught in the centre of attention it needs to be acted upon, until it is tamed, sidelined or transformed" (20). Doubt, in other words, necessitates a kind of agency. I would agree with most of what Pelkmans says here. This book is an ethnography of the agency that arises out of what Pelkmans calls "the restlessness of doubt" (20), a critical investigation of the relationship between doubt and agency as seen through the lens of witchcraft.[9] However, this book seeks to explore in detail the question opened by Pelkmans whether "doubt can be at rest" (20). The ethnographic claim of this book is that sometimes, and in spite of people's most desperate hopes and sustained efforts, doubt cannot be "tamed, sidelined or transformed" (see also Bloch 2013). Witchcraft in Buli is an instance of doubt's undomesticability, as it were. Doubt is part of the experiential, sensorial, mythical conventions of Buli engagement with witchcraft, which is at once inaccessible and ineradicable. Over the last century, people have continuously struggled to rid their daily lives, their community, and their own sense of themselves of the figure of the *gua*. But so far these efforts have been unsuccessful. The chapters that follow will trace the long history and intricate sociality of the attempts by Buli people to rid themselves of the *gua* by converting to those modern institutions and discourses that seemed to offer the hope of eradicating witchcraft. Witchcraft, I will show, is a condition of doubt that is "never at rest" but which, far from rendering Buli people passive and despondent, has produced a form of historical agency in which hope and failure, promise and disappointment, are constant themes. The history of witchcraft in Buli is therefore also a particular history of hope and the failure of its imaginative horizons (Crapanzano 2004; Miyazaki 2007).

I will employ Jacques Derrida's concept of aporia to interrogate the "restlessness of doubt" within witchcraft, and the relationship between doubt and agency, hope and failure, that attends it. Derrida uses the concept of aporia to point to "an interminable experience" (1993:16), an experiential conundrum that has no resolution and that cannot be determined, categorized, or placed within a meaningful order. Aporia marks an impassable situation, where understanding and the will to knowledge fail; aporia is a "not knowing where to go" (12). Experience therefore remains, painful and troubled. The aporia is a threshold that cannot be fixed as an object in space or as an identifiable problem in time. An aporia is not in Pelkmans' sense "a dubious object" that can be delineated and tamed or sidelined. An aporia has no clear presence as an "object" in the first place and cannot readily be handled by a subject. Rather, an aporia is a fracture in space-time itself, before which the subject's own identity begins to dissolve. An aporia essentially signals the impossibility of stable identity, our own and that of others. In the words of Derrida, it marks the point where "the very project or problematic task becomes impossible and where we are exposed . . . in our absolute and absolutely naked uniqueness, that is to say, disarmed, delivered to the other, incapable even of sheltering ourselves behind what could still protect the interiority of a secret" (12). I suggest that witchcraft—in Buli and possibly elsewhere—is an aporia in Derrida's sense. It is "an interminable experience" intimately entangled with the problem and impossibility of identity, with the discomfort of a subjectivity that is disarmed and delivered unto the other as well as with the dangers of the other within oneself. Witchcraft, in Buli at least, is an aporia (or a set of aporias) that, paraphrasing the quote above, exposes naked identity and makes its maintenance as a safe interior space impossible. I will explore the usefulness of the concept of aporia to study witchcraft in more detail in chapter 1.

## Witchcraft and the Domestication of Doubt

Witchcraft is a particularly apposite place to begin an anthropology of enduring doubt, because doubt occupies a crucial but awkward place in the anthropology of witchcraft: always at its center and always sidelined. Since the publication in 1937 of E. E. Evans-Pritchard's brilliant and rightly canonical book on witchcraft among the Azande the anthropology of witchcraft has been dominated by what one might call an "explanatory paradigm," a paradigm that perceptively identifies doubt as ethnographically central to people's perception of witchcraft, only to then sideline this doubt analytically by suggesting that witchcraft functions as an "explanation." Evans-Pritchard inaugurated this paradigm by famously arguing that witchcraft, above all, explains the world to those who believe in it. Witchcraft, as conventional anthropological wisdom has put it ever since, explains why illness, death, and misfortune afflict certain people and not others; it explains, in the celebrated example from Azande, why the granary collapses at the very moment when people sit under it to seek shelter from the sun (Evans-Pritchard 1976:22–23). This book seeks to challenge this paradigm of witchcraft as a clearly delineated and institutionalized object that functions as a form of explanation. It does so by taking the radical doubt that is constitutive of witchcraft seriously. This entails also a critique of witchcraft as a kind of belief.

When witchcraft becomes belief and meaning, doubt is sidelined. Take Evans-Pritchard's celebrated account of how he once saw "witchcraft on its path" (1976:11). He described it as a strange light that passed through the banana garden that surrounded his house, only then to disappear mysteriously. Evans-Pritchard continues: "There did not lack ready informants to tell me that what I had seen was witchcraft. Shortly afterwards, on the same morning, an old relative of Tupoi and an inmate of his homestead died. This event fully explained the light I had seen. I never discovered its real origin, which was possibly a handful of grass lit by someone on their way to defecate, but the coincidence of the direction along which the light moved and the subsequent death accorded well with Zande ideas" (11). Witchcraft is here presented as a form of rationality, a set of beliefs. And as a set of beliefs, witchcraft "fully explained" certain events (misfortunes and accidents), it structured practices (divination and magic), and it legitimated certain forms of social organization (the power of diviners, princes, and courts). The notion that Azande *believed in* witchcraft was the foundation of Evans-Pritchard's argument here. Indeed, the theme of belief is emphasized repeatedly in the very first sentences of his monograph: "Azande believe that some people are witches and can injure them in virtue of an inherent quality. . . . They also believe that sorcerers may do them ill by performing magic rites with bad medicines. . . . The relations between these beliefs and rites are the subject of this book" (1). The notion that Zande witchcraft formed a system of belief allowed Evans-Pritchard to reach what was in 1937 a highly innovative and controversial assertion—namely, that witchcraft contained a rationality of its own that provided an encompassing and systematic cosmology. But seeing witchcraft as belief also entailed a divide between reality and fantasy, between modern science and cultural imagination. This divide meant that Evans-Pritchard had to sublimate Zande doubts about witchcraft in order to reach his conclusions about witchcraft as a set of beliefs that explained events, or that served a function in one overarching system of social logic.

It is thus not that Evans-Pritchard ignored Azande people's ambivalence or doubt. On the contrary, the ethnographic parts of his book are sprinkled throughout with descriptions of the doubts that Azande express about witchcraft: the doubts about details of witchcraft that only a witch could know (1976:12) and the doubts voiced by people accused of witchcraft about whether or not they were, in fact, witches (61). "I have frequently been struck," Evans-Pritchard noted, "when discussing witchcraft with Azande by the doubts they express about the subject, not only in what they say, but also in their manner of saying it, both of which contrast with their ready knowledge, fluently imparted, about social events and economic techniques. They feel out of their depth in trying to describe the way in which witchcraft accomplishes its ends. . . . Only witches themselves understand these matters fully" (31). Evans-Pritchard, however, did not pursue these doubts in any detail. Indeed, I submit that he could not do so for theoretical and epistemological reasons. Thus, in all instances where Evans-Pritchard brings up the issue of doubt, he cites doubt as evidence of an Azande disinterest in witchcraft as an intellectual and abstract phenomenon, or even as a general expression of their unfamiliarity with logical and consistent thought about witchcraft. For Evans-Pritchard, Zande doubts became proof that witchcraft in Azande was not an abstract and reflective issue, but a practical concern, "imprisoned in action" (32). Doubt is thereby also firmly locked up in belief. "Azande," as Evans-Pritchard put it, "have to state their doubts of the mystical powers of witch-doctors in mystical terms. . . . Their idiom is so much of a mystical order that criticism of one belief can only be made in terms of another that equally lacks foundation in fact" (1937:194). It was such inconsistencies that for Evans-Pritchard disqualified Zande witchcraft from the realms of our reality, as the philosopher Peter Winch (1964) would later point out. While scientific theories of reality were constituted by a basic intolerance of internal inconsistencies and driven by a mode of thinking and reasoning that was premised on doubt and skepticism, Zande ideas of witchcraft had no such interest in inconsistencies. As Mary Douglas noted (1980:108), this capacity to tolerate self-contradiction was not, as for earlier theories—such as that of Lucien Lévy-Bruhl (1966)—a sign of mental deficiency. Rather, internal contradictions could be tolerated exactly because they were encompassed systematically by an institutionalized system of belief. In Evans-Pritchard's view, Zande doubts about witchcraft were therefore always circumscribed by belief and could not be evidence of epistemological skepticism. "Scepticism," he noted, "far from being smothered, is recognized, even inculcated. But it is only about certain medicines and certain magicians. By contrast it tends to support other medicines and magicians" (1937:475). Zande skepticism in that sense becomes *proof* of the force of their beliefs. It is paradoxical that Evans-Pritchard should reach this conclusion about Zande doubts, since it was Evans-Pritchard's own doubts that afforded *him* a logical distance from these beliefs—even, and especially, when he was inclined to be sucked into their world, such as in his encounter with the "light of witchcraft." In short, Evans-Pritchard's doubt gave him distance from Zande beliefs, while Zande doubts were evidence of their "imprisonment" in a social system of mystical explanation and belief.

My account of the absent dog in the preface is intended as a kind of counterpoint to this alleged connection between visibility and reality that allowed Evans-Pritchard to make a comfortable distinction between "real" fact and "belief." My concern here is not, as many recent anthropologies of witchcraft have advocated, to rehabilitate the "reality of witchcraft." Rather, it is to question the idea of witchcraft as belief, and to emphasize doubt as a shared condition of witchcraft. It was by not seeing a dog that I began to entertain the possibility of a shared doubt. While doubt is readily shared, beliefs tend to be exported to an "other" . . . but always at a cost.

Indeed, Evans-Pritchard's distinction between Azande beliefs and his own skepticism was a delicate fabrication. In his wonderful analysis of the trick that Evans-Pritchard performed to reveal the trickery of an Azande witch doctor, Michael Taussig shows how Evans-Pritchard's maintenance of an Enlightenment distance from witchcraft in effect contained its own magic. When Evans-Pritchard revealed the witch doctor's ruse, explains Taussig, he did not gain the Enlightenment distance he had hoped. Instead, he may merely have been "doing little more than the culturally appropriate thing" in a society like Azande, where skepticism, as Evans-Pritchard himself repeatedly pointed out, was endemic (Taussig 2003:300).

There are two critical ways of reading Evans-Pritchard's study of witchcraft. One can see Evans-Pritchard as Winch (1964) does: as a rationalist whose confidence in the ultimate veracity of a scientific worldview prevents him from truly understanding witchcraft. For all its critique of science, however, this position shares with Evans-Pritchard the notion that witchcraft is a matter of belief: it is ultimately because witchcraft is about belief that it, also for Winch, remains "incommensurable" with science (see Tambiah 1990). Alternatively, one can see Evans-Pritchard not as a scientist but as a magician who conjures up the difference between science and belief by magical means. This is the route that Taussig takes. He demonstrates how Evans-Pritchard's attempt to understand witchcraft scientifically, to unmask its magic, ends up collapsing under its own weight. For it turns out that it takes a lot of magical trickery to unmask magic, just as it takes a lot of magical belief to maintain Azande skepticism as radically different: "Certainties dissolve into ever more mystifying contradictions magically dispelled, momentarily as it were, by the author's self-assured explanations of the multifarious aspects of magical phenomena" (Taussig 2003:295). What Taussig is pointing out here is exactly that it takes a magical trick to maintain the Western monopoly on skepticism and to uphold the difference between Azande doubts and Western doubts in witchcraft. This opposition is a fiction, but in the early twentieth century it was a necessary fiction that enabled the emergence of the distinctive, anthropological perspective on witchcraft as a coherent, explanatory, and cosmological system of belief.[10]

As the archetypal primitive belief system, witchcraft had to be belief "without a doubt." It was this emphasis, on witchcraft as a system of belief that provided moral explanations for misfortune and served a variety of social functions, that was to be Evans-Pritchard's lasting legacy to witchcraft studies. "Following Evans-Pritchard," Henrietta Moore and Todd Sanders argue, "an entire generation of anthropologists aimed to demonstrate, in varied ethnographic locales, that 'witchcraft is something more than meaningless superstition'" (Krige 1947:8; quoted in Moore and Sanders 2001a:6–7). This interpretive will to see in witchcraft a meaning-making system of belief runs through other theories of witchcraft, too, including the sociological theories of the functionalist and structural-functionalist schools, which held that witchcraft, as a set of beliefs, reflected and helped maintain social control, and including the affective theories, which saw witchcraft as a set of beliefs that helped individuals cope with life, illness, or psychological disorders (Ellen 1993b:18; Kluckhohn 1944; Lévi-Strauss 1963). In his book on Navaho witchcraft, Clyde Kluckhohn writes, for instance, "One of the manifest 'functions' of belief in witchcraft is that such belief supplies answers to questions which would otherwise be perplexing, and because perplexing, disturbing" (1944:82).

Doubt might be everywhere in the ethnography of witchcraft, but in the theory of witchcraft doubt is domesticated because it never leads to "the perplexing" or "the disturbing." Instead witchcraft is made to lead away from it. In the end, doubt is analytically domesticated into explanation. The same domestication of doubt, though for different reasons, arguably remains at the core also of the contemporary anthropology of witchcraft. This may seem to be an odd statement. After all, a growing number of recent ethnographies have begun to highlight how witchcraft is constituted precisely through ambivalence, doubt, contradiction, interruptions, uncertainty, and plasticity (Ashforth 2000, 2005; Geschiere 2013; Niehaus 2013; Parés and Sansi 2011; Sanders 2003; Stoller and Olkes 1989; West 2005; White 2000). As Parés and Sansi, for instance, aptly put it, witchcraft or sorcery operates "not by fully demonstrating its power, but by opening a possible doubt; one is never fully sure it is not true" (2011:2). And let there be no doubt: I find much to applaud in these recent studies, in particular this deliberate focus on doubt as the working dynamic of the spiritually occult. For instance, Adam Ashforth's evocative description of what he calls "spiritual insecurity" in Soweto, a term that refers to "the dangers, doubts, and fears arising from the sense of being exposed to invisible evil forces" (2005:1), encapsulates the starting point of this book. At the same time, it is my distinct sense that in the contemporary anthropological emphasis on the importance of doubt, ambivalence, and contradiction in witchcraft, ambivalence and doubt are still ultimately made to make sense analytically, to serve a purpose, to reflect some outside condition. Belief and interpretation still provide the explanatory link between witchcraft and world. Morten Axel Pedersen has aptly referred to this tendency to see the spirit world as imbued with a certain kind of hermeneutic power to explain the world as a "symbolic functionalism" (2011:33). Suggesting that sorcerers and anthropologists are "colleagues" of a sort, both seeking an "interpretation of the world's workings," Harry West, for instance, writes, "Through sorcery discourse, Muedans [in northern Mozambique] reflected upon the complex truth that the world they made sometimes eluded their grasp, sometimes turned around and made them, and sometimes became suddenly and unexpectedly responsive to their whims" (2007:81, 70). The contradictions of sorcery and witchcraft, West appears to say, interpret life. They allow people to reconcile themselves with the workings of a complex and contradictory world—much like interpretive anthropology. But along the way, contradiction, it appears to me, has acquired a new hermeneutic function as explanation or reflection; doubt, in other words, has been redomesticated by meaning. I suggest this is because West and most other anthropologists of witchcraft, like Evans-Pritchard, remain wedded to the paradigm that witchcraft is a form of belief. To be fair, I do follow West some of the way in his argument. Indeed, West is one among a growing number of anthropologists who have opened up a new and fruitful avenue of research by suggesting the need to take people's (often tortured) beliefs in witchcraft realities seriously (Ashforth 2000; Favret-Saada 1980; Niehaus 2012; Stoller and Olkes 1989; West 2005). They do so in an attempt to cross the great divide between

*[handwritten margin notes:]*

*the historian is not the demonologist. The historian is the witch. (Ango?)*

*especially the witch who resists — + finds a story to tell (although almost all do tell stories)*

*She is to easier*

Western knowledge and native beliefs, to see local belief less as "bad science" and more like "rhetorical art," as West, quoting Kenneth Burke, puts it (2007:23). "For me," Paul Stoller writes, "respect means accepting fully beliefs and phenomena which our system of knowledge holds preposterous" (Stoller and Olkes 1989:227). I concur with the intention of this sentiment but find its premise untenable. The problem is that it continues to uphold an awkward and ultimately unnecessary distinction between the beliefs of others and the knowledge of the West. It was this same distinction between "their beliefs" and "our knowledge" that undergirded Evans-Pritchard's analysis. And the distinction continued to live on in the so-called rationality debate about how to describe the apparently irrational beliefs of others (Hollis and Lukes 1982; Sperber 1996; Tambiah 1990; Wilson 1974). The rationality debate, which dogged anthropology for decades and continues to frame its understanding of witchcraft, was characterized by two hostile fronts, which, their disagreements notwithstanding, agreed on one thing: putting doubt and skepticism firmly on the side of Western rationality while wedding witchcraft to belief and meaning.

An analysis of witchcraft in terms of "belief" is ultimately unhelpful, I think, because it is built on an "epistemology of presence" in which witchcraft is assumed to be unproblematically "real" or "there" to those who "believe in it." Belief always domesticates doubt by transforming the question of reality into a matter of presence. But witchcraft is never simply "there" (or "not-there") in any simple sense, as my encounter with the dog-that-wasn't in the preface sought to illustrate. Belief is therefore the wrong paradigm, if one wants to explore doubt's restlessness. For nowhere is doubt more restless, I suggest, than in witchcraft: "it needs to be acted upon" but it cannot be "tamed, sidelined or transformed" (cf. Pelkmans 2011b:20). If witchcraft is an occult reality, we need to find novel ways to truly come to terms—analytically, theoretically, and ethnographically—with its "occult nature," its invisibility, and its inaccessibility, as much as we need to recognize its reality. Focusing on witchcraft as doubt rather than as "reflection," "explanation," "meaning," or "belief" entails, I suggest, a break with an epistemology of presence, in which objects either "are" or "are-not," as well as with the hermeneutic functionalism that attends it.[11] This also means rethinking the relationship between witchcraft and modernity.

## Witchcraft and Modernity Revisited

If witchcraft is not an answer to, a function of, or a commentary on the world, but rather an aporia to which solutions are sought in a changing world, this poses a challenge to the overt or implicit causal relationship between modernity and witchcraft that structures many recent studies of witchcraft in Africa (Comaroff and Comaroff 1999, 2000; Englund 1996; Ferme 2001; Geschiere 1997, 1998; Moore and Sanders 2001b; Niehaus 2001; Smith 2008) as well as in Melanesia, the Caribbean, and Asia (Klima 2002; Knauft 2002b; Morris 2000b; Romberg 2003; Schram 2010). These analyses, which interpret witchcraft as a "gauge" of or a "discourse" on the problems or "hidden mechanics" of global modernity, have done much to highlight the coevalness of witchcraft with modern forms of political, economic, and social enchantment (Comaroff and Comaroff 2000; Geschiere 1997). They have thereby helped to de-exoticize witchcraft by dispelling the idea that witchcraft is unique to traditional or premodern societies, and allowed the study of witchcraft to be the starting point for a critical analysis of modernity's own account of itself (Kapferer 2003; Meyer and Pels 2003; Parés and Sansi 2011). Key proponents of this approach are Peter Geschiere and Jean and John Comaroff, who in a partly overlapping endeavor have highlighted how "symbolic excess," "ambivalence," and "indeterminate meaning" are at the heart of witchcraft, thereby marking an important break with the tradition after Evans-Pritchard that saw witchcraft in terms of coherence (Comaroff and Comaroff 1999, 2002; Geschiere 1997, 1998). I have the greatest respect for the novel momentum that this approach has brought to the study of witchcraft by highlighting its fragmentary and ambivalent nature, its contemporary and modern modes of reproduction, and its relevance for an understanding of global production and injustice. At the same time, this approach remains wedded to the social anthropology of Evans-Pritchard and his followers. Witchcraft may now be seen in terms of ambivalence, plasticity, and indeterminacy rather than coherence, but local ambivalence about witchcraft tends to be emphasized in order to highlight how it serves the same social functions as coherent belief did. "In its late-twentieth century guise," Jean and John Comaroff, for instance, write, "witchcraft is a finely-calibrated gauge of the impact of global cultural and economic forces on local relations, on perceptions of money and markets, on the abstraction and alienation of 'indigenous' values and meanings" (1993:xxciii–xxix). Whereas the analytical idea of "coherent witchcraft beliefs" for Evans-Pritchard functioned to explain misfortune in general, witchcraft in the approach of Geschiere and Comaroff and Comaroff is a discourse of "symbolic excess" or "indeterminate meaning" that explains the misfortune that is modernity (Comaroff and Comaroff 2002:798). The rise of witchcraft and other "occult economies" is thus "overdetermined" by the contemporary condition of global capitalism and its impact on local relations (Comaroff and Comaroff 2000:317), and represents a vernacular attempt to comprehend the experience of "labor lost, factories foreclosed, communities crumbling" (Comaroff and Comaroff 2002:798). As witchcraft is thereby turned into a kind of vernacular *Zivilisationskritik*, the approach simultaneously conserves witchcraft as a system of belief and means. "New situations . . . demand new magic," as the Comaroffs put it (1999:283; quoting Gluckman quoting Evans-Pritchard). Innovative and fascinating as it is, however, this emphasis on witchcraft as a discourse of ambivalence through which "people try to deal with modernity's dreams and threats" (Geschiere 1998:817) runs the risk of assigning to ambivalence the same social function as "coherent belief" had in the work of Evans-Pritchard. Whereas witchcraft formerly explained misfortune, handled kinship tensions, and supported the power of princes, witchcraft has now—in what Todd Sanders (2008) has aptly called anthropology's "seductive analytics"—predominantly become a tool to handle and critique the discontent of modernity and global inequality. My concern here is that too much emphasis on witchcraft's "tool-like" qualities may end up abrogating an analysis of the central role of doubt and ambivalence in witchcraft, a role the approach of Geschiere and the Comaroffs so perceptively diagnosed in the first place.[12]

Buli witchcraft for me thus constitutes an ethnographic challenge. I cannot make it fit into the argument that witchcraft has proliferated as a discourse of ambivalence because it explains or makes comprehensible the novel conditions of modernity. Witchcraft in Buli provides no apt discourse, no workable tools, no reliable means. No power, money, or respect can be harnessed from its "indeterminate meaning" (Geschiere 1998). The ethnographic problem, then, is this: why is witchcraft experienced as proliferating in Buli if it has no social function, makes no sense, and explains nothing? I suggest that an answer to this question can be found by taking the radical doubt that infuses witchcraft seriously. By focusing on the aporetic rather than the explanatory aspects of witchcraft, I argue, it is possible to get a potentially novel perspective on the "modernity of witchcraft" (Geschiere 1997). Instead of modernity being the new social conditions of ambivalence, and witchcraft a partially traditional discourse that allows people to come to terms with these conditions, I suggest the relationship between witchcraft and modernity is the inverse: witchcraft is the ambivalent aporia, the interminable problem; modernity, meanwhile, appears to allow a certain kind of explanation of this aporia and, as such, is mined for answers to it. The existential ambivalence that is witchcraft has historically motivated people in Buli to search their world for an answer—for a way of "taming" their doubt, as it were. Modernity seemed to provide such a method of taming.

Despite the many analytical problems associated with the concept of modernity (Cooper 2005; Englund and Leach 2000; Knauft 2002a), I use "modernity" here as a heuristic cover term, an informant term, for the changes associated in Buli with

Christianity, the nation-state, and capitalism. In Buli, the various institutional incarnations of modernity—the church, the state, and the mining company—have appeared for more than a century to be holding out a promise of some kind of answer or solution to witchcraft. In Indonesia, the notion of "the modern" (I. *yang modern*) has always been what Frederick Cooper calls "a claim-making concept" (2005:115): Christianity, capitalism, and the nation-state all came to Buli with a certain claim about transformation and change, of propelling the backward and the traditional into the future.[13] I therefore follow Cooper's proposal to treat "modernity" as an informant term and to trace through it "the different ways people frame the relationship of past, present, and future" (149). The teleological promise of a radical break with the past that characterized modernity throughout Indonesia was taken in Buli to harbor the promise of a future without witchcraft.

This promise was an enticing one from the beginning (chapter 3). It has also proven a promise that, once harbored, has been hard to give up. Therefore, even when the various institutional incarnations of modernity in Buli fail—as they have consistently done so far—to deliver on their alleged promise to bring an end to witchcraft, in my experience people remain surprisingly loyal to modernity. In Buli this loyalty applies to state modernity as much as it does to Christianity and global capitalism—all of which are called upon in an attempt to respond to the aporias of witchcraft. I would suggest that in Buli it is this promise that confers upon modernity—whether in the shape of conversion to Christianity, incorporation into the nation-state, or inundation by capitalism—its particular enchantment (Bennett 2001; LiPuma 2001; Meyer and Pels 2003).

## Suspending Belief

My critique of witchcraft as belief extends from Bruno Latour's (2010) critical appraisal of the notion of belief in modernity. In its own account of itself, so Latour argues, modernity has been accompanied by the loss of "belief." In return for our lost beliefs, we moderns instead got knowledge. By giving up our belief in "fetishes" as it were, we moderns acquired "facts." Belief has therefore become what distinguishes the nonmodern from the modern. The nonmodern others have belief, while moderns do not; indeed, it is through his belief that the nonmodern other is distinguished as being different from the modern. In an intriguing twist of this modern ideology, Latour suggests that it might in fact be the moderns who believe: moderns need to believe in the belief of the other to maintain their own account of themselves as nonbelievers. Moderns "believe in belief in order to understand others" (Latour 2010:7). In this sense the existence of belief among the nonmodern others has itself become a declaration of faith in the

*[handwritten marginal notes:]* modernity to end? as belief + the dawn of fact

*but what if no-one believes anything?*

*(this would also work for early modernists + students of similar "beliefs" in Europe)*

modern constitution. "Our" modern facts may prove the falsity of "their" beliefs, but ironically we still need these beliefs in order to remain "in the right." Moderns believe in belief.

This opposition has direct consequences for the study of witchcraft. The notion of witchcraft as belief upheld a particular paradigm of knowledge, to which witchcraft was opposed. This opposition between belief and knowledge applied to those who needed witchcraft belief to confirm their own beliefs in the veracity of knowledge. But the opposition also forcefully structures the arguments of those anthropologists who, like Stoller, want to demonstrate their respect for witchcraft's reality by "accepting fully beliefs and phenomena which our system of knowledge holds preposterous" (Stoller and Olkes 1989:227). Indeed, because this attitude of seeming respect for belief through a suspicion of disbelief has become so dominant in the anthropology of witchcraft, it is worth interrogating.

Anthropologists who advocate this stance of respect for other worlds or ontologies thus often exhort others to "suspend their disbelief" during fieldwork, especially when studying the fantastical, the occult, or the "unbelievable" (Badone 1995; Dwyer 1977:146; Kapferer 2001:343).[14] The concept of the "willing suspension of disbelief"—now a cliché in cultural studies, performance studies, and anthropology for the attempt to understand the exotic, the different, and the fantastical—was coined by the British poet Samuel Taylor Coleridge. Founder of the Romantic movement in England, Coleridge was steeped in the Counter-Enlightenment and concerned to recover the appreciation of beauty, spirit, and tradition that he and his fellow romantics felt had been lost in the Enlightenment pursuit of reason. Coleridge argued that in an age of disbelief it was the task of the poet to supply an experience of belief, beauty, and mystery through a "willing suspension of disbelief" (Abrams 1958). The "suspension of disbelief" was "willing" because it involved the pursuit of what Coleridge called "poetic faith" through "an investment in communication despite a measure of initial distrust" (Tomko 2007:244). For Coleridge, poetic faith was, in other words, not naive—like the beliefs of "the primitives"; rather it was a "Synthesis of the Reason and the Individual Will" (Coleridge, quoted in Tomko 2007:244). Poetic faith was not blind but a kind of willed knowledge: "a Light, a form of Knowing, a Beholding of Truth" (244). The romantic suspension of disbelief, as a result, was therefore always momentary, never permanent; always guarded and "experimentative," never absolute (245).

In short, the notion of the "willing suspension of disbelief" rested firmly on the same putative opposition between modern, rational disbelief and premodern belief that was at the heart of Enlightenment rationality itself. Therefore, although I am sympathetic toward the anthropological exhortation to suspend disbelief as a general rule, I nevertheless find it deeply problematic, since it upholds the illusion that disbelief is the monopoly of modernity. Belief, meanwhile, is in this view characteristic of the lifeworlds of nonmoderns, of the lost worlds of tradition, of other ontologies. These different lifeworlds, so the argument runs, can be accessed only through a willed suspension of modern disbelief. While modern rationality celebrated the loss of belief, and Romanticism lamented it, both the Enlightenment and the romanticism of the Counter-Enlightenment shared the same "belief in belief." However, in order to access the skepticism, doubt, and acknowledged impossibilities that characterize witchcraft, at least in Buli, one needs to move beyond the modern idea of belief that characterizes romantic modernity as much as rational modernity. I suggest therefore that a "suspension of belief" (in the beliefs of the other) is a much more urgent, and difficult, anthropological task than the conventional "suspension of disbelief."

## Doubt, Therefore Witchcraft

Focusing on doubt may, in short, help us suspend our disciplinary belief in witchcraft as a system of belief. In my own endeavor to do so, I have been greatly inspired by recent studies in history that have sought to break with conventional approaches to European witchcraft. Conventional historical accounts of witchcraft in Europe have long maintained that doubt was a poison to witchcraft, and that witchcraft beliefs began to decline when scientifically and religiously grounded doubts about its reality increased (Kors and Peters 2001; Thomas 1973; Trevor-Roper 1969). Europeans, so the account went, formerly believed in witchcraft for the same reasons that contemporary people outside Europe do: not being modern, they did not doubt. With the advent of modernity and its doubts, however, beliefs (including beliefs in witchcraft) began to fade.

Recently, however, historians of European witchcraft have begun to challenge this conventional assertion that it was modern doubt that led to the decline of witchcraft beliefs (Bond and Ciekawy 2002; Clark 1997). In a fascinating study (2002), historian Walter Stephens has suggested that it was actually modern doubt that drove *the rise* in European concerns about witchcraft. Stephens analyzes the legal obsession in fifteenth- and sixteenth-century Europe to get direct confessions from women accused of having had sex with demons. He suggests that these confessions from "demon lovers," the title of his book, were important to early modern, European Christian clerics as part of a desperate and roundabout attempt to prove the reality of God. Such proof had become increasingly important in the face of a general crisis of belief that was set in motion by the influence of Aristotelian science on Christianity during the Renaissance. Stephens's argument is, basically, that it was modern skepticism that fueled these trials. Witchcraft concerns were, in other words, not driven by belief; they were driven by a "crisis of belief," by doubt. Stephens's argument runs as follows: Aristotelian logic, as rediscovered by the Christian church in the Renaissance, called for reality to be proven empirically. This logic put mounting pressure on the church to find ways of aligning faith in God with these new criteria for knowledge. In this climate, the early modern clerics felt that the existence of God could be asserted indirectly if the corporeal reality of the devil was proven by direct testimony. That is to say, witch confessions became one of the ways that one could prove the existence of God by proxy. If demons were real and could assume a corporeal form, then God, although invisible, was likewise real. Stephens asserts that what drove the witch trials, with their focus on confessions of carnal knowledge of the devil, was not a belief in witchcraft but an anxious and skeptical attempt to prove the occult reality of God *through* the existence of witchcraft. According to Stephens, in the fifteenth and sixteenth century, "witchcraft theorists did not suppose that their theories [about the existence of the devil] corresponded with reality: they were *testing* to discover *whether* a correspondence existed and dreading that it might not" (2002:10, italics in the original). If the reality of the devil could not be proven through testimonial evidence, then the reality of God was in doubt as well, according to Aristotelian criteria for objective truth. Renaissance witch trials, it seems, were built on the paradox that only if these doubts could be dispelled, could the existence of God be proven. In order to believe in God, one needed to believe in the veracity of those women who said they had had sex with demons. Trial by torture was a desperate means of trying to ensure the truth of their testimony. It was in other words the clerics' doubts as to whether such confessions could truly be trusted that gave the witch trials their brutal urgency and legalistic obsessiveness. Early modern doubt and a crisis of belief, it would seem, played a central role in the rise of European witch trials and the extraction of confessions from accused witches after the fifteenth century: "Witchcraft theory and witch-hunting *were caused* by skepticism, not by belief or credulity" (364, italics in the original).

By pushing skepticism from the Enlightenment back into the Renaissance, historians like Stephens have suggested that it is possible to loosen doubt from its Cartesian moorings (Broughton 2002) and explore the many forms of doubt that live beyond the Enlightenment.[15] My ethnography of witchcraft and doubt in eastern Indonesia is a contribution to this endeavor. I argue that an investigation of the reality of witchcraft in terms of absence rather than presence, in terms of ontological doubt rather than ontological certainty, and in terms of existential aporia rather than social function or commentary, opens up to an appreciation of traditional forms of reflexivity that may not be so different from those we tend to reserve for the late modern West, in self-congratulation or in self-deprecation. Doubt, skepticism, and reflexivity are not the cognitive or institutional monopoly of late modernity or indeed of a reinvented, critical anthropology. Doubt is institutionally reproduced as part of social life in many forms, also outside of the late modern West, and as such, doubt, uncertainty, and skepticism can well be the object of comparative analysis (Bubandt 2005b; Douglas and Wildavsky 1982). Witchcraft—at least in Buli—is a phenomenon around which doubt is being reproduced in a continuously failed attempt to understand and manage it. This aporia of witchcraft—its absent presence—imposes, I argue, a persistent instability on everyday life, existential reality, and social history in Buli—a persistence that I propose to follow ethnographically and historically.

**Figure 1.** A *gua* (or *setan*) drawn by Fanda Guslaw (ten years old). Photo by author.

So long as we doubt, So long we also believe — in witchcraft (+ other things?)

What would happen, this book asks, if we turned conventional notions about the relationship between modernity and witchcraft, and between the real and the ideal, on their head and took seriously my Buli informants' sense that witchcraft was the problem, and that modernity entailed the promise of an answer? What would happen, if our analysis was premised on the possibility that witchcraft was the problematic reality, and that what gave modernity its appeal, its special magic, was its seeming promise to provide an end to witchcraft? What if witchcraft was problematic because its reality was simultaneously inescapable and unknowable, and if modernity's promise of an answer was consistently being undermined by this paradox and therefore had to be continuously renewed? Then it would not be a matter of highlighting either how witchcraft disappeared in the clear light of modernity or how it was being retooled to understand the injustices of a modern world, but rather a question of understanding how modernity's appeal historically has depended on its apparent ability to provide some answer to the doubts of witchcraft. Instead of determining whether witchcraft is vanishing or increasing with modernization, we would undertake the ethnographic task of tracing how modernity is experienced as succeeding or failing under the conditions of witchcraft.

## Arriving at Witchcraft

Straddling the equator in the northeastern corner of Indonesia, where the Indian Ocean meets the western Pacific, Halmahera is the largest island in North Maluku, a province of around one million inhabitants (see map 1).[16] At around 18,000 square kilometers, Halmahera is the size of Israel or Slovenia. Its four tentacle-like, mountainous peninsulas give the island a K-shaped contour and provide some degree of shelter for three large bays: Kao Bay facing northeast, Weda Bay facing southeast, and the Bay of Buli opening up to the east.

Buli is an Austronesian-speaking and predominantly Christian group numbering some three thousand people.[17] The Buli-speaking settlements include the village cluster of Buli as well as the villages of Tewil, Wailukum, and Tatangapú. Buli Christians form a minority in the administrative district of East Halmahera, where in 2009 some 90 percent of the overall population of some sixty thousand is Muslim (BPSPMU 2010:142), a statistical balance between Christians and Muslims that reflects almost exactly that of Indonesia as a whole.[18] Buli people are a minority also in linguistic terms. The Buli language is one of the six Austronesian languages spoken on and around Halmahera, which belong to a group of languages known as the South Halmaheran-West New Guinea subgroup: Buli (and Wayamli), Maba (and Bicoli), Patani, Weda (and Sawai), Giman, and East

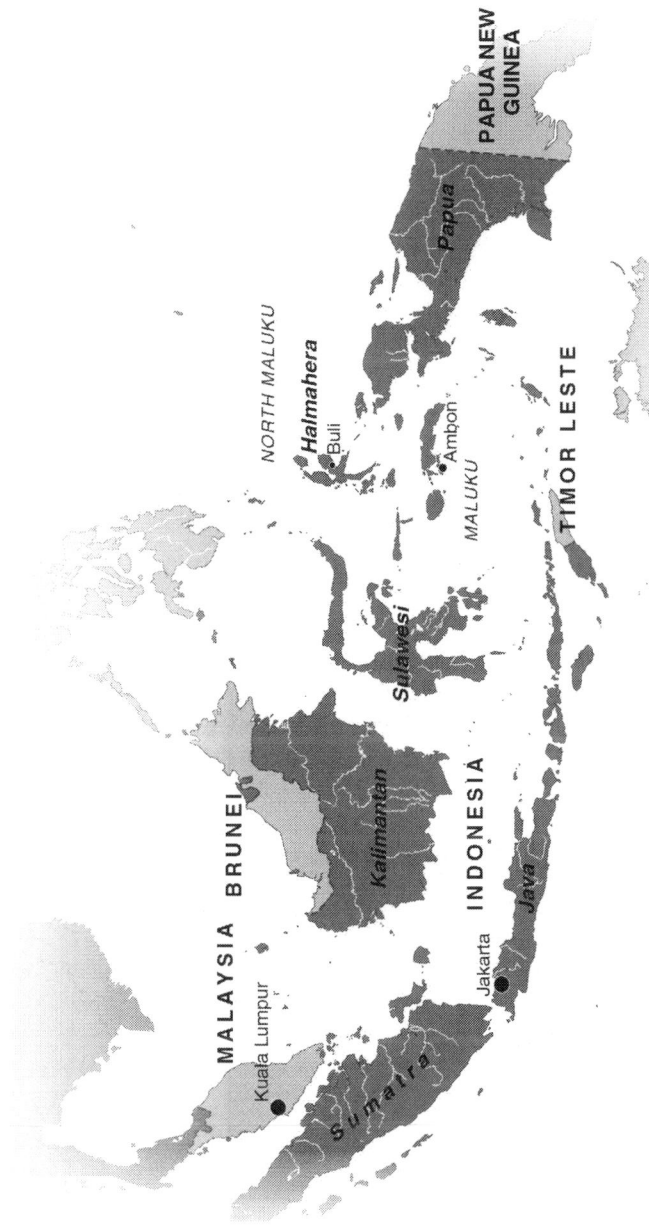

Map 1. Location of Halmahera in Indonesia.

Makian (Blust 1978; Wurm and Hattori 1983).[19] A number of Papuan languages are also spoken on the northern peninsula by some of the dominant cultural groups in North Maluku: Tobelo, Galela, Ternate, and Tidore (see map 2). The linguistic complexity of Halmahera, where sixteen languages, many with several dialects, from two distinct language families are spoken, is also in many ways a microcosm of the ethnolinguistic mosaic that is Indonesia, a country where some seven hundred languages are spoken.[20]

Apart from being the name of a language, Buli is also the name of a village cluster on the almost triangular Bay of Buli, which opens into the western Pacific Ocean (see map 1). In the early 1990s this village cluster was a sleepy place. It consisted of three adjacent villages: Buli Serani, the administrative capital of the Maba subdistrict (I. *kecamatan*); the mainly Muslim village of Buli Islam; and the Christian village of Waiflí, where I conducted my fieldwork.

Waiflí—literally "the Place of the Sago-Bark Container"—is the name Buli people use to refer to the village that is officially known in Indonesian as Buli Asal, or "Original Buli." In the early 1990s, life in Waiflí was similar to that in many other remote villages in eastern Indonesia. The economy was predominantly oriented toward subsistence swidden farming, hunting, and fishing, supplemented by cash crops like coconuts—introduced by Dutch colonial officers in the first decades of the twentieth century to replace *damar* resin as the main means of providing a cash income, and enabling the locals to pay taxes—as well as cocoa and cloves. Marine products (such as bêche-de-mer, lobsters, hawksbill turtle shells, shark fins, and anchovies) and forest products (such as hardwood, rattan, and deer antlers) were also sold to provide households with a small amount of cash for trade-store goods, school fees, clothes, and consumer items like plastic furniture, watches, TVs, and video CD players (VCDs). Sago was the main staple, and fish the most important source of protein. Garden products like bananas, corn, cassava, sweet potato, taro, and ferns also featured regularly in the Buli diet, as did rose apple, cashew, breadfruit, Lansium fruit (I. *langsat*), mango, lemon, and other fruits and nuts. Delicacies like green turtles, sago grubs, *palolo* worms, wild pig, and deer would always cause excitement in the household. Unlike the ethnic groups in the northern part of Halmahera, Buli villagers and their neighbors in central Halmahera do not grow dry rice, so high-status foods such as rice and flour-based cakes also had to be purchased in stores to be offered to guests or used as prestations in the exchanges that are an essential element in marriage and burial ceremonies.

I first came to Waiflí in 1991 as part of a PhD project that focused on ethnic relations among marginal groups in the central part of Halmahera. I knew very little about the area. I did know that Maluku (then still one province known in the older literature as the Moluccas) was an economic backwater in the eastern part

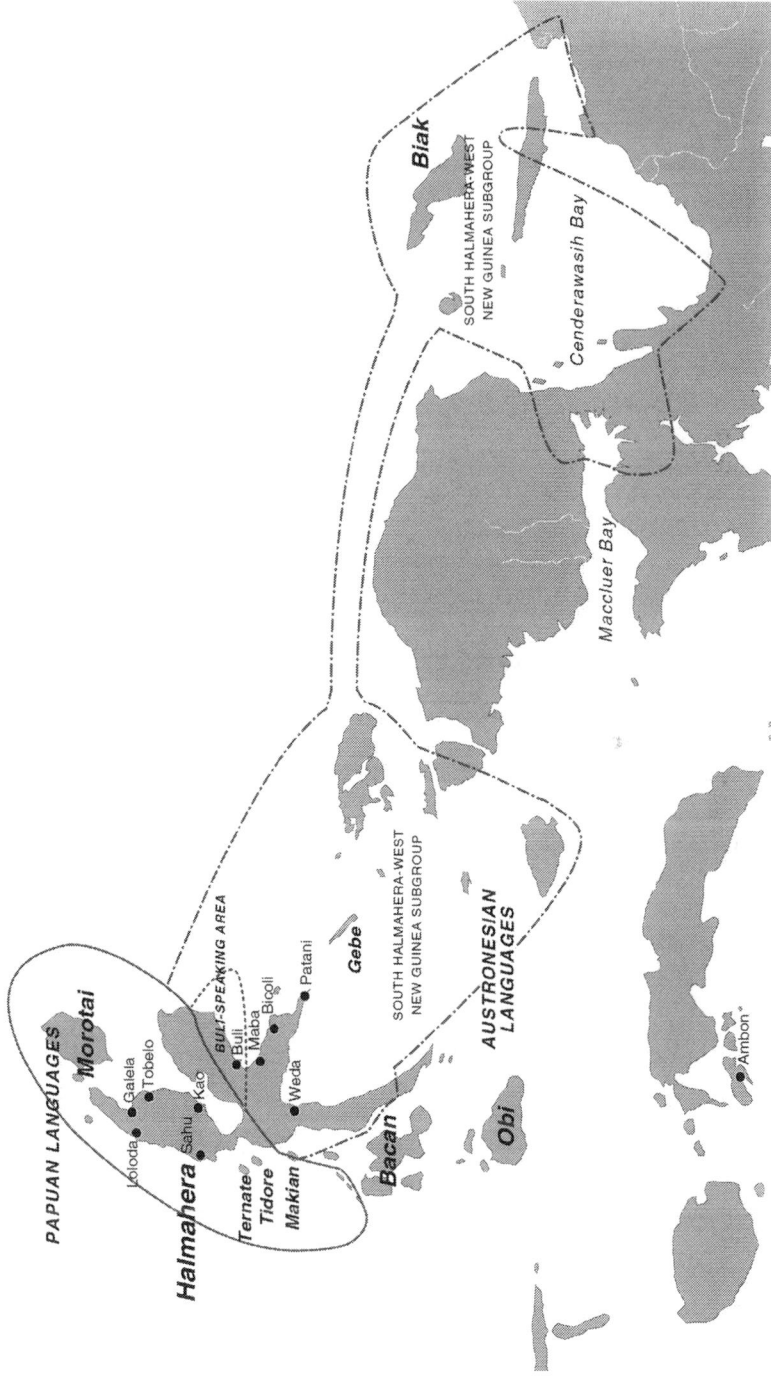

Map 2. Linguistic map of North Maluku.

of Indonesia (see map 1), a country established in 1950 after a protracted armed struggle against the Dutch (Ricklefs 2008:248). The northern part of Maluku, I knew, had for centuries before the arrival of the first Europeans in 1511 been ruled by four sultanates (Andaya 1993) and held a central place in the European Renaissance imagination as the fabled Spice Islands. I was also aware that Buli had formerly been under the rule of the sultanate of Tidore; and that it had since 1900 been a mission field of the Utrecht Mission Union, a Calvinist mission society of the Dutch Reformed Church, one of whose missionaries had produced a Dutch-Buli dictionary and grammar (Maan 1940, 1951). Other than that, my knowledge was based on the little the 1989 copy of *Indonesia Handbook* in my backpack could tell me. And the thousand-page guidebook had only the following brief entry about the central part of Halmahera: "Maba, S of Buli, is the heaviest black-magic area" (Dalton 1989:949). This should have alerted me to the importance of the occult in this part of Halmahera, but the surfer slang of the entry meant that I did not really pay it any heed. As a result I only "arrived" at witchcraft as an analytical topic after fieldwork diverted me there.

Installed in the house of Kenari, who at the time was the deputy village head and often went by the name of "Deputy" (I. *Wakil*), I still remember my frustration during my first few months with what appeared to me to be an obsessive need to control my movements. "Where are you going?" Kenari would ask me whenever I ventured outside. Asking where someone is going (*aum deluá ga?*) is a conventional greeting in Buli, and indeed throughout North Maluku where the phrase *mo kemana?* (Where are you going?), pronounced in the distinctively intimate North Malukan Malay dialect, is a common, inquisitive salutation. It is, however, an inquiry that does not necessarily demand a precise answer. It encapsulates an ethos of village existence where information about the actions, intentions, and whereabouts of other people—what fish they might have caught, who they might be going to see, or which sources of betel nut or palm wine they might have procured—goes into the social capital of "the give and take of everyday life" (Schieffelin 1990). Answering the common greeting of where one is going is therefore a delicate balancing act of deciding what to say, and to whom. To relative strangers (*smat nesa*) who are not "friends" (*ni del*) and who are outside of the vague circle of one's "house" (*ebai*)—bilateral kin and affines—one should not reveal too much (because one would thereby risk that one's fish, palm wine, or betel nut would have to be needlessly shared), whereas one could also easily offend if the other perceived the response as withholding too much. Kenari had appointed himself as my adopted father, and as such he tolerated no vague conventional answer: he wanted to know exactly where I was going.

In the 1990s Indonesia was ruled by the New Order regime under the leadership of Suharto. Authoritarian, centralist, and modernist, the New Order for three

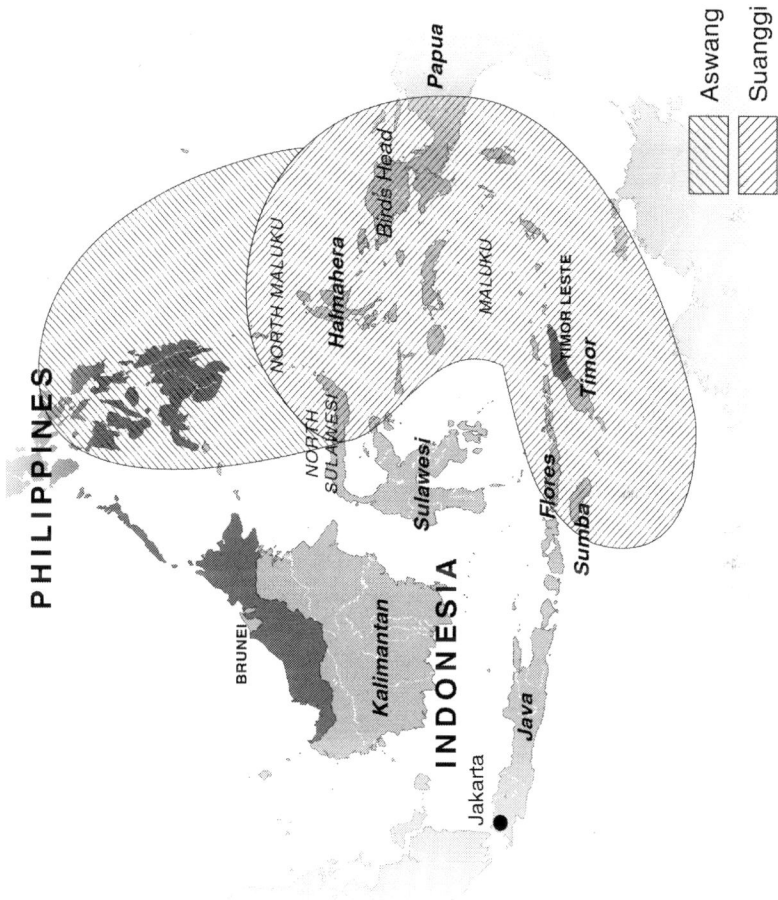

Map 3. Approximate geographical extension of the terms *aswang* and *suanggi*.

semantic variations of the *suanggi*, for one, were simply too great (Ellen 1993b), in some places being a sorcerer who learns technique, in other places a cannibal witch. Equally important, however, to the failed comparative ambition were its theoretical bearings. The part-whole relationship between social structure and evil figure that Van Wouden postulated simply did not hold. I suggest it is time to reassess the complexity of the *suangi* complex in particular (and of witchcraft in general) by releasing it from the social part-whole relationship within which it has been trapped.[23] Hopefully, what I have to say about the corporeality, inaccessibility, and doubt associated with witchcraft in Buli may find some comparative purchase not only in the eastern part of the Indian Ocean but also beyond.

## The Story of Witchcraft in Three Soundscapes

Three revolutions characterize Buli history in the twentieth century: the conversion to Christianity after 1900; the incorporation of Buli into the Indonesian nation-state in 1950; and the discovery of minerals and the introduction of a monetized economy in the late 1990s. All three revolutions have been associated with hopes for a better future, and indeed all are seen in Buli today as major steps on the road to becoming modern. Despite and over the course of these three revolutions, however, witchcraft has persisted—obstinately, embarrassingly, and incomprehensibly. Under the new conditions promoted by these shifts, witchcraft continues, even as people keep hoping for its demise.

This book is organized around three ethnographic sound bites, three "auditory landscapes" that fix these historical revolutions at three specific moments in Buli history: 1933, 1993, and 2004. I outline these historically situated soundscapes, as Alain Corbin has suggested, "with a view to detecting, rather than dictating, the passions that stirred them" (1999:xx). Like the sound bite in the preface featuring the masticating but absent dog, the soundscapes from 1933, 1993, and 2004 are voices from particular historical moments when political power and existential anxieties came together in a contentious relationship that invariably revolved around hopes and concerns about the *gua*. Witchcraft in Buli is not an unchanging phenomenon; it is a historically changing social aporia, a reality full of dilemmas that have different contours and to which different solutions appear to present themselves in each historical moment.[24] I propose that historically the appeal of the outside world to people in Buli has largely correlated with the extent to which it seemed to offer a solution to the problem of the *gua*. A certain historical constant haunts this appeal, however: As a changing world appeared to offer new solutions to the aporias of witchcraft, the implementation of these solutions appeared to produce new versions of the same aporias. At every turn the *gua* seemed to steal its way into these new conditions. Those relations of attachment people maintain "to compromised conditions of possibility whose realization is discovered either to be *im*possible, sheer fantasy, or *too* possible, and toxic" amount to a "cruel optimism," in the words of Lauren Berlant (2011:24, italics in the original). The three soundscapes that begin chapters 4, 6, and 8, respectively, seek to depict three historical moments in the cruel optimism that adheres to Buli hopes of ending witchcraft.

After a theoretical discussion of the relevance of the notions of doubt and aporia to anthropology and the study of witchcraft, read through a particular case of witchcraft in chapter 1, I present an outline of Buli myths about the origins of witchcraft in chapter 2, suggesting that myth constitutes an institutionalized form of doubt. Chapter 3 traces the long history of political protest that rippled through North Maluku in the eighteenth and nineteenth centuries against the legitimacy of the sultanates of Tidore and Ternate, protests that were fueled by a political ambition to resurrect the sultanate of Jailolo. The ambition gradually developed strikingly millenarian overtones, as it became linked to an expectation that the dead would come back to life. This hope for the resurrection of the dead—a hope that was closely connected to the dream of bringing an end to witchcraft in Buli—became a key factor in the enthusiasm with which people converted to Christianity in 1901. The first auditory landscape, which opens chapter 4, comes from 1933. It describes the noise made by a group of angry Buli people as they try to drown out the Christian sermons of the village's first missionary by drumming and dancing. These people were animists who in 1901 had enthusiastically converted to Calvinist Christianity because, for a short while, it seemed to offer deliverance from death and witchcraft. This promise, or so these people felt, soon revealed itself as a lie, however, and they apostatized in disgust. When the Calvinist mission returned to Waiflí in the 1930s, it was therefore a provocation, and the animists made a last stand. To the animists it was evident that adopting the Christianity of the Dutch colonial masters did not mean the end of death and witchcraft; instead converted Christians seemed to behave like witches, and witches concealed themselves by converting to Christianity. Chapter 5 delves into the corporeal dimensions of witchcraft, a perverse corporeality that is the basis of its horror. I describe how witchcraft targets all the central sites of embodied existence. In a world where the body is the auspicious measure for the correct manufacturing of most socially significant objects—houses, boats, weapons, and traps—the viscerality of witchcraft is itself a form of world unmaking, and this is arguably a pivotal aspect of the horror of the *gua*. It is the visceral and world-unmaking horror of the *gua*, I suggest, that has historically impelled people in Buli to look to the outside world for possible ways of dealing with it, understanding it, and perhaps eradicating it.

The second soundscape is from 1993 and opens chapter 6. It is the call of Sami, who from her sickbed deliriously and desperately implores the police and army officers to shoot the suspected witch that has made her ill. Like Christianity before it, New Order development appeared to Buli people from the mid-1960s to the late 1990s to offer a solution to the problem of witchcraft, this time through inclusion in the political order of the modern Indonesian state. Centralist, authoritarian, and controlled by the former lieutenant-general Suharto, the New Order regime (1967–98) practiced a form of development that combined a growth-oriented, but also clientist, economic policy with a form of political control that sought ideological homogeneity (Hill 1994; Schwarz 1994; Siegel 1986). As a number of excellent anthropological accounts have shown, on the nation's periphery the focus was economic (but highly monopolized and corrupt) development and the domestication of all forms of cultural, ethnic, and religious expression that were seen to constitute a political challenge (Acciaioli 1985; Antlöv 1995; Aragon 2000; Keane 1997; Kipp 1993; Li 2000; Rutherford 2003; Spyer 2000). For the most part loyal to the developmentalism of the New Order regime, people in Buli hoped that the state and its project of development (I. *pembangunan*) might bring an end to witchcraft. Far from rooting out witchcraft, however, the New Order state seemed to offer greater protection to witches than to their victims, and it widened the scope of what witchcraft could be in the first place by demonizing the guardian spirits or *suang*, a main source of traditional protection against witchcraft. The result is the production in Buli of witchcraft as a form of "cultural intimacy" (Herzfeld 2005), a rueful but central aspect of the image Buli people have of themselves as "backward" and not truly modern. In many ways, it is precisely the persistence of the *gua*, in spite of all their attempts to rid themselves of it, that for Buli people has come to define them as essentially "backward."

Chapter 7 presents an analysis of the fundamental opacity that characterizes the Buli notion of subjectivity and sociality. The minds of human beings are fundamentally opaque (Robbins and Rumsey 2008), to each other and to themselves. It is in this opacity that witchcraft operates and out of which it is constantly reproduced. In light of the fundamental unknowability of humans to themselves and to each other, tradition advocates a constant ethics of care (*istiár*). While chapter 2 outlined the mythical contour of witchcraft as an aporia, chapter 7 looks at the traditional social practices through which the aporias of witchcraft are managed but simultaneously also constantly reproduced. Buli tradition (*adat re atorang*) is essentially an ethos of "care" or "caution" that seeks to conjure up proper sociality and conviviality through a morality of exchange and an ethical care of the self in the full awareness that this is an impossible ideal. Unlike Christianity and the Indonesian state, Buli tradition never promises any solutions to witchcraft, only a pragmatics of caution.

The third and final soundscape is from 2004 and begins chapter 8. It is my frustrated account of the ear-splitting noise of music, motorbikes, and TVs that completely transformed the sonic landscape of village life after 1997 as people found new sources of wealth through land compensation and jobs in the newly opened nickel mine in Buli. The money in turn allowed them to acquire new consumer goods, many of them producing electronically or mechanically enhanced forms of noise. Life in Halmahera changed dramatically during the late 1990s when vast deposits of lateritic nickel were discovered in the regions of Buli, Maba, and Weda. The Indonesian mining company Aneka Tambang (Antam) opened its first strip mine in Buli on the island of Gei in 1997, and since then half a dozen other mining sites have sprung up in the area. The arrival of commercial mining in Buli almost coincided with the fall of the New Order regime in 1998, along with the gradual democratization of Indonesia. In the first decade of the new millennium, the combined effect of mining and democratization caused a demographic, economic, and social revolution in Buli. In the village of Waiflí alone the population grew sevenfold from around 200 in 1991 to more than 1,400 in 2010. As mine workers, petty traders, and government officials from other parts of Halmahera and Indonesia have flooded to Buli in search of good fortune and prosperity, the place has transformed from a sleepy village cluster with a population of around 2,000 into a bustling pioneering town with a population of nearly 10,000 people. But in spite of the fact that venture capitalism was accompanied by severe environmental degradation in the region, and that democratization began with a protracted ethnoreligious conflict between 1999 and 2001 that killed several thousand people and poisoned relations between Muslims and Christians in North Maluku, the Buli people I know mainly see the upside of these radical changes.[25] Buli is finally becoming part of "the modern world" (I. *dunia modern*).

The new kind of modernity that came to Buli in the first years of the twenty-first century seemed, in other words, to beckon with a particular vista—namely, inclusion in the world of modern technology and wage labor. In part at least, this new vista—like the vistas opened by Christianity and by state order before it—is attractive, I argue, because it suggests, yet again, the possibility of an end to the *gua*. The electric lights and noises of modernity, Buli people hope, will drive away the *gua*. But like the modern vistas before it, for many people in Buli the sociotechnological landscape of the new millennium appears not only to harbor hopes of an end to witchcraft but also, ironically and tragically, to establish new conditions for its reproduction. Witchcraft changes, invariably and constantly, as it diffuses into, and even thrives within, the very conditions that were supposed to signal its end. Witches, as one woman complained to me in 2004, are cleverer than university professors, and appear to change at least as fast as social life itself in Buli. Witchcraft, it appears, is as plastic as the modern changes that seemed to hold out the promise of its disappearance. That is the irony of both witchcraft and modernity in Buli.

For more than a century the attempt to get a grip on the aporias of witchcraft through an encompassment of the outside world has been a constant concern and continuous source of both hope and disappointment in Buli social history. The doubts that make up the only possible human engagement with witchcraft are part of a historical world-making in Buli, a key factor in the historical engagement that Buli people have with the outside world. Buli people's attempts to solve the unsolvable, understand the inexplicable, and perchance banish the unbanishable are constitutive of a Buli "worlding" in Tsing's sense (2010): their historical engagement with themselves, modernity, and the world at large in a contextual mutuality. Witchcraft regarded in this sense is not a belief system that has responded to or been a reflection of historical change. Quite to the contrary, "witchcraft doubts" have been a driving force in the shaping of Buli historical agency and change, in their varying attempts to make the outside world available as a solution to their problems, to accept and to read into historical changes that have arrived on the shores of Buli the possible hope of handling, or even eradicating, witchcraft.

This book, then, is an ethnographic account and a cultural history of an aporia over the *longue durée*. It is an account of the existential, moral, visceral, and social dilemmas that congeal around witchcraft as an impossibility and a reality, and it is a description of the many ways that people in Buli during the last century have engaged each other, their own tradition, and modernity, as this was offered to them, in an attempt to deal with witchcraft as an existential *problematique*. The *gua* is an aporia, a condition of being without a path—blocking Buli people, in their own view, from achieving proper conviviality as demanded by tradition (*adat re atorang*), from maintaining corporeal integrity and comfort, and from becoming truly modern.

-if only we could put all the witches
in the meatgrinder (Dahl)

# I

# WITCHCRAFT, DOUBT, AND APORIA

No society can live without in a sense opposing its own
value system: it has to have such a system, yet it must at the
same time define itself in contradistinction to it.

BAUDRILLARD, *The Transparency of Evil* (1993)

It was July 1999 and two years into the Southeast Asian economic crisis. The parliamentary elections in June, the first since the collapse of the New Order regime in 1998, had launched a race for the next president of Indonesia. The incumbent, Jusuf Habibie, was pitted against three contenders: Megawati, Gus Dur, and Amien Rais. The victor would turn out to be Gus Dur, the sage of traditionalist Islam and a vocal reformer (Barton 2002).

The late 1990s were full of promise and anxiety. The student protests that had brought down Suharto in May 1998 had been driven by a wave of ardent enthusiasm for a new and democratic future. But throughout Indonesia, economic crisis had stoked political tensions that since the fall of the New Order regime had reached a boiling point, causing several instances of social, religious, and ethnic turmoil. In Ambon, the capital of the province of Maluku, to which Buli still belonged in mid-1999, there had been fighting between Christians and Muslims, locals and immigrants, for six months. The violence appeared to have abated for some weeks, but then suddenly in July it erupted anew, reaching hitherto unseen levels of brutality. In Buli, some 500 kilometers to the north, news of these events appeared to augur a new era. As the end of the millennium drew near, the grim overtures of democracy in Indonesia blended with local concerns (Bubandt 1998a). A few months later, the paranoia generated by the violence in Ambon would play an integral part in the violence that flared up throughout North Maluku as well (see chapter 8).

In July 1999, however, the immediate concern in Buli was the rain. All year the rains had been unusually heavy, incessant even. A world off-kilter always means too much rain. Some blamed the inundation on the violence in Ambon, while others felt the cause was more local. There were rumors that the ancestors (*smengit*) and the mythical hero of Buli, Íyan Toa, were upset. The national Indonesian mining company, Aneka Tambang, had recently begun nickel excavations on the small island of Gei, located just off the coast of Buli village, and some speculated that it could also be this unauthorized disturbance of the forest that had caused the unprecedented rainfall. Something had to be done.

Coincidentally, the mining company had recently approached the Kapita, the ritual guardian of the shrine of Íyan Toa, to ask that a "traditional ceremony" be performed. This was part of a strategy used by most mining companies in the region to ensure the solidarity of "the local population" (I. *penduduk setempat*). The strategy was hatched from the modernist and condescending notion that "traditional people" would accept mining operations if traditional ceremonies were performed. And the strategy worked, although not for the intended reasons. The request strengthened Buli ideas that the company was in operational and financial trouble and now required assistance from Íyan Toa. The idea that a large mining company might need the help of a local mythical ancestor to prevent rain from obstructing production, and to raise the nickel content of the ore, implied a new recognition of local spirits, spirits that were otherwise conventionally frowned upon by modernist bureaucrats and Christian ministers alike.

The abnormally heavy rains in July 1999 were not the only symptom of ancestral dissatisfaction. There was also a strong sense in the village that there were markedly more instances of illness and death than usual. Indeed, the two problems, rain and illness, appeared to be linked. Like the rain, the recent cases of illness could be indications that Íyan Toa no longer "stood in front of" (*tiban*) his human descendants to protect them from the *gua* witches that often caused people to fall ill or die. The illness of a young woman named Lisa appeared to support this bleak hypothesis. Lisa's infirmity was originally divined to be related to a recent childbirth, a case of insufficient attention to the purifications needed to expel the "raw blood" (*lafláf ululif*) that accumulates in the womb during pregnancy. But when a second divination (*failál*)—later supported by a third—revealed that Lisa had been attacked by a *gua*, a cannibalistic witch, the number of somber statements grew.

The reappearance of the specter of the *gua* after several months without any attacks seemed to bring a tension back into the social life of the village, and to lend an urgency to everyday conversation that I had experienced in Buli many times before. People would make sure to venture into their gardens only in pairs, and at night small groups of men and women would form, as if by coincidence, as people made their way toward the stream to urinate or defecate. Parents would be extra careful to warn their children not to roam around alone after dark, and Lisa's illness became an additional reason for them to prohibit their school-age children from going to the shops of one of the Bugis traders to watch television till long past their bedtime.

As people tried to take precautions to avoid further attacks, the social terror of the *gua* began to take on comical forms as well. Laughing, a young man told me how he had been nearly frightened to death earlier in the day. He had been clearing his swidden garden when he was surprised by a sudden, loud thump behind him. Turning with his knife held, ready to face the attacking *gua*, he realized it was the sound of a bamboo, exploding from the heat of the fire. In aporia, fear and fun, tragedy and comedy, are never far apart.

## Theoretical Excursus 1: Experience without End

The word *aporia* means "puzzle" or "without a path." It is used in Greek philosophy to denote a puzzle that generates a state of perplexity. *Aporia* derives from the word *poros*, meaning "path," particularly one associated with water, such as a sea route or a route down a river (Kofman 1988:10). Gareth Matthews, for instance, translates *aporia* as "without a means of passing a river" (1999:30). It refers to the act or difficulty of passing, the problem of dealing with something difficult, or the impenetrability of an enigma. This association of the aporia with the dangers of water and rivers in Greek thought resonates closely with the Buli analogy between witchcraft and barnacles hidden in the river. Witchcraft is an invisible danger hidden by the reflection of reality's surface, as it were. An existential bewilderment is at the heart of witchcraft in Buli that also runs through the notion of *aporia* in ancient Greek thought. *Aporia* thus refers to the feeling of being at a loss, of being perplexed, or of being embarrassed when confronting such problems (Liddell and Scott 1990:215). These various meanings developed historically, it would appear, within Greek thought and were incorporated into philosophy at different times and for different purposes. Initially taken to refer to a numbing embarrassment, a place from which no roads led out and where thinking was therefore stuck, the concept of *aporia* arguably came into its own philosophically with Aristotle. Instead of denoting an impassable hindrance or an embarrassment, for Aristotle *aporia* came to signify the productive essence of existential philosophy—the necessary beginning of thought itself (Matthews 1999:118; Rescher 2001). Aristotle's thesis was that *aporia* constituted the beginning of philosophical inquiry. *Aporia*, in the Aristotelian understanding, designated the kind of puzzle that needed to be sought out and stated clearly in order for philosophy to commence. Jacques Derrida pushed this line of thinking further, making it part of his general theory of deconstruction and suggesting that aporias are inescapably part of all Western thought. Indeed, aporias made philosophy possible and impossible at the same time. Aporias, Derrida proposed, haunted the logic of the Western philosophical tradition, always undermining the possibility of stable meaning, of a pure origin. For Derrida, the term *aporia* became a sort of diagnostic device with which to deconstruct Western metaphysics, and he discussed a series of topics through a more or less explicit invocation of the concept of *aporia*: speech and writing (Derrida 1976), gift exchange (Derrida 1992b), death (Derrida 1995), religion (Derrida 2002), and justice and democracy (Derrida 2005).[1] Although Derrida's application of this concept was aimed at deconstructing Western metaphysics, I suggest that its applicability is much broader. Aporia refers to the inherent instability of all systems of meaning, the "blind spots" of any metaphysical argument" (Lucy 2004:1). But how can one focus on a blind spot? In Buli, the *gua* is the embodiment of a "blind spot" in this sense, an invisibility before which meaning and existential certainty fragment at every level: morally, spiritually, corporeally, socially, epistemologically, and historically.

Derrida was perhaps most explicit about his use of the concept of *aporia* in his critique of Heideggerian phenomenology, in which he suggested that aporia was built into the relationship between being and death. There is, Derrida argued, a conundrum that lies at the heart of phenomenological thought: being is a being-unto-death as Martin Heidegger (1962) saw it, and yet it is impossible to experience one's own death. Phenomenology is, in other words, a philosophical inquiry into experience that has to place outside of human experience that which forms its existential basis: death. Phenomenology's notion of being, with its dual but aporetically linked focus on experience and mortality, was grounded on what Derrida calls "an anthropological border" that separated humans from animals: humans are allegedly unique in that we live our lives in the knowledge that we are destined to die (1993:41). Under these conditions Derrida asks, "Is my death possible?" (21). Firstly, is it meaningful to ask this question at all? Does the question appear odd because language is not meant to capture death, or is death not always outside of language? Herein lies the first aporia of death—namely, its impossibility in language. Secondly, does death make sense from the point of view of being-in-the-world? If my death always remains outside of my experience, and if I can experience only the death of another (or of myself as another in my imagination), death "as such" ceases to exist at the very same time that death, as a reified and unavoidable presence in language and the conscious mind, defines my being. As Derrida remarks, "The death of the other comes first, always first" (76). Our inability to approach death as experience means that we constantly return to it as a limit of experience. In Western metaphysics, it seems, life and death are in an oppositional relationship that constantly generates death and its relation to being as a problem or as an aporia (Derrida 1995; Johnson 2008:ix).

Death, for Derrida, is an aporia in a Western phenomenal world because it can never be experienced, and yet it functions as a horizon for an entire philosophy of "being." But this status of death as both impossible and foundational is not universal; it clings to a certain kind of metaphysics that may be uniquely Western. As James Siegel (2006:2) asks, What about societies (indeed, most societies outside the West) where the line between life and death is not so easily drawn? Arguably, in this light it is not death as such that is aporetic, but certain kinds of death, such as "bad deaths" or "difficult deaths" (Hertz 1960; Seale and Van der Geest 2004). Witchcraft in Buli establishes as a real possibility such "bad" or impossible "deaths," and thus I claim that witchcraft in Buli is aporetic for a reason that is similar, if not identical, to death's aporia in Western metaphysics: it represents a nonviability, an impasse, that allows no proper path for understanding, emotional comfort, or experience, and therefore continuously produces perplexity and doubt as its main condition of being-hidden.

"The fear of death," Derrida maintains, "is what gives all witchcraft, all oc-cult medicine, a hold" (2008:23). In Buli it would be more accurate to say that witchcraft, far from promising to soothe the fear of death by somehow providing it with an explanation, is what injects terror into certain kinds of death. Whereas all death is aporetic in Western metaphysics, in Buli—and other places where humans cultivate close and interdependent relationships with the ancestor spirits of the dead—not all death is aporetic in the manner that Derrida's quote sug-gests. In Buli, at any rate, it is not death "as such" that makes witchcraft a problem; rather, it is witchcraft that makes some deaths aporetic. Some deaths are problem-atic or "difficult," not only because of the manner in which they happen, but also because of what comes after. If the causes of these deaths are uncertain, so too are their effects. Some deaths have no end, provide no closure. Some deaths are haunt-ing long before they happen, and long after. Witchcraft illness and death have, in other words, an "afterlife," for they are full of social conflict, physical suffering, emotional agony, and cognitive confusion. Also, and significantly, they are diffi-cult because they are uncertain.

Although Derrida's analysis outlined above is mainly concerned with destabi-lizing Western philosophy and its particular idea of being as presence and death as its limit, I think there is, nevertheless, a general analytical point here: an aporia marks the tipping point at which our very means of capturing the meaning of experience is what estranges us from that meaning. I have no intention, nor am I in any position, to provide a detailed account of Derrida's work or its relationship to phenomenology and Greek philosophy (but see Protevi 1994; Reynolds 2005). It appears to me, however, that Derrida's and Aristotle's understanding of aporia converge on one common point: that aporia is not the end. Rather, it is a beginning—a frustrating and agonizing beginning, but a beginning nonetheless.[2] The reason is that an aporia can never be left alone, it *"can never simply be endured as such"* (Derrida 1993:78, italics in the original). An aporia poses a problem to experience, a limit. For is it possible to experience an aporia as such (3)? One senses that the answer for Derrida is no: it cannot be experienced "as such," but must become something else. An aporia is and is-not at the same time. It withdraws from experience yet still presents a limit, a horizon. This indeterminacy is what is both unavoidable and unendurable, and when confronted with an aporia, an impossibility, we are obliged to seek a path where there is none. An aporia therefore commands constant attention and work, even though this work is always already impossible. I will venture to say that this experience—that conceptual and emotional existence may find itself up against a limit at which it is in danger of dissolving—is not the monopoly of Western metaphysics but has itself, as a condition of experience, a broader applicability (although this formulation probably reveals that I am precisely the kind of phenomenologist against whom Derrida employed the concept of *aporia*).

Aporias in this sense are useful as analytical entry points into the experiential problems of intersubjective existence, Western or otherwise. Aporias can be characterized as those concerns that chafe the heels of the central dilemmas of how self, sociality, and time are made and unmade. While aporias may be a general fact of life, they naturally grow out of and feed upon particular conceptions and practices of being, and they are also embedded in particular historical, political, and cultural conditions. Because aporias can never be endured as such, when facing them people need to continuously produce solutions, however partial and inadequate those solutions may be. In Buli, the solutions are constructed in a *bricolage* fashion, composed out of the cultural matter and materials made available by changing historical, political, and social conditions. The aporia and its partial solutions are thus part of the same unstable and emergent whole.

*"She saw the* gua *with her own eyes, so it must be true . . ."*

At times, aporias—offering "no path," no way out—command all attention. So, too, in July 1999 in Buli. Daily conversations in the village would, inevitably, turn on whether there was any news about Lisa. One afternoon I found myself sheltering from the rain with five other people in the kitchen of Hitam and his wife, Roda. Besides Hitam, Roda, and myself, there were Roda's two sisters, Dika and Tila, and Kenari, their next-door neighbor.

The three sisters had gathered to grate coconuts in order to make cooking oil, and they were chatting and generally enjoying each other's company. Hitam, meanwhile, was not quite himself. Three days earlier, while on a trip to collect sea cucumber (*moka*) to sell to the local Chinese merchant, he had stepped on the dorsal fin of a poisonous stonefish (*nof*) and had received a potentially fatal and exceedingly painful sting to his foot. Initially there had been some fears that the sting would kill him, but after three days of serious illness, Hitam was now recovering. Divination had suggested that it was the ancestral spirit (*smengit*) of his deceased father who had "pushed" (*taf*) him onto the stonefish, angry that Hitam had not honored the forefather ritually for some time. As Hitam sat quietly nursing his swollen foot, conversation among the rest of us assembled in his kitchen eventually centered on Lisa.

"She saw the *gua* with her own eyes, so it must be true," Kenari began. A few days earlier Lisa had told the family members who were tending her how the witch attack on her had happened, and the story had immediately leaked throughout the village. Lisa had been walking to her garden patch a few weeks earlier with two younger nieces when a large black dog had suddenly jumped her from behind. As she looked up, the dog—walking upright on two legs—had turned away. As it did so, the figure's reflection (*gurumin*) had flickered—like a television image when

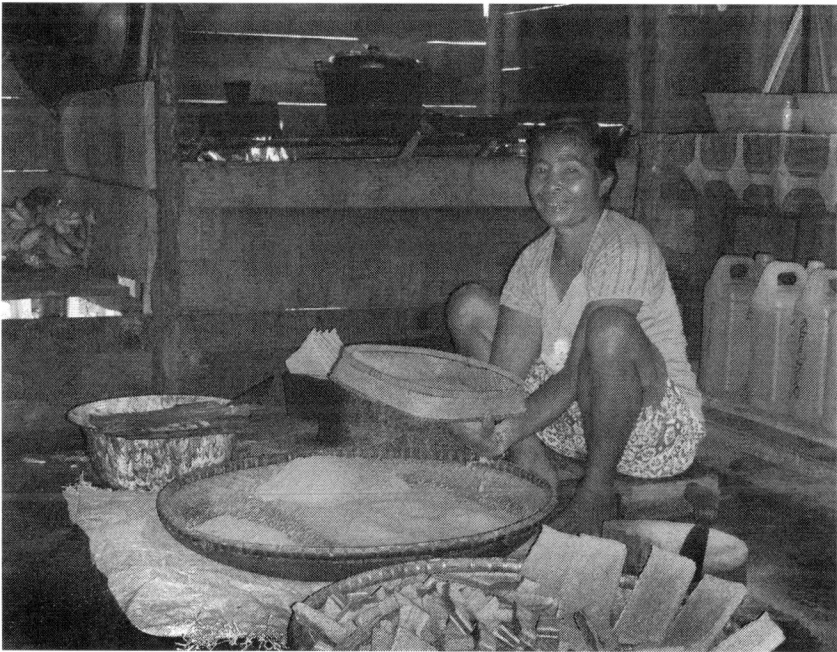

Figure 2. Hatanuna Lukam baking sago bread. 2007. Photo by author.

the reception is poor—and as it did so, it briefly transformed into Lisa's aunt, Yantima (see fig. 3).[3] After getting back on her feet, Lisa had continued along the path to her garden, only to be attacked by the black dog a second time, and then a third time. During the final attack Lisa had lost consciousness, and perhaps it was here that the dog ate her liver, as the *gua* are wont to do. Regaining consciousness, Lisa had heard the dog speak to her, saying: "It is your mother"s grudge (*singan*) that brings you this. If you tell anyone, you will surely die."

Later, Lisa had forgotten about the event. In Buli, one's shadow/reflection (*gurumin*) is also one's consciousness and memory, and people say the witch takes away the victim's shadow during its violent attack. The victim therefore has no knowledge of the attack. Indeed, Lisa's young nieces similarly had no recollection of meeting either dogs or relatives in the garden. So it was that the incident—memorable as it otherwise was—had been forgotten. Now, however, Lisa had regained her memory of the events. As the Buli expression has it, "Her inside had hit upon it" again (*ulor ya neto*). Convention has it that "one's inside" can "hit upon" a witch attack only because the witch has made memory possible by returning the *gurumin* (shadow) to the victim. But the witch's returning the shadow consciousness to the victim, and with it memory, is full of spite. The *gua* allows memory to return only when it is already too late. For this reason, recalling a *gua* attack is always alarming; remembering it is potentially a sign of one's imminent death. At the same time, memory of the event is the most reliable route to recognizing the cause of the illness and the identity of the *gua*. In other words, the witch occupies an aporetic nonspace between memory and forgetfulness, between event and ignorance, between consciousness and oblivion. Memory of a *gua* attack is, simultaneously, an omen of death and the best road to a cure.

Lisa's account of the attack had opened a serious rift between her family and that of her aunt. Her narrative had quickly reached also the ears of the accused family of Lisa's aunt. Soon after, a public quarrel had broken out between Lisa's

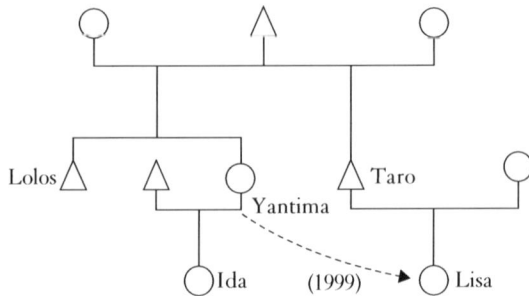

**Figure 3.** The attack.

mother and Ida, the daughter of the aunt presumed to be a *gua*. "Raw! Raw blood! That is what it is. She is crazy, crazy [because she hasn't sought treatment for her postnatal condition]," Ida had shouted. Ida's public assertion that rawness was involved not only served as a defense of Yantima, her mother; it also implied moral laxity on Lisa's part. Lisa had two children with two different men, and Ida publicly insinuated that promiscuity and Lisa's lack of attention to "women's things" (*maping riri*) were at the root of her illness. Lisa's mother, meanwhile, had hotly retorted: "We do not know the work of the *gua*. Are you a *gua* yourself since you know what happens in this house?"

As talk in Hitam's kitchen turned to the details of this public dispute, a more general conversation about *gua* began to develop. I was partly responsible for instigating the conversation. I had brought a video camera, because I wanted to make amends for my regrettable tendency to never record interviews, a tendency that made me feel I lacked documented evidence for the many assertions, guesstimates, and pronouncements about the *gua* that I had heard or witnessed over the previous eight years. So I asked a deliberately ignorant question, hoping that the presence of the camera would encourage a kind of self-objectification, a need to be understood by the eye of the camera, which would transcend the awkwardness that ordinarily surrounds public talk of witchcraft. As it turned out, my question generated a conversation that showed the wide range of emotional responses that witchcraft, in my experience, always generates: embarrassment and anger, frustration and doubt, self-justification and self-deprecation. In that sense the recorded conversation is not unusual at all: it highlights the highly reflexive and theoretical problem that witchcraft constitutes in Buli, which is a far cry from conventional anthropological representations of witchcraft as a merely practical and empirical concern. The conversation also reveals witchcraft's aporetic nature in Buli—the impossibility of translating the experience of witchcraft into soothing explanation, as every attempt to comprehend it generates new uncertainty. To illustrate the way people endeavor, continuously and unsuccessfully, to domesticate witchcraft, this chapter tacks between the concrete story of Lisa's illness and a general discussion about the many dilemmas, difficulties, and contradictions of the *gua* in Buli, thereby emphasizing how acutely aware people are of these difficulties and contradictions, and of their insolvability.

Witchcraft is as ubiquitous in Buli as E. E. Evans-Pritchard reported it being in Azande. But unlike in Evans-Pritchard's account of Azande, in Buli it is not the object of a "natural philosophy by which the relations between men and unfortunate events are explained" (Evans-Pritchard 1937:63), a philosophy that was "not incommoded" by its internal contradictions (28). Rather, in Buli, witchcraft is the object of an explicit and self-conscious philosophy of uncertainty that seeks to grapple with the epistemological, ontological, and reflexive aporia of witchcraft. People are in fact extremely "incommoded" by the contradictions of witchcraft, and they worry a great deal about their irreducibility. Therefore—and again, unlike in Azande, where Evans-Pritchard reported that it "is no use saying to a Zande 'Now tell me what you Azande think about witchcraft,' because the subject is too general and indeterminate, both too vague and too immense, to be described concisely" (70)—my question that afternoon in 1999—"What is witchcraft, really?"—sparked a lengthy discussion about witchcraft, in practice as well as in general. In fact, I propose that Buli people engage explicitly in this kind of general speculation *precisely because* "the subject is too general and indeterminate, both too vague and too immense, to be described concisely." It is this excess of vagueness and indeterminacy—the absence of explanations and stable meaning—that makes general speculation necessary in the first place. It is because the *gua* is "an interminable experience" (Derrida 1993:16) that it cannot be left alone, and for the same reason it can never be resolved or function as an explanation. Witchcraft is a general, epistemological, and ontological problem because it is acknowledged to be so "difficult" (I. *susah*), so fraught with contradictions.

NILS: What is the *gua*, really? How would you explain this to someone who does not know anything about it?

KENARI: That is the question: "What is the *gua* in reality (I. *sebenarnya*)." This is what the police also ask: "What is the *gua*, really?"

TILA: The *gua* is a *setan*, a devil who eats people, a ghost (I. *hantu*) [*laughing*].

KENARI: For the police, the *gua* does not make sense, so they have to ask.

RODA: You know, one or two of the police officers believe, too.

KENARI: Oh, they must, because every village has its own *setan*. This is what I told the police officers who came here when my wife died [a few years earlier, also allegedly because of a *gua* attack]. I said: "Pak, there are two perspectives on this. I know that you in your duty as a policeman have to follow the letter of the law (I. *hukum*). But when we speak about you and me as people, it is a different matter. We do not know about these things. This is a fact of life (I. *itu soal biasa*). And therefore we also have to follow traditional law (I. *hukum adat*) in these matters." So the matter of the *gua* is difficult (I. *susah*).

RODA: Very difficult! For one thing we cannot see them.

KENARI: When the *gua* spears or eats someone, that person may or may not see the *gua*. We do not know. But people do not normally see the *gua*. Only when the *gua* comes to attack you do you see it.

TILA: And then you faint and do not know anything anymore [*laughing*].

Seeing and not-seeing, believing and not-believing, knowing and not-knowing, making sense and not-making-sense: these aporias of witchcraft in Buli are made all the more difficult by the fact that customary ways of trying to understand and manage the reality of the *gua* are being challenged by Indonesian legal institutions. The law makes no concessions to the reality of the *gua*; rather, it insists on dealing with witchcraft by denying it. This denial appears to Buli people, well versed as they are in the power of true faith after a century of Christianity, to hold a promise of its own: perhaps if one denied the reality of the *gua* with sufficient conviction, it would cease to exist? At the same time, this promise is highly tenuous, for the same police officers charged with the official act of denial often affirm the underlying reality of witchcraft, when they translate the *gua* into their own *setan*.

In this context, Roda's assertion that one or two of the police officers "believe, too" (*dela bená*) and Kenari's immediate response that "they must" are striking. It seems as though for both Kenari and Roda the belief of powerful outsiders provides a modicum of a grip on what they themselves can only doubt. It would appear, in other words, that Latour's (2010) notion of "the belief in belief" is not reserved for Western moderns. For Buli people, their belief in the police officers' beliefs in witchcraft (beliefs that the police can never publicly admit) takes on the quality of a "proof" of something in which Buli people themselves find it impossible to have faith. Since "proof" concerning witchcraft is so hard to come by, people must seize upon it wherever possible, even if this "proof" is the belief of outsiders who can never publicly admit to it.[4]

If the beliefs of the law enforcement officers provided one kind of tenuous proof of the *gua*'s reality for Buli people, the law itself seemed to offer another kind—namely, the recognition that came through the notion of "traditional law." It is thus a historical irony that the very national law (I. *hukum*) that is now rejecting witchcraft has historically created, as its own shadow, the institution of "traditional law" (I. *hukum adat*), which can sometimes be called upon, as it is by Kenari, to assert the reality of witchcraft with at least some semblance of juridical authority. The term *hukum adat*, understood as referring to a system of traditional laws and customs, became entrenched within the colonial scientific vocabulary in

Indonesia during the last decade of the nineteenth century, in particular through
the efforts of the Dutch legal scholar and Orientalist C. Snouck Hurgronje (Sonius 1981:li). Hurgronje and others identified a variety of local customary systems
throughout the Dutch colony, known as *adat*, which appeared to them to have the
character of legal systems. They increasingly felt, however, that these systems of
"*adat* law" were being undermined by direct rule and modernization. Beginning
in the early twentieth century it therefore became the role of the Dutch colonial
administration to protect these local systems of law. Generations of colonial officers were schooled in local law and culture before taking up positions in "the
Dutch East Indies," the colonial name for what would eventually become Indonesia. As a result, "scientific knowledge" of local *adat* law became part of the newfound moral grounding for colonial rule during the twentieth century (Bubandt
2005a:202; Sonius 1981:xxix). To a large extent, independent Indonesia copied this
legal dualism between national law, built on the principles of Dutch Roman law,
and *adat* law, perceived to be unique cultural systems specific to the local communities that had fostered them (for analyses of this, see Benda-Beckmann 1995;
Davidson and Henley 2007; Evers 1995; Li 2000; Lukito 2012). *Adat* law *(hukum
adat)* can therefore be invoked by Kenari and others in Buli as a kind of "paralegal
system"—a cultural law without the status of proper law, but nevertheless officially recognized—to assert witchcraft as "a fact of life," a *soal biasa*. The state's
acknowledgment of *adat* law is thereby translated into an indirect recognition of
witchcraft as a paralegal fact of life.

As a consequence, the aporia of witchcraft in Buli is not merely a local one. It
is a reflexive and representational aporia of a community vis-à-vis a nation-state
whose representatives are charged with upholding a state order of reason that denies the existence of witchcraft, but that also, through a twist of historical irony,
becomes implicated in what it denies. Witchcraft and its problematic reality are
thus an aporia deeply entangled in the imaginaries and experiences of Indonesian
modernity and nation building in Buli. Buli people deal with witchcraft in the
awkward awareness that it is simultaneously an official embarrassment, the subject of epistemic denial, and a fact of life—a *soal biasa*. This fact, however, is never
"there" in any simple way. It is a fact that is inherently concealed, and about which
one can only doubt.

Despite several visits to Lisa's sickbed, neither the local nurse from the health clinic
nor any of the three healers *(sowsów)* called in had been able to cure her illness.
Instead her condition had deteriorated. And when Lisa's account of the witchcraft
attack at this time appeared to give a reason for her lack of improvement, it sent

her family, who began to fear the worst, into a rage. Lisa's father, Taro, decided to call the police as well as the local village head (I. *kepala desa*) and persuaded them to force Yantima, the accused witch, to attempt to cure Lisa. Convention has it that the *gua* at fault is able to effect a cure, simply by saying a brief spell (*tawar*) into a glass of water, which the patient then drinks. This simple measure, it is said, will cure the damaged liver, which is the main cause of illness in cases of witchcraft (*ungan*). In spite of her remonstrations that she was not a *gua*, pressure from the police eventually persuaded Yantima to perform the curing ritual—just one day prior to our group conversation at Roda and Hitam's house.

Here, then, is another aporia of witchcraft in Buli: the witch is the optimal healer of its own victim. In Buli, this desperate possibility that the witch can provide the most effective remedy for the ailment of witchcraft is itself unstable, however. It is an inherently untrustworthy path, for how can one trust a witch to truly effect a cure? Perhaps the accused witch will deliberately misspeak the spell, or somehow make sure it is "without (magical) content" (*ni loló pa*). People say that embarrassment (*maimái*) may entice the witch to provide a real cure, but how can a creature bent on eating the livers of family and neighbors possibly be trusted to have human feelings such as shame? In fact, the *gua* is known to sometimes seize such an opportunity to finish off its victim, turning the cure into a poison (see chapter 6 for an example). The ability of the witch to provide a cure that is potentially also a poison entails a radical undecidability, an undecidability that is never resolved but kept in a state of perpetual tension.

## Theoretical Excursus 2: When the Cure Is Also the Poison

In his critique of Platonic logocentrism—the philosophical *epistēmē* that imagines finding, in abstract logic and thought, places of stable meaning that act as a kind of cure (Greek *pharmakon*) against unreason, confusion, and aporia (Stocker 2006:50)—Derrida points out that the Greek word for "medicine" (*pharmakon*) is itself polysemic and unstable. Not only can *pharmakon* mean both remedy and poison; it is also associated semantically with the witch or wizard (Greek *pharmakeus*) and the scapegoat (Greek *pharmakos*) (Derrida 2008:133). The imagined remedy for confusion (reason) is inherently colonized by and entangled with its opposite: witchcraft and poison. This, Derrida suggests, points to an aporia within the epistemic logic of Western Platonic thought. Logos as a cure (*pharmakon*) for confusion may itself also be a poison (*pharmakon*). In a famous passage from Plato's dialogue *Meno*, which I will discuss below, the young aristocrat Meno accuses Socrates during a debate of being a *pharmakeus* (a wizard) (Derrida 2008:119). Derrida uses this accusation to suggest that Western rationality is founded on a

*[handwritten marginal note:]* le fact that words have same are show aporia

paradox or an aporia: that Socratic reason actually looks suspiciously like witch-craft. While logic presents itself as a cure for confusion and ignorance, it may in fact also act as a poison on itself. This poisonous, dark side of logos must always be denied, however, for epistemic reason and stable meaning to endure.

For Socrates and Plato, aporia is a transitory stage, a philosophical prop of sorts. Aporia is a rhetorically induced state in one's opponent that can be turned into a conduit to real knowledge. Aporia has no real place in the Platonic "epistemol-ogy of presence"; it remains outside of reason, always available to domestication by epistemic reason. Derrida, however, uses the discussion about the internally poisonous nature of logos to suggest that aporia may be less easily removed or obviated than Socratic reason imagines.[5] Meno's experience of being bewitched is in this sense turned against Socratic reason. It highlights the lingering poison at the heart of palliative reason. Instead of being a minor obstacle to the inexorable advance of reason, Derrida argues that aporia is an irreducible experience of the impossibility of pure reason as such.

The same possibility that a poison is concealed in the cure clings to witchcraft in Buli. The fact that the most effective cure of witchcraft comes from the witch him- or herself contains a desperate irony, inherently full of uncertainty: the witch is the best doctor against the deadly illness it has cannibalistically induced. This irony—that the cure is also a poison—is not restricted to witchcraft healing; it has also been very much a part of Buli's historical experience. Christianity and moder-nity were received in Buli as a cure for witchcraft, seemingly offering the possibil-ity of doubt's end, but neither the conversion to Christianity nor the conversion to modernity has yet brought the final cure that it seemed to promise. Christianity and modernity may have introduced the hope for an epistemic cure for the *gua*, but these cures entailed their own forms of poison, allowing the *gua* to continue to live, and even to thrive, under those very conditions that were supposed to banish it (see chapter 4). As a consequence, Buli people agonize over the aporias of witch-craft, explicitly and on an almost daily basis.

*"First the grudge . . . then he eats you!"*

If the curing of witchcraft is full of aporia, so too are its causes:

NILS: Why do you think *gua* eat people, eat their liver (*yatai*)?

KENARI: There has to be a grudge, a foundation, first. Let us say, for in-stance, that I am a *gua* or a sorcerer (*mahapayao*). If you and I do not al-ready have some issue with each other, I would not attack you. There has to be a basis or a foundation (*ifif*) first.

TILA: First the grudge, and then the attack—then he eats you!

KENARI: Our ancestors used to say, "Whoever is not a *gua* will become one, and whoever is not a sorcerer will become one." It is because of this thing we are talking about: you are disappointed, "your inside breaks" (*ulor namgói*), and you become angry.

Grudges are the cause of witchcraft—that is clear enough. But grudges themselves are less clear. In most cases, in fact, they appear to be absent altogether. In sixty-one of the ninety-one cases of witchcraft-contingent illness and death on which I have obtained most data, I was unable to ascertain any grudge. Indeed, in many cases people said that there was no grudge. They may have said this for many reasons, of course. Perhaps they wanted to forget the grudge in order to make the attack all the more unreasonable. Perhaps they preferred not to say. Perhaps they really did not know. The problem is not so much the lack of possible grudges in every instance of witchcraft; it is more than there could be so many grudges. Thus, even the smallest, most forgettable, resentment could potentially cause an attack: a sarcastic remark between women washing clothes in the river, a water bucket that someone borrowed without permission, a dispute over who owns a banana palm. In practice, grudges (like the witches themselves) are therefore invisible. This renders any attempt to identify a grudge after an attack very difficult, and any attempt to foresee a grudge impossible. Hence, Kenari's claim that "there has to be a grudge" is more like a guess about what motivates *gua* than it is a statement of certainty. Knowing what grudge caused a particular attack takes a lot of reconstruction, a lot of guessing. Anger, after all, gnaws away on the inside of a person, not the outside.

An example of the invisibility of grudges (*singan*) is provided by the death of Selena, Kenari's wife and my adopted mother in 1996. According to Kenari, Selena had been beaten and her liver eaten by a married couple, Barbara and Kamadi, who were close neighbors. It had happened when Kenari and Selena had been on a two-day excursion to collect turtle eggs on the island of Gei. Barbara and Kamadi, meanwhile, had been night fishing (*fagaso*) nearby and, according to Kenari, attacked his wife while she was washing on her own by a stream. The grudge was, according to Kenari's family, the slightest possible—namely, the refusal of one of Selena's nieces to receive a betel nut from Barbara's daughter, joking that it might be poisonous. According to Kenari, this insinuation of sorcery was enough to set off the attack several months later when an opportunity presented itself. I knew Barbara and Kamadi well, and their account of Selena's death also involved a grudge, one in which I was involved. At the end of my first stint of fieldwork, I distributed my belongings to people I had come to know well. I decided to give my food cupboard, in which I stored food out of reach of dogs, rats, and cats to Annie, Kamadi's sister. Selena had been upset about this decision. I had built the cupboard myself, but the wood had come from an abandoned pile of planks owned by Kenari and Selena. Therefore, Selena argued, the cupboard rightfully was theirs. After my departure Selena had approached the *babinsa*, the noncommissioned military officer, accusing Annie of stealing the cupboard. A widow, Annie had few supporters, and she had been forced to give up the cupboard to Selena. Upset about the event, Annie's brother, Kamadi, had made a donation (I. *derma*) in church, swearing an oath that if his sister Annie was lying about the cupboard the donation should come and "get" her (*nyal i*). If, however, Selena, was in the wrong, God should "get" her. "And get her He did," Kamadi noted dramatically, "less than four months later." The irony is that if the reason for Selena's death was divine punishment, it was for an event that everybody remembered well. If, however, Selena's death was caused by witchcraft, the grudge was an event that most people had long forgotten, an event that had to be laboriously re-collected. Witchcraft always appears to absent itself, to hide its own reality from people.

Sometimes witchcraft itself can be the grudge. Such, it appeared, was the case with Lisa. Indeed, the *gua* dog that attacked Lisa had referred to this grudge during the attack when it announced, "It is your mother"s grudge (*singan*) that brings you this." This grudge went back to the marriage between Taluku and Ida. Ida was the daughter of the suspected perpetrator, Yantima. Taluku, meanwhile, was Lisa's cousin on her mother's side (see fig. 4). Lisa's mother, in particular, had been strongly against the marriage.

The reason for her opposition was that Ida's mother, Yantima, and her brother were accused of being the *gua* responsible for the death of Gora, Lisa's uncle, back

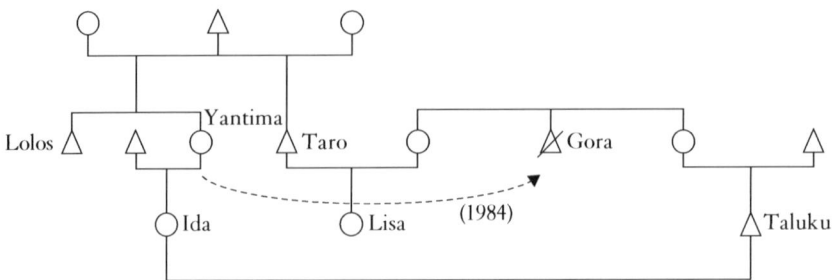

**Figure 4.** The grudge.

in 1984. "What are you doing marrying her? Her family ate your uncle!" Lisa's mother had protested to Taluku when he married Ida. The conflict was complicated by the fact that Lisa's father, Taro, was also Yantima's half brother (see fig. 4). When Yantima was accused of causing Gora's death in 1984, however, Taro had sided with his wife's family and broken off relations with his half sister. The marriage between Yantima's daughter and Lisa's maternal cousin five years after Gora's death had brought the painful consequences of this decision into the open. For the marriage meant that the two families would become in-laws (*paing*) and had to sit across the table from each other during the marriage negotiations—something that Lisa's parents had been quite unwilling to do.

Many families in Buli face problems similar to those of Taro and Taluku. Buli kinship is bilateral. This means that you are related both to people in your patri-line, called *ebai pusa* (trunk-house) or *fam*, and to members of your *ebai bangsá*, your "house of relatives" (the extended lineage beyond the immediate patrilineage, including the relatives of your mother as well as the maternal relatives of your father). The combination of bilateral kinship and the endemic nature of witch-craft means that Buli people are frequently related to both the accused witches and the victims of witchcraft attacks, either through blood or through marriage. Witchcraft feeds on, intervenes in, and frequently becomes a force in the making and breaking of such consanguineous and affinal relations. Buli custom (*adat re atorang*) is built on the decorum and ritual etiquette demanded by such relations. This proper etiquette makes and defines Buli society and subjectivity. Indeed, it is *adat re atorang*, literally "custom and rules," that protects against witchcraft by ex-horting people to adhere to proper conduct and exchange (see chapter 7). If every-one were to conduct themselves according to custom, there would be no grudges and therefore no witchcraft. Such is the ideal. Yet time and again witchcraft un-threads the fabric of proper sociality and conviviality. Witchcraft is indeed, as Ges-chiere (2003) has aptly put it, the "dark side of kinship." But in Buli witchcraft relations and kinship relations are so entangled that one cannot separate them in order to relink them causally in any clear fashion. So in Buli it would be inac-curate to suggest that witchcraft highlights "kinship tensions" as the structural-functionalist paradigm holds (Marwick 1990), just as it would be wrong to main-tain that witchcraft somehow explains or provides meaning to kinship misal-liances, as symbolic anthropology tends to claim (Douglas 1970). In Buli, there is no hint—for its inhabitants or for me—that witchcraft, the existence of the *gua*, somehow explains, regulates, or mediates kinship tensions. Rather, and disturb-ingly, witchcraft produces these tensions, undoing kinship relations in the process, tragically and unpredictably. Indeed, the grudge that has to be present for witch-craft to exist often does not become clear until after the attack is remembered. Seen in this perspective, witchcraft comes first, grudges second. Witchcraft is the primary reality around which kinship is forced to navigate. But given the inaccessible and invisible nature of witchcraft realities this is an impossible task.

Like all *gua* attacks in Buli, the death of Gora had left a long trail of social problems in its wake, which stretched on for years and transformed along the way. Difficult as the marriage negotiations had been, the marriage between Taluku and Ida had nevertheless, at least temporarily, forced the two families into cordial social relations, and Ida, though not well loved, had at least been accepted by Taluku's and Lisa's family. Lisa's illness broke this truce, however, and was an embarrassment to Ida in particular. Now she and Taluku would have to choose sides between her mother (who was accused of witchcraft) and Taluku's family (which, by extension, was the victim). Ida's attempts to mediate a few days earlier had failed miserably, ending in the public quarrel with Lisa's mother, during which Ida, too, was suddenly accused of being a witch. This possibility was likely because the ability to become *gua* witches runs along genealogical lines. Ida might well have inherited the seed of witchcraft from her mother.

> NILS: If we look at people in the village, most people are not *gua*, even though people get angry quite a bit.
>
> TILA: That is right; only very few people are *gua*.
>
> KENARI: To say that even ten people are *gua* in this village would be too high a number.
>
> NILS: But why, then, are they *gua* and the rest of us not?
>
> TILA: That is something people do by themselves. They steal and they hide.
>
> DIKA: They hide food, like bananas such as these [*laughing, picking up a bunch of small bananas from the table*].
>
> KENARI: They are too focused on their food, they want food for themselves. . . . It is this that makes someone a *gua*.
>
> RODA: The *gua* spirit will begin to flirt with them (*ncero si*)!
>
> DIKA: Like if you dream about food, and you decide not to tell.
>
> TILA: That is the *gua* spirit tempting you!
>
> KENARI: I have said this to Adam [a neighbor and classificatory son] already: "With your kind of behavior you will become a *gua*, too!"

RODA: Does he hide food?

KENARI: He does! He goes fishing and sells the whole catch, while his father and mother sit hungry in the house.

HITAM: His parents are old and no longer strong.

KENARI: And they sit there hungry! He will keep only enough fish for himself and his children and will sell the rest. My God! (I. *astaga firullah*!) So I have said to him: "Once upon a time, your father was a *gua*, so you have the 'seed' (*geo*) in you. One of these days this seed is going to grow in you with this kind of behavior. Suddenly, one day you will find yourself attacking them in the garden." The pit falls from parents to children, and some of them will get it. That is the reality. Would you not say this is difficult (I. *susah*), Nils?

Kenari's use of the word "difficult" here is interesting. *Susah* is Indonesian and means "difficult" or "bothersome," as when something is associated with great effort or pain (Echols and Shadily 1989:536). *Susah* can also mean "troubled" or "unhappy" and carries, much like the Greek notion of *aporia*, a wider sense of general distress. *Orang susah* (troubled people) is often used to refer to people who are poor or bereaved or who have experienced some calamity.

The *gua* is "difficult" in the dual sense of being both the cause of calamity and a painful, problematic enigma. The *gua* is existentially, socially, as well as epistemologically *susah*. It lurks beyond human comprehension and is the cause of all manner of illness and death that in turn generate hardships involving one's own neighbors and family and, often, the authorities. The seed of witchcraft is both real and hidden. Some get it, and some do not. Knowing who has got it, and handling the tough dilemmas this entails, is indeed *susah*, difficult.

The witchcraft attack on Lisa bore out the truth of this: Lisa's father, Taro, was obliged to distance himself explicitly from his half sister, Yantima, and his half brother, Lolos, when they were accused of "eating" Gora in 1984. This act of distancing himself from his own family was fraught with ambivalence, however. There was general agreement in the village that the *gua* seed had probably been passed on to Lolos and Yantima from their father, Pariama. But Pariama was also Taro's father (see fig. 5). Pariama—one of the last people in Buli to convert to Christianity, in 1972, shortly before his death—had been married twice. His first marriage, to Taro's mother, had produced three children. After the death of Taro's mother, Pariama had married again, resulting in the birth of Lolos and Yantima.

After growing up together, Taro and his younger siblings, Yantima and Lolos, had explicitly turned against each other when, in the early 1980s, the first

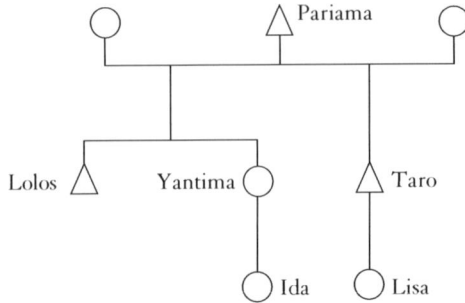

**Figure 5.** The seed.

accusations of being *gua* had been raised against Yantima and Lolos. The contentious death of Gora, Taro's wife's brother (*tamái*), in 1984 had been the decisive event causing this rift. In this context, the accusations made by Lisa's family against Yantima were full of paradox, for as the family charged that Yantima was a witch and might even have passed the seeds of witchcraft on to her daughter, Ida, the accusation also reminded everyone that the seed had been passed down to Yantima from Pariama, who was also Taro's father—with Taro in turn being Lisa's father. If Ida was a witch through her mother, Yantima, then Lisa could equally well be a witch through her father, Taro. The only thing that distinguished Taro from Yantima was his carefully managed image of himself as someone whose behavior and emotional "inside" were the very opposite of a witch. But this distinction was tenuous at best. As the Buli proverb has it, "The old people used to say, 'Whoever is not a *gua*, may become one, and whoever is not a sorcerer may become one.'"

*Gua* characteristics are inherited in the form of a kernel or a seed (*geo*) from either parent. However, the kernel becomes active in the child if he or she has an avaricious character. Therefore not all children of a *gua* necessarily become *gua* themselves. On the other hand, an inherited kernel is not strictly needed to become a *gua*. According to another Buli saying, "If one 'looks for it [i.e., the *gua* spirit],' one will find it, even without a 'seed.'" Certain types of conduct are in themselves enough to precipitate a metamorphosis into a *gua*, because parsimonious, secretive, greedy, and unsociable behavior attracts *gua* spirits. In addition to becoming a witch by inheriting the seed, or by adopting certain kinds of behavior, one can also become a *gua* by accident. This may happen through dreams, or because a protective spirit actually turns out to be a *gua* spirit. Some myths also relate how people have paid a *gua* to give them the seed. Finally, one can become a *gua* by infection or contagion. Living and eating alongside a *gua* may in itself be enough to make a person a *gua*, since the spit of a *gua* is regarded as highly infectious (ZCR 1922 [71]:3). Furthermore, a *gua* may deposit a small tick or aphid, known as *glum* or *blewing ni ut* (lice peculiar to the dusky scrubfowl [*Megapodius freycinet*]), on someone to turn that person into a *gua* as well.

This multiplicity of ways in which a person can become a *gua* makes the possibility of becoming a *gua* as likely as becoming its victim. As much as daily life is concerned with protecting oneself against becoming the victim of a *gua*, it is also about convincing others and oneself that one is not a potential *gua*. Arrogant, greedy, parsimonious, and lecherous behavior, for instance, is just as likely to make you a witch as it is to make you a victim of witchcraft.

## Theoretical Excursus 3: The Politics of Inaccessibility

"Any one may be a witch, but it is of no importance so long as he does not direct his powers against his neighbours," Evans-Pritchard noted about the Azande (1935:419). In my experience of Buli society, nothing could be further from the truth. It is in fact of great importance that "whoever is not a *gua* may become one." In a society where the witch constitutes the worst imaginable form of being, it undermines moral certainty to know that anyone may potentially incarnate it. Evans-Pritchard's statement comes as part of the argument that witchcraft in Azande constituted "a system of moral philosophy" that defined "moral sentiments" and had "great influence upon conduct" (419). Witchcraft formed, in other words, the basis for a moral system in Evans-Pritchard's functionalist analysis. But no such function runs through Buli witchcraft. On the contrary I suggest, the Buli moral system is continuously undermined from within by witchcraft's potential omnipresence. Because of witchcraft's potential omnipresence, no unequivocal and firm moral grounding (to denounce the witchcraft of others, for instance) can exist. The existential and moral doubts that accompany life in a world in which anyone may be a witch are worth pondering a bit further (see also chapter 7).

With an analytical impulse very similar to the one that drives this book, Siegel has made this very dilemma the starting point in his recent and immensely inspiring work *Naming the Witch* (2006). Based on interviews with people after the event, Siegel's book analyzes a spate of mob lynchings in East Java where more than one hundred people, suspected of being sorcerers (*tukang santet*), were killed over a period of just a few months between late 1998 and early 1999. Siegel extends to the study of witchcraft Derrida's insight that any language (especially moral language) always fails to capture that which it seeks to label.[6] Calling someone a "witch" or killing someone for being a "witch" never brings any comfort or solution, Siegel argues. Naming (or indeed killing) the "witch" is a "failed attempt at signification" (Siegel 2006:21), because witchcraft is essentially unknowable and inaccessible. Siegel seeks to get at the inaccessibility of witchcraft (and other types of indeterminate, eerie, or "traumatic" experience) through the Freudian notion of "the uncanny"—a concept that in many ways overlaps with my notion of aporia as an experience that refuses to yield to language, understanding, or the senses. The uncanny nature of East Javanese notions of witchcraft, in Siegel's reading has a clear political history. The collapse of state order (and state oppression) in May 1998, Siegel claims, meant the sudden absence of a strong state that for three decades had taught people how to know themselves. In this uncertain climate, anyone could be a witch. Siegel's claims that the murder of suspected sorcerers, under these circumstances, demonstrated how society was pursued by "bad dreams" of the political father, by "Suharto as nightmare" (189). It was essentially because people, after three decades of political authoritarianism, felt the absence of the state to be uncanny, that they looked for a substitute, fearing what they would find and being unable not to look: "In East Java, when relations to the state were feared to have been broken and national categories felt not to apply, witchcraft emerged. Wherever one turned, there was lethal menace rather than consolidated conflict. Anyone could be a witch" (207). This idea of the witch as a stand-in for an absent state constitutes an elegant twist on Siegel's earlier analysis of New Order politics. In a previous work (1998), Siegel had thus convincingly shown how the New Order state elite was "haunted" by the image of the "masses" (I. *massa*), and how the state devised its draconian policies in an unsuccessful attempt to eradicate what it feared within society itself.[7] And yet society was also celebrated by the New Order (as the "people" or *rakyat*) and formed the basis for its legitimacy. The New Order state was haunted, in short, by "society as a ghost," society being both a necessity for and a danger to the state's legitimacy. *Naming the Witch* suggested that with the disintegration of a state that had for three decades claimed to know its "people" better than they knew themselves, the source of social identity—recognition of who one was socially—also evaporated. The effect was a reversal of a haunting: if authoritarianism had been haunted by the "people," democracy began by being haunted by the absent authoritarian leader.

Siegel's book is a fascinating exploration of witchcraft as a kind of political aporia. But whereas Siegel's book provides a political history of the inaccessibility of witchcraft, this book seeks to provide an ethnography of it. Siegel focuses, after the event, on those important but also extraordinary moments when witchcraft becomes unbearable enough to warrant mass murder, when witchcraft turns into witch hunt. I focus on the everyday life of witchcraft as it unfolds, and suggest that the "uncanny" or "aporetic" nature of witchcraft is neither a historical exception nor solely an effect of New Order politics. Witchcraft's inaccessibility or aporia in Buli grew out of a history that is older than the New Order (see chapters 3 and 4). In Buli, it was not the collapse of the New Order that made witchcraft unbearable. On the contrary, the collapse of the New Order in Buli came with a renewed

promise that witchcraft might end (see chapter 8). Ironically, the same promise
had accompanied the New Order itself (see chapter 6).

The politics of witchcraft's inaccessibility in Buli is, in other words, not causally tied to the state in any simple fashion. Witchcraft in Buli cannot neatly be
said to be "the form Suharto took when he vanished from the political center"
(Siegel 2006:189).[8] Rather than a state effect, witchcraft's inaccessibility in Buli is
an existential aporia that people constantly but unsuccessfully endeavor to understand. The continued conversation on the rainy afternoon in Buli in 1999 was to
highlight this.

### "The difficulty is that we do not really know the work of the gua"

NILS: The *gua*, I have noticed people saying, are not just greedy (*magolojo*)
and stingy (*matungtúng*). They are also arrogant (*combong*). Once they
have eaten someone, they will tell the victim that [the victim] is going to
die.

RODA: They caution them (*petngo si*). They let them know: "On this day
you will die!" So it is the sick person himself who remembers: "Oh, on this
day I was attacked, and the *gua* was this or that person."

TILA: In these circumstances it is very hard not to believe what people say.
You know, they have seen it themselves, and they relate what has happened.

KENARI: But believing it is also difficult (I. *susah*)!

RODA: Yes, believing what people say is difficult. But not believing is difficult, too.

KENARI: The difficulty is that we do not really know the work of the *gua*.
We cannot know. All we have to go by are the habits (I. *kebiasaan*) of our
grandparents, habits that fell to our parents and that have now fallen to us.
If we would only stop following these habits . . . but we cannot. It is this
that causes problems.

It is difficult not to trust what the victims of witchcraft say: they are, after all,
the only witnesses to a reality that is hidden from sight. Even so, it is also difficult to trust what the victims say because their memory of the witchcraft event is
"given" to them by the witch. A similar dilemma runs through the other source
of authority on witchcraft: tradition. Tradition is all people have to go by, and it
is tradition that provides the information on the *gua*, its characteristics and its
nature. Yet people are also painfully aware that the "habits of the ancestors" are

*more on this desire to admit/show of...* [handwritten marginalia]

partial by nature, guesses at best (see chapter 2). It is difficult to trust tradition because no human really knows the work of the *gua*. To make matters worse, Buli people have learned that these habits of the ancestors are "backward," "pagan," and "superstitious," and as such not to be trusted.

Witchcraft is doubly difficult because it captures people in a reality to which neither experience nor tradition provides reliable access, but which nevertheless is inescapable. As the saying goes, "If there is witchcraft at play, it will become real/ revealed" (*gabe gua ni hal, musti kenyataan*). The reality of one instance of witchcraft is revealed by the eruption—before long—of another instance of witchcraft. Only witchcraft truly proves the reality of witchcraft: this is the fundamental indeterminacy of witches. And yet, despite their occult indeterminacy, one sure thing applies to witches: they cannot change their ways. "The shit-eating dog," as the Buli proverb has it, "will always eat shit" (*in nan cicaya, na cicaya, fun ce*). Witchcraft always remains.

Lisa eventually recovered. But the reason for her recovery remained unclear. Indeed, it would be impossible to find any consensus in the village as to what healed her. Perhaps the pills the nurse had given her had cured the illness. Perhaps the illness was due to postnatal problems, and the ritual cleansings to banish the raw blood had worked. Perhaps, as others maintained, rituals to appease the wild boar, the animal spirit (*suang*) of Lisa's family, had effected a cure. From this perspective, Lisa's illness was caused by the decision of her family to raise a wild pig in their garden, even though the wild pig is the guardian spirit of Lisa's mother's family and therefore should not be eaten or even touched by them. Then again, the illness could also have been due to a *gua* attack (*ungan*). This interpretation, though contested, appeared to be the majority opinion in the village, especially in light of Lisa's own account of the attack. Perhaps the combined efforts of the three healers had had the desired effect (see fig. 6). Perhaps the magic of the glass of water that Yantima had been compelled to prepare had cured Lisa. Or perhaps Yantima had entered Lisa's bedroom at night in the *gua*'s spirit form and cured her, as *gua* are said to sometimes do when they are too ashamed (*mai*) of what they have done, or when they fear the repercussions if their victim dies.

Buli life is full of disquieting and inchoate events, such as Lisa's illness, in which the *gua* is a central specter. In everyday life, the *gua* is a constant menace that Buli people cannot afford to entirely forget, but toward which they still also easily adopt attitudes of mockery, hilarity, irony, and denial. At intervals, however, the *gua* asserts its presence through illness, death, or strange interventions in social

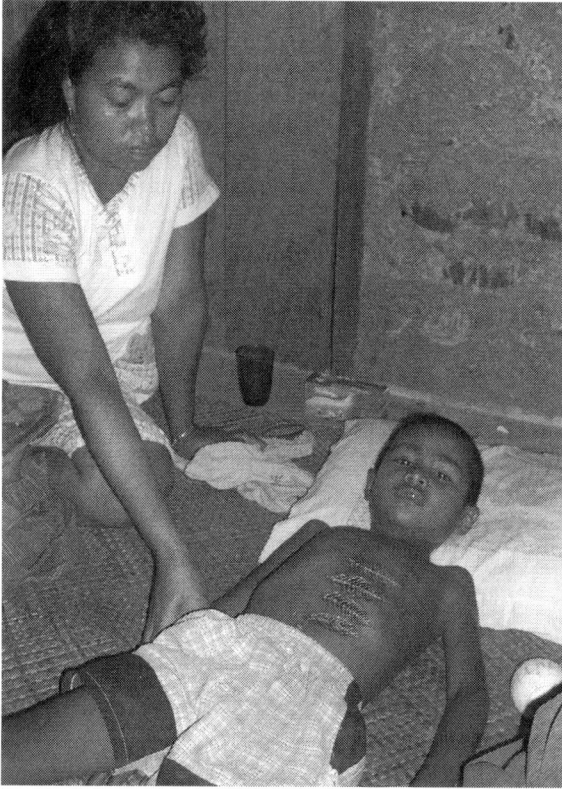

**Figure 6.** Elvis Guslaw being treated for *ungan*. 2004. Photo by author.

life with shocking undeniability. Such *gua* events are full of tension, anxiety, and desperate attempts to understand them; yet somehow they always seem to evade comprehension. These events affect most aspects of social life; yet despite their best efforts, people in Buli are unable to control or even fully grasp them. Each incident of witchcraft is therefore open to multiple interpretations and constantly changing, for such is the nature of the *gua*: its presence calls out for interpretation, which constantly fails because witchcraft is fundamentally unknowable. The reality of witchcraft is undeniable, yet the inaccessibility of the *gua* both to the senses and to common sense makes certainty about any given attack impossible. Thus, while the implications of its presence are highly significant, the *gua* itself appears to be frustratingly beyond any meaning. It remains an enduring experience of the impossible, and implicates people in aporia—a "not knowing where to go" (Derrida 1993:12)—at every turn.

### Theoretical Excursus 4: Does Aporia Travel?

By now it will be apparent to the reader that my use of Derrida is naive. It is naive because it is ethnographically rather than theoretically motivated; it has an empirical motivation of which Derrida himself was highly suspicious (Morris 2007:369). It is also naive because, rather than having a deconstructive aim, it takes a toolkit approach to Derrida that will employ a few of his concepts (like *monstrosity, undecidability,* and *aporia*) for their analogical usefulness in approximating what I take to be Buli experiences of witchcraft. Finally, it is naively comparative. One might reasonably object that aporia in Derrida's analysis arises solely within the crevices of Western metaphysics, and that aporia, therefore, is specific to Western philosophy, law, and literature. As such, my use of the concept to designate Buli experiences with/of witchcraft seems misguided. Is aporia not wedded to Western metaphysics, and does my attempt to transplant it to an eastern Indonesian village therefore not constitute a form of ethnocentrism, asserting an implicit metaphysics in a place where there is none? Can aporia, one might ask, travel as an analytical category?

My response would be that this line of reasoning that wants to reserve aporia for the West repeats a fallacy that witchcraft studies has been teaching us all along—namely, that witchcraft is practical and contextual, not theoretical and metaphysical. Systemic doubt and aporia, thereby, become a monopoly of the West. This approach, as I have suggested, reproduces a "great divide theory" (Latour 1993:99) and sets up ethnography to provide what Derrida has called "a false exit" from the strictures of Western thought itself by positing an idealized terrain "outside the West"—a place that has no Western metaphysics of presence, no *epistēmē*, and because of this also has no aporia. In the spirit of symmetry (Latour 1993), I will venture the claim that aporia is useful as an analytical category that names that which troubles a system of meaning, any system of meaning (Deutscher 2005). "No society," as Baudrillard points out, "can live without in a sense opposing its own value system: It has to have such a system, yet it must at the same time define itself in contradistinction to it" (1993:66). In Buli, the *gua* is the embodiment of this contradiction.

By suggesting that aporia may form the basis of a comparative anthropology of doubt, I do not imply that all metaphysics are the same. The metaphysics that the *gua* undermines and opposes in Buli is not a Western one. While Western logocentrism appears to operate only to the extent that it denies the aporias of its own making, Buli tradition acknowledges that the aporetic nature of the *gua*, its undecidability and ultimate unknowability, are woven into tradition itself, its origin (chapter 2) as much as its mode of reproduction (chapter 7). I suggest therefore that Buli tradition operates on an explicit "metaphysics of doubt": when it comes to the gua, we can only guess (*rai*). Christianity, as chapter 3 will demonstrate, for the first time offered a new kind of metaphysics, a "metaphysics of certainty" that promised to end witchcraft, to abolish death. Later incarnations of modernity, the state, and venture capitalism appeared to promise the same.

### Witchcraft and/as Aporia

Whether this ethnographic use of Derrida "under erasure," a ~~Derrida~~-inspired analysis of witchcraft in terms of aporia, is in his spirit or not, I will leave it to the reader to decide. It is, however, worth noting that witchcraft and aporia are, in fact, closely linked in Greek philosophy. Therefore my suggestion that witchcraft is aporetic is not entirely arbitrary. The link arises in a particularly interesting way at the center of the magnum opus of Western philosophy, Plato's *Meno* (Plato 1964). At one point in Plato's rendering of the dialogue between Meno and Socrates, Meno—frustrated with the Socratic method of guided inquiry (Greek *elenchus*) that systematically uses perplexity as a mode of philosophical debate—"describes his [own confusion or sense of] aporia as the effect of witchcraft and enchantment . . . and he proceeds to warn Socrates to stop his method of inducing aporia in other people lest he be 'arrested as a wizard'" (Politis 2008:95). As Sarah Kofman describes Meno's reaction, "Only magic and witchcraft can leave a man like Meno speechless and directionless . . . and if this had been anywhere but Athens Socrates would most likely be arrested for sorcery" (1988:18). The accusation, although undoubtedly just rhetorical banter, was still serious enough. Witchcraft, magic, and sorcery were real threats in the ancient Greek world (Flint et al. 1999:xiii; Harrison 1961; Ogden 2002), a reality that also presented itself to Plato and Socrates, for all their skepticism (Collins 2008:43–44). Meno was a native of Thessaly, which at the time was renowned as a region where witchcraft was rife. In his poem *Pharsalia*, for instance, the Roman poet Lucan claimed that "no monstrous fantasy surpasses" the Thessalian witches, whose power emanates from the "deleterious herbs" that the Thessalian earth brings forth (Ogden 2002:121). Witchcraft, it appeared, was an autochthonous feature of Thessaly itself.[9] With his Thessalian background Meno would have had direct knowledge of the social power of both witchcraft and witchcraft accusations. More than likely, then, there was also a serious note to Meno's rhetorical accusation of wizardry against Socrates.

The witches of Thessaly were notorious for their ability to reverse the natural order of the universe (Ionescu 2007:30). Likewise, the use of aporia in the logic of Socrates, so Meno charged, was a reversal of proper logic as Meno understood it. Aporia, Meno claimed, was essentially a form of witchcraft—a poison to logic rather than a cure for the lack of it. Indeed, Meno was not the only one to suggest that Socratic reason was more a poison than a cure, and that it numbed people through wizardry rather than providing a logical antidote to ignorance (Derrida 2008:119). Aristophanes had done the same in his play *Birds* of 414 BC, mocking the rhetoric of Socrates as being akin to necromancy (Ogden 2002:27). It was this special kind of "wizardry" embodied in Socrates's ability to sway souls through rhetoric that would eventually lead to the philosopher's trial and execution in 399 BC (Brickhouse and Smith 1990:30; Derrida 2008:120).[10] In a comment on this crucial passage in the *Meno*, R. S. Bluck has noted, "Socrates' elenchic procedure no doubt contributed to the unpopularity which brought about his arrest" (1961:270).

Having accused Socrates of wizardry, and attempting to hold his own against the Socratic use of aporias, Meno counters Socrates by posing an aporia or paradox of his own (Plato 1964:8). Meno proceeds by challenging Socrates to explain how it is possible to inquire into matters of which one has no prior knowledge: "How will you inquire into something, Socrates, when you don't at all know what it is? Which of the things you don't know will you suppose it is, when you are inquiring into it? And even if you happen upon it, how will you know it is the thing you didn't know?" (Fine 1992:205). This aporia of how one inquires into the unknown, often called "Meno's paradox," is a paradox very similar to the one that lies at the heart of Buli engagement with witches. It is a paradox that I seek to trace without aspiring to make any suggestion as to how it might be solved. Indeed, my main argument is that in Buli this paradox, the unknowability of the *gua*, is and remains an unsolvable paradox. Witchcraft is aporetic because it is an impossible experience without the comfort of meaning. Indeed, Sarah Kofman's definition of aporia comes very close to the experiential inescapability and impossibility that characterizes witchcraft in Buli. Kofman describes aporia as "the place where one comes into contact with inextricable bonds that are impossible to break, with a realm of shadows without exit" (1988:10–11).

In the Platonic tradition, however, Meno's paradox had to be solved; an exit had to be found. In many ways the solution to Meno's paradox of how it is possible to know the unknowable is the very beginning of Western rationalist philosophy. Socrates sets out to solve the aporia by essentially sidestepping it. In one of the most famous passages in Western philosophy, Socrates in response to Meno's question calls over one of Meno's uneducated slaves, and using guided inquiry on him, he proceeds to demonstrate that the slave already has knowledge about the basic principles of geometry. This proves the Socratic contention that it is possible to inquire into the unknown, because some knowledge (*anamnesis*) is a priori or innate to the soul, even though it is initially unknown to the person in question (Plato 1964:290–291). This passage about a priori knowledge that can be recovered by means of a dialogue that clears away perplexity and aporia would go on to become the master narrative of Western rationalism and logocentrism, one that proceeded by denying or obviating aporia. As Derrida notes, for Plato the antidote for the kind of witchcraft (Greek *thaumatopoia*) that clings to ambivalence, mimesis, and representation is always the *epistēmē* (2008:140). Epistemic reason or rationality as epitomized by modern science and philosophy is the antidote, the *alexipharmakon*, that enables a careful weighing, measuring, and counting. Reason frees the mind from being at the "mercy of an appearance" and at the mercy of the perplexity (aporia) engendered by polysemy, an excess of meaning: "The cure by logos, exorcism, and catharsis will thus eliminate the excess" (131). This obviation of excess and of aporia to arrive at truth is foundational to Western epistemic rationality and metaphysics; it is an obviation that Derrida's concept of *aporia*, as I understand it, seeks to overturn. In opposition to rationality's account of itself (and of its own salvation from aporia), Derrida suggests that aporia was only seemingly eliminated by logos; for the cure of logos against aporia is always also a poison (witchcraft?) to logos itself.

Witchcraft, so it seems, is present at the very origin of Western rationality—as a half-forgotten accusation and as an obstacle that had to be cleared away by reason. But as Derrida notes, the very act of clearing away aporia makes reason indistinguishable from poison, from witchcraft.[11] The accusation of witchcraft—Meno's and Derrida's—therefore clings to the very rhetorical means by which rationality seeks to ensure a space unto itself. Aporia is at the heart of this accusation against rationality. It is there as a lack and an excess at the same time: aporia is, simultaneously, too little medicine and too much poison. It is this simultaneous lack and excess that also runs through Buli witchcraft: as much as it disconcertingly absents itself from human attempts to understand and capture it, there is an excessiveness to its corporeal reality. I therefore contend that Meno's paradox, a paradox at the historical cusp of Western rationality, is a useful entry point into witchcraft (in Buli and elsewhere). Instead of simply dismissing this paradox, as Neoplatonic reason has insisting on doing for centuries, we need to explore its implications and take seriously the way in which the paradox points to the impossibility of human certainty—especially certainty about those things that one does not or cannot know. I suggest that for a long time now, perhaps too long, witchcraft studies has followed the path of Socrates and Plato and tried to obviate the paradoxes and the inaccessibility of witchcraft in an attempt to reclaim solid epistemological ground. Perhaps it is time to take a cue from Meno rather than from Plato when it comes to witchcraft.

Meno's aporia—of how it is possible to know things about which one knows nothing—reintroduces, within the register of European philosophy, the problem of radical alterity that was inherent in the image of the empty nautilus shell, which I introduced at the beginning of this book. In Buli there is no easy epistemic antidote, no *alexipharmakon*, to witchcraft. Rather, the aporia of witchcraft is built into reality itself, into the notion of self and other, into the limits of the senses and of common sense, and into intersubjective existence. The fundamental unknowability of the other is thus uncomfortably closely related to the fundamental unknowability of oneself. Herein lies what Bruce Kapferer, following Sartre, calls "the magicality of human existence" (Kapferer 1997:2). Sartre's notion that "man is always a wizard to man" (1948, cited in Kapferer 1997:2)—its now quaint-sounding gender-blindness notwithstanding—already suggests the possibility that one is a wizard to oneself as much as to others. The-other-as-witch therefore always entails the possibility of oneself-as-witch. It is this intersubjective problem of alterity as "already a problem of the self" that the witch embodies in Buli. And yet the witch (as self or as other) is ever inaccessible.

As the next chapter will show, this insistence on the uncertainty that clings to witchcraft reaches into myth as part of a general epistemology of doubt. Myth in this sense provides no ontological certainty, no firmness to the universe. Witchcraft is not held in place by myth. Rather, myth in Buli confirms the existence of a fundamental "restlessness of doubt" upon which witchcraft thrives.

# 2

# THE ORIGINS OF WITCHCRAFT AND THE DOUBTS OF TRADITION

When it comes to witches and sorcerers, we humans
know nothing. We can only guess.

BANUS, JUNE 2002

"One doubts on specific grounds," as Ludwig Wittgenstein phrases it. Then he continues, "The question is this: how is doubt introduced into the language-game?" (Wittgenstein 1969:60e). I suggest that doubt is mythologically grounded in Buli. There are at least three myths about the origin of witchcraft. These myths, individually and together, suggest something that is fundamental to all aspects of the *gua*—namely, that it continuously recedes from human attempts to understand or manage it. "When it comes to the *gua*," Banus, a local healer (*sow-sów*) once told me, "all we can do is guess (*rai*)." The Buli word for "to guess" is either *rai* or *fatailo*. *Fatailo,* in particular, is interesting. The word means "to guess" in the sense of "to aim at something without seeing it clearly, to shoot at something blindly" (Maan 1940:30). Guessing is like trying to hit something while blindfolded. In Buli, all guesses are in that sense accompanied by impossibility—blind conjecture infused with the expectation that it is off the mark. The mythical accounts of the *gua*'s origins are instances of an "epistemology of guessing" that runs through all aspects of Buli attitudes to witchcraft. As I will explore further in chapter 7, this epistemology of guessing—particularly but not solely in the face of witchcraft—is connected to what Joel Robbins and Alan Rumsey (2008) have called "a doctrine of the opacity of mind," an explicit and shared sense that the inside of other people is ultimately unknowable. I believe that Bronislaw Malinowski was fundamentally right when he famously suggested that "myth serves principally to establish a sociological charter, or a retrospective moral pattern of behavior" (1948:144). But in Buli, myth is a charter, authoritative and defective at the same time, of an explicitly unknown terrain. It is a charter that advocates "caution" (*istiár*) as the most suitable form of behavior, and "guessing" (*fatailo*) as the only available form of knowledge when it comes to witchcraft.

Like all guesses about witchcraft, myth is explicitly recognized as only partial and probably faulty "guesstimates" about the nature of the *gua*, its actions, its raison d'être. Myth (*kayat*) and tradition (*adat re atorang*) can therefore never give a complete template of the *gua*, and people repeatedly emphasized to me the inherently incongruous and ultimately inscrutable nature of the *gua*. Everything that can be known about the *gua* is likely to be contradicted by something else. Therefore no knowledge about the *gua* is stable or completely trustworthy. In the face of the fundamental unknowability of the *gua*, caution (*istiár*) and doubt are the best means of protection. Doubt about the truths that myth can deliver, and that humans as a consequence can access, runs through and across Buli mythical accounts about witchcraft. This grounds what I call an "epistemology of guessing," an institutionalized ontological uncertainty that is not so dissimilar to the kind that the social sciences normally reserve for late modernity. Focusing on the doubt that myth grounds, the argument of this chapter aligns with insights derived from the emergent anthropological interest in "traditional reflexivity" (Kordt Højbjerg 2002b), skepticism (Gable 2002; Taussig 2003; Whyte 1997), and doubt (Pelkmans 2011a; Schielke 2012) to critique the conventional sociological insistence on myth as a delivery system for ontological surety.

## Myth 1: Witchcraft and the Creation of the Land

According to a myth that Buli people share with their Maba and Tobelo neighbors, witchcraft is as old as the island of Halmahera itself. In fact, the island was created by witchcraft when a giant called Watowato was killed by a giant *gua* named Papudou. Tangkea Guslaw told the myth to me in 1994, and it runs as follows. Watowato had asked Papudou to make him some new iron arrow points and a new knife blade. While he was forging the arrow points in the fire, Papudou enticed Watowato into drinking large amounts of palm wine (*wo*). Eventually Watowato got drunk and fell asleep—fatefully unaware that Papudou was also a witch (*gua*). While Watowato was asleep, Papudou tore open his stomach and devoured his liver. Then he plunged the red-hot knife blade he was forging into Watowato's breast. Awaking in shock and distress, Watowato frantically sought to cool the burning in his abdomen by drinking water from a nearby river. He drank the river dry and proceeded to the next river and the next, until he had drained every major river on the island. It was futile. Watowato was dying. Before he expired, however, Watowato managed to grab his bow and launch two arrows at Papudou. The arrows hit Papudou in the eyes, and he died as well.

Papudou's dead body became a mountain that lies north of Buli, and the corpse of Watowato became the highest peak on Halmahera's northeast peninsula. Known locally as Watowato, it rises some 1,440 meters above sea level. The two dead bodies gradually began to smell (*pupúi*), and after three days the stench became so overpowering that Watowato's slave and two wives succumbed to it and also died, turning into named mountains as well. One wife, Watileo, formed the mountain at the foot of which the three Buli villages still nestle. Watileo's physical features—her pregnant stomach and her legs, breasts, vagina, and head—as well as the three giants stones of the fire place (*cit*) where she expired are still recognizable features of the landscape today (see fig. 7), even as the mountainous area is being scarred by mining companies in search of nickel.

The myth describes the beginning of the world and the beginning of witchcraft, and suggests that the topography of Halmahera is intrinsically linked to the actions of *gua*. It was, in other words, an initial act of witchcraft that set in motion a whole chain of events upon which human existence could later be established. Human life and settlement on the island would not have been possible without the witchcraft death of Watowato and his companions (Bubandt 1998b).

**Figure 7.** Sefei and Ipsan Raja with Watileo Mountain in the background. 1993. Photo by author.

Ironically, the myth suggests that the *gua* lies at the basis of human existence in an eponymous topography—at the same time indispensable and deadly. The legend of Watowato exposes a fundamental ontological double bind at the heart of human existence in Buli: the *gua* is constitutive of the beginning of human life on Halmahera, and yet, since time immemorial, it has consistently and outrageously jeopardized the very human conditions that it made possible on the island. Herein lies a central mythical paradox, an aporia, in the nature of the *gua*, for the myth of Watowato indicates that while the *gua* is antithetical to Buli existence, it is also its topographical condition of possibility.

## Myth 2: Witchcraft Shadows

The beginning of the world and the beginning of witchcraft are also related in another account. According to this myth, which Kenari told me several times, first in 1992, at the beginning of time the world was the inverse of its current form: the land was sea, and the sea was land (*batang ca olat fare olat ca batang*). This "first world" belonged to the *jin* spirits.[1] The *jin* created the world as it is today by turning the world around so that ocean and land were in their current locations. By doing so, the *jin* "gave birth to this world" (*sil ta rtub dunia taie*). The beginning of the world populated by *jin* spirits, however, is also associated with the origins of the *gua*. The *gua* spirits are a kind of *jin* that escaped from the time when the world was inverted. Like the *jin*, the *gua* spirits slipped from the "first world" into the current world at the moment of its "birth," and populated the forests and the small coastal islands. Here they lie in wait (*tantano*) for a human body that they can possess and turn into a witch.

The *gua* spirits are a kind of wind (*latan*) or shadow (*gurumin*) that roams the world (*sawsawal*). The world in Buli is generally full of different kinds of *gurumin*, "shadows." The ancestors (*smengit*) and guardian animal spirits (*suang*) are shadows, just as Íyan Toa, the cultural hero of Buli society, is a shadow. Each human being also has a *gurumin*, or shadow. People are not born with a *gurumin* but acquire it shortly after birth. The attachment of the *gurumin* (simultaneously meaning "shadow" and "reflection") to the body increases as the person grows, gains experience, and becomes aware. The *gurumin* connotes awareness and consciousness as well as life experience and spiritual balance. The shadow-reflection-awareness of the *gurumin* is what makes humans alive and aware. It is their soul, one might say, the condition of their being. Only one kind of animal, the hunting dog, is said to have a *gurumin*. Dogs are therefore said to experience fear and may, like humans, be given magical roots (*aiwáo*) to make them courageous and lose the fear of death (*makés*). Apart from dogs and one other notable exception, only humans, ancestors, and spirits are conscious beings with a *gurumin*. This exception is the witch (*gua*). Witches are shadows on the prowl, shadows that escaped into the world of conscious beings at the time when the world was inverted.

Both the myth of Watowato and the myth about the world turned upside down are what could be termed "ontological accounts" of the *gua*. According to both explanations, the *gua* is endemic to life itself on Halmahera. The *gua* is in the land and on the wind. It is responsible for making human life possible by creating the landscape in which people live, and it is an integral part of conscious life itself, a being made out of the same shadows that make human consciousness and sociality possible.

This ontological origin of the *gua* is full of abjection (Kristeva 1982), however. The *gua* is a shadow very similar to that of the human shadow-soul. It is this similarity that accounts for their mutual attraction, an attraction that is sexual in nature. Human witches are made because the *gua* spirit "flirts" (*sero*) with the human conscious mind, seeking to "tempt" its human counterpart in its dreams of food and incestuous sex. If one has dreams of this kind without telling others about it, one's conscious self or "inside" (*ulór na*) is already beginning an illicit affair with the *gua* spirit (I will discuss this further in chapter 7). The *gua* spirit, in turn, is said to be attracted to anyone who is obsessively greedy (*golojo*), envious (*ulór na mici*), stingy (*matungtúng*), or plain bad-tempered (*ulór na mayai*). The sexual relations that are established when human beings become *gua* are unnerving precisely because of the close links between the shadows of humans and *gua* spirits. The *gua* spirit's flirtation with the human shadow leads away from human subjectivity, morality, and sociality. When a villager is accused of being a *gua*, that person is therefore said to "have ceased to be human" (*smat i pantó*). The *gua* is the only conscious being in Buli ontology that steadfastly refuses to be part of the animist social world of humans, ancestors, spirits, and dogs. Spirits and ancestors may get angry and cause illness, but they are all amenable to ritual supplication and control. The *gua* is not.

The two myths that describe the ontological origins of the *gua* are therefore intensely aporetic. They suggest that the *gua*, the most inhuman of all conscious beings, is similar in kind to the human beings on which it preys. The myths are also strongly pessimistic. They indicate that as long as humans harbor feelings of greed, stinginess, envy, and ill temper, the *gua* will always be around. And since one can never truly know the "inside" of another, there is nothing to suggest that such feelings will go away. The myths of Watowato and the *jin* origins of world entail a frightening and depressing prospect: that as long as there are humans, there will also be *gua*.

## Myth 3: Gua Mané and the First Human *Gua*

A third myth, the myth of Gua Mané, suggests an alternative—namely, that witchcraft is a genealogical and historical fact rather than an ontological one, and that the first *gua* in fact came from a neighboring village. The background for this myth is a prior history of exile and political inclusion since at least the seventeenth century into the structure of sultanate rule in North Maluku.

The first Buli people, according to local folklore, lived at a place called Buli-Tua on the Mabulan River, on the north coast of central Halmahera. It was here that they encountered Íyan Toa, the hero of Buli culture, who provided them with the fighting prowess and male bellicosity that are at the core of Buli self-identity. It was also at Buli-Tua that the sultan of Tidore first arrived to bequeath to Buli the ritual titles that incorporated Buli society into the Tidore political structure and established, in Buli, the morality and rituals of tradition, or *adat re atorang*. These titles comprised the *oloán* (village leader), the *ƙapita* (war leader), the *oƙu* (juridical arbiter), and the four *uat* (elders) who headed the four *gélat* (territorial groups) that descended from the first four families in Buli society.[2] By accepting these titles, the Buli community was incorporated into the political structure of the Tidore sultanate.

In return for this incorporation Buli was increasingly after the eighteenth century obliged to pay tribute to the sultan, to provide tribute service (*coów*) to war expeditions, and to submit to the local *sangaji*, the sultanate representative who resided in Maba. The domain ruled by the *sangaji* in Maba was, in turn, one of "the three regions" under Tidore rule on Halmahera, known as Gamurange (see map 4). The three Halmahera domains of Maba, Weda, and Patani were crucial to sultanate rule, because it was through the Gamurange that the sultanate of Tidore maintained its control over Raja Ampat and the coastal areas of western New Guinea (Andaya 1991; Kamma 1948–49; Rutherford 2003).

The incorporation of Buli into the symbolic and political structure of the Tidore sultanate is a central point of reference in Buli tradition. This incorporation not only established the values, virtues, and moral rules of conduct that make up Buli tradition (*adat re atorang*). The sultanate also provided Buli titleholders with a status that continues to be important in ritual affairs and ceremonies today (see fig. 8). Buli occupied the bottom of the sultanate's symbolic pecking order, a position that is simultaneously the source of pride and resentment. On the one hand, Buli were made ritually subservient to their immediate neighbors from Maba (who were marked as symbolically superior and female). On the other hand, Buli people became "the eyes of the dog" (*ƙaso ma yoma*) in the domain of Maba, and were charged with acting as a spearhead in war—a position associated with courage, masculinity, and magical invulnerability. The absorption

**Figure 8.** Four titleholders in traditional uniform in front of Íyan Toa's spirit shrine: Tangkea Guslaw (*kapita*), Kandati Raja (*uat* of *gélat* Gagáili), Mengapa Barabakem (*uat* of *gélat* Tatam), and Lingoro Veplun (*oku*). 1992. Photo by author.

into the Tidore sultanate gave the Buli community a distinct self-identity vis-à-vis its regional neighbors, a self-identity characterized by belligerence and bravery. Buli mythical accounts proudly tell how it was the Buli warriors who always went ashore first when the war canoes (*kora-kora*) in extirpation raids (Dutch *hongi-tochten*) arrived on the Papuan coasts, and how they were the ones who protected the domain of Maba from attacks by the Tobelo forest people in the service of the sultanate of Ternate. The same male belligerence, associated with the mythical culture hero of Íyan Toa, was also, according to myth, called upon to vanquish the archetypal witch called Gua Mané. Tangkea Guslaw related the myth to me in 1997 as follows:

> Once, a seven-headed witch called Gua Mané inhabited the forests of Halmahera with his wife, where they terrorized the villagers of Maba. The Maba village leader (*sangaji*) beseeched the sultan of Tidore for help. The sultan ordered a warship to sail to Maba, and with its cannons the ship bombarded the monsters' forest abode until the area was completely destroyed. The Dutch captain of the ship then returned to Tidore and reported to the sultan that Gua Mané and his wife had been killed.

However, Gua Mané and his wife were not dead. They had fled before the ship arrived, taking up residence in a large cave far inland from Maba where the cannons couldn't reach. From their new abode, the giant witches would fly out to snatch people from Maba and bring them back to the cave to devour them whole. Eventually, the village of Maba was so decimated by these raids that the *sangaji* desperately turned to Buli for help. Four Buli men answered the appeal and set off along the headwaters of the Usia River, where they built a bamboo raft (*et*). Two of the men, Uláling and Babába, tied themselves to the raft as bait while Ulás and his brother-in-law hid under a mat of leaves with their machetes ready.

Gua Mané and his wife, clad in loincloths of bark, were grooming and delousing each other when, looking down from their cave high above, the monsters spotted the raft with the men floating on the river. "Be careful not to puncture their testicles (*lalaya*). I want to eat them," said the wife of Gua Mané as her husband flew down to grab Uláling and his brother.

While Gua Mané was trying in vain to snatch up Uláling, who was firmly tied to the raft, Ulás emerged from his hiding place and cut off one of the monster's heads. "That doesn't matter; I still have six left," Gua Mané taunted. Ulás then cut off another head. "It doesn"t matter; I still have five left," Gua Mané jeered—just before Ulás cut off a third head. This banter went on until all seven heads floated in the river, and Gua Mané was dead. Then Gua Mané's wife attacked, mad with rage. Ulás killed her, too.

When Ulás and Uláling went to inspect the cave of Gua Mané, they found a large heap of bones that exuded an unbearable stench, and not far from the bone mound they found a second, smaller cave that turned out to be the dwelling place of the adopted daughter of Gua Mané, an adolescent girl named Bincawái.

Full of precaution, the men decided to leave the girl in the cave and paddled back to the coast to tell the *sangaji* in Maba of their victory. The *sangaji* thanked Ulás and Uláling and gave them usufruct rights of the extensive sago swamps behind Loipoh. When people from the Maba hamlet of Soa Loipoh emerged from their hiding places, they decided to go and inspect the monster's caves, and there they discovered Bincawái. Bincawái was a beautiful girl, and one Maba man decided to take her back to the village. Here he married Bincawái, and it is because of her descendants that some people are *gua* today.

According to this myth—and my sense is that today it is the best-known account of the *gua*'s origin—some people become *gua* because the "seed" (*geo*) was passed into the community of humans through the marriage between Bincawái and a man from Maba. From the point of this ill-advised mythical marriage, the *gua* ceases to be associated with monsters and giants and crosses the threshold into human society.

While the myth of Watowato and the narratives about the time when the world was inverted account for the origins of the *gua* in ontological terms, the myth of Gua Mané explains the origins of the *gua* in genealogical terms. The myth places the origins of the *gua* within a political and genealogical time frame. It also explains why some people are *gua*, while others are not, and it hints at why human *gua* tend to cluster in particular families. The myth establishes and confirms the convention that people become *gua* because they have the seed (*geo*). In the myth the origin of witchcraft is, however, also conveniently externalized. The first *gua* "seed" (*geo*) comes from outside Buli itself and is associated with sultanate rule and the imposition of a cultural hierarchy that gave Maba, the allegedly timid neighboring ethnic group, traditional authority over Buli. The origin of the *gua* is thereby relegated to the world outside Buli society, and pushed onto the effeminate but also symbolically superior Maba people.

The myth of Gua Mané is essentially optimistic. The origins of the *gua* are here placed clearly in time and space. The myth also suggests that Buli people were in a position to handle and kill the *gua*, which was a feat neither their politically superior Patani and Maba neighbors nor the Tidore sultan and the Dutch colonial authorities had been capable of achieving. The *gua* is represented as a monster that can be handled using the same means of war and belligerence with which Buli people engaged their traditional enemies. In its animal-monster form, the *gua* can still be vanquished with the fighting magic that Buli people had inherited from Íyan Toa. Once the *gua* blends into human society, however, control by means of fighting magic is lost. Instead of a seven-headed monster, an enemy that can be slain, the form of the *gua* shifts into the mundane. The *gua* becomes a master of disguise (*mef*). As Peter Geschiere (2013) has convincingly shown, anxieties about witchcraft are closely associated with the betrayal of trust and intimacy. In its contemporary, inaccessible form, the *gua* is the uncanny expression of the intimate and the mundane gone awry. It can assume the shape of almost anything in village life: a banana tree, a motorbike, a dog, a neighbor, or a relative. The main difference between the *gua* today and the *gua* in the myth is thus the opacity with which the contemporary *gua* endures among the living—it is unslayable.

The three origin myths of the *gua* contain a central contradiction. If people become *gua* because they get the "seed" from a parent, as suggested by the myth of

Gua Mané, then the problem of the *gua* can be traced genealogically and is limited to certain families. If, on the other hand, the *gua* is conceived of as a "shadow" being from the beginning of the world that flirts and entices people into becoming *gua*, then witchcraft is endemic to human life in Buli. The myth of Gua Mané implies that the problem of the *gua* is limited, traceable, and can be contained genealogically. The myth of Watowato (like the mythical notion that *gua* escaped from the "first world") suggests that the problem of the *gua* is endemic, untraceable, and an ontological condition of being. The former myth places the *gua* in a historical time frame and within particular families. It holds the optimistic implication that the problem of the *gua* may also have an end. The latter places the *gua* within an ontology and a topography from which, pessimistically, there is no escape. The former, "genealogical," explanation holds out the view that only particular people become witches: "For someone to become a *gua* there must be a seed." The latter, "ontological," explanation implies the opposite—namely, that anyone can become a witch: "As the old people used to say, 'Whoever is not a *gua* will become one, and whoever is not a sorcerer will become one.'"

A particular kind of reflexivity develops in these mythical attempts to grasp the aporetic nature of the *gua*. The myths of Watowato, Gua Mané, and the reversal of the world try to come to terms with some of the questions about the *gua* that become acutely relevant in every witchcraft illness and accusation—questions such as the following: Why do people become *gua*, and how? Who may potentially become a *gua*? What drives their attacks, and how does one protect oneself against them?

People in Buli are very specific about the two ways of becoming a witch. One can become a *gua* either by inheriting the seed from a parent (*gua turunan*) or because of one's emotional inclinations, essentially because one "looks" for it (*gua ningo*). As we were able to glimpse in chapter 1, the two different accounts of the origins of *gua* are basic to most contemporary discussions about *gua*, not only in debates about specific cases, but also on a more general level, because the two accounts articulate very different diagnostic and prognostic ideas about witchcraft and its futures. In the space between the genealogical and ontological accounts of the origins of the *gua*, there is ample room for interpretation. Myth, it would seem, provides little comfort when it comes to the *gua*. Instead it provides a disconcertingly wide interpretive horizon.

Each of the three myths about the origin of the *gua* gives a very different account of the degree to which witchcraft is rooted in Buli existence, and hence provides a different scenario about the possibility of imagining a future without *gua*. Christian and modern discourses have suggested new kinds of answers to the question of whether a world without *gua* is imaginable, while the mythical accounts deal with the question but provide only equivocal answers. The myths of the origin of the *gua* therefore speak directly to contemporary Buli modernity. The expectations and anxieties, hopes and fears, and desires and worries associated with modernity in Buli are closely interlaced with questions about the beginning of witchcraft, its ontology, and its possible end. Rather than a single, clear-cut answer to these questions, the multiple myths about the origins of the *gua* provide several answers, each of which suggests its own specific conditions of possibility and scenarios for the future. Just as the various myths provide very different answers, cautiously optimistic as well as worrisomely pessimistic ones, to questions about the ontological status of witchcraft and the prospects for one day ending it, so the contradictions inherent in each myth hint at the very problem of ever obtaining any certain knowledge about the *gua*. The *gua* is the point where Buli social, moral, and ontological understanding of the world meets a kind of impasse. This is where the very fundamentals of the givens of the world are shattered, pushed into a state of tension, or called into question. The *gua* is a symbolic vortex that swallows and distorts all certainty. In the orbit of this existential black hole circulates a mythical logic of doubt.

## Equivocal Myths and a Tradition of Doubt

Mathijs Pelkmans has argued that there might be at least four ways of dealing with doubt, and putting it to rest: "(a) diverting one's attention, so that the object of doubt is no longer in the spotlight; (b) reinterpreting the object of doubt in a way that makes it less 'dubious'; (c) denying that doubt is doubt; or (d) removing the alternative when confronted with two possibilities" (2011b:20). Buli myth appears to offer none of these. The myth of Gua Mané perhaps comes closest to a form of domestication, reinterpreting the *gua* as a monster that can be handled through Buli fighting prowess. But then the *gua* steals back into society through marriage. Sometimes doubt cannot be put to rest. As Maurice Bloch paraphrases the attitude of his Zafimaniry informants on Madagascar when it came to the question of the spirits and how they manifest themselves in dreams, "We are in an area in which we are in doubt and where we shall remain in doubt" (2013:53). In Buli myth doubt is not tamed or sidelined. Rather, myth "remains in doubt." Thus, I suggest that it is in myth and through witchcraft that doubt, as Wittgenstein has it, is "introduced into the language-game" (1969:60e).

Myth provides no alternative to "remaining in doubt" because it speaks directly to the inscrutability and contradiction built into witchcraft. The multiple origins and the divergent futures of witchcraft charted by the myths have the effect of cultivating doubt, highlighting it as the only possible and only wise attitude to adopt in a world of witchcraft. The myths alert people to the fact that when it comes to witchcraft they are guessing (*fatailo*), shooting blindly at a target out of sight.

This notion of myth and tradition as institutionalized forms of doubt and contradiction—as a domain in which mythological worlds are "built up only to be shattered again" (Franz Boas, as quoted in Lévi-Strauss 1955:428)—stands in stark contrast to conventional notions of tradition, particularly in contemporary sociology. Think, for instance, of Charles Taylor, who in his magisterial work *A Secular Age* describes the transition to modern secularism as a shift from a traditional world in which belief "is unchallenged and indeed, unproblematic, to one in which it is understood to be one option amongst others, and frequently not the easiest to embrace" (2007:3). If modernity is fluid (Bauman 2000; Berman 1982), then by contrastive inference, tradition must be firm, fixed, solid—propped up by a worldview that never questions itself but remains "unchallenged and indeed, unproblematic."

Perhaps the best-known example of this image of tradition within critical sociology comes from Anthony Giddens, for whom tradition provides a basic "ontological security." Tradition, according to Giddens, establishes "a sense of firmness of things. . . . The world is as it is, because it is as it should be" (1991:48). Giddens paints this picture of tradition in order to set up his portrayal of modernity defined as a "post-traditional order," in which the certainties of tradition have been replaced by the radicalization of doubt. His notion of tradition as characterized by certainty, and late modernity as pervaded by doubt, was, of course, a reaction to an older, conventional Western prejudice—namely, one in which certainty and unassailable truths were the preserve of Western society. It was this "comfortable view" of Western knowledge and existence that E. E. Evans-Pritchard's generation of social scientists had expressed: Western science provided a stable and consistent worldview through a form of logical thinking that was intolerant to contradiction. Giddens instead focused on doubt. Doubt, Giddens would agree with Evans-Pritchard, is the monopoly of the West, but then Giddens goes on to claim that doubt did not lead to truth and certainty, as earlier generations of social scientists believed. Instead, so he argues, Western critical reason entailed a radicalization of doubt that seeped into all aspects of Western institutional and existential life.

While this reversal of Orientalist stereotypes was refreshing when it emerged in the early 1990s, as Vassos Argyrou has noted, it also came at a "time of profound crisis" for the idea of an opposition between tradition and modernity, "precisely to deal with this crisis" (2000:29). Giddens essentially replaces one kind of "great divide theory" with another (Latour 1993:97). In so doing, he also ends up corroborating a very conventional notion of tradition—inside as well as outside anthropology—which, like earlier models, insists on analyzing tradition in terms of order, norms, and structure. In anthropology this view of tradition as order has been dismissed from many different angles (Abu-Lughod 1991; Bourdieu 1977; Clifford 1988; Clifford and Marcus 1986; Jackson 2000; Ortner 1984). It appears to me, however, that Giddens's opposition also obscures the extent to which tradition may, in fact, be constituted by doubt and institutionalized reflexivity, features that Giddens reserves for late modernity. Doubt, since Giddens at least, has become the watershed in a new Great Divide theory.

The Buli people I have come to know since 1991 are not traditional in any ideal-typical sense, and hence Buli is by no means a "counterexample" to Giddens's descriptions of the late modern West. Buli society is so implicated in global economic relations, postcolonial history, and geopolitical realities that it would be nonsense to speak of it as "traditional." But it would be just as misleading to speak of Buli as posttraditional, whether in the commonsense understanding of the word or in Giddens's more restricted sense, which refers to late modern Western society. My point is this: ideal-typical notions of traditional and posttraditional societies may be a useful way to think when engaging in an analysis of Western modernity, but the distinction loses its analytical acuity when confronted with the realities of life in "zones of awkward engagement"—which is where most people in what used to be called the Third World live out their lives (Tsing 2005).

Witchcraft in Buli has historically been shaped with (and has given shape to) a particular kind of institutionalized reflexivity that—provided one is convinced by this argument—undermines Giddens's assertion that institutionalized reflexivity is reserved for the posttraditional condition. This would mean either that Buli has "always been modern" or that we should consider widening our comparative scope regarding institutionalized reflexivity and ontological uncertainty (Ashforth 2001; Bandak and Jørgensen 2012; Bubandt 2005b; Kordt Højbjerg 2002a; Whyte 1997). The reservation of institutionalized reflexivity to a Euro-American late modernity is problematic because it bars an analysis of lives outside, or on the margins of, this late modernity in terms of existential ambiguity, ontological uncertainty, and experiential paradox. By default it suggests that traditions (and witchcraft) constitute systems of meaning that ensure an ontological stability and certainty, but within which doubt plays no central role.

The origin myths recounted above are, I would argue, part of an institutionalized reflection about the *gua* where no knowledge can be entirely trusted, for all knowledge is opposed by other knowledge. Buli myth, in that sense, is an "expert system" at odds with itself. As such, myth and tradition actively cultivate an ontology of uncertainty and doubt in Buli. Modernity, however, does not. In fact, modernity is in Buli historically associated with the end of doubt. Christianity, the first incarnation of modernity to arrive in Buli, thus appeared to offer a magical kind of certainty. As the next chapter will show, the appeal of Christianity in the early twentieth century was exactly a promise of certainty, a promise that Christianity would bring an end to death and witchcraft. This was a possibility that was so at odds with the ineradicable and inaccessible nature of witchcraft in Buli thinking that it was immensely appealing and therefore was sought out with great enthusiasm.

# 3

## HOPE, CONVERSION, AND
## MILLENNIAL POLITICS

Now, they say, the dead have risen from their graves in Kao
and have already destroyed parts of Halmahera.

VAN DIJKEN, NOVEMBER 1874

It was with high hopes that W. Tutuarima, a Christian catechist (I. *guru je-maat*) from the island of Ambon, arrived in Buli in June 1899. During the first part of that year several delegations of Buli animists had made the perilous and weeklong journey to Tobelo in their outriggers to visit Anton Hueting, the resident Dutch missionary. There, they pleaded with Hueting to place a missionary in Buli. Many of them had even cut off their long hair and taken off their traditional red headbands as signs of their willingness to completely abandon local tradition (*adat re atorang*). Buli enthusiasm to become Christian converts to the Utrecht Mission Union (UZV), a mission society of the strongly Calvinist Dutch Reformed Church (Nederlandsch Hervormde Kerk),[1] was part of a sudden explosion of conversion fever in otherwise predominantly Muslim North Maluku. All over Halmahera animists were eagerly, almost impatiently, converting to Christianity in the late 1890s. Tutuarima came to Buli from the north Halmaheran congregation of Kupa-Kupa, near Kao, where the entire village had converted suddenly in 1898 (Haire 1981:175). On a single day in September 1898, Hueting himself had baptized 360 people in Tobelo, and within a few years the number of baptized Halmaherans reached 3,200 (176). Tutuarima's visit to Buli in June 1899 was his second. Following a first and very successful visit, he was now returning to prepare for the placement in Buli of the Dutch missionary F. van Beekman (182). The mood in the Dutch mission was buoyant. In a letter from June 1899, a mission colleague of Hueting's wrote optimistically to the congregations back in the

Netherlands supporting the UZV financially that in Buli a "great working area is opening itself to Brother van Beekman" (*BUZ* 1900 [4]:58).[2]

Given his expectations, it came as a shock to Tutuarima that upon his return to Buli he was received by angry Maba representatives of the Tidore sultanate. The sultanate representatives vehemently rejected his presence and claimed, much to Tutuarima's astonishment, that he wanted to set himself up as a new king (*BUZ* 1900 [13]). The animists in Buli in turn reacted violently to these protests and assaulted their Muslim sultanate superiors. Only Tutuarima's intervention prevented the sultanate representatives from being killed (Hueting 1935:183). Upset by the unexpected turn of events, Tutuarima speedily returned to Tobelo and reported the incident to Hueting. After the colonial government in Ternate had "made it abundantly clear" to the sultan of Tidore "that it is the wish of the Government that Christianization was not to be disturbed anywhere, provided it is carried out by honest means" (*BUZ* 1900 [13]:153), Van Beekman, under the protection of a colonial army escort, took up his post as the first Dutch missionary to Buli in 1901. Before the end of the year, virtually all animists in Buli had converted to Christianity. This chapter seeks to trace the history of this enthusiasm for Christianity among the animists of Halmahera as well as the sultanate resentment of it. This is a history that is at once political and cosmological.

## The Cosmo-Politics of Conversion

Local enthusiasm for Christianity in the late 1890s was a remarkable and sudden turnaround for the UZV in Halmahera. Since the establishment of its first Christian mission station in Halmahera in 1866, local suspicion against the UZV had been high, and conversion had as consequence been excruciatingly slow. However, in the last decades of the nineteenth century the local attitude toward Christianity had begun to change gradually, and by 1898 interest had turned into outright fervor. In his history of the Christian church on Halmahera, Hueting calls this change "a God's miracle" (1935:98).

To the devout Dutchmen the sudden success of the mission was divinely preordained. Halmaheran enthusiasm for Christianity seemed, in fact, to be a local repetition of the "great awakenings"—waves of religious enthusiasm—that had rocked Dutch Protestantism since the eighteenth century and been crucial to the formation of the Dutch Reformed Church (Bos 2010; Ward 2002). Indeed, the notion that the goal of the mission was to instill a great awakening of faith in the converts to enable them to pursue a chaste and pious life figured strongly in the basic theology of many Dutch mission societies, including the UZV (Haire 1981:127). In 1899, Halmahera seemed to be experiencing its own awakening.

The Dutch mission in Halmahera was, however, painfully aware that local enthusiasm also had another source, a prehistory. The nineteenth century was thus perhaps the most tumultuous period in the history of Halmahera, in many ways even overshadowing the ethnoreligious violence that wreaked havoc throughout North Maluku between 1999 and 2001. It was a period rocked by a series of political rebellions, during which Halmahera more than ever before became directly and intimately involved in the political machinations of the two ruling sultanate centers in the region, Ternate and Tidore. Part of an overall narrative of political discontent with sultanate rule such as it had become under the pressures and constraints of indirect rule by the Dutch colonial administration, these rebellions had taken on distinctly millenarian characteristics by the 1870s. The 1870s was also the decade when the Dutch mission began experiencing its first noteworthy successes. This was no coincidence.

Between 1870 and the late 1890s, the missionaries of the UZV were, to their own considerable displeasure, increasingly connected to millenarian promises of a return of the ancestors. Indeed, when Christianity was initially embraced in Buli, it was borne on a wave of enthusiasm about the new religion's apparent ability to bring the dead back to life. This idea that Christianity entailed the return of the ancestors had, as this chapter will trace, grown gradually out of a series of political rebellions beginning with the so-called Nuku revolt in the 1780s (Widjojo 2008). Increasingly important to the appeal of these revolts among local people in Halmahera was the ambition to resurrect the sultanate of Jailolo, the fourth and "lost" sultanate of North Maluku (Andaya 1993). The resurrection of the sultanate of Jailolo sought to recreate a lost cosmic and political balance in the Spice Islands, a goal that during the 1800s increasingly began to hinge on the return to life of Mohammad Arif Bila, the vanished sultan of Jailolo (Leirissa 1990). It was this goal with which the resurrection of the dead, and in turn Christianity, gradually became associated.

Although there are several published accounts of the politics of the Nuku rebellion from 1780 to 1805 (Andaya 1993; Katoppo 1984; Widjojo 2008) as well as of the history of conversion to Christianity in Halmahera from 1866 onward (Haire 1981), there is to my knowledge no account that connects the intertwined threads of cosmology and politics that tie the rebellions of the 1700s and 1800s to the dynamics of conversion in the early 1900s. This chapter is my attempt to do so by highlighting the synchronicity between the history of political protest and the history of Christian conversion, a synchronicity that in Buli linked Christianity to millenarian expectations about a new kind of death. And, as the next chapter will spell out, in Buli the promise that death would end was also a promise about the end of witchcraft. The existing archival material on "the Spice Islands" of North Maluku, bestowed on posterity by a long-standing colonial presence that dates back to 1511, offers in this regard a rare opportunity. It not only enables us to provide a history of the conversion to Christianity over the *longue durée*. By extension, it also offers a unique, long-term historical perspective on witchcraft, its problems, and the promise of its resolution.[3] The hope of ending witchcraft was, as I will show, a radically new possibility, one that very much motivated Buli enthusiasm for Christianity between 1898 and 1901. While this enthusiasm, as the next chapter will show, was to end abruptly a few months after the entire Buli population had converted, the passionate appeal that Christianity gained in Halmahera had its own fascinating history. As this chapter will demonstrate, the remarkable success of Calvinist Christianity in Halmahera after the late 1890s grew out of a long history of political rebellion dating back to the late eighteenth century, out of which arose millenarian movements that are among the first of their type to be recorded in the Pacific Ocean.

The connection between millenarianism and conversion to Christianity is well described and has received particular attention in Melanesia, a region on whose western fringe North Maluku is located. In Melanesia, millenarian motives are often associated with conversion to charismatic forms of Christianity (Lattas 1998; Robbins 2004) or are identified as arising from local mythological charters (Burridge 1960; Lawrence 1964; Worsley 1970).[4] In North Maluku, millenarianism is neither purely Christian nor entirely homegrown. Instead, it is the product of an interaction between local cosmology, Christian eschatology, and anticolonial protest. It developed through historical connections and mutual influences that spanned the regions under the political control of the North Malukan sultanates of Ternate and Tidore (Kamma 1972; Rutherford 2000, 2006). The chapter will outline the history of more than a century of political protest, which tried to inscribe "the figures of spirituality on the grounds of politics" (Foucault 1981:8). This inscription of the figure of spirituality on the grounds of politics would, in turn, link Christianity to a new kind of death and the hope that witchcraft would come to an end, a hope that would resonate into the twenty-first century in Buli and fashion a form of historical agency.

## The Beginning of Radical Hope

Christianity as it arrived in Buli in 1899 delivered a new kind of imaginative horizon, a new kind of anticipation, rupture, and hope (Crapanzano 2004; Miyazaki 2007). The promise that Christianity could bring back dead ancestors entailed the realization of the ultimate animist dream: direct and unmediated communion with the spirits. But the Christian promise also implied another radically new possibility—namely, that witchcraft might have an end. Hope is "radical," Jonathan

Lear argues, when "it is directed towards a future goodness that transcends the current ability to understand what it is" (2006:103). Christianity, I suggest, appeared in the late 1890s to hold out such radical hope to many in Halmahera. At a time when people had come to expect that the world was going to be radically renewed, be turned "upside down," by the arrival of the "Just Ruler" of the sultanate of Jailolo, the millenarian idea that conversion would also make the ancestors come to life and halt witchcraft and sorcery constituted a radical possibility, the anticipation of which explains the exuberance, desperation even, which with people converted after 1898. Their willingness to cut their long hair, an emblem of masculine bellicosity in animist Halmahera, and burn the ritual paraphernalia associated with spirit worship indicates their investment in this hope (see fig. 9).

Hope, as Aristotle noted, "is a waking dream" (Crapanzano 2003:6). The hope for an end to witchcraft was a dream that Buli people entered warily. The idea of a life without death was already intimated in Buli myth, but the hope about a world without witchcraft that Christianity seemed to hold out clashed with Buli mythologies of witchcraft's ontological foundations (see chapter 2). The hope of gaining ultimate control of the *gua* was radical, and transcended people's "current

Figure 9. "Cutting the hair of a converted *alifuru* (animist) on Halmahera." Circa 1920. Tropenmuseum, Amsterdam. Reproduced with permission.

ability to understand what it is" (Lear 2006:103), because it was so at odds with the mythological emphasis on the inaccessibility and ineradicability of witchcraft. While traditional epistemology of witchcraft was grounded in doubt and guesswork, the possibility of an end to witchcraft, illness, and death in one stroke, and possibly an imminent stroke, was a hope that Buli people learned from Christianity. In a sense, one might say that it was Christianity that gave people in Buli hope. Indeed, in Buli the missionaries focused intensely on the concept of hope, and hope was one of the key words in Calvinist theology (Moltmann 2002). The missionary G. Maan, who served Buli from 1908 to 1919 and wrote a Dutch-Buli dictionary and a Buli grammar, employed the Buli word for "hope" or "trust," *mauláng*, to also denote Christian belief in God, a meaning that this word still retains today (1940:62). In the Buli language "believing in God" (*maulángo Jou*) therefore has the implied meaning of "staking one's hope on God" or "trusting God (to be honest)." Today, Hope (*Mawláng*) is still the name of the main church in the administrative town of Buli, which stands on the site of the very first church built during the early twentieth century.

Hope, Vincent Crapanzano notes, is always "embedded within historically and culturally specific understanding" (2003:15). When hope is transplanted from one cultural bed to another, unexpected transformations of its meaning may sometimes occur. This, I argue, is exactly what happens to Calvinist hope in Halmahera. While Calvinist theology sought to temper hope, the mission still inadvertently spurred hope's radicalization in Halmahera. There is an exquisite historical irony to the fact that the Calvinist mission on Halmahera not only owed its success to millenarian ideas about the return of the dead, but also, largely unbeknownst to itself, came to be critically implicated in efforts to realize these ideas. For, as Webb Keane has noted, the Dutch Calvinists who had their mission field in eastern Indonesia "are among the least puzzling or flamboyant of Christians. They are not millenarian or even revivalist" (2007:30). Nevertheless, the history of the success of the Protestant mission in Halmahera is the story of how a "circle of reverend men on whose knowledge, wisdom, and piety the church can safely rely" (Bos 2010:118–119)—a group of missionaries whose measured piety was about as far from millennial fervor as one can imagine—came to be seen as shamans with a great deal of potency (*barakát*), and closely connected to a millennial movement that anticipated the imminent return of the dead. This chapter is an account of this historical irony that was to have important consequences for how Christianity, modernity, and witchcraft would become entangled within the same anticipatory horizon.

## The Nuku Revolt and the Four Realms

From the thirteenth century onward, Maluku was ruled by four sultanates: Ternate, Tidore, Bacan, and Jailolo (Andaya 1993). The power of the sultanates derived from the sale of cloves, which were endemic to the region. After landfall of the first Europeans in 1511, the spices attracted a steady stream of Portuguese, Spanish, English, and Dutch adventurers and merchants who became increasingly embroiled in sultanate infighting. This was to change the distribution of power among the sultanates. A combined Ternatan-Portuguese force sacked the town of Jailolo in 1551, and the last descendant of the Jailolo sultanate dynasty died in 1684 (Andaya 1993:215). Thereby, the sultanate of Jailolo was for all intents and purposes eliminated as a political force. In the centuries that followed, however, the absence of the sultanate of Jailolo came to represent the loss of a cosmo-political utopia, an ideal world of just rule, as Leonard Andaya has convincingly shown.[5] Andaya's work is particularly valuable in showing the importance of the absence of the Jailolo sultanate from the world of the four realms to political rebellion in the sixteenth to eighteenth century.[6] My account will trace the continuing importance of the absence of the Jailolo sultanate, suggesting that its significance actually increased with the passing of time and came to play a crucial role in the rebellions of the nineteenth century as well as in the mass conversion to Christianity at the cusp of the twentieth century.

The Dutch East India Company (VOC) had controlled North Maluku since the beginning of the seventeenth century.[7] During the eighteenth century, however, Dutch support—political, financial, and military—for the sultanates of Ternate and Tidore had grown considerably, allowing the two sultanates to lay a firmer, if always contested, claim to its traditional domains in Halmahera and Papua. Ternate claimed the northern half of the island as well as its southern tip, while Tidore ruled the central half of Halmahera as well as the northern coastal regions of Papua (Kamma 1948–49). Buli, located within the domain of Tidore, was subject to the sultanate representative or *sangaji* of Maba (see map 4).

VOC's support came at a price, however, as it began to interfere more directly in sultanate politics and made ever more insistent counterdemands. It was in protest of this intervention that the so-called Nuku revolt began in 1780 (Widjojo 2008). This rebellion, which was the first to take up the theme of resurrecting the mythical Jailolo sultanate, began as a succession controversy.

In 1779, the VOC deposed and exiled Jamaluddin, the ruling sultan of Tidore, suspecting him of conspiring with the English (Andaya 1993:219). Passing over Jamaluddin's sons Kamaluddin and Nuku, the Dutch installed first Gaijira—an uncle of Jamaluddin—and, when he died a year later, the pliant Patra Alam, son of Gaijira. Defiant, Nuku fled to Halmahera. There he began to rally support for

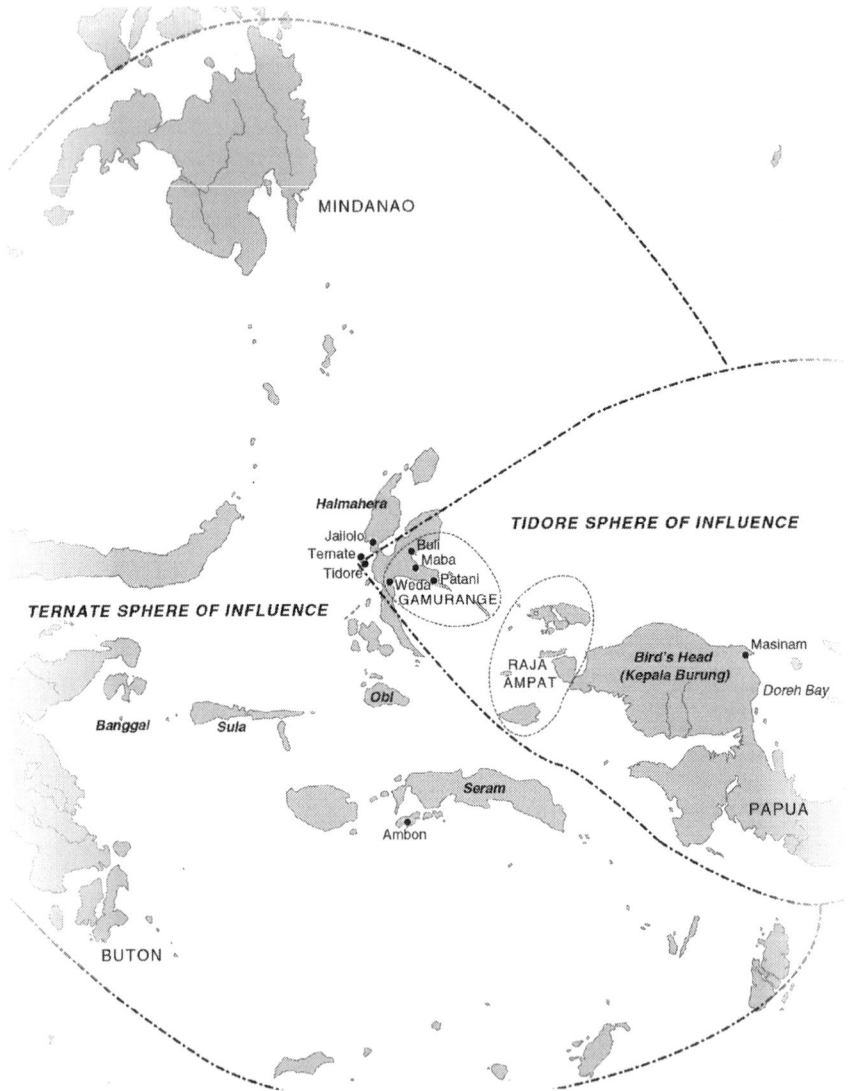

**Map 4.** Approximate spheres of political influence of the sultanates of Ternate and Tidore during the eighteenth century.

a long-standing rebellion against the Dutch and their choice of sultan. Nuku's most ardent supporters were Papuan and Halmaheran villagers, in particular in "the three regions" (*Gamurange*) of Weda, Patani, and Maba (to which Buli also belonged; see chapter 2) (Andaya 1993:109; Haga 1884a: 315).

The support and active participation of Maba and Buli in the Nuku uprising against the Dutch and the Tidore crown had been generated by local indignation over the Dutch-Tidore punitive expeditions that since the late 1600s had sought to enforce the Dutch ban on raiding in the area. Raiding trips provided an important anchor for cultural self-identity for the Halmaheran subjects of the North Malukan sultanates, and they were a means by which sultanate power was both exercised and accommodated (Widjojo 2008:110; see also Rutherford 2003). But the Dutch were eager to stop what they saw as illicit raids, which interfered with their effective control of the spice trade, and through a series of contracts in the late 1600s the Dutch sought to oblige the sultan of Tidore to stop the raids (Widjojo 2008:110). This imbalance in what was perceived as unfair sultanate rule came to be associated with the absence of the Jailolo sultanate, and the idea that Nuku's rebellion would seek to restore fair and just rule to North Maluku by resurrecting the lost kingdom of Jailolo was to be important in ensuring Halmaheran support (Andaya 1993:109; Widjojo 2008:212).[8] Rumor had it that a slave in Buli, who looked exactly like Nuku, was used to lead the Dutch search parties astray by appearing in places far from Nuku's last known sighting (Katoppo 1984:71).

In 1801 the English assumed control of the Dutch East Indies during their first interregnum.[9] One of the first actions of the new English rulers was to formally crown Nuku as sultan of Tidore in return for his support in their struggle to get a foothold in the Malukan spice trade (Andaya 1993:237; Widjojo 2008:200). Even before his coronation, however, Nuku fulfilled his promise to reestablish the lost unity by appointing one of his military commanders, Mohammad Arif Bila, a legal magistrate (*gogugu*) from Makian, as the sultan of Jailolo (Haga 1884a:374). It was this man who would become a mythological linchpin for a millenarian tradition, known under the toponym Djelolo—the man fusing with the place.

Nuku died in 1805 after only four years as the sultan of Tidore, but Mohammad Arif Bila continued Nuku's fight as the sultan of Jailolo and in 1806 staged an attack on Tidore in an attempt to take the crown, and in direct defiance of the Dutch (who had returned in 1803 at the end of the first English interregnum). The attack failed, and Sultan Arif Bila escaped into the forests of Halmahera, where Dutch archival records claim that he died (Haga 1884a:440). Among the local population of North Maluku, however, rumor had it that he had merely "disappeared" and would return in the near future. It is from this condition of occultation that Arif Bila or Djelolo was to become a major millenarian figure in North

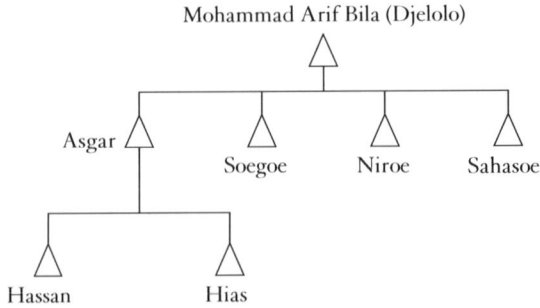

**Figure 10.** The genealogy of Hassan and Djelolo.

Maluku, and indirectly responsible for the success of Christianity in Halmahera after 1898.

Asgar, the son of Sultan Arif Bila, continued the rebellion against the Dutch in his father's name, also entitling himself Djelolo. Asgar was eventually apprehended and exiled to Ambon in 1811 (Haga 1884a:458). But in Asgar's absence, one of his brothers continued the struggle, using the name Djelolo.[10] By the 1820s, political unrest had become so endemic in the archipelago between Halmahera and Seram that the Dutch in exasperation promised to establish a kingdom for Asgar on the island of Seram (see map 4) as a substitute for the Jailolo kingdom on Halmahera (Haga 1884b:4). The kingdom in Seram was to last for only seven years. Sedition in Halmahera continued, and in 1832 the Dutch punished Asgar by exiling him and his family again, this time for life to Java (4). Asgar took his family with him into exile, including his young son, Hassan (Kniphorst 1883:475) (see fig. 10). It was this Hassan who would go on to reignite the political rebellion in North Maluku in the 1870s, when he claimed that his grandfather, Djelolo, had come back to life to rule as "the Just King" (I. *Ratu Adil*) and oversee the resurrection of the dead. The Hassan revolt turned political rebellion into millenarian fervor, a fervor that would in turn engulf also the Dutch mission.

## The End of the World and the Return of the Dead

In November 1874, rumor reached Galela that the dead had come back to life in Kao. Among those revived was Djelolo, the last sultan of Jailolo. The resurrected sultan had reportedly built "many forts in the forest" in preparation for a massive rebellion (*BUZ* 1875 [7]:122). In Galela and Tobelo, rice was left unharvested on the hillsides, and the Christian community in Galela prepared to save itself from the Apocalypse by hammering stakes into the ground. Holding onto these stakes would "prevent them from sliding into Hell" (122), as the world was turned "up-side down" (see chapter 4). Been, the UZV missionary to Kao, reported, "A big revolt has broken out on Halmahera under a certain Hassan, a descendant of the Sultan of Jailolo who calls himself Muhammad Hassan, Prince of Jailolo, and who claims to be the rightful heir to the island" (*BUZ* 1877 [2]:17). Hassan was allied with a prophet in Kao who called himself Adil, "the Just One." Adil claimed to have learned from a gold and pearl bird descending from heaven that a solar eclipse was imminent and that during the eclipse many villages would sink into the ground (*BUZ* 1876 [1]:10).[11] Inspired by Adil, several other prophets sprang up in Galela and in Tobelo, telling of the impending end of the world and the return of the dead. Some eighty houses were built in the forest to accommodate the dead (*BUZ* 1876 [5]:67). In a letter to the UZV mission journal Been reported:

> The Alifuru[12] [animist] people are convinced of the truth of [Hassan's] promise that the new ruler, of whom he has told so much, will arrive within a few days. . . . On the orders of Adil, the Alifuru have thrown away the corpses of their deceased [traditionally placed in shrines in the village], because the newly arisen dead cannot dwell among them if they see the elevated shrines with bones and corpses. The Alifuru have, with this act, completely broken with tradition. At the moment, they are feasting fran-tically day and night; but the worst part is that the population is following Hassan. They say he is not the real ruler, but that he must conquer the island for his grandfather, who has risen from the dead and who stays with the fanatic [Adil] deep in the forest. Hassan himself is in Weda, from where *kora-kora* war boats are going to bring him to Kao, Galela, Tobelo, and the surrounding areas. Hundreds of Alifuru from these places are to accom-pany him under the deception that those who do not follow him will die. The population has become very brutal; now and then one of the robbers from behind Miti [near Kao] appears to quickly murder and rob whom-ever they can find. The confusion is great. I am alone here [in the village of Kao]. All the Chinese and Muslim people have fled. (*BUZ* 1877 [2]:18)

Hassan was the returning king, the envoy of his grandfather, the sultan of Jailolo, come back to life to establish just rule. This was an extremely powerful message that grabbed the imagination of most Halmaherans. No fewer than six hundred people were present to greet Hassan on the island of Miti, and another eight hundred reportedly assembled to receive him in Kao. The mere fact that Hassan himself arrived in Tobelo with one thousand men and fifty war boats (*BUZ* 1877 [2]:26) shows the huge scale that his movement had assumed, at least by Halmaheran standards. According to Hassan's own estimate, by November 1876 his movement totaled thirty thousand people, ten thousand of whom were prepared to follow him to Ternate to put his demands for the reestablishment of the Jailolo sultanate before the colonial government and the sultan of Ternate (*BUZ* 1877 [3]:35).[13]

General mayhem spread to most of Halmahera. Two colonial officials and seven Ternatan sultanate representatives were murdered, and a Chinese merchant mutilated. As a consequence, neither Chinese merchants nor Muslim sultanate representatives dared to sail along the coast of eastern Halmahera (*BUZ* 1876 [5]:66).

By the end of 1876, news of the prophet of Kao and the rebel Hassan had also reached the north coast of Papua (*BUZ* 1877 [11]:174; Kamma 1972:41). In October, a local ruler on the small island of Masinam, a trading post and mission station in Doreh Bay (see map 4), accompanied a large and enthusiastic delegation of Masinam people to Halmahera to join the prophet (Kamma 1972:121). The delegation headed for Maba in east Halmahera, where Hassan was said to await its arrival (Kniphorst 1883:482).

The north coast of Papua had long historical links to Halmahera. Both were part of the domain of the sultanate of Tidore, and both were missionized by the UZV.[14] The area is well known in the anthropological literature of millenarianism because of the myth of Mansren, the famous figure of the Papuan millennial movements and cargo cults. Mansren had disappeared in mythical times "to the West," whence he would return after being heralded by a *konoor* (shaman and magician) to initiate the coming of Koreri—a utopian era in which the dead return to life, and illness no longer exists (Kamma 1972; Rutherford 2003; Worsley 1970).

Peter Worsley has called the millenarian movements of the Papuan north coast "the earliest instance of a millenarian prophecy in Melanesia" (1970:136), but I would contend that one might profitably look west, toward the sultanates of North Maluku and the beginnings of Calvinist rule there, when writing the earliest history of millenarianism. Freerk Kamma, who was the first to see this link, writes: "It is tempting to make a comparison between the *Koreri* [movement in Papua] and the *Adil* movements [in Halmahera]. For diffusionists several footholds are offered, and it is true that the formal elements do not differ much, while there is proof of historical contacts. . . . We . . . suggest that in their mythical character the *Koreri* movements may be more dependent on Halmahera than has been assumed till now" (1972:123).

The similarities between the Adil prophet and the *konoor* (shaman) who would herald the coming of Koreri were also obvious to the people of Masinam in 1876—so obvious, in fact, that the two were seen as rival prophets. Kamma describes how news of the Hassan revolt actually worked to undercut the power of a *konoor* in Masinam: "It seems that the inhabitants of Moom in Masinam had heard that in Djilolo [Jailolo] . . . an even greater *konoor* had made his appearance" (1972:120–121). It was this more potent shaman that the expedition from Moom set out to join.

The millenarian movements in North Maluku and along the north coast of New Guinea were, in other words, similar in their cosmological and political circumstances. Both combined the prophetic heralding of the return of the ancestors with an end to death and the establishment of a political utopia; both emerged in regions under sultanate rule—or, to be precise, in symbolic and political opposition to it (Kamma 1972:106); and both took place in the mission fields of the UZV.

By late 1876, the colonial government was seriously alarmed. Inspired by the Hassan revolt, piracy—long endemic in the region—began to focus entirely on Ternate and Tidore vessels, while other ships sailed the waters unharmed. In the course of just two months, between December 1876 and January 1877, pirates killed forty-six crew members from Ternate and Tidore (Kniphorst 1883:487). A problem that the colonial administration had initially seen as local unrest had swelled into widespread regional rebellion and unrest. The colonial government put a price of 5,000 guilders on Hassan's head (489), equivalent to more than ten times the annual wage of an unskilled Dutch laborer at the time. On 21 June 1877, Hassan surrendered along with the dissident sultanate representatives (*sangaji*) of Maba and Bicoli to the captain of the steamboat *Banka* (494). Hassan was sentenced that same year to exile in Muntok, off Java (Clerq 1890:185). Although the Hassan rebellion was quickly relegated to the footnotes of history (Campen 1884:8), it was to have important and direct consequences for the way in which Christianity was perceived and received in Halmahera in general, and in Buli in particular. Because of the Hassan revolt, Christianity itself came to have special power (*barakát*), even power over the dead.

## A God's Miracle

The mission had experienced a remarkable change of fate during the 1870s that coincided with the Hassan rebellion. The Halmaheran reception of the Christian mission was initially hostile and suspicious, but by the 1870s the early missionaries began to notice a remarkable change. Instead of rejecting or fearing the power of God, it seemed that the locals were beginning to attribute to the missionaries and the Christian God a certain power over the indigenous universe. During the Hassan rebellion, Hendrik van Dijken's church in Galela was always packed with people, and even "pagans" asked him to preach to them (*BUZ* 1875 [12]:202). But it was a success that was premised on the local idea that the Dutch missionaries were powerful sorcerers and had some power over the imminent millenarian events of which the Hassan movement foretold. The "heathens" Van Dijken had complained about in 1874 see in the missionary nothing but "a Christian sorcerer" (Dutch *een christen-toovenaar*) (*BUZ* 1876 [7]:123). At one point in 1876, Van Dijken had an attendance of fifty-six "sorcerers" or shamans (*o gomatere*), many of whom were local prophets and assistants of Adil, at a sermon arranged at the urging of the Galela population (121). As rumors of the Hassan rebellion reached Galela, six hundred people came to ask Van Dijken to be their king and to destroy the Ternatan officials. In effect, much to his own horror, Van Dijken was regarded as the "popular leader and ally" of Hassan (Haire 1981:26). The missionaries were, in other words, seen to be conveyors of a potency (*o giẖiri* in Tobelo and *baraẖát* in Buli), the appeal of which appeared to resonate with themes already present in the millenarian motivation underlying the Hassan rebellion.

The association between missionaries and shamans that the Hassan movement had powerfully established continued to grow between the 1870s and the 1890s. The crucial event in this transformation of Calvinist missionaries into millenarian prophets took place in 1897. There had been minor, sporadic revolts during the 1880s and 1890 that demonstrated that Hassan's messianic promises continued to have currency among Halmaherans.[15] But then, in 1897, a new revolt began brewing, this time revolving around a *sangaji* (sultanate representative) from Tobelo. Claiming to be Hassan's heir, the *sangaji* attracted a considerable following in north Halmahera. He associated himself with a local shaman and professed prophet who also called himself Adil,[16] "the Just King," and the two held nocturnal rituals on the island of Ra, during which they prepared their followers for the imminent return of a messianic figure called "the Great Holder of the Key" (I. *Juru Kunci Besar*) (Haire 1981:174; Hueting 1925:50). As part of these rituals, Adil demonstrated his potency by selling wrapped objects that he claimed would turn into precious valuables at the imminent arrival of "the Just King."

At this time, Tobelo had just become the mission field of Anton Hueting, who had replaced Been (Haire 1981:172). Hueting played an active role in suppressing this final revolt. He traveled to the island of Ra during one of the all-night rituals and convinced the *sangaji* to surrender himself to the local Dutch official (Dutch *Posthouder*) in Tobelo. According to Hueting, he had the greatest impact on the local following when he publicly revealed the shaman Adil as a charlatan (Dutch *bedrieger*) (Hueting 1925:51), by exposing the wrapped gifts as worthless trinkets (Haire 1981:174).

Soon after Hueting had exposed the prophet Adil as a sham in 1897, conversions began to explode as whole villages asked to be baptized. Unlike Van Dijken, his older and more pietistic colleague, Hueting believed in the value of initial mass conversion. Hueting therefore made a point of touring as many villages as possible and of placing mainly Ambonese catechists in strategically selected villages (Haire 1981:173). This allowed the mission to keep up with the growing demand from locals to convert. In the village of Wohia, animist objects were publicly burned on 20 February 1898 in preparation for the mass baptism (175). This total rejection of local *adat* was the same kind of commitment that we saw the Hassan movement had required of its followers in 1874. The Dutch missionary had, it would seem, fully assumed the form of the "Christian sorcerer," who appeared able to fulfill what North Malukan prophets had promised for decades—namely, the end of death and the return of the ancestors. The enthusiasm to convert soon spread across all of Halmahera, including eventually to Buli with Tutuarima's arrival in 1899. It was, as Hueting put it, "a God's miracle" (1935:98).

## (Mis)reading the Gospel in Buli

All the historical ingredients are now present to appreciate the enthusiasm with which the animists in Buli welcomed Tutuarima in 1899 and embraced Christianity in 1901. The scramble to convert that swept Halmahera after 1898 was motivated by millenarian expectations that combined political ideas about the return of the vanished sultan of Jailolo and the reestablishment of the fourth sultanate in the "World of the Four Mountains" (*Moloko Kie Raha*) with an emergent cosmological narrative about the return of the ancestors. The Calvinist mission readily played into this scenario as it propagated its notions of resurrection and the miracle of God through practices of mass conversion, iconoclastic rejection of idolatry, and the unmasking of "fraudulent" prophets.

In light of the seemingly identical millennial messages in Christianity and the long political tradition of insurrection that preceded it, it was only natural that the two should be equated. It is this equation between redeemer and missionary only twenty years after the end of Hassan rebellion—a rebellion that had its stronghold in Buli and surrounding villages in the Gamurange—that explains the repeated appeals by Buli animists for a missionary to be placed in their area. Indeed, as the next chapter will detail, Tutuarima seemed to Buli ears to be merely repeating the prophecies of the Hassan movement: that breaking with their traditional practices, *in casu* by converting to Christianity, would reunite them with their dead ancestors in preparation for the arrival of "the Just King."

The strong objections of both the *sangaji* of Maba and the sultan of Tidore to such a presence in Buli suggest that in Tutuarima they, too, recognized not just a Christian missionary or a representative of the Dutch colonial government, but also a potential catalyst of renewed political insurgence cast in the mold of Nuku and Hassan. More than a century of rebellion against Tidore overrule reverberates in the complaint of the sultanate representative (*sangaji*) that Tutuarima wanted to set himself up as a ruler in Buli. For the *sangaji* as for Buli people in general, the Christian message about a God, who would reunite people with their ancestors, seemed yet another installment of the regional tradition of "the Just King." Iconoclasm played an important role in this elaborate (mis) reading. The prerequisite for the return of the dead appeared to be the same for both the Adil prophecies in 1876 and the promises of a Christian awakening in 1899—namely, the wholesale rejection of tradition. An orthodox Calvinist mission union, the UZV was strongly iconoclastic, politically conservative (Von der Dunk 1978), and fervently anti-Enlightenment in its outlook (Latourette 1959:241). It emphasized the importance of a simple, pious life and the fundamental truth of Christian scripture (Benedict 2002; Keane 2007; McNeill 1954). This general theological background meant that in Halmahera, as elsewhere in the region, the missionaries—who were not educated theologians and ministers of the Reformed Church, but were ordained only for the mission field (Haire 1981:136)—strongly underscored the importance of the Holy Spirit, the sanctity and the literal word of the Bible, and the virtues of hard work and sexual propriety. Conversely, they frowned upon and sought to eradicate those aspects of local tradition that entailed idolatry, sexual licentiousness, or laziness (Keane 2007; Rutherford 2006).

Iconoclasm rests on a strong belief in the falsity of religious worlds mediated by idols. Idols and deceit are therefore inextricably linked. As Bruno Latour has noted, the "classical" iconoclastic stance is motivated by a strong desire to free the believers (that is, those they deem to be believers) of their false attachments to idols of all shapes and sizes. Iconoclasts believe it is not only necessary, but also possible, to dispose entirely of material intermediaries for access to truth, objectivity, and sanctity (Latour 2010:83). The Calvinist missionaries of the UZV represented this "classical" stance. Their fervent antipathy to religious images meant that they took idolatry as the key indicator of paganism. The destruction of idols, such as

**Figure 11.** A lean-to (*ebai peso mar*) in Buli used as a venue for shamanistic divination rituals (*famamá*). Date unknown. Tropenmuseum, Amsterdam. Reproduced with permission.

ancestor figures, ritual paraphernalia, and shrines to honor the spirits (see fig. 11), was therefore often the major ritual event that accompanied mass conversion in Halmahera and elsewhere in eastern Indonesia (Rutherford 2006).

For the missionaries, the animists' willingness to give up the idols of their ancestors was proof not only of the power of God, but also of the power of their belief "that the others—the poor guys whose cherished icons have been accused of being impious idols—believe naively in them" (Latour 2010:84).

Ironically, however, the Calvinists' practice of ritually burning the icons of animism mimicked the destruction of shrines and burial scaffolds that we saw accompanied the Hassan movement. In this way, iconoclasm served to confirm a millenarian promise. For Halmaherans in the 1890s, the destruction of their ancestor figures, cutting their hair, and giving up wearing the traditional red headbands (which signified courage and bellicosity) was a calculated gamble in the hope of cashing in on the promises of the Christian God, a cautious bet against traditional ways of engaging the ancestors, which resembled the bets that people had made throughout Halmahera during the Hassan revolt.

Calvinist iconoclasm also played a second, unintended role in the conversion history of Halmahera. Conversion, as we saw, exploded after Hueting in 1897 had publicly exposed the prophet Adil as a fraud (Hueting 1925:51), revealing his potent wrapped objects as worthless. Idols, it seemed to the missionary, had been exposed for what they were: worthless superstition (Haire 1981:174). But the exposure of the prophet's magical implements by Hueting had a powerful effect on people in Halmahera. As the Irish minister James Haire writes in his history of the Halmaheran church, "The effects of these events were to make strong confirmation in Tobelo of the strength of Hueting's *gikiri* in dealing with the traditional strength or *gikiri* associated with the Tobelorese tribal leaders" (1981:174–175). Rather than defusing the power of the millenarian narrative, Hueting's revelation of the prophet Adil as a fraud transposed its power to the Christian missionary himself.

Revealing the trickery of an indigenous sorcerer, as Michael Taussig has shown, is always fraught with difficulty: "In its unmasking, magic is in fact made even more opaque" (2003:295). Hueting's revelation of a prophet who predicted the return of the dead as a fraud did not undermine the power of this possibility. Instead, Hueting's unmasking of the deception of a false prophet confirmed that the Christian missionary was like a local shaman. In animist cosmology on Halmahera, the shaman mediates between the living and the ancestors. In Tobelo, for instance, the role of the shaman (T. *o gomatere*) was to enter the realm of spirits to protect the shadow of the deceased from the witch spirits (T. *o tokata*) and ensure their proper transformation into an ancestor spirit (T. *o gomanga*) or "strong ancestor" (T. *o dilikine*) (Platenkamp 1988:155). If the shamans failed in this task, the shadow of the deceased would itself "become a *tokata*" witch (159). In Tobelo cosmology, the shaman was therefore intimately associated with the handling of the dead and the transformation of the dead into ancestors (and involved in a cosmic battle with witchcraft). The shamanistic healer (*mamá*) in Buli had the same role of protecting the living from witchcraft through the mediation of spirits. From this starting point, all it took was a small detour through Christian eschatology for people to ascribe to the missionary the power to bring ancestors back to life and vanquish witches. It was this possibility that would so quickly and completely capture the Halmahera imagination.

## Hope, Radical and Rambling

Christianity gave people in Halmahera hope. It was a radical kind of hope that transcended people's "current ability to understand what it is" (Lear 2006:103). For people in Buli, at least, the notion that the ancestors might come back to life, that death could be halted, and that witchcraft would end marked a radical hope in Lear's sense, because this possibility outstripped the epistemology of "guessing" (*fatailo*) that Buli mythology and tradition (*adat re atorang*) espoused. Christianity seemed to hold out the radical hope of a certainty about the unseen world of ancestors and witchcraft that was otherwise unimaginable to an animist. The enthusiasm for Christianity was born, I suggest, from this radical hope.

Now, Calvinism itself was very much a theology of hope, predicated on the existence of God and the deferred future of salvation (Moltmann 2002). Hope, as Hirokazu Miyazaki has shown, shifted in Christian eschatology from being "a concrete hope for the second coming of Christ to [being] an abstract hope for an afterlife" (2007:12). Calvinism worked hard to defer the hope of salvation and the Second Coming from being imminent to being an abstract event. Jürgen Moltmann, the German theologian, quotes Calvin in his magnum opus *The Theology of Hope*: "To us is given the promise of eternal life—but to us, the dead. A blessed resurrection is proclaimed to us—meantime we are surrounded by decay" (2002:4). The promise of salvation, what Moltmann calls eschatology, is tied to the "misery of experiential reality" (Crapanzano 2003:7). Hope "takes its stand" against death and misery in lived existence, but it does not really banish them; for hope, like everything else in Calvinism, must be tempered by moderation; it must not be allowed to run wild. Moltmann continues: "It is in this contradiction [between the promise of salvation and the reality of death] that hope must prove its power. Hence eschatology, too, must be forbidden to ramble, and must formulate its statements of hope in contradiction to our present experience of suffering, evil, and death" (2002:4–5).

Hope must "be forbidden to ramble." And ramble is just what Halmaheran eschatology did in the eyes and ears of the Dutch missionaries. The ideas that motivated the Halmaheran reception of the gospel of hope centered around the exact same problem of promise and death that concerned Calvin, a concern to which the Dutch missionaries in Halmahera were theological heirs—namely, the calibration of "a concrete hope for the second coming of Christ to an abstract hope for an afterlife" (Miyazaki 2007:12). But it "rambled" by seeing hope's fulfillment as a real and imminent possibility. People in Buli and throughout Halmahera concretized Calvinist hope, turning an abstract afterlife into an animist paradise on Earth: conviviality with the ancestors and an absence of witches, sorcerers, and other agents of death. This was a dual hope for the unconditional absence of the absent-yet-present *gua* and the physical presence of the present-yet-absent ancestors. Christianity, in other words, seemed to promise a bulwark against death and the *gua*, making the ancestors all the stronger by making them visible and present. Once people accepted the Christian God, their ancestors would return to life and fully realize their traditional role of protecting the descendants against the *gua*, banishing it for good. In some sense it was the very inaccessibility of witchcraft in the Buli animist universe that gave the Christian hope of salvation its radical appeal. It was, one might say, animist doubt that helped radicalize Christian hope, turning the promise of witchcraft's end into a potentiality no animist would otherwise dare hope for.

I have already quoted Keane's observation that the Dutch Calvinist missionaries in Indonesia are "among the least puzzling or flamboyant of Christians. They are not millenarian or even revivalist" (2007:30). It was therefore historically ironic that conversion to Christianity was accompanied by such millennial fervor in Halmahera. Indeed, the "moderate hope" of the UZV was successful exactly because it appeared through its incorporation in millennial protest to be a radical kind of hope, a radical hope that in the end was more foreign to animist thinking than it was to Dutch Calvinism.[17]

## Conjunctures of Conversion

The association of the Christian mission in Halmahera and Buli with the promise of a return of the dead and a reversal of the world that augured the establishment of just rule was—to employ a concept from a bygone theoretical era—"overdetermined." It was a "structure of conjuncture" that was overdetermined historically, and mythologically, and theologically (Sahlins 1987). But intriguingly, the myths of history that motivated this "historical structure of conjuncture" between Christianity and the return of the ancestors were both Malukan and European in origin. The pietistic Dutch missionaries reluctantly and implicitly accepted the role of new indigenous prophets because it suited their political-mythological ideas about "animist paganism" and its moral state on an evolutionist theological scale. Likewise, the people of Halmahera converted, with a guarded enthusiasm, because the Christian message fitted, unbelievably well, into an emergent political-mythological narrative of political protest and cosmological renewal.

The Dutch missionaries were, in other words, as deeply engaged in a spiritual politics as were the people of Halmahera. Both sides sought to inscribe in the borderland between heaven and earth "the figures of spirituality of the grounds of politics" (Foucault 1981:8). For the Dutch missionaries, Hueting's unmasking of the deceitful nature of Halmaheran millenarianism substantiated their basic belief in the naive faith of the other, and their Calvinist iconoclasm represented the reasonable counterpart to local people's "false attachments to idols of all sorts and shapes" (Latour 2010:83). For the converts in Halmahera, however, Hueting's unmasking of the local prophet served only to confirm the power (*barakát*) of the Dutch missionary, just as Calvinist iconoclasm made its millenarian promise of the return of the dead all the more convincing.

The next chapter will explore how this elaborate mutual misreading was tied to a logic of exchange, revelation, and deception that, in the years and decades after the initial wave of conversion, would come to engulf Christianity itself, when the perceived Christian promise of the return of the dead came to be seen as deceitful. The enthusiasm with which Buli people had mass converted in 1901 soon dissipated. Within the span of a few months, people grew increasingly resentful and eventually apostatized. Christians, many now agreed, were liars. This resentful attitude was to last for decades.

# 4

# CHRISTIANITY AND DECEPTION

Christians are liars . . .
*Kresten madarawa . . .*

DUDU BARABAKEM, EARLY 1930S

## Soundscape 1933

*TAka-taka-TAka-taka-TAka-taka.* The pace of the deerskin drums that accompany the *cakalele*, the North Malukan dance of ritual and war, is fast and gradually builds up speed. Its counterpoint is the slow, sonorous dong of the brass gongs. In 1933, the sounds of the *cakalele* would echo through the village of Waiflí every Sunday outside the house where Mozes Mahulette, the first catechist of the village, was trying to conduct his church service. The source of the noise was a local man named Dudu Barabakem and a large group of recalcitrant animists. They would beat drums and gongs, blow triton shells, cry out *"yeee-hehehe,"* the traditional call of courage, and perform the *cakalele*. Their performance was not just ritual; it was also political. Its purpose was to drown out the slow, pious sounds of the Calvinist service with the fast-paced rhythm of drums that call the spirits into action. "Make noise, make noise (*pei lio, pei lio*)," the dancers would encourage each other, as one usually does when calling up Íyan Toa or one of the guardian animal spirits (*suang*) that each Buli patriline (*fam*) traditionally has. Dudu and his companions were, in effect, doing what one would traditionally do when preparing for war. Armed with spears and dancing shields, one dances (*oa*) in front of the spirit house of one's animal guardian, entreating it to reveal itself by possessing a member of the group and thereby bestowing strength and courage before battle (see fig. 12). Through the fighting magic (*man de wela*) of the animal spirit, one learns to "forget about death" (*to mat pantó*) and becomes invulnerable when confronting the enemy.

The sound of the war drums and the sight of the armed dancers, whose feet barely touched the ground as proof of their magical abilities, was a frightening experience that would have intimidated the new converts who were praying inside the house. Indeed, few people dared to participate in the service. And they had good reason to be frightened, for the Buli dancers were furious about the presence of Christians in their village. There was no way of knowing how far they might take their anger. On one occasion a spear thrown through a window in the house grazed the head of Mozes Mahulette; on another occasion a member of the Christian fellowship was beaten over the head with a dancing shield as he tried to enter the house. As the congregation was calling upon their God inside the house, Dudu and his brothers were calling upon the ancestors and animal spirits in an auditory competition that essentially constituted an invitation to a cosmic show of strength. In striking contrast to the enthusiasm for Christianity that had swept Buli in 1899, Dudu and his brothers were calling for war against Christianity, employing all the magical power (*barakát*) of the very ancestors and animal spirits that people had willingly rejected in 1901 when they converted to Christianity. Instead of fervent hope, the attitude toward Christianity in Waiflí was in 1933 characterized by bitter resentment. This chapter will trace this shift, suggesting that the history of the rise of resentment is as interesting as the history of hope and enthusiasm that the previous chapter explored. Indeed, as we shall see, the two histories are intimately intertwined.

Two men personified the resentful relationship between animism and Christianity in 1933: Dudu Barabakem and Mozes Mahulette. Dudu was a hothead (*makés*) and a hardhead (*boboko ca ncicoal*). In many ways, Dudu was a man with the kind of disposition that Buli tradition idealizes: humble and soft-spoken, but fearsome and belligerent if provoked. These qualities grew out of the proprieties of tradition (*adat re atorang*) and an intimate and carefully maintained ritual relation to the animal guardian spirits (*suang*) and the ancestor spirits (*smengit*). A man committed to the ancestors and the spirits, Dudu was also one of the most visible and audible characters among a large group of Buli animists who, in 1933, did their best to scare away the mission. Mozes Mahulette, meanwhile, was the adopted child of a Muslim Ambonese trader who had arrived in Buli in 1925 to buy copra (dried coconut meat), but had then stayed on. Mozes was confirmed as a Christian by K. A. Bot, the last Dutch missionary to be stationed in Buli. A few years later he married a local Buli woman and moved to Waiflí. Locally known by the nickname Botji, Mozes was tasked by the Dutch missionary to begin mission work in 1933.

The year 1933 marked a new phase in the Christian mission in North Maluku. The region had been the mission field of the Utrecht Mission Union (UZV)
since 1866 (Haire 1981). By the early 1930s, however, the mission was feeling the
effects of the global financial crisis, as funding from the Netherlands dwindled
following the 1929 stock market crash. The UZV closed its school in Tobelo, and
a number of Dutch missionaries returned home. The missionary K. A. Bot, the
last of seven Dutch missionaries who had served in Buli since 1901, left the village
and moved to Tobelo in 1933. With the departure of the last Dutch missionary,
the Christian mission in Buli became an indigenous affair, a process that was
strengthened when the Christian Evangelical Church of Halmahera (I. *Gereja
Masehi Injil Halmahera*, or GMIH) was formally established as an independent
church in 1949 (Haire 1981:53). With much of the mission work outsourced to
Ambonese catechists such as Mozes Mahulette, the Christian mission also came
to the Buli people of Waiflí.

Mozes knew he was facing a difficult task with the recalcitrant animists in
Waiflí. In an account of the missionary's life, read in tribute at his funeral in 1986,
Samadar Batawi provided a local retrospective angle on the mission's early, diffi-
cult times in Waiflí, the village known in Indonesian as Buli Asal:

> At this time most people in Buli Asal were heathen (I. *kafir*), people who
> had not yet accepted religion. When Mozes and his family conducted
> Christian sermons in their house, the heathens would always disturb them.
> They tried to upset the Christian service by beating gongs and pounding
> drums. They would blow triton shells and perform the *cakalele* war dance.
> The purpose was to intimidate the mission and to force it away. In every
> respect—in their attitude, their actions, and their words—the heathens re-
> jected the mission. (Batawi 1986:n.p.)

Dudu and his companions were certainly enraged, and their choice to loudly
protest was animist in nature. But it was not true that Dudu and his group of
protesters had not accepted Christianity. Indeed, every single one of the angry animists dancing and making noise outside the church service in 1933 had for a brief
period several decades earlier been a Christian. Dudu himself had been among the
Buli people who had enthusiastically embraced Christianity in the early 1900s. But
soon after, he and most other Buli people had apostatized in disappointment and
disgust. The resentment that Dudu and his companions felt at the circumstances
surrounding the initial introduction of Christianity was so strong that they were
willing, even three decades later, to employ all the noisy and belligerent measures
that tradition made available to them in their attempt to ward off mission activity
in the village of Waiflí. It was a determined protest against what they perceived

**Figure 12.** Tangkea Guslaw dancing (*oa*) in front of the shrine of Íyan Toa. 1993. Photo by author.

to be the false promises and lies of Christianity, and the bitterness continued for several decades until the last of the village's inhabitants finally converted in 1972.

The pattern of fervent anticipation and bitter disappointment associated with the twentieth-century reception of Christianity in Buli—an ambivalence that continues to inform Buli Christianity today—was founded upon a historically produced set of expectations as to what Christianity could offer. These expectations were and are closely linked to the problem of witchcraft in Buli. Christianity's promise to bring back the ancestors and end death was in Buli related to the ability to bring about an end to witchcraft. Conversion would signal an end to death and illness, the physical return of the dead ancestors, and an ultimate social victory over the *gua* and its control over the living in Buli. When this promise of eradicating death was revealed as empty during the months following mass conversion in 1901, most of the initial converts apostatized in bitter disappointment. For these people, including Dudu, the Christian gospel became synonymous with lies and deception. I will show that these accusations of lies and deception are part of the ambivalence with which people in Buli today regard both themselves and the Christian beliefs they have adopted.

In chapter 3 I described how Christianity introduced radical hope to Buli. This chapter will describe how it also introduced bitter disappointment. Disappointment is an unavoidable fact in human existence (Craib 1994). One might say that

disappointment is hope's twin; it is born with hope. Hope always entails an encounter with the unexpected. As Derrida has noted, "If one could count on what
is coming, hope would be but the calculation of a program" (1994:169). In Buli,
Christianity offered an unexpected and almost unbelievable promise, which, in
the years just after the turn of the twentieth century, people could not help but
jump at: the return of their ancestors and an end to witchcraft. When their hopes
of an end to the *gua* were dashed, trust and hope were replaced by anger and disappointment at every broken promise. The apostatized Christians fled in disgust.
The early twentieth-century rift over Christianity and its control over witchcraft
and death came literally to determine the modern spatial layout of Buli and its division into a village cluster consisting of three separate segments. While a few Buli
people remained with the mission in the village that gradually grew to become
Buli Serani (Christian Buli), the district capital whose main church still bears
the name Hope (*Mawláng*), Dudu and most other Buli people apostatized and
fled the mission in disgust. By the 1930s they had established the village of Waiflí
a few kilometers up the coast from Buli Serani as an animist stronghold against
Christianity. The new satellite village of Waiflí accordingly came to be known in
Indonesian as Buli Asal, or "Original Buli." Between the main village and Buli
Asal a third village section was known as "Muslim Buli" (Buli Islam).

Dudu's noisy protests in 1933 were a historical reverberation of the disappointment of 1901, and the fact that resentment remained strong after three decades is
an indication of the intensity with which it was felt. I suggest that disappointment
with the promise of Christianity persisted as a "fuzzy horizon" for Buli experience
of the outside world, throughout the twentieth century and into the twenty-first
(Crapanzano 2004:2). Buli people's high hopes for, and bitter disappointment with,
Christianity encapsulate an experience of "thwarted hope" (Miyazaki 2007:31),
which sedimented into an evolving historical pattern: an expectant but continuously frustrated hope that the outside world might be able to offer to the people of
Buli that which their own tradition could not provide—namely, a radical solution
to the problem of the *gua*, certainty of its absence. This is a pattern that I believe
has become formative for Buli engagement, not only with Christianity but also
with modernity as they understand it—the replication of "a past unfulfilled hope
on another terrain," as Hirokazu Miyazaki puts it (139).

## Converting, Waiting . . .

Tangkea Guslaw, grandson of Dudu Barabakem, was born in 1929 and was too
young to remember the loud and angry protests that reverberated throughout the
early years of the 1930s. But Tangkea clearly recalls Dudu later telling him the

reason behind his anger. It had all begun back in 1901, as Tangkea explained to me, when the new religion still seemed to hold great promise:

> My grandfather said he had been told: "If you convert to Christianity, your fathers, mothers, and children who are dead will return (*ue*)." "We should become Christian," my grandfather had said to himself. "Christians only have to go to church on one special day per week, and they do not have to feed God all the time like we have to do with the ancestors and animal spirits in return for their protection against sorcery and witchcraft (*payao re gua na*). Also, God does not punish us the way the ancestors do if we do not honor him." So they all became Christian. Simply everybody! They converted to Christianity and "waited cautiously" (*tantano*) to see if the dead would return.

In the animist universe, the ancestors (*smengit*) and the animal guardian spirits (*suang*) are, along with the culture hero Íyan Toa, the most important spirits. Associated with particular patrilines (*fam*), the ancestors and the animal spirits act as protectors of their descendants against other spiritual forces, such as *jin* (wild spirits), *ibilis* (evil forest spirits), or *puntiana* (dangerous female spirit). The ancestors and animal spirits also provide fighting magic and give knowledge about and "blessing" (*barakát*) to medical herbs and roots. But the arguably most important function of the ancestral and animal spirits is to protect against sorcery and witchcraft. In return they are associated with dietary taboos and have to be ritually honored on a regular basis with offerings of tobacco, betel nut, incense, and palm wine (see also Valeri 2000). The spirits are, however, also notoriously fickle and regularly punish the living or withdraw their protection if they have been angered by transgressions of dietary prohibitions or ritual neglect. We saw an instance of this in chapter 1, when an offended ancestor spirit pushed Hitam onto a poisonous stonefish. The relationship to the spirits is therefore not without its costs and risks.

Christianity offered a new deal, a deal that at first glance seemed vastly better than ancestor worship and animism. Instead of the deal represented by the ancestors (*smengit*) and animal guardian spirits (*suang*)—who offered a pragmatic way of "making do" with witchcraft and sorcery in a fragile and high-maintenance exchange relationship—Christianity seemed to promise a new metaphysics. This was a metaphysics in which death was no more, in which the ancestors would return to the world of the living, and in which the power of sorcery and witchcraft would end. This was almost too good to be true, and doubt therefore attended the enthusiasm of conversion from the beginning. Tangkea Guslaw quotes Dudu as saying the converts "waited cautiously (*tantano*) to see if the dead would return." *Tantano* is what the hunter does when he waits—stealthily, expectantly, and alert—for shy prey to approach. *Tantano* is also the kind of waiting in which the witch engages when it waits for its victim in a secluded spot. *Tantano* is about the chance of prey that may never be fulfilled, and it is about catching unsuspecting victims or game. The hunter's luck is fickle, but the bounty is always worth the wait. Disappointment and hope, for the hunter, are intimately connected. Indeed, in 1901 the converts had to wait only a few months until the great metaphysical promise of Christianity was revealed as a lie. Dudu's account of his conversion in 1901, as told to Tangkea, continues:

> They waited one month, two months. But the dead did not return. Instead the ancestors and animal spirits began to punish them with sickness, and the *gua* began to eat more people than ever before. So people got angry. They "threw away" (*topa*) Christianity, and fled into the forest. "Christians are liars (*kresten madarawa*)," my grandfather used to say after that. My grandfather and four of his brothers were so angry that they went off to the island of Cef and began making large amounts of spears. They were joined by many others. At night there were so many fires burning that it looked like a city on the island. They said they would kill anyone who came to talk to them about Christianity. They remained there for many years.

The mission's written accounts confirm this sense of bitter disappointment. As the missionary W. Stade, who served Buli between 1919 and 1922, put it, "They surmised from this that if they became Christian, they would see their deceased relatives again and many converted to Christianity. It had to end with disappointment. Every day they asked when the dead would return, and after what was probably an epidemic broke out, they thought their ancestors were angry and they reverted to paganism" (*ZCR* 1923 |81|:n.p.).

What Stade refers to as "an epidemic" could in Buli terms be nothing other than a spate of sorcery and a *gua* attack. From the Buli perspective, they had been promised the return of their ancestors, and so they enthusiastically turned to Christianity and began, with some caution and doubt, to "wait with their eyes open" (*tantano*) to see if the ancestors really did return. When the ancestors withdrew their protection, and the witches began to roam more than ever, people's expectations turned to bitter disappointment and a profound sense of betrayal.

The continuation of death after their conversion to Christianity suggested two things. First, it became apparent that the ancestors and the Christian God were not united in one project, but were instead deeply divided. Angered by the people's decision to turn to Christianity, the ancestors and the animal spirits had withdrawn their protection, giving free rein to attacks by *gua* and sorcerers (*mahabod-iga*). Second, the Christian God did not appear to be able to protect humans from the *gua* and other agents of death, as people had expected. With each suspicious death, the *gua* manifested its continued existence even in a Christian universe. As it turned out, Christianity did not end doubt; it could not banish death or the *gua*. As this became increasingly obvious, people began to flee the village and reverted to honoring their ancestors and animal spirits. And Christianity became associated not only with the promise of a definitive solution to the problem of death and the *gua*, but also with deception, lies, and betrayal.

The very same people who had enthusiastically accepted Christianity in 1901 became, as one mission report put it, "hermetically closed towards the Gospel" (*BUZ* 1915 [11]:175). Each new death served only to confirm Christianity as a lie (*darawa*). The missionary Stade wrote in 1923, "The shamans once asked a teacher and me, what was the point of becoming a Christian if one did not see one's deceased [relatives] again anyway?" (*ZCR* 1923 [81]:n.p.).

After its initial success, the mission in Buli began to languish during the first decades of the twentieth century. In 1910, G. Maan complained, "Heathendom in Buli is very tough, and although three-quarters of its followers were the ones who in 1901 initially joined the Christian movement, they quickly fell back" (*ZCR* 1918 [26]:n.p.). By 1920, the number of Buli people who had taken Holy Communion had still not passed sixteen (Magany 1984:164). In one of his final reports to the mission society from 1922, Stade declared:

> Much time, patience, and faithful dedication is required of the missionary; nay, more than that: he must pray and struggle mightily to instill the workings of the Holy Spirit into the hearts of our Christians in Buli, before they let go of the belief in the *gua* [witches]. This belief is still frequently the cause of apostasy and decline [in the number of converts]. Whenever a young person dies, people point to this or that *gua* and think that our God was unwilling or unable to help. They show their indignation with God by withdrawing from the congregation and church services. (*ZCR* 1922 [71]:3)

Dudu himself remained defiant till the end. He died, as did many of his kinsmen, without converting. However, Dudu's relationship to Christianity was anything but straightforward. On the one hand, he hated Christians with a passion until his death in the mid-1950s, and he would publicly mock Tangkea, his grandson, and other young people when they gave up their sarongs and bark-fiber loincloths (*pelpelet*) in favor of modern clothes and began attending Christian school: "Who do you think you are? Christians?" On the other hand, Tangkea also recalls that Dudu knew the entire Lord's Prayer by heart—an incantation he had memorized when he had embraced Christianity in 1901. Tangkea remembers how his grandfather would recite the prayer to himself when he thought he was alone . . . almost like a spell.

I do not know how to interpret Dudu's prayer. Was Dudu, the ardent critic of Christianity's lies, still in awe of its power, hoping as he had in 1901 that Christianity might still offer the hope of putting a stop to witchcraft? Or had he incorporated the Christian God into the pantheon of spirit beings of his animist universe, treating its prayers as a magical spell? Whichever it might be, Dudu's attitude—resentful yet hopeful—is for me testimony to a more general ambivalence that characterizes Christianity in Buli, because of its unique historical trajectory where bitter rejection followed enthusiastic conversion. Joel Robbins has usefully suggested that conversion may be seen a two-stage process, in which people initially come to Christianity "for locally defined utilitarian reasons" but remain with it for intellectual reasons, "because they are looking for new ways to explain, predict, and control the world around them" (2004:86). No such clear structure appears to order conversion to Christianity in Buli, where a long history of contact has blurred the distinction between locally defined reasons and "new intellectual ways to explain and control the world." And yet, the Buli conversion history may still be usefully described in all its muddled ambivalence in Robbins's terms. People like Dudu initially came to Christianity because of a specific "locally defined reason" of sorts—namely, the hope that Christianity might constitute a new way to control witchcraft. This intellectual hope of control (part of Robbins's second stage of conversion) was, as the previous chapter demonstrated, not in any strict sense "local." Rather, it was a coproduction of Calvinist theology and a millennial history of political protest. Dudu apostatized when he found Christianity's promise of control to be lacking, and yet for all his resentment against Christianity, he added Christian prayer to his panoply of spells, thereby perhaps also changing both himself and the animism he so vehemently defended. Today, Buli people denounce Dudu and his contemporaries as "stupid people" who misunderstood Christianity. And yet, they remain Christians in the utilitarian hope that Christianity might still protect them against witchcraft as they struggle to understand why there continues to be witchcraft in a Christian world. The paradoxical history of conversion in Buli may be summarized as follows: people came to Christianity for intellectual reasons that were Calvinist and anticolonial as much as they were "local"; and they remain Christians for utilitarian reasons that continue to fail. For witchcraft from the beginning stole its way into Christianity.

## Christian Witches

It was one thing that the Christian God did not seem to protect against witchcraft. Worse still, the lies (*darawa*) of the Christian missionary, who said that his religion could bring an end to witchcraft and death, appeared to mimic the deception (*da-rawa*) of the *gua*. This apparently paradoxical idea of Christians as *gua* is encapsulated in the frequent accusation that those who converted to Christianity appeared to flaunt all traditional morality and conduct themselves in ways that resembled the *gua*. "Look at those who have converted," Tangkea remembers his grandfather saying. "They have sex with the wives of other people (*yal sal*), they steal, and they lie. So what is the point of Christianity?"

Indeed, there are several examples of suspected *gua* being among the very first converts. In 1996 a man from Waiflí killed a wild pig in the forest behind the village. The dead pig, however, mysteriously disappeared while the hunter was searching the surrounding forest for rattan vines with which to fashion a harness so he could carry the carcass back to the village. When dead deer and pigs disappear in this fashion, it is always an indication of witchcraft. It is said that the hunter has accidentally killed a *gua* that had disguised itself in one of its animal forms. If a *gua* is killed in its animal form, convention has it that although the spirit *gua* will vanish with the dead animal, the human-host *gua* will, at the same time, be mortally wounded. Proof comes when a suspected *gua* in the village dies soon after. This is precisely what happened the day after the perplexed pig hunter returned to the village in 1996: an elderly woman suddenly collapsed and died. As it happened, this woman was not just any old lady. She was the granddaughter of the first Buli inhabitant to convert to Christianity in the 1930s. This man had been a close friend of Mozes Mahulette, acting as his stalwart supporter at those sermons in 1933 that Dudu and his group protested so fiercely. Several of this initial convert's family members, including his son and granddaughter, were also suspected of being *gua*. It is, of course, easy to see why conversion to a high-status faith that denied the existence of witches would be an attractive proposition to someone roundly suspected of witchcraft (Hefner 1993). But the tendency that suspected *gua* were often the first to convert nevertheless tainted conversion to Christianity in the eyes of many Buli people, and it served to lend credence to Dudu's suspicions about the *gua*-like behavior of the new Christians.

The charge that conversion might in itself also promote adultery, theft, and lying—all behaviors that decidedly went against proper traditional behavior (*adat re atorang*) and that led straight toward becoming a *gua*—was a directly inverted picture of the missionaries' discourse about Buli, in that the puritan Dutch missionaries regularly bemoaned the loose morality of Buli people. In 1916, for instance, the missionary Maan complained: "Whereas adultery and offenses against morality in general are severely punished in North Halmahera, there is no punishment against them in Buli tradition. The inhabitants of the Bay of Buli and

Weda are morally on a very low level. Social conscience as we think of it is dead here and this leads to the most woeful conditions" (*ZCR* 1916 [7]:1).

Sexual permissiveness and laziness were particular areas of concern for the missionaries, because they went against the Calvinist emphasis on the importance of sexual restraint and hard work to Christian virtue (Rutherford 2006).[1] It is interesting that Dudu and the missionary agree on moral laxity being a problem in Buli. But whereas the missionary places the problem of immorality (seen from a Christian point of view) with Buli tradition or *adat*, Dudu inversely places immorality (seen from the point of view of Buli *adat*) with Christianity. Christians, it seemed to Dudu, were the worst adulterers, thieves, and liars—people driven by gluttony, and with an unrestrained desire for what belongs to others. As a Buli moral rule of thumb has it, "Other people's things and spouses are their own; other people's foodstuffs are their own" (*Smate ni, smate ni; smate na smate na*).

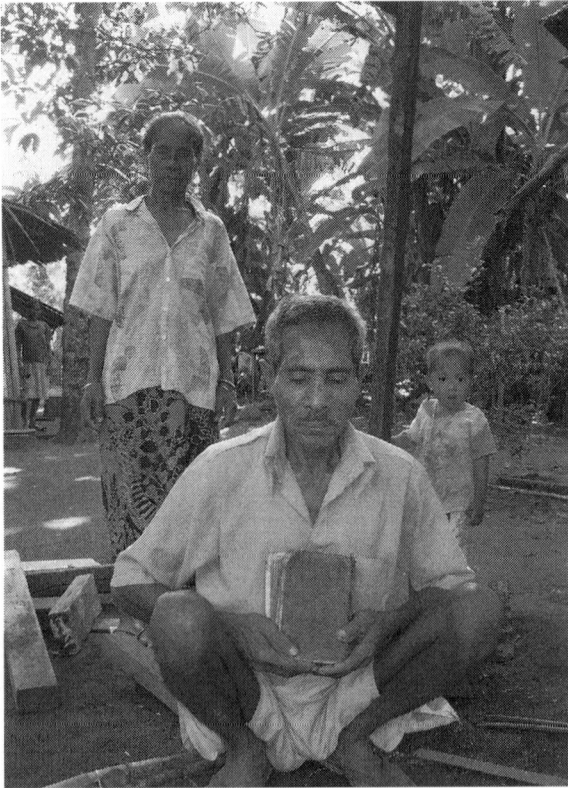

**Figure 13.** Laskap Tayawi holds the Bible that his father received when he converted to Christianity in 1972. 2004. Photo by author.

This is a rule that people break on a daily basis, as a matter of course, when they have affairs or pick a low-hanging fruit from someone else's garden. But some people seem to be incapable of restraining their sexual and material desires, and those are the people most likely to become witches.

Dudu's charge of Christian adultery, theft, and lies is therefore also a poignant condemnation and rejection of the Christian promise to rid the Buli world of *gua*. Not only was Christianity unable to deliver Buli people from the presence of the *gua*; Christianity appeared to promote the same kind of behaviors—stealing, lying, committing adultery—that were themselves the initial signs of the *gua*. In other words, it was as if Christianity itself became a safe haven for witches. It is this feeling of being doubly deceived that made the anger of the traditionalists so strong that it persisted for decades after 1901. Not until 1972 did the last three households in Waiflí convert to Christianity (see fig. 13). They did so, as we shall see in chapter 6, under the political pressure to adopt one of the five world religions sanctioned by the early New Order as a perceived ideological inoculation against Communism.

## On Stupidity

Today, Tangkea Guslaw represents tradition. He is the custodian (*Kapita*) of the shrine to Íyan Toa that is still located centrally in Waiflí. Íyan Toa, the supreme guardian spirit of Buli people, was right at the top of the list of guardian spirits that Dudu and his brothers called upon in 1933 to help them against Christianity. But Tangkea also sees himself as a devout Christian. He is a former member of the Church Council in Waiflí, and his youngest son has become a minister. For Tangkea as for other Buli people, Christianity represents a new age of modernity, progress, and knowledge. Conversion to Christianity is therefore also a conversion to modernity (Aragon 2000; Keane 2007; Spyer 2000; Van der Veer 1996), a transition from the ignorance of tradition to modern knowledge and self-awareness.[2] Here is how Samadar Batawi, in his written tribute to Mozes Mahulette, describes the years after the 1933 clashes between traditionalists and Christians:

> With the help and power of the Lord, the attitude and behavior of the animists in Buli Asal of their own accord gradually weakened. The heathens came to their senses and little by little began to take part in worshipping the Lord in the house of Mozes Mahulette, so that in the end they themselves began to understand Christianity. Mozes Mahulette was an exemplary model, and because of him the majority of people in Buli Asal are now Christian. They have houses with cement walls, and we are

witnessing how they work tirelessly to build a more modern Church in the village. (Batawi 1986:n.p.)

The power of the Lord, it seemed, manifested itself in physical form as modernity, represented by such elements as cement houses and a new church (see fig. 14). Indeed, the house of Mozes had been the first house with cement walls in Waiflí: technology, modernity, and Christianity all rolled into one. For many people this was a very attractive and highly compelling package, as I will elaborate in chapter 8. Tangkea recalls the story that old man Gamsaya, one of the first converts in Buli, told about his visit to the house of K. A. Bot. It seemed to Gamsaya that the clock hanging on the wall of the missionary's home commanded him to convert. Every hour on the hour, the clock would strike, chiming notes that to Gamsaya's ears sounded like it was chanting: "Convert to Christianity! Convert to Christianity!" (*Mcung serani! Mcung serani!*). Old man Gamsaya was so impressed with this technological wonder that he eventually followed the wall clock's injunction. Nevertheless, according to Tangkea, Gamsaya never entirely abandoned his suspicion that this might be just another one of Christianity's deceitful tricks.

Today, the people of Buli are unanimous in their view that it was right to convert to Christianity, and this view is accompanied by a strong sense that conversion

**Figure 14.** "The Congregation in Buli Serani, Halmahera." 1937.
Tropenmuseum, Amsterdam. Reproduced with permission.

marked a transition from ignorance and stupidity to knowledge and modern insight. People also acknowledge that their forefathers often converted with the wrong ideas in their heads. This picture of "the stupid ancestor" is not one-dimensional, for the ancestors also represent the virtues of Buli tradition that no one seems to have today, and they continue to punish their Christian descendants for their immorality. However, in relation to Christianity—the most explicit marker of Buli's entry into the modern, outside world—knowledge is the main differentiating factor between "then" and "now." Tangkea does not mince words in this respect when he talks about his grandfather's generation. Dudu may have been a fearsome, undaunted, and courageous man of tradition, but he was also a very ignorant man: "I am not trying to offend our ancestors, but really, they were very stupid (*fuma tua*)! And my own forefathers, my great-grandfather and my grandfather, they were among the stupidest. They were so stupid that many of them spoke poorly—eehh, it is true, Nils."

Tangkea proceeded to mimic the slow stutter of his grandfather: "You, you, you, where are you going?" This ancestral stupidity today provides an explanation not only as to why Dudu and his generation so enthusiastically embraced Christianity in 1901, but also as to why they so fiercely resented it in the decades that followed.

The narrative of the earlier generation's backwardness and stupidity was also the narrative that the Dutch missionaries used to explain the mission's difficulties in Buli during the early decades of the twentieth century. Describing the Buli belief that "the dead would return during the last days [before the end of the world]" (*ZCR* 1923 [81]), Maan called them "foolish ideas about Christianity" (Dutch *dwaze denkbeelden van het Christendom*) (*BUZ* 1909 [22]:86). They were foolish because they were based on fear, and fear in turn was bred by ignorance. As Maan notes in a letter to the mission journal, describing the presence of the *gua* in Buli, "They know nothing about sin and guilt, but plenty about fear. It is from fear that the animist who receives Jesus Christ is first absolved. Deliverance from fear and terror is a glorious gift of the Gospel" (1912:216).

The problem was not ignorance itself, but the fact that people stubbornly failed to acknowledge their ignorance. And it was in this stubbornness that their ignorance truly lay. The Calvinist missionaries were generally critical of the Enlightenment, but their mission of bringing the knowledge of God to the pagan peoples of the world was still born out of the Age of Reason in its struggle to remedy the ignorance of the other. As Bernard McGrane argues, "Enlightenment knowledge consists in awareness of ignorance and ignorance consists of non-awareness of ignorance. Not knowing about ignorance is the very being of ignorance. The ignorance of the Other consists of the ignorance of ignorance. The alien Others are seen as ignorant because they don't know what they don't know. What they don't know is the nature of ignorance" (1992:71–72).

Dudu's stupidity lay in not realizing that he was stupid, and in insisting fearfully on the reality of his own world of darkness, in which ancestors and animal spirits protected their descendants against outside enemies as well as against witchcraft. Christianity, as he understood it, had opened up a new possibility in this existence, a new metaphysical possibility, in which the Christian God could replace the ancestors and animal guardian spirits and offer not partial but complete and unconditional protection from death and witchcraft. However, this misunderstanding as to what Christianity might offer—based on ideas about Christianity that the missionary Maan called "foolish" (*BUZ* 1909 [22]:86)—was far from based on an absence of knowledge. The idea that death itself was historical rather than inevitable was a reading of Christianity that Buli myth already prefigured.

## The Beginning and End of Death

The Christian message did not furnish people in Buli with a new heaven (Burridge 1969). The Malay word for the Christian heaven (I. *surga*) that W. Tutuarima, the first Christian catechist to arrive to Buli, would have used when speaking about Christianity was thus the same word as the one already used in Buli for the place of the ancestors: *sorogá*, a word they had likely adopted from their Muslim neighbors. The two places were conceptualized in very different spatial terms, however. Traditionally, the place of the ancestors was indicated as being in a "downward" direction, below the sea (*nap*). It was therefore customary for people in pre-Christian times to be interred in the hulls of their outrigger canoes. The canoe hulls would bring them to "the place below the sea." The Christian idea of heaven placed the ancestors "up" (*puis*) rather than "down below" (*pap*). Therefore the message that people heard, and quite logically for them, was that their ancestors would be "relocated upward," so to speak, to commune with the living in this world. Buli people already communed with the ancestral spirits (*smengit*), but the spirits were not directly visible. One sees the spirits only in dreams. Christianity appeared to offer a physical communion with the spirits, a new kind of world. So the perceived promise was that the Buli ancestors were going to "return home" if people converted to Christianity.

The Christian promise that the dead would "return" also unwittingly played into preexisting Buli ideas about death. When a child dies in Buli, it is said that "the child has returned home" (*wawái ca nue i*). For adults, however, "returning home" is used about the people who come back from *sorogá*. The unborn appear to have an attachment to the world of *sorogá*, which is where they come from in the first place in animist thought, and this often makes them want to return home. Older people, on the other hand, have an attachment to the world of the living, which keeps them attached to it even after death, and which makes them want to "return home" to be among the living. This also explains the interest that the ancestors continue to have in the world of the living.

Christianity's promise that "the dead would return home" was, in other words, eminently in sync with Buli eschatological ideas. These ideas were premised on a narrative that speaks of the mythical time when the dead always "returned home to the living after death." This myth, called "The Old Woman and the Child" (*Ngolo ca fare Ntu ca*), takes place in a mythic past, and this is how Kenari told it to me in 1999:

> Once, a woman went sailing with her son. Inside the dugout canoe the child was playing with a stone and a piece of dried sago stem (*ba*). The woman told her son to throw the light sago stem into the water but to keep the stone. "If you throw the stone into the water, it will sink, and we will no longer return home once we die (*tmat, tuwe pantó*). So throw the sago stem into the water and we will return." The child sat for a while repeating to himself: "Throw the stem or throw the stone?" (*topa ba, topa pat?*), but then suddenly threw the stone into the ocean. The stone sank out of sight. Ever since that time, people do not see their deceased relatives again because they follow the stone to *sorogá* "below the sea."

The ostensible Christian message of the potential return of the ancestors acted like a magnet on the people of Buli, because it suggested as a certain and imminent future something that myth merely treated as a vague semiotic possibility: that the ancestors might return (*ue*). At the same time, myth made the promises of Christianity understandable and attractive in all their world-renewing magnitude. The world would literally be turned "upside down" (*dunia nfulas i*), bringing the place of the ancestors down below the sea "up" into the same world as the living. The expression the world will "be turned upside down" (*bon fulas i*) is still used to describe the events of the Second Coming of Christ and the end of the world (Bubandt 1998a, 2004b).

As Michel de Certeau has warned, rather than "assum[ing] that the masses are transformed by the conquests and victories of expansionist production, it is always good to remind ourselves that we mustn't take people for fools" (1984:176). Indeed, the fool's knowledge is merely a "subjugated" and "disqualified" knowledge, a block of knowledge that remains disguised (Foucault 1980:82). My attempt to sketch a genealogy of this disguised knowledge suggests that not only did the Buli people's "foolish" ideas about Christianity make eminent, even necessary, sense within the Buli historical experience. These ideas also seized upon something essential about the Christian idea of hope—namely, its predication on the omnipotent agency of God, a "transcendent agency, which in turn implies limits to human agency" (Miyazaki 2007:17). As they converted, the people of Buli consciously put their own ritual agency "in abeyance," to use Miyazaki's expression, and waited cautiously (*tantano*), like a hunter for prey. Upon their conversion, Buli people were waiting for the return of the dead and an end to death, just as the hunter waits in hiding for his prey: expectant and cautious at the same time. Against this background of hope's arrival, it is perhaps easier to understand the sense of betrayal that developed from it and that remained strong with Dudu and his contemporaries three decades later in 1933. The appeal of Christianity to people in Buli was the equation between Christian faith and Buli notions of hopeful expectation and trustworthiness: belief entailed a trust in the termination of doubt and the hope that death might end. This is a hope (*mauláng*) to which Buli people continue to commit themselves and explore to become better Christians. The central question in Buli Christianity today is whether this hope was, in fact, a lie (*darawa*).

## The Impossible Gift of Hope

In his analysis of the relationship between hope and Christianity in Fiji, Miyazaki argues that the hope of receiving compensation for the loss of ancestral land—a hope that was maintained (and thwarted) for more than a century—was born with the Fijians' conversion to Seventh-day Adventism in 1898 (2007:36). Hope, however, also figured prominently in Fijian exchange relationships, as gift-givers hoped for a return-prestation from gift-receivers. Miyazaki argues that a homology exists between these two kinds of hope, and that the Fijian hope for land compensation was the replication of "a past unfulfilled hope on another terrain" (139). Just a year later, in 1899, as we saw in the previous chapter, a similar kind of synchronicity of hope and conversion took place in Buli on the western fringes of the Pacific. And like the Fijian synchronicity, the new hope that Christianity enabled in Buli was also made readable through the logic of exchange. The Dutch missionaries in Buli themselves claimed that they were bringing a gift, the "glorious gift of the Gospel," which would deliver Buli people from the "fear and terror" of ignorance and superstition (see also Aragon 2000; Maan 1912:216). To Buli ears, this gift from the powerful white missionaries also promised deliverance from the *gua*. Theirs did indeed appear to be a glorious gift. Moreover, it also appeared to be a free gift. "We should become Christian," Dudu had said to himself in 1901. "Christians . . . do not have to feed God all the time like we have to do with the ancestors and animal spirits. . . . Also, God does not punish us the way the ancestors do if we do not honor him."

The gift of the Gospel appeared to be a gift of life without the *gua*, and as I will explain in chapter 7, seemingly it did not require the kind of exchanges or contain the kind of dangers that Buli exchange did. In a society where exchange is at the heart of what proper ritual, tradition, and conviviality are all about, accepting the apparently free gift of the Gospel was tantamount to discarding a whole way of life. The rejection of the ancestors and the animal spirits, the possibility that witch-craft could be eradicated, and the hope of getting all of this for nothing (or rather, by merely going to church, as Dudu had put it, "on one special day every week") made sense within the context of the overarching expectation that the end of the world was imminent, and that everything was going to be turned "upside down."

Vicente Rafael has suggested that conversion in the context of colonialism in-volves "a fishing for meaning" (1988:3), angling in the discursive and symbolic waters of the powerful other for those elements that "render the other understand-able" (211).[3] Conversion in Buli was enabled, and later interrupted, by a series of "mistranslations" that grew out of this particular kind of fishing (211). The "fool-ish ideas about Christianity" that allowed Buli people to imagine conversion as the only requirement for the ancestors and the end of witchcraft to materialize essen-tially "hooked" an element in Christian eschatology that made it understandable and highly attractive. This element was not "caught" out of the blue. The hope that Christianity offered was closely connected to a messianism that was central to "the glorious gift of the Gospel" in Protestant theology. As much as their ideas might have been considered "foolish" by Dutch missionaries, Buli hopes for/trust in (*maulángo*) an end to death and witchcraft were nevertheless congruent with a certain programmatic messianism of Christianity, one that Calvinist theology had sublimated but not eradicated through its notion of hope. Protestant philos-ophers since Calvin had thus placed hope at the center of Protestant theology as the premise of faith and the possibility of salvation: "Hope is nothing else than the expectation of those things which faith has believed to be truly promised by God" (Moltmann 2002:6). The "foolishness" of the messianic interpretation that Buli people read into the Calvinist gospel was so acute for the Dutch missionaries precisely because messianism was an element of Protestantism's own theological heritage—a legacy that Protestantism had constantly struggled to rid itself of, though always unsuccessfully (Campion 1994; Thompson 1996).

## A Brief History of Deception

Prophecy and deception, millennial hope and disappointment, are intrinsically linked (Festinger et al. 1956). This link between hope and deception appears at least twice in the history of North Malukan conversion to Christianity. As the previous chapter has shown, it was partly through the revelation of trickery that the Christian mission took on the mantle of the Hassan movement and appeared to promise the return of the dead. This trickery, as we have seen in this chapter, returned to haunt the mission itself when the perceived promise was not kept. The idea that the introduction of Christianity was based on deceit lingers to this day. A Buli elder, Ponco Batawi, gave me this Buli perspective on the politics of mass conversion as advocated by Anton Hueting: "In former times, in order to get people to accept Christianity, the missionaries would lie a little and deceive a little: 'If you become Christians, your parents will return.' That is politics. Its purpose is to get people to enter Christianity first and later teach them the actual content." Buli people are, as it happens, not alone in making this link between deception and conversion. The two are also linked theologically. In 1920, Maan described the initial fin-de-siècle conversion in Buli as follows: "I doubt that the propagating catechists [NB: Maan no doubt meant Tutuarima here] always worked with tact since the lack of missionaries meant that they could not be adequately controlled. I know for certain that they sometimes used miraculous ways and strange means, and that they sometimes said and promised things that made a great impression on the natives, but which were completely wide off the truth, just as many people misunderstood many things" (1920:344).

Maan, in other words, here blames the "foolish ideas" about Christianity on Tutuarima. Tutuarima in turn defended himself and blamed the natives, saying that people in Buli were stupid "blockheads" who did not speak North Malukan Malay, the language in which he was preaching (*ZCR* 1923 [81]). But Maan then continues his ruminations on the nature of misunderstanding and describes it as part of a process of gradual conversion. He refers to the German theologian Johannes Warneck, whose mission work in Sumatra had brought him to think of the conversion of animists as a three-stage process (Warneck 1908). In the first stage the animist, according to Warneck, seeks God to be relieved from fear; in the second the convert learns about the grace of God; and only in the third stage does Christianity entail a battle against sin and the renewal of moral life. Maan continues: "And now I think of our Christians in Buli. They converted; that is to say, they turned to God and began to put their trust in Him rather than in their own gods and spirits, whom they had served and honored out of fear. But this in itself did not make them Christians in the full sense of the word. For that one has to move on, and come to the experience of the love of God through Christ, which in turn will teach them about sin as a debt to God" (1920:345). Animists, Maan reasons, are trapped in a world of immediate returns, which is why it will take them time to comprehend the grace of God: "Animist paganism is entirely egotistical and its religious activities are a struggle for a life without love. Therefore it is also so difficult for them to understand the love song of God" (1912:218). This implies that the path to God's love is always initially taken for the wrong reasons, with a view to immediate returns. Conversion, Maan appears to suggest, is by necessity misleading. The animist comes to Christianity for the wrong reasons, with misguided ideas. And yet this deception (guided essentially by the work of the devil) could be turned to theological good. Speaking of the millenarianism of the north coast of Papua, which had close links to the Hassan movement, the UZV missionary J. L. van Hasselt wrote in 1872: "Are we right in denouncing all these legends, which hold out a prospect of higher and better things, simply as deceit of the devil? Might not these things serve as a starting-point for the preaching of the Gospel? I for one do not hesitate to answer this question in the affirmative" (quoted in Kamma 1972:105).

Deception is inevitable in conversion—a necessary part of the Christian theological notion of the difference between magic and religion, animism and Christianity, and hence an unavoidable dimension of the new strategy of mass conversion that the Calvinist mission began in North Maluku in the 1890s when local interest in Christianity soared. There were, in other words, good theological reasons for accepting the locals' millenarian interpretations of their mission as a necessary evil on the path toward eventually teaching the Halmaheran animists "the love song of God."

In the end, the history of hope and deceit that traverses conversion to Christianity in Buli left intact the original problem of witchcraft and its ambivalent presence in the world. As the next chapter will show, the continuing visceral horror of the *gua* gives a "cruel" twist to the optimism that people harbor about witchcraft's end (see Berlant 2011).

# 5

## THE VISCERALITY OF WITCHCRAFT AND THE CORPOREALITY OF THE WORLD

Placenta and intestines,
Pillow and secrets
*Dodomi se galegale,*
*Popoje se rahasia*

NORTH MALUKAN PROVERB (*dola bololo*)

In October 2007, I had just arrived back in Buli when a neighbor, Pineki, came by to greet me. She was on her way to her garden to gather cassava roots for dinner and harvest some edible ferns that she planned to sell in the market the next day. Pineki, a classificatory aunt to the children of the household and therefore also my aunt, sat in the doorway in the old tattered dress that she used for garden work, her carrying basket (*yan*) slung over one shoulder and a towel wrapped around her head to protect her from the hot sun. She sat quietly for a while, looking pensively at the ground. Then, as if making up her mind about something, she swung her head around toward me and said, "My granddaughter, Hilda, has died since you were last here." I had already heard the sad news. Hilda was a spirited little girl who used to run between our two houses and felt equally at home in both. She had often sat in on the impromptu English classes I sometimes conducted in the evening on the floor of the main room, forming the strange words with her lips, but too shy to say them out loud in front of the older children. Pineki launched into the sad story of Hilda's death:

She was nine years and nine months when she died in 2005. She came home from school one day at noon and said she felt hot. She couldn't pee. Said it hurt when she tried. I took her down to the doctor in the health clinic in town. The doctor said it was malaria and gave her some pills. But the pills didn't help. That same night Hilda got worse. Then she suddenly said, speaking in a completely normal voice, "Uri's Mum put a piece of fire-wood into me where I pee, and it came out here." Then she pointed to her mouth, Nils! We called the police and the *babinsa* (the noncommissioned army officer), and they asked her, "Why are you ill, little miss (I. *Nyonya*)?" So she told them the same thing again. Nobody had told her to say this, you know! The child herself said this. The police wanted to get Uri's mother and force her to cure Hilda, but she had disappeared into her garden hut down the coast already, as soon as she heard Hilda was ill. I tell you, the village almost exploded when Hilda died the next day. You know how hot-tempered her grandfather is.

Witchcraft is nothing if not horrible; and a large part of its horror is visceral. Hil-da's death after a female *gua* had assaulted her, eaten her liver, and forced a piece of firewood through her body from her private parts to her mouth—preventing her from urinating and from speaking during the last day of her life—was a total destruction of Hilda's embodied being. It targeted three corporeal sites at once: her shadow (*gurumin*), her liver (*yatai*), and her breath/genitals (*nyawa*). The totality of the *gua*'s corporeal destruction of its victim, its instrumental disassembly of the victim into his or her constituent parts, its cannibalistic reduction of humans into prey, are crucial dimensions of its intolerability, its unthinkability, its abject na-ture. The viscerality of witchcraft is, in other words, at the root of its inaccessibil-ity. The corporeal horror of the *gua* is, as it were, "beyond belief," at once awfully significant and utterly meaningless.

This chapter looks at the two themes that run through the corporeal horror of witchcraft in Buli: the deconstruction of the human body in witchcraft on the one hand, and the desires and repulsion of cannibalism on the other. It delves into the often-overlooked somatic dimensions of witchcraft. Witchcraft in Buli is a matter of eating and being eaten (see also Behrend 2011). An essential dimension of the *gua*'s horror is the fact that it is a cannibal. "Someone ate them" (*isa nan si*) is a common way to referring to the cause of witchcraft-related illness (*ungan*). The viscerality of eating and being eaten is central to witchcraft in Buli, and this corporeality is what sets the witch (*gua*) apart from the sorcerer (*bodiga*). As with every other aspect of the *gua*, this corporeality is ambivalent, undecidable. The witch is thus excessively corporeal and entirely disembodied at the same time. The *gua* is highly somatic, a cannibal spirit that lures and destroys the bodies of human witches and human victims at will. However, this visceral deconstruction of what it means to be human and to live in a human world is carried out by a disembodied spirit that is, itself, inaccessible to the senses and to the logic of embodied existence. Witchcraft is therefore an aporia of embodied being, a corporeal experience that has no solution.

The deconstruction of the human body in a *gua* attack, I would argue, is all the more horrific because of the way the human body is so intimately entwined with the social world in Buli. In every attack the witch essentially perpetrates an act of world destruction. The bodily attack by the witch on the human body is a corporeal violation of ontological proportions, because the world itself is modeled on the human body. It is this world-destructive dimension of witchcraft, I suggest, that infused Christianity's apparent promise of a new world without witchcraft with such radical and enthusiastic hope. The combination of radical hope and radical horror also undergirds contemporary promises of witchcraft's end.

## Signification without Meaning

The *gua* approaches its victim stealthily, and almost always from behind. It then knocks the victim unconscious by kicking or punching him—evicting the person's *gurumin* (the human shadow-cum-awareness). Victims are also said to lose their "inside"—their emotions and feelings—at the mere sight of the *gua*. With both his protective shadow and his "inside" (*ulór*) gone, the victim is helpless and essentially lifeless in the hands of the witch. The *gua* then proceeds to open the victim's abdomen to get at his liver (*yatai*). Squatting on top of the inert body,[1] either in its human shape or in the shape of one of its animal familiars (a dog, certain birds, a pig, or an insect), the *gua* feasts on the raw and bloody liver before molesting the body, sexually as well as physically. After extracting the liver, it seals the wound with water, or by licking it with its long tongue (*ZCR* 1922 [71]:3). The wound closes completely and becomes invisible to the human eye. The *gua* may also spear its victim with whatever is at hand—a piece of wood, a sago branch, or a spear brought along for that purpose—and such a wound will later cause a piercing pain (known as *lebet*). In its frenzy, it may even beat the victim, causing black and blue marks where the punches have fallen, choke it, or try to drown it in a pool of water, which will result in breathing problems during the subsequent illness. A frequent *gua* hallmark is sexual molestation directed at the victim's genitals (*nyawa*). A male *gua* will often rape a female victim and sometimes does so very violently, which is why one frequent sign of a *gua* attack is said to be the laceration of the rectovaginal septum. The genitals of male victims are also often beaten and molested. Swollen and painful testicles are therefore also a frequent symptom of a *gua* attack.

"Being deadly," as Susan Sontag has observed, "is in itself not enough to produce terror" (1988:38). For something to be truly terrifying, it must be deeply

imbued with cultural significance. The horror of the *gua* is linked to the Buli conception of corporeality and stems from the *gua*'s perversion and destruction of the
most significant body sites. The feelings of dread and revulsion arise not merely
from the illness or death of a relative or friend. They are, more fundamentally,
related to the symbolic violence of an attack that systematically and abominably
violates the very corporeal sites that are symbolically vital. In this sense, it is not
death that makes witchcraft so unacceptable in Buli; rather, it is the way witchcraft
deconstructs life that makes it so abhorrent. The *gua* is an abject being because
it violates the boundaries of the body in significant ways. In Buli, I would argue,
abjection finds its manifestation in the *gua*. Julia Kristeva defines the particular
horror of the abject as "[a] 'something' that I do not recognize as a thing. A weight
of meaninglessness about which there is nothing insignificant, and which crushes
me" (1982:2). The *gua* is a creature without a face; and therefore it is essentially
unrecognizable. Victims of witchcraft attacks report that the face of the witch
was "clouded" (*cocomá*) or "dark" (*dororam*). Witches frequently "use the faces"
of other people, so that even when one recognizes the face of a *gua*, one cannot
be sure. If intersubjectivity emerges in the face-to-face encounter, as Emmanuel
Levinas has proposed, if in other words the face of the other establishes the fundamental basis for ethical rapport and for subjective identity itself (Levinas and
Kearney 1986:24; Lingis 1985), then the faceless *gua* undermines this possibility.

In Buli the absence of a face (*ushgnor*) is one of the *gua*'s main characteristics,
signaling its inaccessibility and its inhumanity at the same time. "I didn't recognize them, their faces were dark like that of the *gua*" (*yai fayala si pa, ushn-
gorna dororam laisá gua na*), people will say of strangers they do not know or trust.
Similarly, older children will scare their younger siblings by pulling their T-shirts
over their heads to cover their faces, and young men put on the *cokaéba* masks in
mimicry of the *gua* in the rituals that surround the birth of the prophet Muhammad (*Mawlid*) in many Muslim villages throughout North Maluku.[2] The witch is
always a masked or faceless figure (see fig. 15). Without a face, the *gua* remains a
"something" that one cannot recognize, an undecidable "weight of meaninglessness about which there is nothing insignificant" (Kristeva 1982:2).

It is worthwhile to briefly explore Kristeva's understanding of the difference
between meaning and signification. Signification is related to signs and denota-
tion; it is the importance attributed to entities. Meaning is the link provided between entities in thought or language, which situates entities within a common
context. Signification is concerned with terms, while meaning is concerned with
relations.[3] The *gua* is the negation of relations. It is an "isolate," a faceless entity onto itself that appears to come out of nowhere and from anywhere at the
same time. It breaks all relations and thrives on its own desires. It is completely
"other" to what being human in Buli is all about. And yet it invades human lives

**Figure 15.** Boys wearing *cokaéba* masks made from leaves in mimicry of the *gua*. 1997. Photo by author.

in multiple ways. As such, the *gua* is an aspect of life that has to be continuously abject for meaning to emerge. And yet there is nothing insignificant about the *gua* and its attacks.

As meaningless and incomprehensible as each attack is, it nevertheless artic-ulates an "intolerable significance" that makes the *gua* a central figure of horror (Kristeva 1982:11). I contend that its horror relates to several of the most central di-mensions of existence in Buli. The most basic of these dimensions is corporeality: how the body is perceived and how it interacts with the world. Witchcraft throws into crisis the social symbolism of what Kristeva calls "the primal mapping of the body" (72). It does so because it attacks exactly those sites that are most fundamen-tal to embodied being, and that set up the body as a significant model for many of the most socially important objects in the world. The feeling of dismay and disgust evoked by the *gua* is therefore both somatic and semantic, because it is the horror of the meaningless but highly significant destruction of the victim's body. It is a somatic disgust with a violation of the significant borders of the body—"the nodes where symbolicity interferes with . . . corporeality" (125). In Buli, these nodes are constituted by the vital and visceral sites that the *gua* targets: the genitals (*nyawa*), associated with breath and life; the shadow (*gurumin*), associated with consciousness; and the liver (*yatai*), associated with emotions. Every *gua* attack is therefore a deconstruction of the composite fact of being human, a disaggregation of embodied existence.

## Breath and Genitals

Ordinarily, death is referred to in Buli as "having no more *nyawa*" (*nyawa pantó*). A person loses their *nyawa* when the bodily functions such as breathing, movement, and speech stop. *Nyawa* can, in its most general sense, be translated as "breath" and "life" (Maan 1951:74), or indeed as 'soul" or "vitality," as in being bodily alive. After a normal or "easy" death, the disappearance of the *nyawa* begins a staged progression toward death that lasts three days, a very common phenomenon throughout Southeast Asia (Hertz 1960). During this period the deceased is treated as if he or she is merely asleep, and is repeatedly entreated "to wake up" (*mpaling*) in an effort to persuade the *nyawa* to return.

The word *nyawa*, however, is also used to mean "genitals." In the Buli language, to "remove the *nyawa*" (*salawe i ni nyawa*) is a normal way of expressing that one has killed an animal or a person. But it also covers the double meaning of "removing someone's genitals." In the myth of Íyan Toa, Buli's cultural hero and single most important mythical figure, he kills his enemy, a Bicoli warrior called Mamole Mancaboú, by cutting off or "removing" his penis. In the story the phrase "removing or cutting open the *nyawa*" plays on this double entendre. The myth continues to relate how Íyan Toa then inserted the castrated penis into the mouth of the vanquished enemy and placed a hibiscus plant in his urethra. The plant took root, and a large hibiscus tree now marks the site. This killing is foundational for Buli self-identity because it marks Íyan Toa's rescue of a decimated Buli population, and holds a promise of constant protection. The myth of Íyan Toa relates how, after saving the Buli people from their Bicoli enemies, their hero disappeared into the smoke of a fire, vowing that he would always be there and could be called upon whenever Buli people encountered trouble. As demonstrated in chapters 3 and 4, this theme of disappearance and the promise of return is part of a millennial narrative that resounds throughout Melanesia (Kamma 1972; Rutherford 2003; Worsley 1970). It is a theme that also appeared in the account of the vanished sultan whom the Hassan revolt sought to bring back. And like the absent sultan, the figure of Íyan Toa combines disappearance with the promise of a millennial return. It was Íyan Toa who provided Buli people with their magical fighting prowess, that "little something" (*fapeisá okocé*) that gives them—by their own accounts—the upper hand against their Tobelo neighbors—a fighting prowess that also explains why Buli people were called upon by the Tidore sultanate to protect Maba against Tobelo and the witch-monster Gua Mané (see chapter 2). Essential to Íyan Toa as a fighting man, a hothead (*makés*), is the close link between his slaying of his enemies and his emasculation of them—taking their life and taking their penis.

The explicit association between *nyawa* in the sense of "breathing" or "being alive" and *nyawa* meaning "genitals" is based on Buli ontogeny.[4] The human being is said to originate from menstrual blood that is given human shape by semen (known as "fat" or *mná*). The human body is thus the result of the mixing of fluids from the genitals, blood, and semen (Bubandt 2004a). The aspect of being alive (*nyawa*) is therefore closely related to the genitals, the source of a person's being in terms of ontogenesis. The attraction that human genitals have for witches is therefore not sexual as such. Rather, given the semiotic equivalence between genitals and "life," the targeting of the genital area is an expression of the *gua*'s generalized ravenous hunger for the lives of others.

Interestingly, the *gua*'s attraction to the genitals (*nyawa*) may also be used as a form of protection against witches. If someone is alone and senses that they are being stalked by a *gua*, traditional wisdom has it that they should remove their clothes (*legas*), thereby exposing their private parts. In the *gua*'s eyes, human genitals will shine (*gagám*) green and bright in the same way that other *gua* do. The *gua* will then mistake the genitals for a fellow witch, and will go to prowl elsewhere. The reason this works is that *gua* are said to give off a strong glare, their eyes shining bright green or blue (*bisbís*); indeed, that is often what reveals them to humans. Here the visual and the genitals—the gaze of desire and the object of desire—are inverted. In the world of witches, human genitals shine like the eyes of other witches. This is part of the overall "perverse perspectivism" of witchcraft, the way witches perceive reality from a distinct and inverted point of view (see Vivieros de Castro 1998). This perverse perspectivism pertains to all of the senses, most notably smell, sight, and hearing. In the world of witches, for instance, foul smells are sweet, and sweet smells are repugnant. Witches also walk upside down— a fact that can be ascertained if one applies magical eye drops (*sapói*) and goes to the grave of a recently deceased person, where witches will often gather. Sounds are similarly inverted: An apparently distant sound from a *gua* means that it is really close by, while loud sounds mean that the *gua* is actually some distance away. A common way of portraying the *gua* that alludes to this perverse perspectivism is to hold one's index fingers and thumbs, shaped as two rings, in front of ones eyes, but with hands turned upside down, like an oddly inverted pair of glasses.

Hilda's death was the result of an attack aimed not only at eating her liver and "removing her shadow." In a final act of significant but senseless anger that played on the double meaning of *nyawa*, the *gua* also forced a piece of wood into her genitals (*nyawa*), thereby forcing them into her throat and preventing her from speaking and eventually from breathing (*fawa*). The *gua*'s sexual molestation of Hilda was a perversion of both myth and ontogenesis. It was an unbearable mockery of all that it is heroic and proper in Buli, made doubly ironic by the fact that Hilda's family were the ritual guardians of the village's spirit house in honor of Íyan Toa.

## Liver and Emotions

While the genitals are associated with being alive, the liver (*yatai*) is the seat of emotions, many of which are referred to by lexemes using the root term *uló*. The missionary G. Maan (1940:77) translates *uló* as "the inner core, feeling, heart, consciousness." *Uló* may be glossed as "one's inside," and the word is used to express a wide variety of emotional and cognitive states (see fig. 16).

The liver, in other words, is the embodied site of human emotional and cognitive life. The liver is also precisely the organ coveted and eaten by the *gua*. The *gua*'s extraction of the liver is an act that robs the person of the seat of human qualities such as emotions, thoughts, and character. As a result the consumption of animal livers is fraught with problems. Although livers from sea turtles and larger

**Emotional states:**
"to have in the inner core, to like, wish for" (*uló loló*)
"to be happy" (*uló ya senga*)
"to be troubled or sad" (*uló ya kangelá*)

**Personal character or qualities:**
"to be jealous or envious" (*uló ya mici*)
"to be a good person" (*uló ya mafia*)
"to have a bad inner core, to be a bad person" (*uló ya mayái*)

**Cogntive abilities:**
"the inner core it touches on: to remember" (*uló ya neto*)
"to have many inner cores: to be undecided" (*uló ya lal*)
"not yet have an inner core, to be unaware of a young child" (*uló paubé*)

**Figure 16.** Embodied emotional states.

mammals like deer and pig are eaten with relish, they are referred to as *momoan*, "that which is forbidden," and it is normal practice to blow softly on an animal liver when removing it during the butchering process in order to lift the taboo.[5] This ambivalence toward the symbolism of eating the liver of animals reflects the horror that the anthropophagous activities of the *gua* inspire in Buli. It is perhaps for the same reason that there is little or no use of blood and meat in Buli ritual, and there is no elaborate blood sacrifice of the kind otherwise widely found throughout eastern Indonesia (Howell 1996). Similarly, Buli has no tradition of consuming parts of the liver of slain enemies during warfare, as was customary among most groups in the northern part of Halmahera.[6] In Buli this act was not practiced, and the knowledge that others had such practices inspires the deepest disgust.

## Shadow and Consciousness

Whereas human beings kill by "opening or removing the life/genitals" (*salawe nyawa*) of their victim, the *gua* by contrast is said to kill its victims by "removing the shadow-consciousness" (*salawe gurumin*). Every witch attack therefore begins when the *gua* "removes the *gurumin*." With the removal of his shadow, the victim loses consciousness and all memory of the attack. I began to outline the importance of a person's shadow in chapter 2. The shadow or reflection (*gurumin*) is the perhaps most important aspect of being human. Humans are conscious because they have a *gurumin*, a characteristic that they share with spirits and hunting dogs, as well as with—disconcertingly—the *gua*. A person's shadow/reflection is, in a very real sense, the imprint that their body constantly leaves in the world, and it is both the trace and the essence of their corporeal being-in-the-world. The *gurumin* is accretive, growing more and more attached to a person during his or her lifetime. Newborn babies do not yet have a *gurumin*, and by inference no "inside" (*uló paubé*). So *gurumin* also denotes something akin to "experience" or "awareness." Dreaming (*mahngél*) and visions are effects of the shadow moving off to different places. Sleeping is therefore an inherently vulnerable state, which is seen as ambiguously related to death, whereas dreaming is a condition that is full of potential but also fraught with danger.[7] It is in dreams that the shadow of the diviner is able to approach spirits in the shamanistic *famtúlo* and *famamá* possession rituals that Buli animists previously performed to seek cures for illness. Dreams can also augur good events and misfortunes; and it is in dreams that people's shadows are tempted by *gua* spirits to become *gua* themselves.

The *gurumin* is also essential—without it a person will die. "Wherever we go, it goes, too," a Buli riddle (*cagulu*) asks. The correct answer to the riddle is the *gurumin*. The shadow is the essence of life, and without his or her shadow-consciousness a person is already dead. Witchcraft is exactly the perverse realization of this scenario, resulting in a human victim who only appears to be alive but is really without consciousness, experience, awareness. A kind of living dead. It is said that victims who appear to be alive after a *gua* attack have often died already, and are merely animated by the *gurumin* of the *gua* that attacked them. The tendency for the shadow of the *gua* to occupy its victims naturally adds to the complexities of dealing with victims of witchcraft, and of trusting what they say. Just as disturbingly, this shifts the limits of death into the realm of animated life, as *gua* victims effectively die before they stop speaking, breathing, and moving. Hence, if the corpse of a deceased person decomposes more rapidly than usual, and its smell is more pungent (*pupúi*) than it is normally, it is often taken as an indication that witchcraft was involved.

## Of Bats and Witches

"You know, it's a bit like the fruit bat," Om Ponco declared. Om Ponco was blind, in his late seventies, and in 1992 when I met him was generally held to be the most knowledgeable person in the area. His reference to the fruit bat was the beginning of an analogy; his attempt to explain to me the connotations of the word *ungan*, the state associated with having had one's liver eaten by a *gua*. Fruit bats or flying foxes (*fni*) are a delicacy in Halmaheran cuisine. They spend the day sleeping in large colonies, hanging upside down in the tops of certain trees to which they habitually return. They are hunted on rainy days when the moisture on their wings is believed to hinder their flight. The tree is simply cut down, and the bats collected from its branches. In Om Ponco's analogy, it was the eating habits of the flying foxes that made them such a good analogy to the *gua*:

> It is a bit like what the fruit bats do to the bananas. At night, they fly around among the banana plants, landing on bunches here and there. They test whether the bananas are ripe by inserting their claws into the fruits. After a few days, the fruits begin to rot when fruit flies enter the puncture sites. While the banana looks fresh and green on the outside, it is, in fact, completely rotten and soft (*jakam*) on the inside. The fruit bat then returns a few days later to eat of the rotten fruit.

Like the fruit bat, the *gua* also flies around, often at night, looking for suitable victims, and then settles on its prey. Kireni, who was nine months pregnant with her fourteenth child, woke up one night in March 1992 to find a *gua* crouched on top of her stomach about to eat her liver. Her husband chased the figure away, and although Kireni developed a fever the following day, she eventually recovered. This kind of illness is known as *ungan kakamo i*, with *kakamo* meaning "hand." The hands of the *gua* dig into its victim, causing the victim to rot from the inside in much the same way as the fruit bat causes the banana to rot by digging its claws into the fruit. Once the *gua* has sunk its claws into its victim, it will, like the fruit bat, return several times to eat from the same person. And like the banana, the person may look healthy on the outside, but inside the process of decomposition has begun.

Buli folklore has it that the fruit bat is not entitled to the bananas at all, but steals them from their rightful owners, the birds. A myth (*kayat*) tells of the time when the flying creatures of the sky decided to divide between them all of the fruits that humans had planted: mango, papaya, banana, and so on. The voracious fruit bat was given first choice. Seeing the large fruits on the *lélim* tree, the fruit bat greedily chose that for itself, while the birds agreed on the ownership of the remaining fruits. Although they are very big, the fruits of the *lélim* tree, a species of mangrove tree (*Xylocarpus spp*), are inedible unless they are cooked.[8] Only when it ravenously took its first bite did the fruit bat realize its mistake. Ever since then, the fruit bat has been stealing the fruits that belong to the birds. That is why it is a nocturnal animal: it waits for the birds to sleep before flying out to steal their fruit. During the daytime, however, it hides from the birds out of shame (*mai*). For this reason the birds are said to curse the bat by loudly chirping at it if it flies out during the daytime. Tricked by its own greed, the flying fox is destined to steal what by agreement, by rights, belongs to the birds. The *gua*, in like manner, aims to take or destroy what does not belong to it: people's livers, shadows, and genitals.

The *gua*'s consumption or destruction of these parts of its victim constitutes a violation of the very "nodes where symbolicity interferes with . . . corporeality" (Kristeva 1982:125). In its removal of the shadow, its molestation of the genitals, and its consumption of the liver, the *gua* dismantles the constituent elements of human life in Buli, putting in its place a living-yet-dead victim who has been robbed of consciousness, experience, awareness, emotional subjectivity, and life itself. Essential to the horror and disgust that the *gua* inspires in Buli is the corporeality of its actions: the disembodiment of its victims, the way it makes the bodies of its victims "foreign" to themselves, the manner in which it systematically steals, destroys, and disaggregates the elementary parts of what makes them human. None of it makes any sense, but it is highly significant nevertheless.

## The Body of the Witch

If witchcraft makes "foreign bodies" out of its victims, it certainly also makes foreign bodies of its hosts (Lingis 1994). A person becomes a witch when a *gua* spirit takes the place of his or her *gurumin*, or shadow-consciousness. The *gua* spirit uses its human host as an outrigger boat (*pelang*), transferring to the host its own cannibalistic cravings. The host's hunger for human liver can never be satiated, however. As Tangkea once explained to me, "The *gua* uses humans as its outrigger, its boat; but it only uses their mouths. So when a human *gua* eats liver, it does not fall into the human belly as food; it falls into the belly of the *gua* spirit or shadow." That is why a human being who has become a *gua* has a hunger that can never be satisfied; it is a human mouth with a spirit stomach.

Indeed, the conventional image of a prowling *gua* is that of a disembodied head, a bizarre image of a flying head with "its entrails dangling from the neck" (*hnyao loló kawkawil nap*). Before a human *gua* flies off in search of victims (*amngái*), the head is said to "pull out of its disguise" (*ncibit in ni mef ca*), leaving the headless body of the human host behind.[9] The *gua* spirit, in other words, wrenches the head and entrails from the body of its human host, and it is this perverse and literally disembodied form that takes flight (see fig. 17).

Meanwhile, the body of the human host, which is merely a cloak (*mef*), is left behind in a hidden location while the witch, entrails dangling from its neck, flies off to prowl for victims. The lifeless body is referred to as the *buang*, a hunting expression used in reference to deer and pig. *Buang* designates the carcass left from the butchering process: the backbone, rib cage, and hips. The *gua* essentially butchers its host in order to enable it to go on the prowl. Humans are turned into cannibals only when their own bodies are "butchered," taken apart, by the gua spirit. It is only in its "butchered" bodily form that the human witch is a witch, and constitutes a danger to its fellow humans. But being "butchered" in this way

Figure 17. The disembodied head of the *gua* on the prowl. Drawing by Deice Guslaw (twelve years old).

also has its risks for the human *gua* host. Custom has it that if one fills the abandoned and sleeping body (*buang*) of a human witch with sharp stones, shards of glass, or broken seashells, the human witch will die. So too, in fact, will the *gua* spirit. Rendered "inhospitable," the human host dies, and left without an abode, the *gua* spirit dies too.

The *gua* on the prowl is a travesty of human embodied being. Separated from the *buang*, the *gua* with its head and entrails becomes a parody of a digestive system. The head with its dangling entrails is an embodied figure of insatiable hunger, of greed. The stomach of the human host is never filled, because the human livers that the disembodied head of the *gua* eats will fall through the separated entrails to be consumed by the *gua* spirit. The human host, who is merely the instrument or "canoe" of the *gua* spirit, is therefore left always hungry, forced to continue to prowl, butchering its own body every time it does so, only to find that its own greed for human liver remains unsatisfied. The disembodied head of the human *gua* may eat the liver with its mouth, but only the *gua* spirit will be satiated. In Buli terms, this is the very root of the tragedy of witchcraft. It is the bodily reason why it is so hard for a witch to stop once it begins to crave human liver. Greed is eternally unfulfilled. The *gua* as a result cannot stop. Witchcraft persists: "Once the dog has eaten shit, it will always eat shit" (*Nan cicaya, in nan cicaya, fun ce*).

## Witchcraft as a World Unmaking

Witchcraft is not simply an attack on the human body of the *gua*'s victim and a distortion of the body of its host. It is a "world unmaking." To understand why, I have to make a foray into the material world of Buli architecture, hunting practices, and canoe building. For in a very material sense, the body is the measure of the good life in Buli. This is related to two fundamental aspects of embodied being. First of all, the human body is a felicitous space that is open to the world by virtue of its very construction. The joints and the orifices of the human body open up to exchanges with the spirit world, in ways that can be auspicious as well as problematic. Herein lies the fortune and frailty of embodied being. Second, the human body is also a model for making the world. There is a similitude between bodies and all of the important objects in the Buli traditional universe: boats, houses, weapons, traps, gardens, and medicinal plants. Accordingly, these objects must have appropriate measurements to maintain their auspiciousness, and in this endeavor the body itself is the yardstick. When constructing a house or a boat, one actually imposes or imprints the measurements of one's own body on these objects. Making objects in Buli is essentially a way of "embodying" them, of recognizing their corporeality and providing them with suitable bodily proportions. Embodying social objects is necessary to bestow auspiciousness upon them, but it also enrolls them in the same dilemma of auspiciousness and frailty that resides in the nature of human bodies. The human body informs the body social in a variety of ways that establish an auspicious model for thinking about most of the central activities of Buli life: dwelling, hunting, gardening, and performing rituals, as well as communicating and communing with the spirits.

Witchcraft is part and parcel of this dilemma of auspiciousness and frailty. The activities of the *gua* are a perversion of the embodied nature of the world through which people in Buli seek to ensure auspiciousness. A *gua* attack is not just an attack on a body, but also by extension an undoing of the bodily dimensions of auspiciousness as such, an unmaking of the world. The disgust and horror that the *gua* provokes are related to its fundamental undermining of both embodied being-in-the-world and the embodied being-of-the-world. Gaston Bachelard used the word "topophilia" in his study of felicitous spaces, arguing that felicitous or auspicious spaces that hold comfort and intimacy are also inherently linked to hostile spaces (1969:xxxi). Though hostility and intimacy are opposites, images can lend themselves to both types of experience.[10] Images (of, say, a forest or a house) may, from one perspective and under certain circumstances, be hostile and *unheimlich*, while in a different context they connote homeliness and auspiciousness. The body is, in this double sense, a felicitous space.

## Joints and Their Dangers

The joints that confer auspiciousness on humans and the material world are simultaneously fragile openings into the world of witches. Joints and orifices provide "openings" (*pupúang*) to the world and therefore need to be protected. Toddlers in Buli often have pieces of cloth tied around their wrists (and sometimes around their ankles as well) containing roots or other medicines that protect them against intrusion. These bracelets (*fati*) are usually made of red fabric known as *kasuba*, which is commonly used when dealing with spirits (and in pre-Christian times as headbands of war). The bracelets prevent spirits from entering the apertures of the joints. The size of the interstice varies, and people with widely spaced joints are particularly vulnerable.

Joints and orifices are the main focus of curative practices in Buli, because they are simultaneous points where intruding spirits and medicinal cures may enter, and points through which a person's shadow (*gurumin*) may also return if it has been evicted by a spirit. *Famumi*, the burning of curative leaves, bark, and wood for inhalation, and *aús*, blowing into the bodily orifices, are instances of such practices. When people invoke the aid of a guardian animal spirit (*suang*) or an ancestor (*smengit*), they will frequently pull their fingers so that the joints crack while they make an implosive sound through their compressed lips. This creates a "space-in-between" (*pupúang*) through which the *suang* or *smengit* can enter its protégé. Similarly, the *gua* spirit will depart through the forehead (*mta popó*), once the person identified as its host willingly undergoes treatment.

The term *utó* expresses a situation where there is a matching of joints. When joints "match" or "fit" with one another, contact between humans and spirits is possible. *Utó* can be auspicious. If a person's joints "match" those of a *jin*, for example (*donga na faeteta*), they may be able to obtain knowledge about medicine or fighting magic from the *jin*. A particular form of divination (*failál*) involves a piece of bamboo. The length of the bamboo stick is one fathom (the length between the fingertips of the outstretched arms), and the stick has been magically prepared by a spell (*bobeto*) that invokes a particular spirit with whom the diviner maintains a relationship. A question is then posed to the bamboo stick. If someone's knife is gone, the person might ask, "Did somebody steal my knife?" Then the diviner will grab the stick and measure it against the person's outstretched arms. If the answer is yes, then the person's outstretched arms will match the ends of the stick exactly (*utó*). If the answer is no, his arms either will not reach the ends of the pole completely or will overreach. Spirit contact in general is based upon the same principle of *utó*: it is a matter of establishing a corporeal-emotional "match" in which one's bodily proportions, one's joints (*donga*) and one's "inside" (*uló*), correspond to those of the spirit. The concept of *utó* therefore connotes more than merely coinciding measurements. It also suggests a relationship characterized by openness and generosity, which is necessary when divining or seeking knowledge from benevolent spirits. Contact with the spirits is only possible in a kind of exchange relationship (see chapter 7). It is said that one's "inside" must be able to "give" (*uló ca npo*). Such exchanges between humans and spirits are necessary to ensure an auspicious life, since the ancestors (*smengit*) and the animal spirits (*suang*) protect humans with whom they have "fitting joints," and who are willing to involve themselves in an exchange relationship with the spirits. These exchange relationships entail that spirits provide protection and magical knowledge in return for ritual offerings of betel nut, tobacco, and incense.

While it is essential in benevolent relationships that the inner core "give," the openness or matching of joints that characterizes cases of possession and illness is, in a sense, a matter of "giving too much." Matching joints are therefore dangerous as well, for they precipitate the unwanted intrusion of malevolent spirits into the body, or into the house. Spontaneous possession is explained as a matter of "matching joints." Similarly, sorcery attacks or possession by forest spirits (such as the *meki* or the *putiana*) occur through the joints. The *gua* is likewise said to gain entry into a house by simply touching one of its corners (or "joints"), which then opens up to them like a door. It is common practice to place small bags of salt (which is believed to be repulsive to land-based spirits like the *gua*) underneath the corner posts of a house to prevent the *gua* from entering. The vulnerability of a house to the *gua* is ironically an effect of the very bodily proportions and corporeal structure of the house, which ensure its auspiciousness. The corporeal proportions of houses, boats, and weapons constitute an inherent openness that demands special attention, so it is important to avoid "matches" between the "joints" of the construction and its bodily dimensions to ward off accidents, illness, and misfortune.

## Bodies, Boats, and Houses

The body provides an elaborate system of measurements. These measurements are a natural part of Buli discourse and are precisely designated in the Buli language. Some measures involve the fingers, the feet, or the height of someone standing up or sitting down. The basic units in the Buli system are certain significant joints (*donga*): finger joints, wrists, elbows, shoulders, and hips (see fig. 18).

This is not as foreign as it might appear at first glance. The roots and etymology of traditional units in the United States and in the English system originate in embodied measurements. Leonardo da Vinci's *Vitruvian Man* was based on a general idea in European thought in his day that applied the body as a unit of measure. An *asuna* in Buli corresponds to the old European unit of measurement known as a "French ell," while *kakámo pao* is an "English ell," and *tan* has the same basis as the old English yard (Fenna 2002). Nevertheless, all standardized units of measurement—whether the metric system or the standardized English and US unit systems—impose a particular kind of blindness or tunnel vision (Scott 1998), a blindness that tends to prevent us from appreciating the complexities of embodied units of measurement. Standardized systems of measurement entail a generality and scalability that is unthinkable in a measurement system based on bodily proportions. In a standardized system, space is homogenous and

| | |
|---|---|
| *Lof:* | the length from the fingertips to one's arms outstretched (a fathom) |
| *Elef:* | the length of the outstretched arms but with the fists closed |
| *Asuna:* | the length from the elbow of one arm to the outstretched fingers of the other arm |
| *Kakamo pao:* | the length from one shoulder to the fingertips of the other arm |
| *Tan* ("to eat"): | the length from one's teeth to the outstretched fingers of one arm |

**Figure 18.** Embodied measurements.

general. By contrast, in a world where lengths and sizes are measured using arms, fingers, and legs of different-sized people, space does not have one measure, but a multiplicity. People differ in shape and size, and it is this very difference that makes such a system suitable for measuring space in terms of personal fortunes and usage. People use their own specific measures when building important material objects. The actual proportions of a spear will therefore depend on the bodily size of its manufacturer. In addition, all makers of spears will have specific knowledge of the number of, say, ells, that are most auspicious for a spear, knowledge that was revealed in dreams by spirits (*jin*) or given to them by their parents.

The spear used to hunt turtles (*yafane smo ni mai*), for instance, must be of a specific length if it is to fetch anything. The green turtle is a treasured delicacy and a required offering when performing the ritual to appease Buli's culture hero Íyan Toa and assure his protection. The turtles are hunted by boat and speared when they come up for air. This is a difficult undertaking, and only a few men in the village are successful turtle hunters. Their success is due to a plethora of magical prescriptions and precautions, provided to them by spirits because their "joints match." These prescriptions include ensuring the correct proportions for the spear handle, the tip, and the rope. The specific measurements are always individual. The length of Johnny's spear, for example, is two fathoms, one *sang* (the space between the thumb and the middle finger), one width of his hand, and one width of his bite (*loflú, sangsá, gúgim bahnga, fare tong bahnga*) (see fig. 19). It is the width of his bite at the end that ensures its auspiciousness. The length of the line (*faicáu*) that runs from the spear tip and is tied to the boat also has an auspicious length. In Johnny's case, this is 55 fathoms plus the width of his bite (*tanatlim re loflím re tong bahnga*). The measurements of Johnny's spear and line would not necessarily be auspicious for another man, whose arms would be a different size and therefore would not "match." Every Buli man needs to determine his own specific measures, those that are particularly auspicious for him, when manufacturing the socially significant objects of the Buli traditional universe: machete, spear, boat, trap, house, and dancing shield. If one has not inherited such measures from one's father or acquired them from a spirit, one can ask for measurements from others who have proven themselves as successful hunters and builders—and then test their auspiciousness for oneself.

"Matching" (*utó*) is not always auspicious. The spear of another hunter was "two fathoms, one *sang*, and a bit" (*loflú re sangsá re glé*). Here it is exactly "the extra bit" (*glé*) that ensures auspiciousness. The "extra bit," that one adds "for good measure," as the English expression goes, is especially important when building houses and boats. Houses and boats are like bodies, and so the construction of houses and boats aims to make sure that their joints do not match the physical measurements of their occupants. The conventional rectangular houses

**Figure 19.** Johnny Ibis checking the length of his turtle-hunting spear. 2004. Photo by author.

in Buli mirror the structure and form of a human body. The corners of a house are its elbows, and indeed, since the word for "elbows" (*sasúno*) derives from the word for "corner" (*sasún*), it would perhaps be more correct to say that in Buli the human body mirrors the structure of a house. The gables of the house are its "chest"; the posts in the middle of the walls are its "hips," and the ridgepole is its "backbone" or 'spine' (*long hapaluan*). It would be extremely inauspicious if the backbone were placed at the exact center of the house. Avoiding the centerline of the house is a cardinal tenet of Buli house building. The ridgepole therefore has to be placed slightly off center to the left or right. In similar fashion, the "hips" or center poles on the long walls of the rectangular house must not be placed in the exact center between the corners or elbows of the house, but be offset "an extra bit." This "extra bit" (*glé*) ensures that the "joints" of the house are not weakened by the poles. If the poles and the joints "matched exactly" (*utó*), it would be tantamount to inviting malevolent spirits, illness, and misfortune into the house.

The same precautions are needed when building an outrigger canoe. As one man explained to me, "The outrigger is like a house. If you know how to make an outrigger canoe, you also know how to make a house. The house has the same measurements as the planked boats, such as the *pelang pakpák* or the *pelang lataf*." The *pelang lataf* is a planked boat constructed by attaching one or two rows of planks (*sapi*) onto the hollowed-out tree trunk that forms the lower hull. Alternatively the hull can consist entirely of planks, as it does in the *pelang pakpák*, which is considered to be the fastest, lightest, and technically most difficult outrigger to construct.[11] The planks simultaneously raise the gunwale and extend the length of the keel, making the craft larger, lighter, and more seaworthy than the normal hull of a dugout canoe (*pelang ayu*). The planks are joined together with dowels (*loan*), also referred to as "tongues" (*papléor*). It is the location of these "tongues" that must be guarded carefully to prevent them from piercing the joints of the boat. The main point to avoid when placing the "tongues" or dowels in a boat is the "backbone," the exact center between the boat's bow and stern, measured with a piece of string folded in half once. The other joints of the hull are located halfway to the backbone from the bow and stern, respectively, with their locations established by folding the string in half again. The string—in the case of a *pelang lataf* I saw being built—is folded repeatedly to chart five joints on either side of the backbone, each halfway between the end of the boat and the previous, more central "joint." Once the joints are marked out, holes for the dowels are drilled, and carefully offset "an extra bit" (*re glé*) from them.

All of these precautions are necessary because there is a basic homology between the house, the boat, and the human body, a homology that must be carefully observed when fashioning the socially significant object of the Buli traditional universe.[12] This homology is dialectical: it works in both directions. So just as the outrigger boat must have body-based dimensions to be auspicious, a vital aspect of the body itself—the entrails, of both humans and animals—is configured like an outrigger boat. Thus the entrails of animals and humans are said to form an outrigger. The liver, heart, and lungs are attached "as one string" (*wala pusa*) to the throat, and form the central "hull" of the body. The kidneys, meanwhile, lie on either side and are said to form the "floats" (*eri*) relative to the other organs. When butchering an animal it is considered inauspicious to cut this "one string." In a similar way, the spine (*long hapaluan*), literally "the center bone," also represents the central hull of an outrigger.[13] The liver (*yatai*) and the *nyawa* (the breath/genitals) are located along the axis of this "center bone" and represent the goods carried in the boat.

It is this image of the body as a boat that the *gua* transforms into its own perverse assembly (see fig. 20). The *gua* uses the body of its host as a boat (*pelang*), just as other spirits may use animals as their boat. However, in the case of the *gua*, it literally exposes the "body boat" of its human host when it "pulls out" (*sibit*) the head from the body at night. From this head the human entrails that constitute an outrigger boat—liver, heart, and lungs on the "one string" (*wala pusa*) being the hull with the kidneys/"floats" attached—dangle in mockery. The Buli word for these nightly jaunts is *amngai*. The word *amngai* also refers to the swift speed

OUTRIGGER                    HUMAN HOST OF A *GUA* SPIRIT

Bow (*seselá*)                              Head

Outriggers (*eri*)

Heart (*popolulu*)

Liver (*yatai*)

Kidneys

Genitals (*nyawa*)

Stern (*hamulé*)

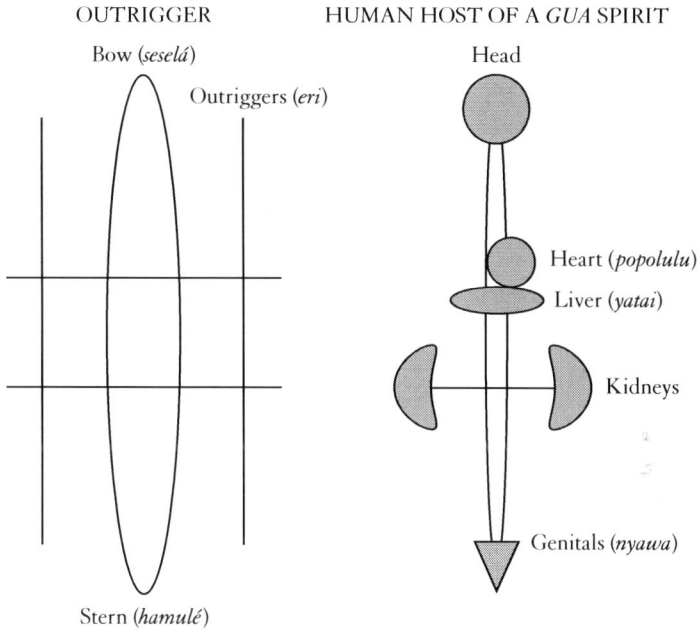

**Figure 20.** The canoe-like shape of the flying *gua* witch.

of a boat at night. A boat, so people say, travels much faster at night because of the steady night winds that often blow in the Bay of Buli. Consequently, journeys by sea (such as the one described in the preface) are often started before dawn to take advantage of these winds. The *gua* undertakes an uncanny version of these nightly voyages when it uses only the head and entrails of its host as perverse "canoes," a set of body parts that has lost all bodily auspiciousness.[14]

## Houses and Boats as Social Groups

A bodily series of fundamental homologies set the embodied parameters for life's auspiciousness in the spirit-filled world in Buli: the body is a boat-that-is-a-house. This homological series is in turn extended to most other objects fashioned by humans: spears, shields, traps, medicinal plants, and gardens all have a structure that mimics that of their human makers. The body has dimensions that are suitable for most artifacts, which means that these artifacts come to be compatible with, and in important ways resemble, the body of their owner and maker. Buli people fashion the socially significant objects in their own image, as it were. This homology between body and objects extends further, however, infusing the organization of society as well. In essence, bodies, objects, and social collectives have comparable shapes and proportions.

As is typical in many Austronesian societies, lineages in Buli are bilateral and are referred to as "houses" (*ebai*). This widespread tendency to conceptualize social groups as houses has in anthropology given rise to the concept of "house societies" (Fox 1993; Lévi-Strauss 1987), and to a realization of the profound links in these societies between architectural structures, social organization, and embodiment (Carsten and Hugh-Jones 1995). Because of the homology between "the house" as a physical structure and as a social group, both are often seen in terms of the human body. "House societies" are very much "body societies." In Buli the house is a social group on two levels. One's closest patrilineal relatives and the in-married women of the ascending generation are known as one's *ebai pusa* (or "trunk-house"). After the Dutch concept of *fam* or family was introduced, probably in the early twentieth century, it began to be used synonymously with the patrilineal core of the *ebai pusa*. The "trunk-house" is complemented by the *ebai bangsá* ("house of relatives"). This refers to the extended lineage beyond the immediate patrilineage and includes the relatives of one's mother (such as her siblings and parents) as well as the maternal relatives of one's father (his mother's family and his sisters) as well as their in-laws. These groups are especially important in the ritual events that accompany marriage and death.

The homology between houses and boats also extends to social organization and ritual. For instance, in the context of marriage negotiations, the equivalence between houses and boats is signaled in several ways that emphasize the importance of the outrigger canoe to coastal peoples like the inhabitants of Buli. Each of the house groups that are being linked are represented as outriggers, just as the prestations they offer each other frequently assume the symbolic shape of an outrigger. At marriage negotiations, two bilateral lineages or "houses"—representing the groom (known as "the man's side," *man ci*) and the bride (known as "the woman's side," *mapíng si*), respectively—face each other (*fabobó*) to negotiate the bride price (*kaimulo*) and the mutual exchange that accompanies it. Each side or "house" (*ebai*) is represented by a ritual elder who leads the negotiations and "carries the talk" (*ut mauting*). The ritual elders of the two houses are known as the "bow of the boat" (*seselá*). The house that engages another house in marriage negotiation is symbolically seen as a boat or outrigger. The male representative of the "trunk-house" (called *uanlí*) is symbolically seated in the middle of the outrigger (*pomúl*), while the male representative of the "house-of-relatives" (*keráp*) is seated in the "stern" (*hamulé*). The ritual elders of the two lineages or houses are said to resemble the crew (*masanái*) of the war canoes, known as *juanga*. During sultanate rule these vessels of the Tidore sultanate were manned by corvée laborers, men drafted from Buli and other areas under Tidore rule to perform a preset period of tribute labor (*coów*). The war canoes were sent out on regular tribute and slave raids to the coasts of western Papua.[15] The outrigger is therefore a powerful symbol of sultanate rule, of its raiding expeditions, and of its political organization, an organization within which the Buli people stress their own gendered role as warriors—"the eyes of the dog" (*kaso ma yoma*)—male protectors of the female but superior Maba people (as described in chapter 2). The ceremonies and exchanges that go into marriage replay a number of the central and gendered themes of sultanate rule, such as raiding (marked as a male activity) and tribute payment to a female superior. Here, the outrigger is a symbol that organizes and encompasses the asymmetrical but constantly reversible values of male and female.

In this vein, the bride price (*kaimulo*) that the man's side gives to the woman's side is itself conceptualized as forming an outrigger. The *kaimulo* is a sum of money that consists of two parts: *kaimulo hak*, which comes ideally from the patrilineage or "trunk-house" of the groom, and *kaimulo bangsá*, which comes from the maternal side or "house-of-relatives" of the groom's side.[16] This prestation of money is said to form the "hull" of the prestations from the man's side, while two other components, consisting of large cooking pans, are said to represent the "floats" of the presentations.[17] Taken as a whole, the prestation consisting of money and pans, hull and floats, forms an outrigger canoe (see fig. 21).

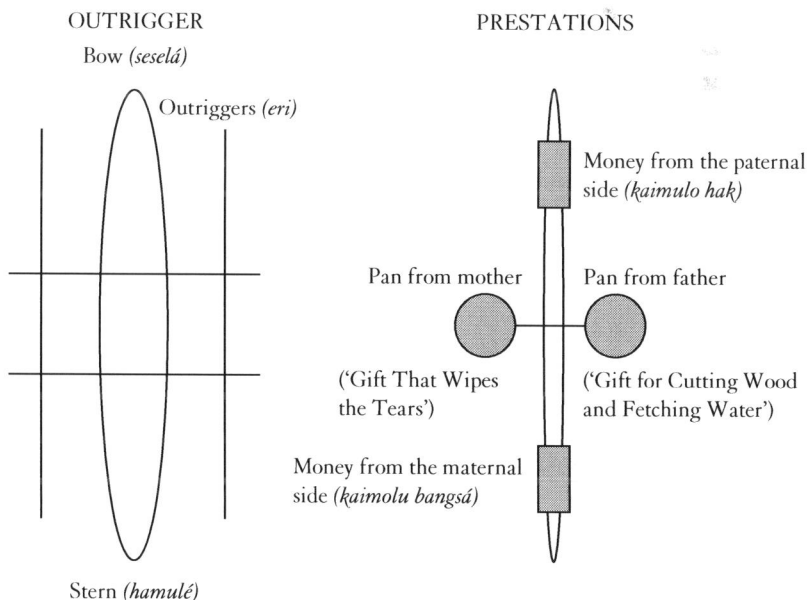

Figure 21. The canoe-like shape of marriage prestations.

## Witchcraft and Embodiment

I have highlighted these homologies between the human body, architectural structures, boat constructions, hunting implements, social groups, and ritual exchanges to demonstrate the thoroughly corporeal nature of the Buli universe. My purpose in doing so is to outline what might be called "an embodiment theory of witchcraft" and to argue that horror, like auspiciousness, is somatically driven in Buli. The *gua* is implicated—in meaningless yet significant ways—in the comprehensive destruction of embodied being in a Buli world where significant objects, social groups, and ritually significant exchanges themselves have bodily dimensions.

Numerous recent studies have explored witchcraft in relation to state politics and a global neoliberal economy (Ashforth 2005; Geschiere 1997; Niehaus 2001; Romberg 2003; Siegel 2006; Smith 2008). I will also attempt to do this for Buli in chapters 6 and 8. This chapter, however, has tried to draw out the links between witchcraft and body politics—the symbolic orders that guide the proper boundaries of embodied being. These orders, I suggest, are systematically undermined by the *gua* in ways that not only destroy the basic conditions of corporeal being, but also constitute an unmaking of the world. The unmaking of the world through witchcraft is brought about by its interruption and perverse mimicry of the symbolic orders that strive to ensure auspiciousness through a series of homological relations between the human body, social objects, and social collectives.

The central truth of these homologies is contained in the crisp yet enigmatic proverb in the Ternatan language that began this chapter, which people would often recite to me: "Placenta and intestines, pillow and secrets" (*dodomi se galegale, popoje se rahasia*). The proverb speaks to a public secret of ontogeny—namely, that the newborn and the placenta are actually siblings.[18] The fetus and the placenta share the same pillow in the womb, as it were. The proverb also has a wider semantic horizon, however. "Stomach and liver" (*hnai re yatai*), people would often respond when hearing the proverb, nodding in assent to its basic truth. It always seemed to me as if they were providing the answer to a riddle contained in the proverb. Thinking about this "answer," it strikes me first that the statement "Stomach and liver" (*hnai re yatai*) speaks about a visceral fact—namely, that inside the belly, the stomach and the liver share the intestines as their secret pillow. And indeed that is what people would tell me they meant. But the statement connotes more than just anatomy; it relates to a basic social truth in Buli. The stomach, after all, has to do with eating, and the liver, in Buli, has to do with feelings. Eating together and feeling together, commensality and community, are inseparable in Buli. In that sense, the statement "Stomach and liver" refers to an unalterable social fact: eating together and feeling together are linked; they are the real "secret bedfellows" of the proverb. Conviviality is established by eating together, by sharing food (a theme I expand on in chapter 7). There is, in other words, a direct viscerality to sociality, and a direct organic truth to conviviality and "good companionship" in Buli. The human body and the body social are intimately linked (O"Neill 2004).

It is this corporeal life-world that the *gua* destroys when it turns the liver, the organic seat of feeling (together), into an object of consumption. An analogous destruction of the bodily dimensions of the cosmo-political world runs through all aspects of a *gua* attack: The *gua* turns humans into "intestine boats" (*pelang*) and spirits them on predatory sailing trips that parody the raiding expeditions of the sultanate of Tidore. The *gua* enters the houses of its victims through their corners or "joints," perverting the way humans communicate with spirits. It decomposes the human body from within, like the disowned fruit bat rots the banana. It extends death into life by animating its victims with a false shadow-consciousness (*gurumin*). It eats the liver, turning the organic site of emotion-toward-others into the object of its ravenous feeding, and it molests life (*nyawa*) itself when beating the genitals of its victims. In a world that is social and auspicious because it is based on corporeal dimensions, it is the perverse disaggregation of bodily existence that enables the *gua* to engender such visceral horror.

I find Kristeva's notion of the abject useful to denote how the *gua* destroys in the most visceral ways every aspect of corporeal auspiciousness in Buli, while withdrawing itself from this same corporeality, from tangible reality. An abject, for Kristeva, is neither subject nor object. Rather it marks "the place where meaning collapses" (1982:3), a place toward which one is drawn and from which one is repelled at the same time. The abject is-not. This same kind of impossible reality marks the *gua*, its existence on the very edge of the perceivable world. And yet, for all its intangibility and meaninglessness, the actions and effects of the *gua* are corporeal and significant in the extreme. Conforming to the category of the abject, the *gua* is an "intolerable significance" (11). It is, as Kristeva puts it, "[a] 'something' that I do not recognize as a thing. A weight of meaninglessness about which there is nothing insignificant, and which crushes me" (2). In chapter 2, I traced how the *gua* is—impossibly—a primordial being in Buli, a cocreator of the local universe. In some mythical accounts the *gua* is a spirit being that emerged from the time of the *jin*; in other myths it is responsible for the creation of the island of Halmahera. At the same time, as I have sought to demonstrate in this chapter, the *gua* is a world-destroyer. By targeting those "nodes where symbolicity interferes with . . . corporeality" (Kristeva 1982:125), a *gua* attack is aimed not only at individually embodied beings but at the Buli universe as such, a multifaceted assault on a world where human bodies, boats, houses, traps, spears, shields, and social groups enable each other.

# 6

# NEW ORDER MODERN

About the world these days I cannot speak . . .
*Dunia oras taie, yai fasebut pa . . .*

CONVENTIONAL FIGURE OF SPEECH USED AS A PREAMBLE TO
PRONOUNCEMENTS ON TRADITION IN RITUAL SPEECH

## Soundscape 1993

"Lolos did it. He is a witch. A witch! . . . No, go away. Go away. They did it. Why don't you do anything? They did it! They will kill us all! Call the *babinsa* officer. Let him shoot them, let us shoot Lolos and Minggus!" The screams of Sami pierced the night. Her shrieking was loud, incessant, unnerving. Sitting up on her sleeping mat, Sami was wild-eyed and incoherent. As she yelled, she flailed her arms constantly, as if she were fending off an unseen assailant. Her screams were unnerving because they seemed to be a live report from a witch attack currently under way. But they were also highly embarrassing because they publicly made accusations that for months had been voiced only in private, for fear of retribution from the police. The people who had begun gathering outside the house where Sami sat, ranting and raving, whispered among themselves and shuffled their feet in discomfort, pulling their sarongs—in which most people sleep—tight around their shoulders against the cool of the night, and against their mounting unease. Sami Barabakem was an attractive woman in her late twenties. In 1981 she had married Herman Batawi and moved into his house in a neighboring village. By 1993 the couple had two young children, a seven-year-old boy and a girl of five. They had come to celebrate the New Year with relatives in Waiflí and to bring their son back to the primary school he attended in Waiflí, after spending the Christmas holidays in their garden hut near their home village.

Sami's ravings began on the night of 5 January 1993. The evening had marked the culmination of the New Year celebrations, and everyone in the village, including Sami and Herman, had taken part in the communal feasting. Women's *walit* singing and men's *cakalele* dancing had gone on till late under the tarpaulin suspended in front of the minister's house, accompanied by liberal consumption of tea, cakes, and palm wine. Around two o'clock, after almost everyone, including Sami, had gone to sleep, she had suddenly awakened and sat up on her mat on the floor. Without warning she had gone into a catatonic stupor, eyes staring blankly into space. She looked, as someone later described it to me, "as if she had forgotten something" (*laisa in talinga fapaisá*), before suddenly flying into a violent rage. As she was spending the night in the house of a classificatory brother, Noah, just opposite the minister's house at the center of the village, her cries had roused most of the village people from their sleep.

## Madness and the Truth of Witchcraft

There was a general consensus that Sami's high-pitched accusations were the result of madness (*pongpongol*). But it was a madness that made acute and painful sense to the bystanders. First of all, the catatonic stupor followed by a rage driven by a mad and embarrassing lack of restraint was an obvious indication of witchcraft. It is well known that the *gua* removes the shadow or *gurumin* of its victim during an attack. This loss of the *gurumin*—simultaneously one's experience, consciousness, and awareness—marks the moment of both imminent death and oblivion. One has just experienced a deadly attack, but has simultaneously been robbed of the ability to know it. This state of oblivion is, however, often changed by another intervention perpetrated by the witch. In an almost unbearable act of arrogance, the *gua* "makes its victim remember" (*fauló ya neto*) the witchcraft attack by returning its shadow-consciousness. This "recovered memory" is the only way that humans can know directly about witchcraft, but witches simultaneously warn their targets that they will die immediately if they relate this knowledge to others. This puts the human victim of witchcraft in a double bind: the person has knowledge of the attack but will die if he or she shares this knowledge. And yet it is this very knowledge that family members and healers who are called in to attend a sick person will strain to decipher in the whispers of the afflicted person, knowing full well that this may, in fact, hasten the victim's death. Witchcraft and its possible cure are, in this sense, a struggle over secrecy and sociality, over memory and its dangers. Just as in Jeanne Favret-Saada's classic study *Deadly Words* (1980), an analysis of witchcraft in contemporary western France, talk of witchcraft in

Buli is an effect of being "caught" by witchcraft. But in Buli speaking the truth, and telling that one has been "caught," are also in themselves deadly. The paradoxical truth about witchcraft in Buli is that the *gua* reveals the truth about itself, but prohibits the enunciation of this truth upon pain of death. So the truth about witchcraft in Buli is intimately and paradoxically entangled with death by witchcraft. Just before the moment of death, the victim gains a revelatory but also deadly insight into witchcraft, an insight that is inherently unstable because it is provided by the witch itself. The dying victim is afforded a unique but at the same time inherently impossible insight into the reality of witchcraft. The memory of a witchcraft attack can ironically be recovered only through witchcraft. This lost but recovered memory, impossible as it is, provides humans with the only available truth about witchcraft.

It was this impossible insight into witchcraft that seemed to explain Sami's disorientation when she awoke that night in January 1993. Instead of whispering her memory of witchcraft as victims normally do, however, Sami publicly shouted out her accusations. Indeed, her public accusations were somehow made more believable by their flagrant violation of proper conduct. Only a person who has lost her *gurumin*, her sense of sociality and awareness of propriety, would behave in this way. Embarrassing as they were, Sami's loud accusations were, in an awkward way, the best evidence of witchcraft that one could get, and as such they were impossible to ignore.

Sami's speech was largely incoherent (*bafeto*), but the crowd assembled outside could clearly make out the statement she kept repeating over and over throughout the night. She shouted that she had been attacked by Lolos, her classificatory uncle, and Lolos's son-in-law, Minggus, under a mango tree at the edge of the village a few days earlier. Lolos had also told Sami that he was going to kill everyone in *fam* Guslaw and *fam* Batawi. If she and these families were to survive, Sami charged over and over, the village had to call in the Indonesian army, personified by the *babinsa* (a noncommissioned officer recently stationed in the village), to shoot the two witches dead.

Sami was from the Barabakem patriline (*fam*). Although this meant that she was not the direct target of Lolos's threat to the Batawi and the Guslaw families, multiple other relationships and events made her a significant nexus for the threat. For one thing, Sami was married to Herman, who was from the *fam* Batawi patriline. In 1986, Herman's father, Mani Batawi, had been eaten and killed by Lolos, or so the family was convinced. And two years before that, in 1984, Sami's own father, Gora Barabakem, had also died after a gua attack by Lolos (see chapter 1). Sami's mother was from *fam* Guslaw and the classificatory sister of Tali, a ritual elder (*uanlí*) of the Guslaw patriline. Sami was therefore Tali's classificatory daughter. I stood next to Tali that night in January 1993 listening to Sami's accusations, and I saw how sadness, panic, and outrage fought for control in his face. In the ramblings of his classificatory daughter a terrible possibility seemed to emerge—namely, that witches had it in for the Guslaw patriline and that the deaths of Mani and Gora were linked to deaths in Tali's own immediate family (see fig. 22). On that evening in 1993, therefore, Tali could not help but remember that death of Karo, Tali's brother-in-law, in 1991, a tortured death that I will describe in this chapter.

It is the conjuncture of these three previous attacks that made Sami's eerie illness so significant. Sami's body became the site of inscription of "a particular spatiotemporal horizon of meaning" (Munn 1990:5) that allowed a search backward in time even while creating a certain potential interpretive range for future action. Using Nancy Munn's notion of "event history," I suggest that the unintelligibility of witchcraft incites people to construct histories of this kind in a frustrated search for answers to the interminable experience of the *gua*. It is the aporetic nature of the *gua*, its inaccessibility, that necessitates a constant quest to assign meaning to it. But contrary to Lévi-Strauss's (1963) famous example about the sorcerer who heals by assigning one meaning to an illness with too many meanings, I suggest that in Buli the attempt to understand witchcraft, and perchance to heal, is a much more fraught one. It is essentially the impossible attempt to assign meaning to events that are full of significance but ultimately devoid of meaning. Life with witchcraft in Buli furnishes few of the conceptual and existential comforts that structuralist analysis conventionally seeks to assign it. The kind of witchcraft event history that I will trace in this chapter in this sense repeats therefore, at a microlevel, the incessant but impossible quest to cope with the aporia of witchcraft that has driven historical agency in Buli over the longue durée (see chapters 3 and 4).

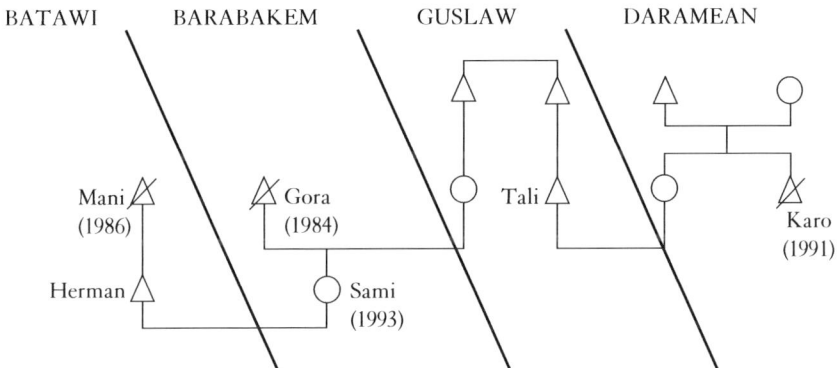

**Figure 22.** Three deaths connected.

## Political Complicity and Its Ghosts

Intimately connected to the impossible event history of these three witchcraft deaths was the New Order, the authoritarian and developmentalist regime of President Suharto that governed Indonesia between 1966 and 1998. Occurring as they did at the height of New Order rule, both Sami's fit of madness in 1993 and Karo's death in 1991 involved continuous appeals to local representatives of state authority to intervene against witchcraft. As this chapter will demonstrate, these appeals—voiced so desperately in Sami's pleas for the army officer to shoot the *gua*—speak to a larger fact—namely, that an important part of the attraction of New Order ideology for people in Buli was the promise of a development process that would render the *gua* a thing of the past. Accordingly, people appealed to the local authorities to live up to this promise. The authorities did so ambivalently, however, being caught—at certain times—in the very witchcraft realities they denied, and appearing—at other times—to aid and abet the witches rather than assisting their victims.

A series of excellent studies has begun to unearth the many hidden ways in which the spirit world both haunts and facilitates the politics of the modern nation-state in Asia, its past problems and its hopes for the future (Cannell 1999; Figal 1999; Kendall 2010; Kwon 2008; Morris 2000a; Pedersen 2011). The exploration in this chapter of the links between state imaginaries and witchcraft realities seeks to contribute to this expanding field of "spiritual politics" in modern Asia, focusing on the unintended consequences of political attempts to eradicate the spirits of the past in the spirit of modernism (see also Bubandt 2014). In considering these connections, I present two parallel arguments.

I argue, firstly, that the "high modernism" of the New Order state had a unique appeal because it seemed to come with the promise of ending witchcraft, and that this appeal undergirded Buli complicity with state ideology. The implementation and imaginaries of development in Indonesia have been the subject of a number of important recent studies (Aragon 2000; Brenner 1998; Collins 2007; Dove 1988; Li 2007; Rutherford 2003; Siegel 1986; Spyer 2000; Tsing 1993). These studies demonstrate how the fabric of New Order development ideology, although blanketing the entire archipelago with political hegemony, continued to be frayed by the wear and tear of social life as its individual threads were woven into local concerns and priorities. I believe that this simultaneous process of blanketing and fraying also occurred in Buli as development ideology and witchcraft concerns became increasingly entangled. The relationship between state concerns and witchcraft concerns, I argue, is one that is more fruitfully conceptualized in terms of complicity and frustration than in terms of power and resistance. Buli attitudes to New Order modernity, like those throughout much of the Indonesian periphery, were not characterized by opposition and resistance—an attitude restricted to urban elites on the faraway island of Java that rarely penetrated to the Halmaheran frontiers of New Order nation building. Rather, there was an engagement in Buli with Indonesian modernity and the Indonesian state that sought to domesticate and placate outside power, as people had always done, through hypercomplicity and encompassment (see Tsing 1993).

"Who are you going to vote for?" I once asked my sister just before an election. Her reply was "For whoever wins!" This answer gestures, I think, to a general feature of politics in Indonesia, especially during the New Order. There was in Buli—as indeed throughout Indonesia—a comprehensive complicity with the "antipolitics machine" of the New Order (see Ferguson 1990). Politics was something the elite handled. And this politics was a politics of the future, a politics of radically breaking with the local past. The New Order rhetoric that was espoused by local authorities in the 1990s held that the modern world (I. *dunia modern*) was just on the brink of arriving in Buli in the form of asphalted roads, timber, and mining companies, as well as, not least, permanent electricity (see chapter 8). In this world there would be no room for devils (I. *setan*), no place for evil spirits (I. *iblis*), and no possibility of witches (*gua*), because people would learn to abandon their 'superstitious beliefs." This promise, I venture to say, was immensely powerful in Buli, for historical reasons explored earlier, and it became the foundation for a basic loyalty to the New Order project of betterment through development.

Loyalty was, however, coupled with a sense of betrayal as the state proved itself unable to live up to its own promises, delivering instead a "permanent deferral" of the modern world (I. *dunia modern*)—a world that was always about to arrive, but continually moved beyond reach again with every new *gua* attack. A dimension of Buli complicity with state power was thus a continuously frustrated expectation that state authorities would apply themselves to the eradication of witchcraft, by force if necessary. Sami's exhortations that the army and police should shoot the witches that had attacked her were one such desperate attempt to hold the state to its promise. Mad and embarrassing as Sami's outburst was, it nevertheless expressed an essential truth about Buli expectations of modernity.

New Order development ideology was, in Halmahera, a policy of change, a policy that generated almost millenarian expectations about the advent of sociotechnological change. When, in the mid-1990s, Suharto announced that the year 2000 would be the time when Indonesia would "take off" (I. *tinggal landas*) economically, in Buli this fed into and also helped to heighten existing Christian and local expectations and anxieties about the new millennium (Bubandt 1998a). It is probably not wrong to see these expectations of modern development in light of the history of millenarianism that had developed on Halmahera over the previous two hundred years (see chapter 3). However, their immediate context was what

Michael Taussig has called a "Third World cult of the modern" that the New Order cultivated, at least in the margins of the nation that were deemed to be "less developed" (Bubandt 2004b; Taussig 1987:278). "Development" (I. *pembangunan*), as it was talked about on Halmahera in the 1990s, seemed to denote a future that was always on the threshold, just about to arrive. It was a future characterized not just by economic progress and technological advancement. Development also implied a new society. This was a society inhabited by a new kind of "aware" (I. *sadar*) subject—a "development-oriented human being" (I. *manusia pembangunan*) who had voluntarily stepped out of "backward society" (I. *masyarakat terbelakang*) and into a new, Pan-Indonesian model "family society," which was characterized by mutual aid (I. *gotong royong*), deliberation (I. *musyawarah*), and unanimity (I. *mufakat*) (see Nicholson 1994).

The present chapter argues, secondly, that these attempts by the New Order representatives to domesticate the backward spaces and "evil spirits" (I. *setan*) of local custom (*adat re atorang*) generated their own forms of ambivalence, in which these spirits came to countercolonize and haunt the imaginaries of the always incomplete New Order project of centralized stability and harmony (see also Pemberton 1994; Schrauwers 2003; Siegel 2001). State attempts to eradicate witchcraft in Buli had the unintended consequence of giving the *gua* a new and more concrete social reality. Buli complicity with New Order modernism, therefore, continuously generated its own frustrations and failures, whenever New Order ideology seemed unable to deliver on its promise of a modernity freed from the ghosts of tradition. For New Order development not only seemed unable to curb the incidence of witchcraft; it seemed to even provide the climate for its upsurge.

I suggest that the reproduction of witchcraft through the attempts made to end it arose out of an ambivalence within the antipolitics machine of New Order development (Ferguson 1990). Development (*pembangunan*) was an antipolitics machine, because it transformed political questions of how society was to be organized into an administrative, technological, and moral matter. New Order repression was not political at all in this understanding, but the administrative organization of society according to a "modern" and morally necessary model of the family. Yet this antipolitics machine was constantly and, throughout Indonesia, pervasively haunted by its own ghosts as the politics that was denied came back to haunt its representatives as spirits (see Bubandt 2014; Heryanto 1999; Siegel 1998). It is therefore quite telling that in the early 1990s, when New Order power was at its zenith, the *gua* appeared to many Buli people to be stronger than ever. As one man commented a few days after Sami's attack, "The issue of the *gua* is not present in the law, because those people [civil servants and police officials] are afraid, too: it would end in war. Because witchcraft does not just happen once. Problems with the *gua* happen every single day."

Sami's blaring accusations bore out this sense of being engaged in a war against witches in which the state itself was intimately but ambivalently involved. As I will show in the last part of this chapter, witchcraft was made more present and real by the New Order's ascribing ever more dimensions of Buli tradition to "witchcraft." By way of example, a basic feature of New Order "high modernism" (Scott 1998), to which people in Buli worked so hard to remain loyal, was that it demonized much of Buli tradition (see Meyer 1999), including the veneration of ancestor and guardian spirits; the use of *jin* spirits for shamanic healing rituals and other medicinal purposes; and the application of garden magic. As the New Order succeeded in reassigning these aspects of tradition to the work of devils (I. *setan*), it also demonized aspects of tradition that had conventionally protected people against witchcraft. Indeed, it was as if the very attempts of the New Order to stamp out witchcraft beliefs and maintain social order became the conditions under which witchcraft in Buli was able to flourish. The result has been the establishment of witchcraft as a particular Buli "cultural intimacy," an embarrassing but also irreducible part of what it is to be Buli (Herzfeld 2005). As the *gua* came to represent the cultural intimacy of being Buli—witchcraft being what killed Buli people at the same time as it defined them—this ironically served to confirm traditional ideas about the *gua* as both violently destructive and somehow nevertheless constitutive of existence (see also chapter 5).

As my account of Sami's madness and its backdrop will demonstrate, people in Buli were New Order citizens with the same mixture of enthusiasm and resentment that they were Christians—attracted by the hope that if only they were devout or loyal enough, state modernity, like Christianity, would stamp out witchcraft; and disappointed by the apparent inability of both projects to follow through on what was perceived as their alluring promise.

## Modernity Deferred

Two days after the onset of Sami's madness, two well-known healers (*sowsów*) from the nearby hamlets of Tewil and Gau arrived to treat her. As usual, their diagnoses were ambivalent in ways that highlighted the complexities of witchcraft. They suggested that while witchcraft was definitely involved, it was not solely to blame for Sami's illness. One healer divined that the guardian spirit of Sami's patriline, the wild pig (*bou*), was angry with her. Several symptoms, widely discussed in the village, had already suggested as much. Sami's swollen joints and neck seemed to be reminiscent of the swelling that affects a pig caught in a sling trap (*sisirá*). Sami also frequently became obsessive about the arrangement of pillows in her bed, insisting they be arranged into what some

people saw as an equivalent of the nest (*samas*) built by a wild sow in preparation for farrowing.

Sami's husband, Herman, seemed to have caused the anger of the spirit guardian (*suang*) because he had caught a pig in a sling trap and brought it with them
when they came to Waiflí for the New Year celebrations. Normally, spouses do
not touch or eat each other's spirit guardians, and Herman should not have done
so either, but he had been unable to give up the pig-hunting skills for which his
own patriline was renowned. As a result, Sami had been obliged to sit next to the
dead pig in the outrigger for the five hours it took the family to paddle to Waiflí.
Both healers worked from this diagnosis and applied the crushed leaves (*bobara*)
and prepared their magical drinks (*táwar*) to soothe the angered spirit guardian. In spite of their efforts, however, Sami's condition did not improve, which
strengthened the family's determination to maintain the truth of her publicly
voiced accusations against Lolos.

One night the following week, I was startled awake by a gunshot at about one
o'clock. The police had arrived from Buli Serani to arrest six men who had allegedly entered Lolos's house in search of the owner. The shot was fired into the
air when nobody seemed willing to reveal their whereabouts. The men were subsequently arrested, loaded into a truck—at that time still the only motor vehicle in
the district—that was requisitioned from a road construction project, and taken
down to the detention cell in Buli Serani. An entourage of younger men followed
the truck on foot to protest against the men's arrest. The attempted assault on
Lolos by the men was a sign of desperation. Sami's condition had not improved
over the previous week, even after three different healers had attended her. She
continued to stare at people without any expression or recognition, and her speech
was either garbled or high pitched and full of complaints and accusations. At this
point, the local minister from the Christian Evangelical Church of Halmahera
(GMIH) was called in to see if he could help. The minister held several communal prayer meetings by Sami's bedside and instructed that the Bible (*Buk ca*, "the
Book") be kept under her pillow. Over the following days, Sami would regularly
replace the turmeric (*popóa*), which the previous healers had told her to clutch in
her hand as defense against the angered spirit of the pig, with the Bible, which she
would hold tight against her chest.

The following Sunday, the heads of both the police force and the army appeared in church after the sermon. Accompanied by the minister from the main
settlement of Buli, the police chief (I. *kapolsek*), himself a Christian from Ambon,
delivered an energetic speech in which he strongly advised people to stop letting

backward beliefs (I. *kepercayaan terbelakang*) be obstacles to safety (I. *keamanan*), development (I. *pembangunan*) and the Christian religion (I. *agama Kristen*). "This cannot go on," he continued. "Mutual accusations and suspicions (I. *kecurigaan*) are unfit for people who are Christian, and it is harmful for development and progress. If this does not stop, I will stop it. Even if I have to arrest every single person who makes these accusations."

The church was the perfect venue for the police chief's speech. Church services are the main communal events in all Christian villages on Halmahera, and the place where all collective messages and announcements are delivered (Platenkamp 1992). The choice of venue was also in tune with New Order modernity, which emphasized monotheism as the first of its five political pillars in the state philosophy known as Pancasila.[1] Hence, it was natural that the church should serve as the platform for the voice of state authority, a voice that articulated the New Order link between religious heresy and state subversion. And even though the speech concluded with the outrageous threat that Sami would be arrested and charged with obstructing development and disturbing the social order, it was still ironically very much in tune with Buli expectations. People expected the state and the church to be fierce in the battle against witchcraft, and even though the police chief targeted its victims rather than its perpetrators, it was decisive action of this type that people expected and demanded from the institutions of modernity. Buli people were (and remain) "Christian moderns" (Keane 2007) for whom the conversion to Christianity during the course of New Order rule increasingly also came to betoken a conversion to modernity (Van der Veer 1996). The persistence of the *gua* despite this double conversion was a problem that very much belonged in the church. The issue at stake, however, was how one saw the mechanism through which witchcraft obstructed modernity.

For the police chief, it was witchcraft that was hindering New Order development from coming to Buli. The people I knew in Buli could not agree more. But whereas witchcraft was an instance of obstinate, backward belief for the police, for the local people it was an obstinate, backward reality. In either case, however, modernity was being deferred by witchcraft. As Tanya Murray Li has suggested, "permanent deferral"—a situation in which inclusion is accompanied by a continuous production of reasons for exclusion—is a central feature not only in the civilizing project of colonialism but also in the logic of postcolonial projects of societal improvement (2007:15). The issue of witchcraft was pivotal in the production and the experience of "permanent deferral" in New Order Buli. For state bureaucrats and police officers as well as for army commanders, charged with the dual function (I. *dwifungsi*) of guarding national safety and sociopolitical order, backward superstition was among the main reasons why development could not proceed properly, whereas for many Buli people the continuing presence of the *gua* was a sign that development had been deferred. People in Buli suffered, one might say, from a "state deficit."[2] They wanted more state power than they could get. They wanted state power, and they wanted it to kill all witches, once and for all. The disagreement in the church about whether modernity was being deferred by the superstitious beliefs of recalcitrant pagans or by *gua* realities that the state failed to properly address was therefore not a disagreement about the basic ideology of the New Order. It was a disagreement about how state power best lived up to its own promises.


## New Order Dreams

During the early 1990s—the heyday of New Order rule, when annual economic growth rates were above 7 percent and criticism of the Suharto government's state cronyism was firmly held in check—active state intervention offered a convincing discourse about a new political future as well as a powerful institutional attempt to engineer such a future. *Pembangunan* or "development" was the shorthand name that people during the 1980s and 1990s had learned to give to this project (Hery-anto 1988). It was a name that most people in Buli accepted, even welcomed, less for the benefits it had demonstrably delivered than for the promises of a better future that it held out. The new modern world (I. *dunia modern*) that development would bring about was one of economic riches, education, public employment, and a sanitized social life. In the early 1990s this project generated particular expectations of modernity in Buli people: dreams about being connected to the electric grid of the PLN generator, which operated from 6:00 p.m. till 12:00 p.m.;[3] dreams of corrugated iron on their houses; of a private TV set; of securing a job as a civil servant (I. *pegawai*) for their children. It was a world in which people, as the state ideology expressed it, had been "becoming aware" (I. *sadar*), a world that entailed a farewell to superstitious beliefs, not just the belief in guardian spirits (*suang*) but also, centrally, that in sorcery (*payao*) and in the witch (*gua*). Through state-engineered progress (I. *kemajuan*), so it seemed, the *gua* would finally disappear.

    The attempts to weed out witchcraft that characterized the New Order in Buli were built into a robustly modernist belief in centrally organized development, economic improvement, and social engineering. They were also coupled with a cultural arrogance toward the backward beliefs of the marginalized people of the Outer Islands, expressed in the concept of "mental guidance" (I. *pembinaan mental*) (Li 2007:58). "The law does not acknowledge magic (I. *ilmu gaib*)," Syamsul Alam, the police chief in Buli, told me in 2004. Pak Syamsul had a BA in law: "This is a leftover from Dutch Roman law, so the hands of the police are tied. All we can do is to take preventive measures (I. *tindakan preventif*) to hinder revenge attack by victims of witchcraft and to provide general guidance (I. *pembinaan*). Perhaps [things will change], when people become more aware (I. *mungkin dengan adanya kesadaran*)."

## New Order Nightmares

Ironically, however, the implementation of "mental guidance" had the effect of making the *gua* more visible, more problematic, and in a sense more real than ever. Part of the reason for this was that the state project of modernist development was carried out by local state representatives who were often themselves not entirely dissuaded of the reality of witchcraft, and who were therefore ambivalent modernists at best. The *babinsa* (the noncommissioned law-enforcement officer) stationed in Waiflí was one of these state representatives caught between state ideology and Buli witchcraft. I knew this officer quite well. He and his family occupied a government-sponsored house originally built for a primary-school teacher who never showed up. Their house was not far from mine, and he regularly came to borrow my typewriter to type up his reports to the military headquarters. The *babinsa* was from Galela in the north of Halmahera, where witchcraft was also a reality. He and his Ambonese wife had two young children. One night in March 1993, I awoke upon the sound of gunshots very close to my house. The shots had been fired by the *babinsa*'s Ambonese wife. Their young son had been ill for some time, and there was widespread speculation in the village that the illness was caused by witchcraft—and that the *gua* responsible for the attack was none other than Lolos. On this particular evening as the *babinsa* and his wife were returning from a visit with fellow army officers in the administrative town of Buli Serani, the couple had repeatedly heard the call of the *cokaéko*—a bird form that the *gua* sometimes assumes (see chapter 8). Indeed, it had seemed to them as if the *cokaéko* was following them all the way home. The witch-bird had eventually settled in a large breadfruit tree just outside their house and continued its ominous calling. Eventually, this had become too much for the *babinsa*'s wife. Grabbing her husband's semiautomatic gun, she went outside and fired five shots into the treetop where the offensive bird had come to perch. The calls had ceased, but by then the entire village was awake. Few people got any more sleep that night. Shortly after this episode, the son of the *babinsa* died, and as the already considerable pressure on Lolos increased, the *babinsa* threatened to kill him. The young boy's death hit the *babinsa*'s family very hard, and the couple eventually divorced. Soon after, the *babinsa* was recalled to the military barracks in Buli Serani.

Sami's mad plea to persuade the *babinsa* to shoot Lolos and Minggus sprang in other words from a shared sense of threat—even though it came a few months before Lolos was said to have caused the death of the *babinsa*'s son. At least this army official, so people would tell me approvingly, acknowledged the reality of the *gua* and was willing to wield state power to eradicate it. As I have already suggested in chapter 1, the bitterly acquired beliefs in witchcraft held by outside authority figures such as police and military officers in many ways helped to prove the reality of the *gua*, and also raised hopes that the state might actually be able to control it. The (imagined) beliefs of outside figures of authority sanctioned an inaccessible reality that Buli people could afford only to believe in. The best they could do themselves, as I have already suggested, was to doubt.

## Police Beliefs and the Problem of Proof

Pak Suleiman was another figure of authority who was given much credit for believing. Pak Suleiman had served as the police chief (I. *kapolsek*) in Buli between 1982 and 1987. When I spoke to him in 2004, he was a frail, elderly retiree living in Ternate, who could look back on many witchcraft-related cases during his posting in Buli. There had, for instance, been the boy who had stepped on the thorn of a wild coconut. The wound had become infected, and eventually gangrene had set in. Feverish from the infection, the boy had related how a man called Jumat had attacked and eaten him in the garden. The house of the afflicted boy had been crammed with people who wanted to kill Jumat. Pak Suleiman said he had convinced people that it was indeed gangrene, but the local medical clinic (I. *puskesmas*) had run out of antibiotics, and without this treatment the boy had eventually died. So in the end, Pak Suleiman admitted, people had not been persuaded by his explanation. The securing of proof (I. *bukti*) was the main problem, Pak Suleiman reflected. Once when a man from Buli Serani said he had been speared by a *gua* in his coconut grove, Suleiman had sent his officers to look for forensic evidence. They had brought back a coconut leaf with dark stains resembling blood. But these turned out to be droplets from a ripe coconut, and the case had to be dropped. I asked if Pak Suleiman himself thought that witches (*suanggi*) existed. "From a professional point of view there are no witches, because there is no proof," Pak Suleiman replied. "As a police officer, it is my task to calm people down and create peaceful relations, that is all." He paused for a while to take a pensive puff of his cigarette. Then he continued, "My neighbor in Bastiong on Ternate was a witch (*suanggi*)," and proceeded to tell the following story.

One afternoon while Pak Suleiman's daughter was running a high fever, he noticed a large cat on the rooftop of his house. Certain that it was a witch in disguise, he decided to chase it. Eventually, he had managed to catch it, but as he was trying to strangle it with his bare hands, the creature had fought fiercely and torn painfully at his arms. Throwing the animal onto a rock in pain and disgust, he had seen it run off into a cluster of pineapple bushes. He had then fired a shot at it with his service revolver, but it had vanished without a trace. The next day, Pak Suleiman's neighbor had complained that her cat had been attacked. "Stop harming my cat, or I won't let you draw water from my well," the neighbor had threatened. "Who needs water, if we're all dead anyway?" Pak Suleiman had retorted, before returning the threat: "I don't believe in witches (*suanggi*), but if I see one I will shoot it." The neighbor had not answered, and Suleiman concluded with satisfaction that her silence proved him right. A few days later Pak Suleiman had caught a glimpse of the neighbor woman through her window. Something was weird about her: her normally short hair now reached to her hips, and she was carefully combing it, mirror in hand. That was proof for Suleiman: "This woman is a *suanggi*." After that the conversation turned to other topics for a while. As I got up to take leave of my host, Pak Suleiman lowered his voice: He knew a certain spell (I. *ajimat*) that would make a *kokók* bird fall from the tree in its human form. He had learned it from a man in Buli. One day, he might pass it on to me . . .

People like Pak Suleiman and the *babinsa* command great respect in Buli. It was on authorities such as these that people staked their hopes during the New Order: authorities who navigated the muddy waters of witchcraft realities with the same measure of doubt and desperate conviction that Buli people had; authority figures who insisted that New Order modernity eventually would make the witches go away, but who were still willing to use their power and their guns to make it do so. It was these kinds of people who came closest to fulfilling the promise of New Order modernity.

Along the internal frontiers of the national development project, the New Order state had fuzzy borders, as others have also pointed out (Antlöv 1995; Tsing 1993). The project of New Order development was transformed in the very contact zones where its implementation was deemed most necessary. The fuzziness was created by a strong ideology of modernity that consigned the *gua* to the realm of superstition, but was simultaneously belied by the practical enrollment of many figures of state authority in the reality of the *gua*. This ideology under erasure allowed a particular hope to grow—namely, that the state could still somehow bring about the eradication of witchcraft. Wishing to believe in the state ideology that in a modern world there where no devils, people in Buli hoped that those figures of authority who knew from experience about the reality of the *gua* could be persuaded to use the power of the state to implement a world without witches.

## Madness without a Cure

A week after Sami's attack, a fourth healer, a man with a reputation for specializing in *ungan* (witchcraft), arrived by boat from the nearby village of Tewil. He
made it clear that this was a complicated case. Sami's lack of response to treatment
meant that no single cause was responsible. The possibility that Sami had been
attacked by a *gua* was maintained, but attention now turned to the reasons why
her protective and ancestral spirits had allowed such an attack to happen. The
anger of the wild pig was one such reason. The diagnosis of the fourth healer
offered more. It appeared that Herman had not observed the taboos associated
with his own *suang* either. As a result, both the eel (*mnu*) and the shark (*woi*) of
his patriline were angry, and this combined anger had made the attack possible.
The main wound on Sami's body, furthermore, was not on her stomach in the
area around the liver, as was usual in cases of *ungan*. Instead, the invisible wound
was located at the small of her back, explaining why the crushed medicinal leaves
placed on her stomach by the previous healers had not brought any relief. The
unusual wound site seemed to be connected to the additional involvement in her
sickness of a *putiana* spirit.

The *putiana* is a Buli version of a figure known throughout the Southeast Asian
archipelago. Named variously *puntianak*, *pontianak*, and *kuntilanak*, it is a female
demon who has died during childbirth and who roams the world in search of a
replacement for her lost child. Often featured in television ghost stories and horror movies (Bubandt 2012; Tan 2010), the *pontianak* poses a particular danger to
pregnant women, but may harm all women out of spite and envy. The *putiana*
was said to have entered Sami's body after the *gua* attack and left its dead child on
Sami's liver (*yatai*), which was already damaged from the witchcraft attack. The
dead child "sat on the wound" (*totongo yabat ca*), preventing it from healing. The
presence of the ghost child, which also explained Sami's ongoing delirium, was
an acute danger to her life, for according to convention, the *putiana* would return
at a later stage to reclaim her child, at which point Sami would die. The healer
decided there was no prospect of healing Sami in Waiflí, so he took her back to
Tewil, where treatment continued over the following months.

Gradually Sami became better. She was not entirely cured, however. In the
years that followed she continued to have an odd look in her eyes—as if she were
still contemplating a certain something that she had lost—and the cause of her affliction was never truly established. As usual, the witchcraft attack remained an indeterminable fact. Sami's madness may not have had a clear cause or cure, but it did
have one clear outcome: it cemented a particular "event history" by connecting a
series of witchcraft incidents into one single narrative, witchcraft incidents in which
the state played the same central yet reluctant role as it had in Sami's madness.

## Witchcraft as Proof of Itself

As Nancy Munn has shown in her study of Gawa in Melanesia, witchcraft provides a culturally meaningful but continuously changing way of connecting events in an intelligible series or line, an "event history" (1990:4). Sami's madness allowed for the creation of just such an emergent event history, which was forged by the very unintelligibility of the attack itself. On its own, like every *gua* attack, Sami's madness was an incomprehensible event. Even so, a particular intelligibility is made possible when the uncanny is given a place. This intelligibility is not one that concerns the origin of the particular witchcraft attack, but one that through connection to previous cases makes a certain seriality possible, so that one instance of witchcraft death, however uncertain, comes to constitute the proof that offsets the uncertainty of previous instances in the series of events. Witchcraft comes to be the proof of itself in a way. But it is an awkward kind of proof. For, as Siegel has noted about the usage of the word "proof" (I. *bukti*) in the East Javanese witch killings of the late 1990s, "proof" is an indication of equivocality more than anything else. Proof means that something strange but expected happened. *Bukti* is tied to an awkward trajectory, a strange historiography: "In effect, to say 'proof' is not to say 'He did it, here is the evidence' but 'I knew it.' After the fact, the uncanny even is claimed to have been anticipated" (Siegel 2006:118).

Witchcraft proves something to have been rightly anticipated, but only after the fact. The strange temporality built into the notion of "proof," which fits so well with the inaccessible nature of witchcraft itself, is, as Siegel has pointed out, one that was very much shaped within the New Order political imagination, where the notion of proof was always an index of power rather than of an authentic event (Siegel 1998; Strassler 2004). The Buli search for the "proof" of witchcraft relied therefore on an uncanny historiography that was adopted from the New Order political imagination. Far from stabilizing witchcraft as superstition because no "proof" could be found, "proof" became the site where witchcraft gained its own kind of uncanny historical reality.

I argue that witchcraft cases come to be connected by the same mechanisms that Michel de Certeau has suggested for events in historiography. Events, Certeau claims, function by "providing the uncanny with a place *useful* for a discourse of intelligibility, by exorcising what is not understood in order to make of it a means of comprehension" (1988:96, italics in the original). It is out of the uncanny fabric of events that are in themselves opaque that history is made, in a piecemeal fashion. Certeau's notion of the event in history thus comes very close to the contexts I would claim apply to *gua* attacks: "The event does not explain but permits an intelligibility. It is the postulate and the point of departure—but also the blind spot—of comprehension. Something must have taken place right *there*, by means of which one can construct a series of facts, or transport them from one regularity to another" (96, underlined in the original). Like the historiographic event, the witch attack becomes the postulate that permits an intelligibility—if always an unstable one. Inverting Michael Taussig's argument that history may function like sorcery (1987:366), one might say that witchcraft in Buli comes to function as history. As people probe the aporias of an attack, it is made intelligible by being linked to previous *gua* events, making them intelligible in new ways and enabling the creation of "event histories," allowing the transport of what is incomprehensible into a new kind of uncanny regularity. In this way, Sami's body became the site of inscription for an event history that aligned, in one optical continuum, a long series of attacks by Lolos and his sister, Yantima. And this perspective suggested that the entire community might be in peril.

## Event History (Part 1): The Death of Karo

The most recent of these attacks, the memory of which was still raw in the minds of many local people, had led to the death of Karo a year or so before Sami's madness in 1993. Karo was not a direct relative of Sami's. He was, however, the brother-in-law of Tali, the oldest member of the Guslaw family, and Sami was Tali's classificatory daughter (FBDD). When during her outburst Sami shouted that Lolos wanted to kill all members of the Guslaw and Batawi houses, she created a link between three deaths, arranging them within a single order that made terrible sense. The death of Sami's father, Gora, in 1984 and the death of her husband's father, Mani, in 1986 were linked, through Sami's own illness, to the death in 1991 of Karo (see fig. 23). An event history, where witchcraft reconstructed both kinship ties and ties to the New Order state, was in the making.

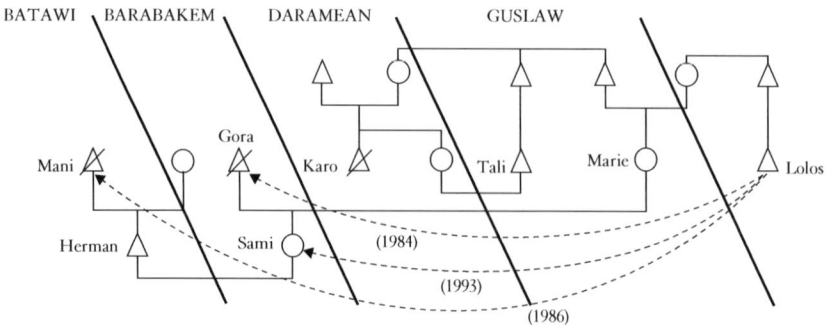

Figure 23. The deaths of Gora, Mani, and Karo connected.

Karo Daramean died in mid-December 1991. His death was not easy—"not easy" (*gampang pa*) being a euphemism used to convey the suspicion that his death was caused by sorcery or witchcraft. Karo's death was also "not easy" in the literal sense that it was an unusually drawn-out, painful, and in the end shocking death. Karo's illness began when his abdomen began to swell. Then he developed painful black marks on his body and got a fever, before he gradually became delirious and his personality began to change. The resident nurse from the district health clinic (I. *puskesmas*) diagnosed his illness as chronic or "old" malaria (I. *malaria tua*) and prescribed the usual set of blue, yellow, and orange pills. Several healers (*sowsów*) had tried unsuccessfully to cure him, and they all agreed that his illness was caused by a *gua*.

Karo identified Lolos as the witch who had attacked him. "My child ate me in the garden" (*fanók ca nan ya poléi bet i*), Karo had whispered one day to those fanning his fever-ridden body. He had then related how Lolos had attacked him and beaten him for a long time. During the attack, so Karo said, Lolos had constantly changed appearance, assuming the shape of a variety of animal familiars. First he was a dog, then a shark, then a scorpion, and, finally, a praying mantis. The account of the beating was substantiated by the many black marks on Karo's body, which resembled bruises.

Lolos was a sturdy man in his late thirties, known for his fishing and iron-forging skills. Until the mid-1980s, when he was first suspected of being a *gua*, Lolos had actively participated in both community rituals and church activities. He was Karo's classificatory nephew (FZSS), a relation (*fanó*) that is regarded as similar to the relationship with one's own child (see fig. 24).

The village authorities had attempted to appeal to this kinship relation to mediate between the two. As is customary in cases of witchcraft illness, the main demand of Karo's family had been that the accused witch should come to cure the victim. The local authorities sought to enforce this demand. In what Lolos must have perceived as an intimidating visit, the village head, his deputy, the Christian

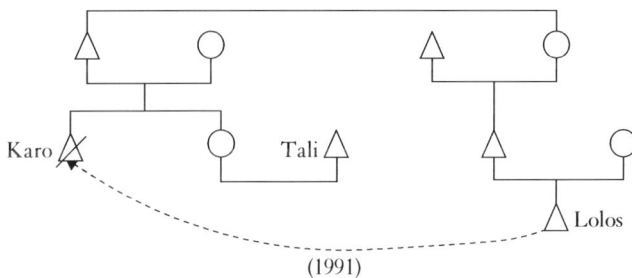

**Figure 24.** The family relation between Karo and Lolos.

minister, and the *babinsa* had turned up at Lolos's home to compel him to attempt a cure. Lolos had initially refused, saying that he was neither a witch nor a healer, and that he knew no cures. After some coaxing, however, an agreement had been reached. As a Christian, Lolos was prepared to make a donation to the church (*topa derma*) and swear his innocence before God. He would also speak a Christian prayer into a glass. Such a prayer is a Christian adaptation of a common healing practice known in Buli as *táwar*, in which a healer whispers a magical formula into a glass of water that the sick person then drinks. This was a solution that all those involved could accept. Lolos could maintain his innocence and emphasize his identity as a Christian, while Karo's family was content that the authorities had managed to sway the man they suspected of being a *gua* to at least try to cure Karo.

The next night, Lolos had gone to the minister's house to whisper his Christian prayer into a glass. The glass was then covered with a Bible and carried in procession to Karo's house. Entering the house, the village head and his deputy, Kenari, had asked Karo if he recognized them. "Yes, you are the village head and the deputy," Karo had replied. "We are not trying to force you," Kenari had continued, "but Lolos has prepared this medicine. Are you prepared to drink it?" "Yes, I will drink it," Karo had responded, and began struggling into an upright position where he would be able to drink. With the help of relatives who supported him, Karo managed to drink most of the water in the glass before he had to lie down again.

Kenari was just about to accept the betel nut the family was offering him, now that the official business was over, when Karo's body suddenly began to convulse violently. The minister and the village head were quickly summoned from the guest room at the front of the house, but they had barely entered the room when Karo stopped convulsing and died. As cries of dismay were heard by those outside—who were all aware that Karo had just imbibed the water prepared by Lolos—pandemonium broke out. This appeared to be proof beyond any doubt that Lolos truly was a witch. His protestations that he was an upstanding Christian had been revealed as part of the "hiding" (*gogan*) at which *gua* are so adept. His Christianity, it was now plain, was merely a disguise (*mef*), in line with the disguises witches use when assuming the shape of an animal or a motorbike, or when employing the faces of other people. "This is going to be major trouble (*masalah mamágal*)," Kenari remembered thinking as he left the house that night, where Kora's relatives were in grief and uproar. Subsequent events would prove him right.

On the third and final night of the burial ceremony for Karo, four women from the throng of mourners had begun pelting Lolos's house with stones. A crowd of men from Karo's immediate family had then entered the house in an unsuccessful

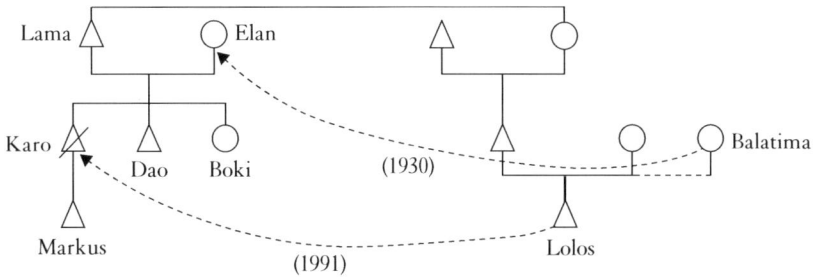

**Figure 25.** The death of Karo's mother.

attempt to find and kill Lolos. Their outrage had a special urgency precipitated by a series of previous attacks. This was not the first time Karo's family had been victimized by Lolos's family. Karo and his siblings, Dao and Boki, had seen both of their parents die following *gua* attacks. Elan, their mother, had been attacked and eaten in the 1930s by Lolos's stepmother Balatima (see fig. 25). According to Karo's siblings, the assault had been motivated by Balatima's envy of the fishing abilities of their father, Lama, who consistently brought home rich catches. The repeated attacks by Lolos's family on Dao and Boki's family were simply intolerable.

## Witches Know No Kin

The resentment that appeared to have caused Lolos's attack on Karo went back several years. At that time Lolos had opened a small trading store next to his house, where he sold consumer items such sugar, salt, soap, and a small selection of clothing. He got the shop items on credit from Menjid, a merchant of Chinese descent in Buli Serani, and sold them at a slightly higher price in Waiflí. On several occasions Markus, the son of Karo, had taken food items from the store, promising to pay when he had the money. Whether it was because others were doing the same or because of general mismanagement, Lolos eventually had to close his shop, as his capital to buy new stock steadily decreased. This pattern of "in business, then bust" is not an unusual one for entrepreneurial ventures in Buli. In 1992 there were four small shops in Waiflí, all owned and run by outsiders. From time to time local villagers would try to set up shops that sold salt and other cheap, basic items before moving on to goods that required more capital input, but they never lasted long. Family members would ask for credit or simply avail themselves of the goods until the stock was gone and there was no capital to restock the shelves. As a result, commercial trade in Buli was completely in the hands of nonlocal people who had few or no family relations in the village, and who were therefore unbound by the moral pressures that accompany exchange relations between relatives (as discussed in chapter 7).

In the view of Karo's wife and children, it was the moral dilemma of these exchange relations that brought on the attack by Lolos. When his shop closed, Markus owed Lolos money for a shirt and numerous food items, and he had still not paid his debt (*yage*) when the attack happened. As the "brother" (FMBSS) of Lolos, Markus was in a good position to ask (*dor*) for these things, and it was not clear whether the shirt and the groceries were to be considered among the host of items that change hands in Buli daily as part of the give-and-take of everyday life, or whether they were commercial items that had changed hands as part of a monetary transaction. It was from the greedy outlook on life that characterizes all *gua*, or so ran the argument of Karo's family, that Lolos had refused to acknowledge the kinship relations between himself and Markus. So instead of seeing the unpaid items as part of the host of exchanged goods that circulate between relatives, Lolos had insisted on monetary payment in return. When this was not forthcoming, he had vented his anger by attacking Markus's father, Karo.

Lolos, who was aware that this version of the story behind Karo's death was being circulated widely in the village, vehemently denied to me that it held any truth: "We are brothers (*tenou*), and we have always borrowed (*bawi*) from each other and helped each other, so why should I get angry because of something like that?" He argued that he had never expected payment for the goods, and that as far as he was concerned, the items were part of the normal helping and sharing atmosphere that ideally pertains between relatives. The break had only occurred with the outrageous accusation leveled against him: "People of the same house (*ebai pusa*) do not eat each other."

Kinship relations, I would argue, are called upon as one of the many means of making witchcraft intelligible, as a moral language to condemn a particular attack or to deny it. "Witches do not recognize relatives (*gua rto bangsá pa*)," the family of victims will complain. "People of the same house do not eat each other," an accused will retort. Family relationships are part of the discursive efforts that seek to make witchcraft attacks intelligible—although, inevitably and predictably, such efforts are doomed to fail. For kinship does not explain anything when it comes to witchcraft. In Buli the relationship between witch and victim, if one exists, only marks a site of the uncanny. Witchcraft tears at kinship relations, cutting them and making them impossible; but it does not do so in a predictable manner.[4] This unpredictability confirms what people in Buli already know: that *gua* attacks can come from anywhere and anyone, kin as well as nonkin. If anything, an attack is most likely to come from someone of your own age and sex, your "brother" (if you are a man) or your "sister" (if you are a woman)—from someone, essentially, like yourself. In that sense, witchcraft reminds everyone who accuses someone else of witchcraft that the witch, the ultimate other, is most likely to be someone like themselves (Siegel 2006).

## The Violence of the Law

Lolos decided to press charges against the four stone-throwing women for willful destruction of property. His decision to do so was, in itself, the result of some pressure from the police. In particular, the deputy police chief in Buli Serani was emphatic that Lolos should stand his ground. In the weeks following the attack, the deputy chief often came to Lolos's house because the atmosphere in the village remained very hostile, and only his frequent evening visits prevented the situation from becoming violent. People suspected that Lolos, as witches are likely to do, was using magic to sway the police to come over to his side. Rumor had it that Lolos smoked continuously when the police visited him as a way of disguising his whispered magical formulas. As one woman put it, "He is using magic to 'steal the inside' of the police, so that they feel sorry for him (*in pei lalao, bo nyal ulor na, bod si masie i*)." The concern of the police and military with the conflicts erupting from *gua* attacks was, however, most likely related to development plans that were under way in the district: Roads were to be constructed, new transmigration sites were to be built, and a mine would soon be opened. The local authorities in Buli were eager to ensure that this newfound economic interest in the area on the part of the central government would not be thwarted by local behavior that was considered incompatible with modernization and development. An example had to be made to show the limits of state tolerance, and a court case would serve this purpose admirably. The police charged the four women in connection with the property damage to Lolos's house, and a court date was set for mid-1992.

People in Buli were flabbergasted and outraged. The state, it seemed, was intent on protecting witches and punishing witchcraft victims instead. As the date of the trial drew near, one of the accused complained bitterly: "First, we get beaten up and eaten by witches, and then we get beaten up, jailed, and prosecuted by the police. It would be much better to live in Iraq than here." The reference to the first invasion of Iraq in January 1991 by a coalition of twenty-eight nations expressed the strong sense of being the victim of a war that was being waged on two fronts: with the *gua*, and with the police. For people who strongly associated state modernity with the disappearance of all devils—*setan, iblis,* and *gua*—it was a moral outrage that the state would want to prosecute those who had already suffered on account of witchcraft.

The court case was as unprecedented as it was frightening. For over a decade no charges from the district of Maba had been brought before the regency court in Soa Sio on the island of Tidore. Then, in 1992 alone, no fewer than six cases from the Maba district were put before the regency court, for offenses ranging from assault to bigamy. Two of these cases were direct results of *gua* attacks. This increase was not accidental. It reflected a new willingness on the part of the local authorities to use the law as a means to stamp out unwanted signs of backwardness, an expression no doubt of the invigorated efforts of the New Order regime at the time to increase political control by intervening in ever-more-minute social matters, even at the lowest levels of society.[5]

The case was finally brought before the court in October 1992, after not only Lolos but also the four accused women from the Guslaw patriline, along with the family's ritual leader, Tali, had been forced to wait for more than a month in Tidore for a vacancy in the court schedule. This waiting period spent in costly and foreign surroundings ruined the two families financially, besides exerting a heavy emotional strain on both sides. In the end, the court gave the women a four-month suspended sentence and put them on a four-year good behavior bond. However, the court rejected Lolos's damage claim of 300,000 rupiah (180 USD), finding the amount disproportionately high.

## Event History (Part 2): New Order Cures

Although the court case had been an intimidating demonstration of state power, it was unclear what exactly it had demonstrated. Concentrating as the verdict did on the issue of property destruction, it did not settle the issue that people thought it might have—namely, the question of whether Lolos was a *gua* or not. As it happened, events transpiring back in Buli already seemed to provide their own proof. As one man told me, "The reality of witchcraft will always reveal itself (*gabe gua, musti ni kenyataan*)." What he meant was that a particular case of illness or death that people suspect is due to witchcraft will be revealed by a new case in the immediate future. It is a telling aspect of the aporias of witchcraft that only witchcraft itself can truly prove the reality of witchcraft. Since every witchcraft event is uncannily devoid of meaning, its intelligibility is established only within a broader event history. The reality of witchcraft is revealed by more witchcraft: when it comes to a phenomenon about which humans can only guess, repetition is tragically the only proof one can hope to obtain.

In quick succession between April and May 1992—while everyone was waiting for the October court date—three men in Buli died from witchcraft. In two of these cases suspicion centered on Lolos's sister, Yantima. During the burial ceremony for the third victim, a man named Hokniel, the victim's classificatory aunt (*fofai*), Pineki, suffered a cataleptic seizure while serving tea for the guests.

Her seizure was immediately ascribed to Yantima, and three young men (a son and two sons-in-law) went to Yantima straightaway to demand that she come and cure Pineki. Yantima, of course, remembered only too well the disastrous result of her brother's attempt to cure Karo six months earlier, and she refused. Later that same night, the men returned and assaulted Yantima, forcing her to go to Pineki's house. Despite a long evening of taunts and threats of physical violence, Yantima attempted no cure that night, and managed to talk her way out of the house.

The next day was a Sunday. But, quite unusually, the church remained empty, as people boycotted the sermon in protest. They demanded that the authorities take action against the wave of witchcraft assaults that had rolled over the village in the preceding months. This was a "war" that the authorities did not acknowledge. "What is the point of going to church? What good is the government?" one man asked rhetorically. After repeated appeals, the police chief eventually arrived from the district capital to personally verify the strangeness of Pineki's affliction. With the police visit, the highly charged atmosphere in the village calmed down somewhat and continued to cool as Pineki began to recover over the following week. Pineki herself afterward recounted how Yantima had returned to her house later in the night after the group of men had tried to force her to cure Pineki. On this second visit, Yantima had assumed her *gua* form as a flying figure with a strangely invisible face. Emerging from the rafters in the ceiling, the creature had descended onto the plaited mat on the floor where Pineki lay and had proceeded to tug on each of her limbs to reset the joints, only to disappear afterward without speaking a word. This simple maneuver had been enough to cure Pineki, and the account convinced people of the value of intimidating and shaming suspected *gua* into performing a cure.

Less than two weeks later, Hengki fell ill. By now it was late May, well into the campaign period for the 1992 general elections that lay just around the corner. Hengki, who was the husband of my adopted older sister, collapsed not far from my house one evening, complaining of unbearable pains in his chest and stomach. He had just returned from the garden, drunk on palm wine, and had stopped by my house late at night to demand that I feed him. I was so irritated by his drunken escapades and brazen demands for food that I refused and sent him on his way home, much to his consternation. The next morning I learned that he had collapsed a few minutes' walk from my house. Many people were initially skeptical about Hengki's claim that he was suffering the effects of witchcraft (*ungan*). Hengki was known for his love of palm wine, and he could be found most afternoons idling near someone's sugar palm (*nau*), waiting for the owner to come and tap it so that Hengki could entice him to share the wine. His wife, in particular, suspected him of wanting to pass off what was most likely a severe hangover as witchcraft. "Who would want to eat him?" she pronounced loudly, the sexual innuendo delighting the bystanders. But when Hengki's illness worsened over the next few days, people became concerned. It is well known that the sourness of palm wine often acts catalytically on wounds inside a person's body, particularly those hidden wounds left on the liver after a *gua* attack. It is for this very reason that palm wine is often used when administering medicine: palm wine carries the curing potions directly to the hidden wound. Then, ominously, Hengki regained his memory about the attack. He recounted how he had been preparing sago in the forest with his five-year-old son when he had suddenly been attacked by Lolos and his brother-in-law, Sepa (Yantima's husband). While Lolos had tried to drown him in a small pool of water, Sepa had speared him in the chest with a sharpened sago branch.

The *babinsa* called Lolos and Sepa to Hengki's sickbed. As before, the alleged witch and his accomplice, were asked to *táwar* a glass of water by whispering a spell or a prayer into it. Lolos had serious misgivings because his last attempt to cure Karo the previous year had failed so dramatically. But the election campaign was in full swing, and it was a high political priority that social calm prevail. The *babinsa* was therefore eager to settle the matter quickly, and he hoped that a curing ritual might achieve this. Under intense pressure from the officer, Lolos and Sepa eventually agreed and prepared a glass of water that Hengki duly drank. The forceful action taken by the *babinsa* suggested to the people of the village that the authorities were beginning to recognize the Buli predicament with witchcraft, and that they supported what was really a reasonable request: that the *gua* should cure its victim. Hengki recovered during the following week, and the New Order seemed to be living up to its promise of helping people deal with the *gua* problem. With the imminent 1992 parliamentary election, however, the constant social disturbance that witchcraft seemed to spawn on a continuous basis in Waiflí was becoming an embarrassment for the authorities in Buli Serani, and the approach taken by the *babinsa* was soon countered. When the police and commanding army officer arrived from Buli Serani later the same day, they sternly admonished people that 9 June, the day of the election, was only two days away, and that no further trouble would be tolerated. All talk of witchcraft had to cease immediately.

## Event History (Part 3): Elections, Petitions, and Evictions

The authorities' intolerance of social disturbances of any kind had its origin in recent events in the national political arena. The campaign of the 1992 parliamentary

election, the fifth under the New Order, had already been marred by scattered
protests across Java. These protests sprang from, among other things, the corruption scandal surrounding the monopoly on cloves secured by the Cloves Support and Trading Board, known as the BPPC. Back in 1990, Hutomo Mandala
Putra—the youngest son of President Suharto, popularly known as "Tommy"—
had managed to obtain ministerial support to establish the BPPC, thereby in effect monopolizing the market for cloves. As cloves were an important cash crop
throughout eastern Indonesia and a vital ingredient in Indonesian *kretek* cigarettes, the monopoly meant that Tommy and his powerful business cronies could
control prices and siphon off large sums of money from the billion-dollar Indonesian tobacco industry. By February 1992, however, just four months before the
election, the clove market collapsed, and Tommy had been forced to admit that
the BPPC, allegedly established to protect small farmers against price fluctua-
tions, had failed to secure the price (Schwarz 1994:156). This failure on the part
of the BPPC made it dramatically clear to rural people throughout the country
that New Order corruption and cronyism could also affect them directly, and
made the BPPC scandal political dynamite, so close to the election. The smallest
of the three political parties contesting the election, the Indonesian Democratic
Party (PDI), had accordingly made the fight against corruption a central issue
in a bold challenge to the ruling Golkar Party, which was controlled by Suharto
(Hill 1992:3). This challenge had already resulted in clashes between PDI members and Golkar demonstrators during the election campaign. The ruling Golkar Party eventually won the election comfortably, gaining—as usual—roughly
70 percent of the valid votes. But voices of dissent were beginning to be heard,
Suharto was increasingly struggling with the army for political control, and the
issue of who might succeed him as the president of Indonesia was starting to be
openly discussed (Bertrand 1996).

The general perception that the hegemony of the Golkar Party and Suharto
was under threat translated into a special but also somewhat vague sense of ap-
prehension (Barker 2001; Siegel 1998). In the lead-up to the 1992 election campaign, the army (I. *ABRI*) therefore instructed all its territorial commands in the
provinces to remain especially vigilant against the activities "of certain groups"
(I. *pihak tertentu*) that would seek to further their own interests by causing trouble during the election (Honna 2001:63). The police received similar instructions. The directives were mainly aimed against former political prisoners and
ex-Communists, but the fear of subversion was so ill defined that "vigilance" (I.
*kewaspadaan*) could be directed toward virtually anything. The fear of subversion
accordingly took on a life of its own in the disciplinary practices of state representatives (Heryanto 1999). For the army and police officers stationed in Buli, who
had no political suspects to direct their vigilance toward, the importance of being

"vigilant" translated into an intolerance of witchcraft accusations as a particular disturbance of the peace and of social harmony. The competition between the army and the police over who was most "vigilant" set the scene for a new level of state intervention into local village concerns about the *gua*.

Hengki eventually recovered from his witchcraft illness (*ungan*). But as soon as he was well enough, he began campaigning to gather signatures for a petition to oust Lolos and his family from Waiflí, a petition that he submitted a few days later to the chief officer of the district army division (I. *koramil*). The petition was an attempt to translate the reality of witchcraft into the language of the state. By demanding that the government remove the two people who were currently under the strongest suspicion of witchcraft in the village, to restore peace and order to the local community, the petition turned the logic of the New Order obsession with social harmony against the establishment itself. Social harmony could be maintained if the state authorities removed the two witches from the village. Witches, the petition declared, were the real threat to social harmony, development, and the peaceful electoral reproduction of New Order rule. The great majority of household heads in the village duly signed the petition: more than 90 heads of families, out of a total of 107 households in the village. Even the village head and the resident minister had signed.

In response to the petition, the district army officer (I. *koramil*) called a meeting on the evening of 14 June 1992. Well before the *koramil* arrived, and the meeting could begin, people were already gathered in anxious anticipation. While the men jostled for space on rickety benches under a temporary roof by the side of the path where the meeting was held, the women sat on the ground in small groups at the edge of the meeting area. Meanwhile, the army officer, the village head, and the minister were seated on chairs behind a small table with tea and a dish of cakes. The *koramil* began the meeting with a stern speech, during which he emphasized that all those present were people with a religion. They were so, he emphasized, because the state ideology, Pancasila, demanded that people must believe in God (I. *Tuhan yang Maha Esa*). All tribes and peoples (I. *suku*) of Indonesia were bound by Pancasila, he asserted, with its dictum of one God and its ideals of social harmony and equality. The order ensured by Pancasila, the *koramil* went on, also meant that the citizens of all tribes (I. *suku*) could freely settle wherever they wished. "This petition," he continued in a firm voice, waving the document with its many signatures in the air, "not only goes against the spirit of Pancasila. It is also a stumbling block to development (I. *hambatan buat pembangunan*). We, the government, are busy bringing development to Buli." He then drove his point home, in no uncertain terms:

> Why, just last week I myself supervised the unloading of the first bulldozer that will build the road to Bicoli. But you people are more concerned about wasting both your own and our time with matters such as these. Every single one of you who has signed this petition now faces a risk (I. *risiko*). I hope you realize this. For it is not in the spirit of Pancasila. The regent (I. *bupati*) [of Central Halmahera] will arrive soon from Tidore on an official visit, and I very much expect that this will be the last time we are going to hear about this matter [of witchcraft].

Then, one by one, all of the men who had signed the petition were called upon by name, and had to confirm that they indeed were signatories as heads of their household (I. *kepala rumah tangga*). Significantly, the signatories also included Taro, the half brother of Lolos and Yantima, whom we already met in chapter 1 and who had signed after pressure from his wife, whose brother, Gora, had died in 1984 because of witchcraft attributed to Lolos and Yantima. The village, in other words, showed an extraordinary degree of consensus in this matter, and no one retracted their signature.

Emphasizing again that this was the last time the authorities wanted to hear of these matters, the *koramil* informed the assembly that he had talked to Lolos and Yantima, and they had declared themselves willing to move.[6] A murmur of approval rippled through the crowd. Yet in return for having persuaded Lolos to move away from his house, the *koramil* said, he expected full cooperation from the villagers: "The next time the village head (I. *kepala desa*) summons you to do communal work (I. *gotong royong*), I expect all of you to be there. When the paths need clearing or the grass around the village meeting center (I. *balai desa*) needs cutting, I expect all of you to be there. I do not want you to be off hiding in your gardens as usual (I. *seperti biasa*)."

People in the assembled crowd emphatically nodded their full approval, and there were smiles all around. No one took offense at the patronizing tone of the speech, which addressed the villagers as recalcitrant children. Almost on the contrary, the petition was itself an appeal to the paternalism of New Order rule,[7] pleading with its local authorities for help and protection. It essentially asked the authorities, in the formal language of New Order bureaucracy, to live up to their own image as the paternal protector of the people (I. *masyarakat*) by recognizing and dealing with witchcraft as a state reality. The *koramil*'s acceptance of the petition was therefore perceived locally as a great victory. An official and administrative solution appeared to have been arranged, and the *koramil* received thunderous applause when his speech finally ended.

The accommodation that people felt they had reached with the *koramil* about the petition in June 1992 turned out to be short-lived, however. In November 1992, rumors began circulating that the police planned to charge all ninety signatories of the petition with slander and vilification (I. *fitnah*). Coming so soon after the court case in October 1992, which had been such a tremendous financial burden on the families of both Lolos and the four women charged with damaging his house, this rumor caused a great deal of anxiety. The costs of travel, lodging, and food on such a trip would be more than most families could ever afford, and so the rumors represented a formidable financial threat. The deputy police chief described to me, in private, that the aim of the charge was to "teach people a lesson" (I. *kasih tobat*). This lesson in state power made the social unrest surrounding *gua* accusations "stand in" for a general lack of involvement in the project of development.[8] Eventually, the issue was resolved in the same way that most such state-society issues in Indonesia are handled: through graft. In late January 1993, the police began to hint that individuals could withdraw their names from the list for the payment of an "administrative fee." The following day, after about forty people had paid in excess of 200,000 rupiah (120 USD) all told, the charges were unceremoniously dropped.

## Sami's Madness Revisited

Sami's madness in early January 1993 occurred while this collective court case still hung unresolved in the air, and while the Guslaw family finances were still suffering in the aftermath of the trial in October 1992. Hence, her loud accusations of witchcraft grew out of a particular historical moment when a recent spate of witchcraft attacks over the previous year had become entangled in various ways with the modernist imaginaries and the corrupt practices of New Order rule. At this historical moment, people in Buli had reason to believe they could hold the local authorities to the implicit promises of New Order modernity, even though this promise had failed several times in the months before Sami went mad.

In the early 1990s, people in Buli were looking loyally but with increasing disappointment to New Order ideology and its state representatives for new kinds of answers to the aporias of witchcraft. In the eighteen months between the death of Karo in 1991 and Sami's madness in early 1993, there were five deaths and seven cases of serious illness in which witchcraft played a major role. Ironically, the establishment of witchcraft as a governmental *problematique* in Michel Foucault's sense—shaped by a combination of state fears of political subversion and a historically motivated loyalty to New Order ideology by people in Buli—seemed to generate more witch attacks than anyone could remember. At the historical height of the New Order, witchcraft appeared to be as intense as ever.

## Witchcraft's Reinvention in the Early New Order

The New Order's complicity in the production and reproduction of witchcraft through its very attempts to eradicate it was not restricted to the 1990s, however. In fact, it can be traced back to the earliest days of the New Order in Buli. In the late 1960s, only a couple of years after 1967, when General Suharto became Indonesia's second president, following Sukarno, New Order began to reorganize local religion throughout Indonesia (Aragon 2000; Atkinson 1983; Keane 2007:105; Spyer 1996). In Buli it was New Order repression of witchcraft that ironically produced the first and so far only self-confessed witch in Buli.

Kenari told me his account of what happened. Kenari had become the deputy village head in the mid-1960s, when he was still in his early twenties. He had begun junior high school (I. *SMP*) some years earlier, but had had to drop out after two years when economic crisis and hyperinflation hit Indonesia in the early 1960s, and his parents became unable to pay the school fees. Even without a high school diploma, Kenari still was one of the best-educated people in Waiflí at the time, and in spite of his youth he was therefore an obvious candidate for the job. One day in 1969, someone had found a *faga* on a nearby beach. A *faga* is a spirit shrine. It is usually a small wooden or bamboo platform on stilts, sometimes covered with a sago-leaf roof, and it is used to present offerings to a variety of spirits, including guardian spirits (*suang*), *jin*, or "wild" spirits (such as *meki* or *putiana*). A *faga* usually contains a plate for tobacco and betel as well as implements associated with the spirits—chiefly the magical roots (*aiwáo*), a knife, a shield, and sometimes a wooden effigy (*táfal*) of the animal associated with the particular spirit (see fig. 26).

One presents offerings to the spirits at the *faga* in return for help in hunting or fishing expeditions, divination and curing, or for magical protection in war or against sorcery and witchcraft. However, a *faga* may also be used to ask the *jin* or forest spirits for help to sorcerize (*payao*) other people. A *faga* is therefore always ambivalent. On that day in 1969, Kenari's own brother and an elderly woman were ill with something that looked like sorcery, and so the discovery caused some worry.

This local concern became significant in light of the mounting political anxiety that characterized the period during and after the nation's transition to the New Order. The late 1960s was a period when animists throughout Indonesia

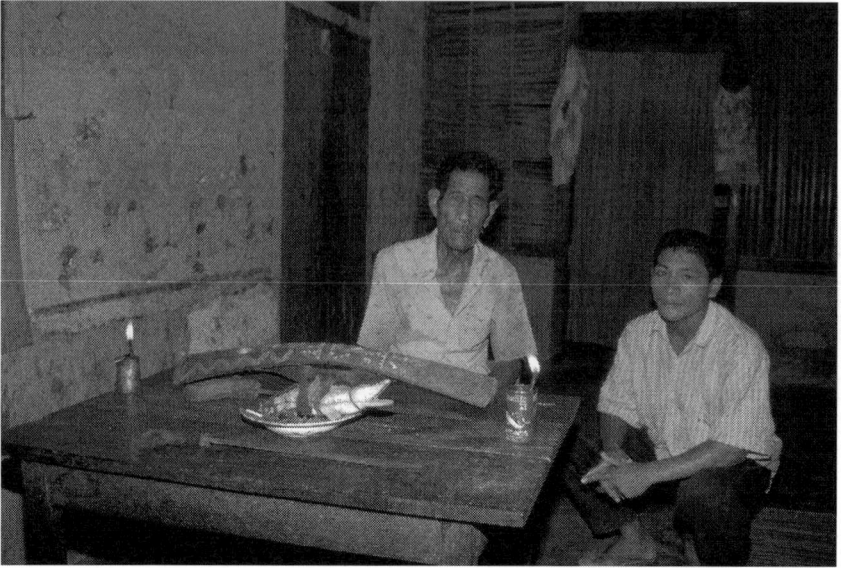

**Figure 26.** Bulia Raja and his grandson with the effigy of the crocodile,
a guardian spirit (*suang*). 1994. Photo by author.

were under intense pressure to convert to one of the monotheistic world religions
as a sign of their commitment to the state ideology of Pancasila. Thus, in the early
years of the New Order, the attitude toward animism was beginning to change
from finding it merely heathen to condemning it as unpatriotic as well. The force
of this argument came out of the way in which the first principle of Pancasila,
belief in one God, became enrolled after 1967 in the New Order's paranoia concerning Communism. President Suharto had come to power in the aftermath of
a series of massacres in 1965–66, during which perhaps as many as five hundred
thousand people were killed on suspicion of being members of the Indonesian
Communist Party (PKI) (Cribb and Brown 1995:106). Indeed, the specter of
Communism gained the status of a "master narrative" for the political hegemony
of the New Order (Heryanto 2006:8; Siegel 1998). As Communism was designated as the main political, but also highly elusive, threat to national stability, all
aspects of Socialism, including its atheism, came to be seen as politically subver-
sive (Stange 1986:80). In the 1960s, Buli and Halmahera were far too marginal
in national politics to be involved in the massacre of suspected PKI members.
Nevertheless, the fear of Communism in Halmahera spilled over into a new kind
of political suspicion of animism, as being somehow akin to atheism in its denial
of monotheism (Aragon 2000). By the late 1960s considerable pressure to convert
to either Christianity or Islam was being exerted on those Buli men and women

who, during the 1930s, had so vociferously expressed their resentment against Christianity (see chapter 4). The church historian James Haire has described the reigning sentiment at the time: "Although these provisions [to politically force animists to adopt one of the five world religions mandated by the New Order] were not strictly enforced in many parts of the nation, in Halmahera they caused considerable fear among the pre-literary religionists, who were therefore inclined to enter one of the religions available in the North Moluccas, Protestantism or Islam" (1981:66).

A look at the numbers seems to bear out this observation. Between 1965 and 1979 the number of registered and baptized members of the main Protestant church in Halmahera, the Christian Evangelical Church of Halmahera (GMIH), rose from around sixty thousand to over one hundred thousand. Although much of this rise derived from either natural demographic increases or immigration from other parts of North Maluku, Haire still estimates that between twenty thousand and twenty-four thousand animists converted during this period (1981:67).

Political suspicion of animism and the concerns in the village about the two ongoing cases of sorcery-related illness congealed into common outrage at the discovery of the spirit shrine (*faga*) in 1969. Although a *faga* could have many purposes, the New Order understanding that all animism was politically suspect added force to local sorcery concerns, and the village head and his staff began an official investigation to find out who owned the *faga*. By 1969, all but a few die-hard animists had converted. Among those who still stood by their animist beliefs was a man called Mangga. His grandfather had been one of the men who, in the 1930s, had followed Dudu Barabakem to the island of Cef in disgust at the lies of the Christian missionaries (see chapter 4). But quite apart from his being an ardent anti-Christian, Mangga had also been accused of sorcery. When Mangga's eight-year-old son revealed that he and his parents had recently been fishing near the place where the *faga* was found, Mangga immediately came under suspicion. A unit of the army (ABRI) happened to be patrolling in Buli at the time, and the Christian army commander, a man from Manado on the neighboring island of Sulawesi, authorized the village head to search Mangga's house. In the bedroom they found another *faga* suspended from the ceiling, in which Mangga kept various magical implements (*jijól*), such as a plate, some magical roots, and a knife.

Such *faga* are essential to traditional masculinity in Buli. They are where the animal spirit guardians (*suang*) are honored and appeased through ritual offerings if family members, as frequently happens, break the food taboos (*momóan*) associated with them. The guardian spirits also underwrite fighting magic and hunting magic, and well into the 1960s they were still used in shamanistic divination rites called *famamá* and *famtúlo*. Finally, the animal spirit guardians, along with the ancestor spirits (*smengit*), are traditionally regarded as the main protectors against

Figure 27. A *faga* suspended in the privacy of a bedroom. 1997. Photo by author.

*gua* witchcraft (see chapter 4). The guardian spirits are therefore crucial to Buli life and livelihood, and many Buli men still keep such *faga* in the privacy of their bedrooms (see fig. 27), even though it is frowned upon and in spite of their conversion to Christianity.

## Mangga's March

Everyone in Buli was, of course, well aware of the fact that animal spirits were honored in secret by most Buli Christians, and Mangga had tried to appeal to this "public secret" (Taussig 1999). He protested that the *faga* was not used for sorcery but to ask his guardian spirit for help in hunting. To no avail. In the moral zeal that arose under the gaze of the Manado army officer, the implements were confiscated as proof of sorcery. In other words, Mangga's animism became, in itself, evidence of sorcery. And under the ardent supervision of the Christian army officer, the charge of sorcery was extended to include an accusation of witchcraft as well.

The following day, Mangga was forced to parade through the entire village. The dried coconut leaves (*mar*) that had decorated his *faga* were hung around his neck. In his right hand he was forced to hold a bamboo tube with palm wine, and in his left hand the small pandanus-leaf offering plate (*buéling*) that had been discovered in the *faga*. As he was marched through the village, Mangga was made to declare loudly and repeatedly: "People on the landside, people on the seaside, come out, all of you! I am Mangga, and I am a witch and a sorcerer." The army officer had written the text for Mangga's public confession, insisting that the admissions be translated and shouted out in Buli rather than in Indonesian, to have maximum impact. Then he had made sure Mangga knew the whole text by heart.

At the end of the involuntary parade, which bore an ironic resemblance to the path of Christ on the way to his crucifixion, Mangga—once again upon the instructions of the army officer—was forced to wade into the sea until the water reached his chest, and to throw away the implements there. Mangga, it seemed, was being made to jettison the "implements of witchcraft" in a way that also mimicked a Christian baptism.

In one swift ceremonial move, animism had come to be equated not only with sorcery, but also with witchcraft. Despite the fact that Mangga had never been suspected of being a *gua*, in the politically anxious times of the early New Order, his animist beliefs were enough to brand him as one. As tradition became shoehorned into being "proof" of witchcraft, the abandonment of witchcraft came to be framed as part and parcel of a conversion to Christianity. This invented ritual made good sense in Buli. Motivated as it was by New Order developmentalist zeal and political paranoia, it helped shaped Buli expectations of New Order modernity, because it replayed in ritual form the expectations, harbored since the early decades of the century, that Christianity would entail an end to witchcraft. The ritual also introduced something new, however. It framed the idea that witchcraft and tradition were overlapping, even possibly identical, and that the rejection of tradition through an acceptance of state-orchestrated, monotheistic modernity could also mean the eradication of witchcraft. During Mangga's cheerless procession, tradition as a whole was demonized in a way that was altogether new.

## Witchcraft and the Awkward Demonization of Tradition

Mangga was the first and, as far as I am aware, the only self-confessed witch that Buli has seen. The application of state power to compel a confession, followed by publicly parading the witch through the village in a performance of self-confession, had the ironic effect of making witchcraft visible and concrete in an authoritative way that went beyond the reasonable doubts that had otherwise always surrounded witchcraft. It did so through a chain of logic whereby the threat of Communism attached itself to animism, and all animism became a form of witchcraft. In the process, features of tradition, such as the ritual honoring of the spirits that conventionally provided protection against the *gua*, became demonized and associated with the very thing against which they conventionally gave protection. Mangga's protests that the *faga* in his bedroom honored his guardian spirits were ignored, because the *suang* in Christian and bureaucratic thinking alike became a *setan*, an evil spirit, and therefore associated with witchcraft. Mangga's parade was the beginning of what became, in Buli, the irony of, and the disappointment with, New Order rule—namely, that it made witchcraft real in new ways while at the same time making people more vulnerable to it.

In spite of all this, the demonization of animism by New Order modernity still made an awkward kind of sense. Nahor, for instance, who used to work in the Office for Religion (I. *Kantor Agama*) in Buli, told me in 1997 that when the last Buli people converted to Christianity in 1972 the pressure had been immense. People who refused to convert were told that nobody would bury them when they died, and that they therefore would not get to *sorogá*, the place of their ancestors (see chapter 4). Without burial a deceased person would not be able to transform into an ancestor spirit (*smengit*), but would remain a wandering spirit called *mum- ing*. Worse, the lack of a burial would put the recalcitrant animists in a struc- tural position that was similar to that of witches (*gua*). In pre-Christian times, a person proven to be a witch by ordeal would be killed by being weighted down with stones and dropped overboard far out to sea.[9] The reason for drowning the presumed *gua* was that the blood of a witch should not be spilt on the ground, this being meant to prevent the *gua* spirit from returning to haunt the village (ZCR 1922 [71]:3). In customary thought, the deliberate omission of burial was, in other words, reserved for witches. It was through this kind of equivalence be- tween witchcraft and animism that the church applied its moral pressure on the remaining animists in the 1960s and 1970s. In the recollections of Nahor, the clerk in the Office of Religion, the sense was very much "that if they did not convert, they were not real people (*smat si pa*)." To "not be human" (*smat i pa*) is also the phrase used about people who are witches. The equivalence between the "back- ward beliefs" of animists and the inhumanity of witches that motivated the last Buli conversions to Christianity in the early years of the New Order established a correspondence between animism and witchcraft and opened up a space for being truly human only after witchcraft (and with it, animism) had disappeared. The irony of this was clear. The New Order demonization of tradition, as prob- lematic as it was, simultaneously entailed the tantalizing possibility of a new kind of humanity after witchcraft. This possibility of a society without witchcraft was eminently recognizable in Buli, because it was the same vista that Christianity had been promising for almost a century. As a result, most people were willing to give up their guardian spirits and enter into the new kind of humanity that the New Order offered, provided that it also meant an end to the "inhumanity" of the *gua*.

For those people who had decided to make this choice, it was therefore doubly outrageous when the New Order also seemed to protect and even produce witches.

Mangga stayed on in the village, and he died some years later without converting. The stigma of sorcery and witchcraft continued to cling to his family. Mangga's son, today a schoolteacher specializing in the teaching of Christian doctrine in primary school, was the object of suspicion on several occasions in the early 2000s. By sending his own children to school and then to the theological seminary, Mangga tried to secure them access to the state and church modernity that had demonized the tradition he himself continued to honor till his death. This is as good an example as any of how well the promise of modernity inserted itself into Buli ideas of tradition, indicating the complicity with New Order modernity that lay even in those who were most victimized by it. Indeed, Mangga's ambivalence is reminiscent of that of Dudu Barabakem, who (as we saw in chapter 4) vehemently denounced Christianity, but who still his whole life would whisper the Lord's Prayer to himself.

In the end, however, Mangga's hopes of freeing or protecting his children from suspicions of witchcraft by giving them a Christian education had the opposite effect of furthering suspicions instead. People say that witches and sorcerers often encourage their children to become schoolteachers and ministers. "The *gua*," one man said, "send their children to the theological college so that people will not suspect them anymore." Because witches "hide" (*gogan*) in the church and behind the police, pretending to be faithful Christians and model citizens, witchcraft finds a place precisely in the phenomena that alternatively deny its existence and claim to eradicate it.

## Political Complicity and Cultural Intimacy

Complicity, it would seem, produces its own kinds of failure. This theme has run through many of the ethnographic accounts given in this chapter: Mangga's march, Sami's madness, and Karo's death were all characterized by urgent calls upon state authorities to help in the "war" against witchcraft. But the loyalty that informed these calls had the paradoxical effect of cementing and multiplying the reality of witchcraft. In chapters 3 and 4 we saw how the aporia of witchcraft was a driving force in the initially enthusiastic, then subsequently frustrated engagement with Christianity. A similar form of historical agency drove Buli complicity with the New Order state. As the New Order, as part of its own project of developmentalism, sought to attend to the problems of witchcraft, it seemed to live up to Buli expectations to relegate witchcraft to the past. It is exactly these expectations—which had grown throughout a century of historical engagement with Christianity—that explain the political complicity with New Order modernism in Buli. However, in the very process of living up to these expectations of modernity, state authorities had to engage with witchcraft, and they regularly ended up falling prey to it. This happened not just literally, as when the son of the *babinsa* died of witchcraft or his wife shot at *gua* birds. It also occurred in more circumspect ways. It happened, for instance, when the authorities were induced, perhaps by magic and perhaps because of a legal system that insists on equal rights, to give shelter to suspected witches; or when local authorities, out of political paranoia and modernist zeal, demonized all animism, thereby making witchcraft more visible and real than ever (for other examples of how the demonization of tradition establishes tradition as a new kind of problem, see Meyer 1999 and Robbins 2004).

The persistence of the *gua* in spite of and within state modernity cemented in turn the sense that witchcraft was somehow, and embarrassingly, essential to what it meant to be Buli. During the New Order, witchcraft increasingly assumed the form of a Buli "cultural intimacy." Michael Herzfeld defines cultural intimacy as "the recognition of those aspects of cultural identity that are considered a source of external embarrassment but that nevertheless provide insiders with their assurance of common sociality" (2005:3). Witchcraft under New Order rule came to mark Buli cultural intimacy in just this way: as embarrassing and essential at the same time. The persistence of witchcraft within the confines of a political order that promised its eradication, but that also insisted that its perpetuation was due to the animism and "superstitious beliefs" of Buli people, meant that witchcraft somehow came to mark an awkward but nevertheless still essential aspect of Buli identity. Complicity, it seems, entails its own aporia, its own impossibility.

In his ethnographic material from Greece, Herzfeld shows how Cretan villagers co-opted the ideal forms of cultural intimacy of a nation-state that they regarded as "intrusive and demeaning" (2005:36). Cultural intimacy in Greece, it would appear, grows as part of a basic resistance to state intervention. I have proposed another possibility—namely, that cultural intimacy may grow as part of a basic complicity with state power. In Buli, the physical oppression and ideological hegemony of the New Order were seen not as intrusive; rather, they were accepted as part of a promise. State-society relations were imagined not through idioms of power and rebellion but rather through (failed) complicity and (frustrated) loyalty. Sami's madness, Karo's death, and Mangga's march are examples of the "raucous and disorderly experience of life in the concealed spaces of public culture," this strange place out of which cultural intimacy grows (Herzfeld 2004:320). The Buli people's acceptance of witchcraft as a rueful but essential dimension of who they were grew out of this loyalty, including the acceptance of the "savage slot" that New Order modernity assigned to them (Li 2000; Trouillot 1991). This acceptance of themselves as "backward," "animist," "not yet aware," because of the persistence of witchcraft, was highly ambivalent, however, for it also entailed a sense of failure on the part of the New Order state itself, failure to deliver a modernity free of witchcraft.

The idea that the contemporary world entails the promise of a radical break with the world of the past is expressed in the epigraph at the beginning of this chapter: "About the world these days I cannot speak" (*Dunia oras taie, yai fasebut pa . . .*). This is how people often begin their sentences when they want to emphasize traditional etiquette, ritual requirements, or conventional rules of conduct. The explicit bracketing of the contemporary world from any claims about insight that derives from tradition is a way to set apart tradition as something distinct from the modern world. This expectation is really a loyal form of modernism that like conventional modernist temporality imagines the future as a break with the past (Koselleck 1985; Kumar 1995). In Buli, this future is, however, constantly undermined by witchcraft. Witchcraft is essentially at the heart of a particular "nostalgia for the future" (Piot 2010), a nostalgia that is common throughout what used to be called the Third World, but that in Buli is driven by the problem of witchcraft. In Buli, it is the *gua* that blocks the future. The following chapter will analyze the context of this impossibility. For the persistence of the *gua* (and with it the impossibility of the future) is embedded in a central feature of Buli life and epistemology—namely, the sense that one can never trust other people. Indeed, concomitantly, one cannot truly trust oneself.

# 7

## SUBJECTIVITY, EXCHANGE, OPACITY

You can measure the sea all the way to America,
Its shallow parts as well as its deep parts.
But with people it is different.
It is difficult to know the inner core of people.

*Olat ca denabe Amerika mngisngo,*
*ni mamaso, ni mlaman.*
*Ga smat tina nculit.*
*Smat(e) ulor na, bot to susa tini.*

KENARI, SEPTEMBER 1997

Over the years, I had gotten to know Lolos fairly well. I had gone fishing with him on several occasions and spent the night in his garden hut a number of times. A self-taught blacksmith, he made the machete (*eta*) and spear (*pegá*) that I still keep under my bed. I saw him regularly during the 1990s as accusations of witchcraft against him grew in both frequency and intensity. A tall and athletically built man in his late thirties, Lolos was married to Kiama, with whom he had three children. Once a respected member of the community, Lolos was now avoided by most of his fellow villagers; and as he spent much of his time in the refuge of his swidden garden, a day's paddling from Buli, to avoid new accusations of witchcraft, he fought a frustrated battle to reconcile, in his own mind, what he knew about himself with what everyone else was saying about him.

The trial following Karo's death in October 1992 had given Lolos a minor victory. Still, the court decision had not answered what most people saw as the real questions: Had Lolos eaten Karo? Was Lolos a *gua*? These were questions that Lolos and his own family had themselves struggled with for several years. Kiama, his wife, had been loyal to her husband throughout (as spouses of accused witches almost always are), even though this had meant that she had severed many ties to her own family, and eventually came under accusations of witchcraft herself. Nevertheless, Kiama was uncertain. Once in 1997, she asked me if perhaps I had a computer or some other device that could diagnose whether her husband was a *gua* or not. Like other people in Buli at that time, as computers were slowly being introduced into government offices, Kiama thought that computers could diagnose illness: one merely typed the question on the keyboard, and the answer, expressed, for instance, as the face of the person responsible for an illness, would appear on the screen. People had heard that this was how the police used computers in the West. Kiama thought perhaps my computer could perform a similar feat and answer the question of whether her husband was really a *gua*. This understanding of computer technology was also supported by local divination practices (*failál*). One method of divination employs a plate filled with water and dried twigs of a wild species of holy basil (*sulasi*), which has a sweet smell said to attract the spirits. Empowered by the spirit (*jin* or *smato*) used by the diviner, the water is said to reveal the identity of a *gua* responsible for an illness when the face of the culprit appears in the pattern of leaves on the water. Lolos had earlier sought the help of such a diviner to settle the question of whether he was a *gua*, but the result had been unclear, he confided in me. The water had been cloudy (*cocomá*)—perhaps, he speculated, because others had used magic to obstruct the proceedings.

Lolos and his sister, Yantima, had also sought other ways of getting some sort of answer or solution to the uncertainty about the nature of who they were. This included seeking out a cure for witchcraft known as *anti*, which consists of three separate treatments. First, in a process called *famumi*, one inhales the smoke of a particular kind of wood, the smell of which is noxious to witches. Then one chews and swallows a number of magical roots (*fatamaga aiwáo*). This will force the *gua* spirit to come out of the forehead of its human host in the shape of either a praying mantis (*gua ni tel*) or a number of other insects, like wasps (*saninipá*), scorpions (*mamnyatif*), and centipedes (*lilifáng*). Lastly, the person is washed (*sisóp*) in water that has been magically prepared by special formulas (*táwar*) in order to cleanse and close the body. Lolos and Yantima said they had breathed the smoke without feeling any sign of unpleasantness or disgust, and that no insects had emerged from their foreheads. To Lolos and Yantima, and the few other people in the village who supported them, this seemed to refute their *gua* alter egos. Other people claimed, however, that the healer who had performed the *anti* ritual procedure was a friend of theirs, and that perhaps an innocuous type of wood had replaced the potent one. In addition to traditional cures, Lolos had also sought Christian proof that he was not a *gua*. He had publicly made a donation to the church (I. *syukur*) and vowed (*sasi*) that he was not a *gua*. Convention has it that God holds people accountable to such a vow and punishes them if their pledge is insincere or untrue. Lolos felt the fact that neither he nor any members of his family had become ill or died since he had made this vow was evidence that he was not a *gua*. Still, he was not totally convinced, and neither traditional divination nor church vows and state rationalism had been able to dispel his doubts. Witchcraft in Buli revolves around this aporia of subjectivity: If other people are essentially unknowable, am I also unknowable to myself? Can I be a *gua* and not know it?

## Subjectivity, Alterity, Opacity

This chapter explores the social and epistemological implications of this uncanny potential in witchcraft: the possibility that anyone can be a witch. Ironically, as this chapter will show, the fundamental inaccessibility of witchcraft is an existential premise for (potential) witches as much as it is for their (potential) victims. Lolos's speculations, his avowals of being a devout Christian, his experiments with traditional cures, and his wife's queries about a possible computer answer sprang essentially from the indeterminable question of whether someone can be a *gua* without knowing it. This aporia necessitates a constant skeptical self-appraisal— one that, I posit, is not unique to those accused of witchcraft but is a generalized existential effect of the "opacity of mind" (Robbins and Rumsey 2008) that characterizes Buli epistemology, the Buli understanding of what can be known. What Joel Robbins and Alan Rumsey call "the doctrine of 'the opacity of other minds'" refers to the widespread perception in many Pacific societies to the immediate east of Halmahera that it is difficult or impossible to know the inner thoughts or feelings of other people (2008:408). This is a doctrine or perception that sets certain parameters for what constitutes sociality, social interaction, and social propriety in these societies. Buli is similarly a society where the opacity of other minds is often remarked upon, and this is presented as one of the problems, and indeed one of the causes, of witchcraft. As one man put it to me, "The ancestors used to say: 'My friends, there is a time for laughter and a time for anger.' One cannot know about this world (*dunia taie yai fasebut pa*), for one cannot know the inside of other people. So be careful, be careful of mutual envy (*fadeldeli*), because that is the origin of the *gua*."

Resentment breeds in hiding. It remains concealed "on the inside," until witchcraft reveals it. One may offend without it being obvious; people may harbor anger about an incident long after others have forgotten it; polite and proper behavior as advocated by Buli customary tradition (*adat re atorang*) may conceal seething envy. One can never know. "One can measure the depth of the sea, but it is difficult, nigh impossible, to know the inside of other people," as the Buli proverb in the epigraph to this chapter has it. But more disconcertingly still, one may also be unable to know the inside of one's own mind. In Buli, the fundamental unknowability

of other people, the opacity of other minds, in other words, has an uncanny corol-
lary—namely, that one may be unknowable to oneself. Lolos was struggling with
this possibility: that an opacity clouded his insight into his own mind, so that he
was a witch without knowing it. The Buli doctrine of the opacity of other minds
therefore carries the uncanny implication that one may be "other" to oneself. This
epistemic uncertainty about the intentions and feelings of others (including the
other that may be *in* me, indeed may *be* me) translates into a series of existential
concerns in daily life. Essentially, these concerns revolve around the questions of
how one avoids witchcraft in social practice. How does one avoid becoming a victim of a *gua*? How does one avoid being accused of being a *gua*? And how does
one avoid becoming a *gua*?

These three questions relate, as this chapter will show, to some of the basic
moral dilemmas about what it means to be a subject in Buli. One avoids becoming
the victim, the accused, and the subject of witchcraft through the same basic social
and subjective measures—namely, through constant conviviality and "good companionship," literally by "accompanying and bringing along" other people (*farerér
re faututi*). In short, one avoids witchcraft by following Buli customary tradition
(*adat re atorang*). Buli tradition, I argue, revolves around a set of moral and ethical
concerns that seek to instill a certain "care of the self" (Foucault 1988a).[1] This
care of the self is intimately linked to the constant attempt to manage the three
dangers of witchcraft. The way one behaves to avoid becoming a *gua*, an accused,
or a victim may be described as the ways in which one actively constitutes oneself
as an ethical subject through particular kinds of morally correct behavior. These
practices, encapsulated in marriage and funeral ceremonies in particular but extending to a host of exchange practices as well, are oriented toward fashioning a
proper self, a "human" (*smat*), through a life-in-others, through a cultivation of a
"we-awareness," as Agnes Heller calls it (1984:13). And yet I will show that these
ceremonies and exchange practices entail strategies that may also lead one to become a *gua*. Buli tradition entails the aporia that the very forms of exchange practices through which one seeks to uphold the conviviality of custom may also lead
one to witchcraft, to the eviction of one's shadow-consciousness (*gurumin*). The
uncanny aspect of this is that one becomes a witch, and loses one's own shadow-
consciousness, without knowing it. This is the witchcraft dimension of the
opacity of the human mind in Buli. Witchcraft, essentially, is inaccessible to the
human mind because the human mind is inaccessible to itself as well as to others. Buli subjectivity, morality, and exchange are, in short, beset by the radical
alterity that is witchcraft. Thomas Csordas (2004) has argued that radical alterity constitutes the kernel of religion. According to Csordas, the object of religion
is to address this "aporia of alterity" (167). Extending this idea that religion is

related to the "aporia of alterity," I suggest that witchcraft is the "aporia of alterity" in its monstrous form: the uncanny danger associated with the otherness that characterizes intersubjective relations to other people as well as every subject's relations to itself.

## Not Knowing Yourself: On Potentially Being a Witch

The last and lingering memory I have of Lolos is the rank smell of death that came from his bed on his last, sad night in 1999. He died surrounded by only a few loyal friends and family members, emaciated from what the resident medical assistant said was tuberculosis. Till the very end however, Lolos and his family held on to the possibility—almost a hope—that the terrible withering of his body was the result of sorcery (*payao*) perpetrated by the son of one of his alleged victims. This was a desperate hope indeed, for no one in their right mind would want an illness to be sorcery. Yet somehow it seemed that if his slow and anguished death was caused by sorcery, it would confirm what Lolos had never been able to prove in life—neither to himself nor to his accusers—namely, that he was not a *gua* after all. Sorcery would demonstrate that he was not a violator, but a victim (I. *korban*) of other people's broken insides (*uló namgoi*). By logical extension, those people who for so long had claimed, themselves, to be victims of witchcraft would in fact have dabbled in sorcery. Perhaps then, the illness they claimed to be witchcraft was actually of their own doing? If you yourself are a sorcerer, then who are you to accuse others of witchcraft in the first place? The logic of this reasoning was far from watertight, as Lolos was well aware. Yet somehow, for Lolos and his family, sorcery became a tool to seek some sort of desperate certainty about his own identity. But it was a blunt tool, a weak form of proof, as everyone knew. For it was common knowledge that victims of witchcraft often use sorcery against the witch. Hence, even as he lay dying from sorcery, Lolos might still be a *gua*, even to himself and those close to him. Witchcraft afflicts everyone with uncertainty—those accused of it as much as those who become its victims. Basically, anyone can be a witch.

Even back when I first met Lolos in 1991, he was struggling with doubts about his own identity. But in June 1992 at a time when more than ninety household heads, representing the vast majority in Waiflí, had signed a petition to have him and Yantima evicted from the village (see chapter 6), his uncertainty was stronger than ever. Lolos received resolute support from several police officers against this petition, and he continued bravely to stand his ground against it, but he was also troubled by a lingering, nagging doubt. The possibility that one might be a *gua* without knowing it—a possibility that most Buli people are presumably impelled to contemplate at one stage or another in their lives—was a pressing problem for Lolos. Did he really know himself at all? Here is an excerpt from his reflections, as told to me in 1992:

> I can feel when I am hungry, and then I will eat. I can feel when I am thirsty, or when I am sick, but I cannot feel anything about being a *gua*. You know, I have given *syukur* [a donation of money] in church, swearing that I was not a *gua*, and just look: nothing has happened. Anyway, I am a Christian, and all this talk about witchcraft is just superstitious beliefs (I. *kepercayaan*). I have never myself accused anyone of being a *gua*. Even when my daughter died after coughing blood for days—she was only three years old—and everyone said that our neighbors were *gua*. Kiama even said they were witches who had eaten our daughter. But I still said no.

For Lolos, many things appeared to support his own feeling that he was no *gua*: God had not punished him when he swore at the altar that he was not a *gua*. Also, Lolos had no personal experience of being a *gua*, and he lacked the emotional inclination to become a *gua*. He had never, even when his daughter died, accused anyone else of being a *gua*—thereby avoiding the kind of anger that can itself lead to witchcraft. Lolos, as far as he himself knew, was not a *gua*. On top of this, Christian theology and educated thinking made it clear that there was no such thing as witchcraft. His lack of accusations against his neighbors demonstrated that he was a good Christian and an upstanding citizen who refused to cause trouble by holding on to backward superstitions. And yet, in spite of these excellent reasons, there was a certain twist to Lolos's denial. A hesitation about his own knowledge of himself.

Lolos, like most men, knew some magic. Before the accusations of witchcraft against him began in the early 1990s, he was a ceremonial elder in the rituals observed to appease the main guardian spirit of the village, Íyan Toa. This position entailed that he was a *makés*, a hothead and a man who knew fighting magic. Lolos believed that this knowledge of magic could even initially have caused the accusations against him: "I have this fighting magic (*ifif*). The guardian spirits (*smato*) that protect this magic can take me anywhere I want to go. People are afraid of it, and they think it is the same as the way the *gua* flies (*amngai*). But they are wrong. This is very different."

In Buli ontology, fighting magic (*man de wela*) and witchcraft (*mahagua*) are indeed very different, even opposed. Fighting magic is underwritten by animal spirits (*suang*) who protect people against witchcraft and sorcery. Although this conception still promotes the use of magic in Buli today, previous decades had, however, also made animist magic appear disconcertingly similar to witchcraft (as described in chapter 6). At the same time as Lolos tried in private to make sense of why he was so roundly accused of witchcraft, this reason could not be invoked publicly. For while these were perfectly sound explanations in conventional Buli thinking, magic had been incorporated during the New Order into the universe of witchcraft. So instead of explaining why he was wrongly accused, any public confession to knowing magic implied, for Lolos, the same danger of confirming his witch identity that Mangga had come to experience in 1969.

Suspecting that his neighbors might themselves be witches, Lolos tried to convince himself and others that he was not. The main basis for his sense that he was not a *gua* was that he had no bodily sensation or memory of being one. If, as he reasonably argued, he could feel hunger, thirst, and illness, then surely if he did not "feel" (*basam*) he was a *gua*, he could not be one?! The problem with this line of reasoning, however, was that in Buli epistemology such experiential testimony is open to serious doubt for reasons that have to do with the way people come to be *gua* in the first place.

## Consciousness and Witchcraft

One becomes a witch after accepting offers of sex or food from a witch spirit. These visitations by the *gua* spirit are said to be like a "flirting encounter" (*sero*) between the *gua* shadow (*gurumin madorou*) and one's own shadow or *gurumin* (see also chapters 2 and 5). If you allow this flirting to continue, the shadow of the *gua* will eventually attach itself to you and take the place of your own *gurumin*, using your body as a "canoe" on its nightly prowling for victims. The *gurumin* of the human *gua* host is only returned, so convention has it, when the *gua* spirit leaves its human host. Since the human *gurumin* or shadow is closely associated with awareness, consciousness, and experience and spiritual balance, its eviction entails a loss of consciousness. The question that people in Buli discuss regularly is, therefore, whether someone who is a *gua* is aware of it, or whether one may possibly be a *gua* and have no recollection or only a faint memory of it. Perhaps, some people suggest, prowling as a *gua* could be mistaken for having a bad dream. Perhaps people who are *gua* forget their perambulations altogether, the same way that people sometimes forget what they dream. Others, however, object to this view. How is it possible, they ask, to dream about assaulting friends and kin, to dream about eating them and violating them, and then not remember? One cannot just forget a thing like that, these people argue. Witches, surely, must know they are witches; they are just too embarrassed (*mai*) to admit it. But then again, even victims forget they have been assaulted and remember only when the witch who attacks them allows them to remember. Perhaps witches suffer from the same amnesia that afflicts their victims.

Becoming a witch and becoming its victim are, in this sense, uncomfortably similar experiences. In both cases the *gua* spirit robs people of the very tool (the *gurumin*) that enables them to know and remember what has happened in the first place. Human witches and human victims of witchcraft are in the same aporetic position: witchcraft is equally inaccessible to both. Lolos's account of not "feeling" himself to be a *gua* is therefore shot through with the same dilemmas that haunt the victims of witchcraft.

Lolos is not alone in harboring such doubt, for this is a general doubt that springs from the association of the *gua* with the absence of one's shadow-consciousness-awareness-experience. How can one have knowledge, awareness, or experience of being something if being this "something" implies the absence of one's consciousness, awareness, and experience (*gurumin*)? As I described in chapter 5, the shadow or *gurumin* is very much what makes one human, because a person's consciousness-awareness-experience is an orientation toward the social other through tradition. The *gurumin* is the "habitus" of tradition, so to speak (Bourdieu 1990). Losing one's shadow-consciousness when one becomes a *gua* is an "unbecoming" of sorts. In chapter 5, I also detailed the bodily dimensions of this "unbecoming": the kind of visceral disassembling of the body of the human host as it becomes a "canoe" to the witch, the head and entrails are "pulled" out of the human host, and only the empty body, the "carcass" (*buang*) of the host is left behind. The eviction of the *gurumin* of the host by the *gua* spirit entails a parallel "unbecoming," in the disaggregation of the host's subjectivity as a conscious, aware, experiencing, and social human being. The cruel irony of becoming a witch is that when you lose your *gurumin*, you also lose the ability to know whether you have lost it. One loses one's humanness to witchcraft without even knowing it. This, I would claim, is a fundamental condition of (im)possibility, the existentially monstrous nature, of witchcraft in Buli.

## The Uncertainty of Naming Monsters

A monster is monstrous precisely because it cannot be experienced as such. It cannot be known, only "mis-known" (Derrida 1990:79). It is its very unknow-ability that makes an unidentified "something" monstrous. But since the self is as unknowable as the *gua*, the monstrosity of the *gua* is also the monstrosity of the self. This is the reason why accusations in Buli are so full of uncertainty and anxious desperation. Victims know that their perception of witchcraft can be only partial, and their identification of the witch never certain. If anything can prove witchcraft, it is only (another instance of) witchcraft (see chapter 6). But the accusers also know that anyone, including they themselves, can be a *gua*, just as they are obliged to acknowledge the very real possibility that whoever is a *gua* may not, and may never, know. That is why "naming the witch" is so fraught with problems; it is a desperate but never fully successful attempt to claim non-witchcraft on one's own behalf (Siegel 2006). James Siegel's captivating analysis of the sorcery-related killings in East Java in 1998 (already discussed in chapter 1) suggests that the uncanny possibility that anyone could be a witch was driven by disintegration of a state that for three decades had claimed to know its "people" (I. *rakyat*) better than people felt they knew themselves. With the fall of the New Order state, Siegel suggests, the source of recognition of who one was also evaporated. Accusing and killing suspected witches was, in that sense, a desperate attempt to reclaim a vanished order that the state had previously guaranteed, and to stabilize an unstable sense of self in a situation where politics could no longer vouch for society or for identity: "The accusation of witchcraft says that whatever it is that one sees of oneself in the witch is not true" (Siegel 2006:203).

The same attempt to deny or forestall the uncanny possibility of one's own being a witch runs through Buli accusations, although, I believe, with a difference. The possibility that anyone could be a witch in Buli is not brought on, as it was in the sudden spate of witch killings in East Java, by anxieties about an absent state. For over a century in Buli, various incarnations of modern political order have promised to domesticate the aporias of witchcraft, only to exacerbate them in the process. So, too, with the New Order state. As we saw in chapter 6, the state in Buli never fully succeeded in safeguarding identity, in living up to its perceived promise to rid Buli of witchcraft. For that reason, the collapse of the authoritarian New Order state in the late 1990s did not lead, in Buli, to a perceived increase in the danger of witchcraft. Admittedly, the collapse of the New Order did bring its own horrors to Halmahera, such as the outbreak of communal violence (Bubandt 2001; Duncan 2005, 2013; Klinken 2007; Sidel 2007), and it did mean that people began scouting for new and perhaps more efficient means of combating witchcraft. As we shall see in chapter 8, the sublime nature of technology and money, both made accessible by wage labor in, and land compensations from, the mining industry, presented itself in the first decade of the twenty-first century as just such a new means. However, since the work of the state in staving off witchcraft had been partial at best during the New Order, its absence was arguably felt differently in the Indonesian periphery than it was on Java. While the possibility that anyone could be a witch was as acute in Buli as it was on Java, this possibility is not an abrupt effect of an absent state, but rather part of a constant atmosphere of uncertainty that suffuses subjectivity and sociality.[2]

## Dreams and the Potential of Being a Witch

"Perhaps you are a witch" (*osta au magua*). The words, teasing and serious at the same time, wafted through my window and mosquito net one morning in 2007. They came from across the street, where Frida and her husband, an Ambonese man who worked as a carpenter, lived in the unoccupied house built by the Social Department to accommodate a government-employed midwife who had never arrived. Frida sat outside the house on a makeshift bench chatting with Heriati, another young mother and neighbor, while Frida minded the small stall where she sold tomatoes, salt, and betel nuts as a supplement to her husband's income. Heriati's indictment, I later learned, had come after Frida had told Heriati about the dream she had had the night before.

Frida had dreamt that she and her husband had sailed out to one of the islands that dot the sea just off Buli, to go on a fishing trip. When they put ashore on the island, they found it was occupied by a large group of people, many from her own family. The group had seemingly had extraordinary hunting luck, for they were busy butchering several sea turtles and a large pig. Frida and her husband had been offered some of the meat and taken it back to the village. This was a troubling dream (*mahngél*). According to conventional wisdom in Buli, offering food in a dream, especially raw meat and fruits, is a standard way for the *gua* to initiate a "flirtation" with a human being. If you accept the food and fail to tell others about it, the *gua* will visit you in your dreams again and again until you eventually become a witch. If you tell others about the dream, however, "then it does not matter, because it was only a dream" (*paisá pa, mahngél be tiná*). It is as if telling makes it a dream, whereas not telling makes it real. The *gua* spirit, it seems, operates in the shadowland between dream and reality, which is another sign of its deviousness, disguising events as mere dreams and tempting the roaming spirit-shadow (*gurumin*) of the sleeping person.

The mythical account of the boy called Tawaigil illustrates what happens if you do not tell others about such dreams. Tawaigil had dreamt that he had been offered raw meat from someone who appeared to be his mother. Instead, the offer had come from a disguised *gua* spirit. Initially declining the offer, Tawaigil had eventually accepted the meat in a subsequent dream and had eaten some of it while saving the rest. The next morning, his mother discovered a piece of raw human liver stuck into a crevice in the bamboo wall. Tawaigil's dream, it turned out, had not been a dream at all, and what he took to be animal meat was actually human liver. Disgusted and afraid, Tawaigil's mother banished her son to an un-inhabited island. Alone on the island, Tawaigil began to encounter the *gua* spirit, who came to him daily in the shape of a shark. One day, the shark approached him and ordered him to eat seven squirrelfish (*gora*) tail first. Struggling with the spiny dorsal fins of the small red fish, Tawaigil eventually managed to swallow the seven fish as ordered, after which he was able to see that the shark was merely a disguise or cloak (*mef*), and that in reality the *gua* had a human-like shape. The food offered by the *gua* in dreams is thus the first in a series of offerings of food items that initiate the person into a kind of "perverse perspectivism" (see Vivieros de Castro 1998)—namely, that of seeing the world as the *gua* sees it while forget-ting one's own humanity, indeed forgetting the world of humans and becoming "unable to recognize family and kin" (*to bangsá pantó*).

Unlike the tale of Tawaigil, who had kept the dream to himself, Frida had done what one is supposed to do after dreaming of generous gifts of food, or hav-ing "dreams of sex with one's father or cross-sex sibling" (*mahngél hma ramau*): she had immediately told her friends and family about the dream, asking them for advice. "If you tell other people about it, there is no shame in it. It was only a dream," Heriati, her friend, explained to me later. People therefore often tell each other dreams and ask about their interpretation—assuring each other that it "was merely a dream" (*mahngél be*). In dreams, one's shadow (*gurumin*) is said to wander, and dreams play an important role in spirit encounters. In pre-Christian times, for instance, dreams were a primary access point for shamans (*mamá*) to commune with the spirits (such as *suang* or *jins*) during divination and curing rites (called *famamá* and *famtúlo*). Dreams also act as omens of bad things to come, or predictions about the future. Kenari was my chief instructor in the danger of dreams. One morning in 1997, while the two of us were on a hunting trip near the site on the Usia River where Gua Mané, the monster witch, was said to have lived in mythical times (see chapter 2), Kenari told me he had dreamt that I asked him to take for himself some of my money in a room next door. He had found the money, three crisp new bills, and had taken them as I had asked. Kenari was dis-turbed by the dream, however. In particular, the crispness of the bills worried him. New bills that look like they have just "been ironed" (I. *baru distrika*) are especially valued for ritual prestations. The fresh, unused appearance of the banknotes was too good to be true, and it seemed to suggest foul play. The *gua* always lures the dreamer with the choicest cut of meat, the largest piece of fruit, the most attractive kinsperson, or the most coveted object. The crisp bills seemed to suggest to Kenari just such a perverse twist to the ordinary logic of exchange. Perhaps a *gua* had used my appearance as a disguise (*mef*) in order to "flirt" with him in the dream. Telling me about the dream was Kenari's way of rejecting the flirtations of the *gua*—of ensuring that it "was just a dream." Witches hover in dreams, turning them inconspicuously into reality. By bringing dreams into social discourse, by exposing one's inside to others, dreams remain "merely dreams."

However, people are also reluctant to relate such dreams, because the account entails an admission that one has had contact with a *gua* spirit, an admission that may later lead to outright accusations of witchcraft. Heriati may just have been teasing her friend when she called her a *gua*, but the joke carried the earnest possibility of later accusations. Indeed, the Dutch missionary G. Maan reported that people in his experience often did not tell others about dreams that were indications of *gua* "flirtation" for fear that they would later be accused of witchcraft (*ZCR* 1922 [1]:2). The account of the night Ena almost became a *gua* may serve to illustrate this point.

One evening in 1994, Ena, a young woman in her late teens, was asleep among her siblings while her parents were out visiting family (*demdemang*). As is common, Ena had locked the door by propping a wooden post up against it to prevent unwelcome guests. In the early hours of the night, however, a neighbor had become alarmed by a sudden racket from inside the house. Ena, apparently still asleep, was hammering on the door and struggling blindly with the post in an attempt to get out of the room. People had quickly gathered to hold her down while Adat, an older woman and healer from the neighboring Muslim village of Buli Islam, was called in to help. Adat divined that Ena was on the verge of becoming a *gua*, her blind panic with the doorpost seemingly motivated by a desire to *amngái* (to fly around as a *gua*). Then Adat had performed an exorcism on Ena using smoke (*taping mumi*). After being cured, Ena explained how two people, a man and a woman, had come to her in dreams over the preceding week. On each occasion they had enticed to her to be alone even more than she was already. When people angrily asked her why she had not told anyone about this, she replied that she had been afraid of being accused of being a *gua*, because both her father and a father's brother had previously been regarded as *gua*.

Dreams of food and incestuous sex implicate people in a moral conundrum: if they relate their dreams, they may later be accused of being a *gua*; if they do not, they run the risk of becoming a *gua*. It was obvious to those around her that in 2007, Frida was troubled by her dream about the hunting luck of her family and was struggling with the moral predicament of the dream. On the one hand, it was a source of embarrassment (*maimái*) to admit that she had been tempted by a *gua* spirit and thereby openly declare that she harbored greedy dreams of food. On the other hand, Frida also clearly worried that if she did not tell of this, then she might in fact become a *gua*. Frida came from a family that had no recent accusations leveled against it, and she therefore had no reason to think she had the "seed" (*geo*) embedded in her body. Nevertheless, both myth and convention suggest that a genealogical link to a *gua* is not a prerequisite to becoming a *gua*. If one "looks for it" (*ningo*), one can become a *gua* even without a seed. As a proverb has it, "Even if you are not a *gua*, you may become one; even if you are not a sorcerer, you may become one." Anyone may become a *gua*. It was this possibility that troubled Frida. After telling her dream to me, she asked me rhetorically what I thought the dream meant, before she continued: "It is clearly a bad thing that I dreamt this, but surely it is okay now that I have told people about it? I would rather tell and have people tease me about it for a while than become a *gua* myself and have someone run me through with a spear."

The possibility of becoming a *gua* is a constant threat to the individual's ability to maintain a safe existence, and it is frequently invoked in everyday life as a rhetorical way of policing behavior. One morning, I was drinking coffee with Kenari while his daughter, Lina, was giving her baby a bath. The bath came after a procedure known as *tarke*. *Tarke* is a ritual act, performed morning and evening on a baby during its first year of life. All parts of the baby's body are squeezed lightly with a warm hand that has been heated by holding it close to the fire. This is said to help the flesh stick to the baby's bones, and to banish its "rawness," which attracts witches and causes illness (Bubandt 1998b). For the moment, however, Lina's one-year-old was squirming in the plastic tub, clearly unhappy about being wet. As Lina's frustrations rose she raised her hand in mock threat, as if ready to strike the child. Breaking off our conversation, Kenari turned to his daughter to admonish her: "You'll become a *gua*, Lina (*Aum magua osta, Lina*)!" Through everyday invocations of the *gua* such as this, certain practices are discouraged and others encouraged. In fact, it is common to reproach others for being in danger of becoming *gua* because they eat voraciously, hide food, or otherwise behave arrogantly. Such warnings are powerful forms of moral critique exactly because people acknowledge that anyone can become a *gua* unless they maintain constant vigilance against emotional attitudes and behaviors associated with witchcraft. The reality of witchcraft in Buli is not only a social and historical fact; it is an existential aporia that demands a particular "ethics of caution" and the deliberate cultivation of a self oriented to others.

Frida's dream highlights how people in Buli become witches when they allow themselves to be turned away from others by accepting gifts of food, but failing to tell others about it. Both accepting the gift in the dream and subsequently remaining silent about it are ways of turning away from the social other, which is the main characteristic of the *gua*. Someone who turns from others by being stingy (*matungtúng*), greedy (*magolojo*), secretive and prone to concealing things (*mahagogan*), gluttonous (*mafaseli*), a pilferer (*lálim*), or a thief (*mahalois*) is likely to become a witch. So is someone who is arrogant (*sombong*), disrespectful (*pandang enteng*), or excessively quiet and withdrawn (*mauting pa*). Being sexually overindulgent (*manafsú*) or lecherous (*cafarune*) are also emotional behaviors that, if cultivated, will lead to dream visits by a *gua* spirit. These forms of undesirable emotional practice all entail an act of turning away from the proper social life of sharing and conviviality, as mandated by tradition (*adat re atorang*), and retreating into self-contained individuality. The *gua* identifies itself, in Agnes Heller's words, solely with the satisfaction of its own "particularistic desires" (1984:12). The witch has no "we-awareness" (13); it is a being-unto-itself, as it were, that withdraws from sociality and common sense.

Witchcraft, in this sense, is the negation of Buli custom (*adat re atorang*), which is built upon the premise that proper subjectivity involves a constant vigilance against speech and behavior motivated by stinginess, greed, arrogance, and disrespect. To ensure this, Buli customary ideas of the proper life consist of an "ethics of caution" (*istiár*) and a morality of exchange, both of which function as navigational tools in the ultimately opaque world into which humans are thrown, and where witchcraft is a constant menace. The remainder of this chapter seeks to describe the dilemmas of this "ethics of caution" and morality of exchange, which before conversion to Christianity and state modernity were the main everyday tools in the struggle to obviate witchcraft.

## The Four Principles of Tradition

Buli tradition (*adat re atorang*) was bestowed upon Buli people by the Sultan of Tidore in mythical times (see chapter 2). This tradition was the framework for political society as well as moral order. Essentially, tradition made human society possible. *Adat re atorang* is supposed to be second nature to humans in Buli; it should infuse every aspect of their conduct and being. Kenari explained *adat re atorang* this way: "Our ancestors said: We are human beings (*smat itet*) because we follow *adat re atorang*. This means four things: 'propriety of speech and action' (*budi bahasa*); 'mutuality and deference' (*ngaku se rasai*); 'politeness and respect' (*sopan se hormat*), 'accompanying and bringing along' (*farerér re faututi*). The world may change, but these dimensions of *adat re atorang* remain." The four principles of tradition, expressed in the sort of couplets so common in the ritual languages of eastern Indonesia (Fox 1988), are all oriented toward what one could call "a cultivation of we-awareness" in everyday speech and behavior. The propriety of speech and action, mutual deference, good manners, and good companionship are the basis of an everyday morality that mandates a kind of self that is a self-unto-others.

It is through these principles of conviviality that humans make themselves and society. Yet people are very aware that the *gua* also participates in this everyday morality, and that as a consequence everyday sociality is treacherous. Both Frida's dream and the myth of Tawaigil have illustrated how witchcraft begins with acts of exchange that mimic the proper kinds of exchange through which witchcraft is otherwise held at bay. The dreams of plentiful offerings of food highlight the fact that sociality, even though it is constitutive of one's own being, is a double-edged sword, in that one can never know when sociality is being faked, mimicked by the witch in order to negate it. Exchange, conviviality, and sociality in a very real sense are always open to capture by the *gua*. Indeed, uncertainty lies at the root of sociality, betrayal at the heart of good companionship, deceit at the basis of exchange. When absorbed by an everyday life ideally governed by *adat re atorang*, a mode of existence that is and should be dispersed into the lives of others, one can never know "what is disclosed in a genuine understanding, and what is not," as Martin Heidegger phrases the ambivalence of being-in-the-world (1962:217). While *adat re atorang* and everyday exchange constitute the morality of a being-unto-others that is accessible to everyone, this public life with others also contains within it the ambiguity that it may generate, among those who are "angry with their share" (*tolea lowat*), a withdrawal from "good companionship" (*farerér re faututi*) into a being-unto-oneself that is the beginning of witchcraft.[3] The being-with-others that *adat re atorang* mandates, in other words, also produces the conditions of possibility for witchcraft. Nowhere is this aporia more visible than in exchange.

## The Political Order of Exchange

Exchange is the essence of *adat re atorang*, the embodiment of proper sociality and conviviality; and yet the everyday tactics that make up the intricate workings of exchange are characterized by subterfuge and obviation. These tactics and forms of subterfuge—such as hiding goods while seeking to entice others to share—are necessary "ways of making do" in exchange (see Certeau 1984:29), at the same time as people acknowledge that such tactics are disconcertingly similar to the modus operandi of the *gua*.

Marriage and alliance have been the focal point of much scholarship on Halmahera (Platenkamp 1988; Teljeur 1990; Visser 1989). Inspired by the Dutch structuralist tradition that during the 1980s and 1990 also dominated the anthropology of eastern Indonesia more generally (Fox 1990; Fox and Sather 1996), this approach saw marriage ceremonies and the symbolism they expressed as "the 'pivot' to a comprehensive organization of cosmos and society" (Fox 1980:3). Marriage ceremonies were rituals in which an entire cosmos was expressed, a cosmos centering on the asymmetrical exchange of objects and people between social groups often conceived of as "houses." Throughout eastern Indonesia, these rituals reflected the political organization of local polities and tended to be organized by a symbolic language of oppositions, such as male/female and younger/elder. These features also run through marriage ceremonies in Buli, and although it is possible to overemphasize the symbolic coherence and the continuing importance of marriage to eastern Indonesian societies, it is certainly true for Buli that it is in ceremonies such as those surrounding marriage that people feel they participate in the making of a social ideal. Marriages are full of competition and fear of committing transgressions that will result in punitive fines, but at the same time it is in marriage ceremonies—when the palm wine flows liberally, when the "soft caresses" of ritual speech are at their most pleasing, and when exchange relations ensure that two "houses" are tied together into one union—that Buli tradition comes closest to delivering the ontological certainty of which Anthony Giddens speaks (see chapter 2 for a critique of this idea of traditional certainty).

Ritual exchange is a fundamentally moral type of action in Buli. It is, still today, the essence of what "tradition" means, and it takes two related forms: ceremonial exchange (*fasima*) and everyday forms of food sharing (*fasuréi*). Ceremonial exchanges are particularly important in connection with marriage and burial. Both are ritual events that are today primarily handled according to Christian liturgy. Even so, parallel to the Christian wedding and funeral ceremonies, a series of traditional rituals take place that all center on the exchange of prestations. A marriage is preceded by a series of bilateral negotiations and exchanges between the families of the prospective bride and groom, to which both the patrilineal relatives (from the "trunk-house" or *ebai pu*) and the matrilineal relatives (from "the house of relatives" or *ebai bangsá*) of the two sides contribute. These exchanges that take place over months and years are said to "tie together" the man's side (*man si*) and the woman's side (*mapíng si*), and to ensure "good companionship" (*farerér re faututi*). One ritual leader expressed this in the following way, "If we build a house, nobody helps us, but see what happens when someone dies or gets married: the whole village stands up." The reason for this cooperation is said to lie in the burden of exchanges that marriage and burial ceremonies place on people. Relatives of both families contribute to the collection of the prestations, and the bilateral character of Buli kinship means that the exchanges that go into any marriage or burial ceremonies involve a substantial part of the village. The man's side "pays" (*palas*) money, clothes, and pans to the woman's side, which in turn reciprocates (*sima*) with clothes, plates, and food.

Marriage ceremonies are in many ways a symbolic rumination on politics because they replicate the polity of the traditional North Malukan sultanate in ritual and symbolic form. Thus the asymmetrical distinction between the "man's side" and the "woman's side" is structured like the political relationship between Buli and the sultanate of Tidore. The woman's side is marked as "female" but also superior, because the family of the woman is symbolically the "ruler" or "sultan" (*kolano*), while the man's side takes the position of the male commoner. This symbolic mimicry of political asymmetry demands from the representatives of the inferior man's side a display of constant respect and humility toward members of the woman's side. It entails, among other things, that they "bow down and honor" (*suba re sijúr*) members of the woman's side before speaking. People from the man's side must also address people from the woman's side as "Lord" (*Jou*). The most obvious sign of this asymmetry is the custom that the future husband moves into the house of his future parents-in-law to work at their bidding for months, until all exchanges have been made, after which the couple moves into the house of the man's parents or into a new home of their own. This period of work for the in-laws is called "hard rowing service" (*kangelá re dao*), and symbolically repeats the tributary labor (*coów*) that people from Buli and other central Halmaheran villages formerly performed as rowers in the war canoes of the sultan of Tidore.

## The Soft Caress of Ritual Speech

Throughout the four separate rituals that make up the marriage negotiations, polite ritual speech is a central component. On these occasions, ritual speech—one of the most admired skills of a ritual elder—is a careful exercise in rhetoric that continually aims to please or "caress" (*safsafa*) one's interlocutor. The way to please is by adding "a little something" (*fapaisá*) to one's speech, by giving it "content" (*ni loló*). This "little something," a term that is incidentally also used about magic (persuasive rhetoric as the ancient Greeks already saw is very much like magic), is characterized by two things: the skillful use of parallel word couplets and a constant play with sexual innuendo. The sexual innuendo is what interests me here, because it is directly related to the ambivalent relationship between tradition and witchcraft. The point I will seek to bring out is that even here, in the midst of rituals designed to bring about conviviality and proper sociality, the *gua* lurks as a shadow.

Ritual speech requires speakers to preface their statements with an apology (*ngara be tiná*) for any references to sexual matters so as not to offend their listeners. This injunction, however, covers even the most implicit reference: one must apologize in advance before making any reference to long objects, to objects that function as food containers, to food items, to the act of eating, or to eating utensils. The same goes for adjectives that may also be used in reference to the sexual act or sexual desire (such as "soft," "slippery," "short," "hard," "slow," or "quick"). Even the most vague reference to objects that resemble the male and female genitalia may cause offense without a proper excuse. The same goes for the use of terms that hint at the sexual act, or terms that are related to the cooking, storage, and consumption of food. To refer to another person's clothes, for instance, one should use the possessive adjective normally employed to denote edible objects (such as the second person singular *anam*, "your") rather than the possessive adjective used for ordinary objects (such as the second person singular *anim*, "your"), since the latter might be taken as a reference to the person's genitals ("your thing," as it were).

Ritual language, in short, is concerned with the same stuff that makes you a *gua* in dreams: food and sex. I suggest that the apology (*ngara be tina*, literally "It is only a door") explicitly brings into language and into collective consciousness a self that handles, politely and through tradition, those very phenomena (food and sex) that attract the *gua*. Food and sex are particularly touchy issues in the context of marriage negotiations—which, after all, seek to organize into a proper *adat* form, precisely food and sex through commensality and conjugality. In this context, the ritual apology, like all tradition, seeks to guard against offense; it is a precaution (*istiár*) against the mutual anger (*fatotolé*) and envy (*fadeldeli*) that are the root of witchcraft in the first place. Accordingly, the slightest infraction of this polite attitude or apologetic form of speech by people on the man's side will "shame" the woman's side, and such "shame" will have to be "covered" by a monetary payment.

Contrary to what one might expect from this description of the touchy nature of sexual innuendo, marriage negotiations are in fact vivacious, often even rowdy affairs. The ceremonies are usually all-night events during which people smoke cigarettes, chew betel nut, and drink sweet palm wine to the rhythm of *walit* drumming. As the participants get increasingly inebriated, the sexual language becomes more explicit, and the gales of laughter and yells of encouragement that accompany every particularly juicy example of sexual reference—appropriately prefaced by an apology—continue till the early hours of the morning. In fact, it is the proper ritual handling of sexual innuendo that marks the truly skillful ritual expert. Such a man might tell a story about a particularly eventful fishing trip, but he will spice up the story by inserting an apology before explaining how the fishing line was "slippery," before noting in passing how he kept the line "wet" in order to "pull it" to produce a distinctive sound that attracts fish, when describing how he grabbed his "lance" to kill the fish in the water, and before relating how it "penetrated" the tail of the fish. It is language like this, apologetic but sexually charged at the same time, that is the true mark of ritual language, and it is greatly pleasing to Buli ears. Sexuality and consumption, bent into the proper, social form, are the basis of Buli tradition (*adat re atorang*). Handled in an improper, greedy way, however, they are the stuff of witchcraft. Marriage rituals are the epitome of tradition, for they establish through exchanges (*fasima*) and through proper speech (*budi bahasa*), deference (*ngaku se rasai*), polite behavior (*sopan se hormat*), and conviviality (*farerér re faututi*) the ideal format for sociality. This is how people should always commune, working to build enduring and pleasant social relations between lineages or "houses" through exchange, polite speech, and respectful behavior. In short, marriage, the primary ritual occasion in Buli, is a careful organization of proper commensality and sexuality through exchange and ceremonial language, the distribution of food and marital relations according to *adat re atorang* in such ways that they do not lead to witchcraft.

## Exchange and Its Tactics

Food-sharing practices are not restricted to marriage negotiations. Ceremonial exchanges (*fasima*) ideally extend into everyday forms of sharing known as *fasuréi*. *Fasuréi* is, in Buli, a part of what Bambi Schieffelin (1990) has called "the give and take of everyday life." Every afternoon women and teenage girls crisscross the village carrying portions of a catch or small servings of cooked food to siblings (*ramau re tenou*), parents (*hma re hnye*), and married children (*nturi*) in households of their own. They also visit affines, in particular a giver's parents-in-law (*ohmó*), daughters-in-law (*malafa*), and brothers- and sisters-in-law (*tamai*). Such "give-and-take" is an important way of maintaining "good companionship," and it should not be subverted. A common skin affliction called *gafgafa*, a kind of psoriasis, is said to develop if one gives food away as part of *fasuréi* but then invites oneself to eat the food one has just given away.

In addition to these exchange obligations between close consanguines and affines (*ebai pusa*), there is an obligation to respond favorably to requests for food from distant relatives (*ebai bangsá*) and even outsiders (*smate nesa*). These requests may take the form of a direct appeal by simply asking (*dor*). Such "demand sharing" (Peterson 1993) is not uncommon, and in some instances it too is ritualized. At one stage in the marriage ceremony, the men of the woman's side can freely ask any of their future classificatory brothers-in-law (*tamái*) on the man's side for anything in their possession. The members of the man's side will have to scramble to get whatever item (say, a knife, a spear, or a drum) they have been asked for, and any indication of "grumbling" (*gurubu*) on the part of the giver can result in a punitive fine.

In general, however, most attempts to implicate others in forms of everyday sharing are more subtle than such outright demands. A range of terms refers to these more subtle forms of exchange in which a sophisticated but largely implicit game of reciprocity, sharing, and withholding is played out. I will take up a few of these terms, all of which are both central to and an undermining of exchange, in order to flesh out how the danger of witchcraft hides in the dynamics of exchange itself. In my analysis, the aporias of witchcraft that beset Buli subjectivity also permeate exchange morality. Ironically, exchange—the means through which proper sociality and conviviality are established, and through which witchcraft is obviated—also embodies the mechanisms for their destabilization by witchcraft. Exchange, although mandated by tradition, is implicated directly in the aporias of witchcraft.

*Bolbolo* is one indirect kind of request. It takes the form of merely presenting oneself, seemingly by accident, when food is present. When someone returns from a fishing or hunting trip, a crowd will inevitably gather to have a look and to lend a hand by carrying the equipment, or by pulling the canoe onto the beach. Inevitably, the "accidental" bystander will comment on the richness of the catch, the fatness of turtle, or the size of the pig, and attentively inquire into the details of how the pig was killed, or where the fish were caught. This kind of friendly and inquiring presence is known as *bolbolo*, and it entails an implicit but powerful request for a share of the catch. One does not ask for a share of the catch outright. Rather, one seeks to stimulate a voluntary offering of food through the performance of conviviality. If the silent incitement to generosity is successful, and the fisherman or hunter offers a small portion of his catch, politeness demands that one refuse the offering. One eventually accepts it, with profuse expressions of reluctance, when the food or gift is literally forced into one's hands. Even though many people today sell their catch rather than share it, *bolbolo* or "tacit appeals to share" are still a conspicuous part of village life just before noon when the fishermen usually return to the village. Those who come down to the returning boats at the mouth of the river to *bolbolo* usually start off insisting they want to buy the surplus of the catch. Often, however, the fisherman feels he cannot sell the catch even to distant relatives, and he will smilingly force his catch upon kinspeople and friends who have come to *bolbolo*, even though it is generally acknowledged that the smile may hide a sting in one's inner core (*uló na pirpír*), and that a fisherman will silently "grumble" to himself (*gurubu*) if he feels that too much of his catch has disappeared before he reaches his house.

"Grumble" is exactly what Wadone did one night, after he and I had been hunting for mud crabs in a nearby mangrove swamp. After two arduous hours wading through the muddy, snake-infested waters to spear mud crabs, the darkness lit only by the light of a kerosene pressure lamp, we returned with a good catch of seven large mud crabs and a couple of decent-sized fish. Although it was late at night and we had tried to sneak unobserved out of the village, several people had seen us depart and had guessed from our gear what we were up to. As we passed through the village on our return, people were on standby to *bolbolo*. Wadone put on a generous face and insisted, despite their strong protests, on giving every person we met one of the largest crabs. It was nevertheless clear, when we reached his house with only four crabs, that he was upset. "This is why I do not go spear fishing ( *fagaso*)," he said. "They are all quite able to receive, but when they catch some fish themselves, they never give any to us."

In spite of the "grumbling" that frequently accompanies it, the tacit incitement to generosity of *bolbolo* has a strong moral foundation in tradition. It is a direct extension of ceremonial exchange relations, and like them it is essential to the maintenance of good companionship ( *farerér re faututi*). G. Maan, the Dutch missionary to Buli between 1908 and 1919, found the practice of *bolbolo* to be such a striking feature of Buli social relations that—in keeping with the general practice of the Utrecht Mission Union to employ indigenous terms to impart an understanding of the importance of central Christian concepts (1912)—he introduced *bolbolo* as the term for "attending a church service" (1940:12). The Christian, so the missionary explained, presents himself or herself to God in much the same spirit as someone who seeks to incite a friend or relative to generosity. God is like the fisherman with the bountiful catch, and church attendance, with all the meekness and modesty that Calvinism thinks appropriate, should take place in the same spirit as those who hope a fisherman will share his catch. The translation reflected how well the Dutch missionaries had recognized the tendency in Buli to see Christianity within a logic of exchange (see also chapter 4), and how, in spite of their basic problems with this interpretation, the Protestant missionaries nevertheless sought to employ it in an exercise of contextual theology.

## The Bodily Hexis of Making Oneself Small

*Bolbolo* is only one term in a wider vocabulary that describes the language games through which people seek to invite others to share. These language games are very much embodied. As Pierre Bourdieu has argued, bodily dispositions are seized upon by every social order to induce a particular embodied conception of the world. Bourdieu refers to the way in which the body becomes the medium of expressing our being as "practical sense" or "hexis," suggesting that bodily hexis is a tacit incarnation of a political worldview: "Bodily hexis is political mythology realized, em-bodied, turned into a permanent disposition, a durable way of standing, speaking, walking, and thereby of feeling and thinking" (1990:69).

"Making oneself small" ( *fanenena it*) is very much a form of hexis in Buli, which embodies the political mythology of *adat re atorang*. The bodily comportment of bowing down, literally and figuratively, before others as a sign of respect emanates from the political order of the sultanate hierarchy, and it has been naturalized into an embodied form of morality. To "make oneself small" is a form of "embodied rhetorics" (Herzfeld 2009) of earnest submission, part of the symbolic asymmetry of politeness integral to rituals such as marriage, and designed to make one's interlocutors feel superior, "on top," "like a ruler." Bowing down (*suba*) is one way of making oneself small, and it is central to marriage negotiations in particular. Before, for example, availing themselves of food, drink, betel nut, or tobacco during marriage negotiations, the representatives from the man's side will lower their head and—in a mimicry of the way in which one addressed the sultan—look diagonally and furtively up at the representatives from the woman's side, and then raise their right hand to their forehead while beseeching them: "Lord marriage partner (*Jou paing*), we enslave (*koro-koro*) ourselves to you. Lord marriage partner, we lower ourselves, we bow down [before you]."

According to Bourdieu, the fact that our practices are structured by hexis (a particular way of comporting our body in order to "do things") causes these practices to appear natural and thereby sensible. To "make oneself small" (*fane-nena it*), one might say, is the political mythology of sultanate rule embodied as part of a morality and structured by the logic and symbolism of asymmetry. In such an asymmetrical moral system, there is a great deal of moral advantage and symbolic mileage to be derived from assuming the inferior position. This applies, as James Scott (1985) has demonstrated, to the class conflicts in rural Southeast Asia; it applies, as Danilyn Rutherford (2003) has shown, to the political relations that marginal ethnic groups maintain to the nation-state; and it likewise applies, I propose, to the micropolitics of village exchange. In Buli, "making oneself small" is not only the essence of proper *adat* behavior; it is also, as we shall see, the best protection against witchcraft.

"Making oneself small" belongs to a general class of deliberate forms of self-denigration that also include "making oneself old and decrepit" (*faleo it*) and "making oneself poor or inferior" (*famayaio it*) in the eyes of the other. All entail a bodily demeanor of "bending down," which is proper to ritual speech and ceremonial comportment but also extends into daily life as an "everyday hexis." Bending over slightly and bringing both hands to the forehead while greeting each other with the honorific term of address *Jou* (Lord) is proper when, for instance, parents-in-law (*paing*) meet and greet each other, even outside of ritual events (see fig. 28).

These days, however, the practice of making oneself small is thought to be disappearing. Older people often lament the casual and disrespectful way of conducting social intercourse in contemporary Buli. This, they complain, has given way to social arrogance. The iconic expression of this arrogance is the bodily comportment associated with Dutch colonial officers and ministers: arms akimbo (*tige hnyao*), feet wide apart, and forehead held high while whistling. It became a joke between myself and Tangkea, ritual leader and social joker, to strut past each other, whistling and arms akimbo, in ludicrous exaggeration of this colonial hexis, after he had told me stories from his childhood about the social arrogance of the

**Figure 28.** Making oneself small during marriage negotiations. 1992. Photo by author.

Dutch. Arrogance of any kind, whether embodied or rhetorical, is not only improper; it is also dangerous. For while the cultivation of self-denigrating speech, behavior (*budi bahasa*), and bodily comportment (*ngaku se rasai*) insulates people from the hidden anger of others, a body that comports itself arrogantly delivers itself directly to witchcraft and sorcery.

Before dawn one morning in 1994, I was awakened by the voice of Selena, my adopted mother, who was loudly scolding her sixteen-year-old son, Willem. Willem had dropped out of school and spent recent months visiting relatives along the coast. He had just returned home, dressed in his finest clothes, carrying a new bag he had gotten from me, and wearing a new pair of shoes given to him by an older brother. Selena was furious because the family was going through what seemed to be an unusual spate of misfortunes. Mateus, one of Willem's older brothers, had developed several large boils that the family felt were due to sorcery from someone envious of the position Mateus had recently acquired at the harbormaster's office in the district capital. Malik, another brother, had recently fallen ill as well, and his illness had prevented him from going to Tidore to take the test to become a government bureaucrat (I. *pegawei*). And Kenari had returned, despondent, from a trip on his anchovy-fishing raft (I. *bagang*) complaining that something was wrong. The *bagang* raft had been beached twice by the tide and almost destroyed in the surf. Furthermore, unlike the rafts around him, his raft had caught almost no anchovies.[4] The family was clearly the target of other people's envy and sorcery. Having been away, Willem was unaware of these recent mishaps, but the carelessness with which he had enjoyed his return, flaunting his new clothes and spending the night away from home, was too much for his mother. She was concerned that her ten children were not taking enough "precautions" (*istiár*), that they were behaving like "big people" and thereby making themselves vulnerable to attacks from witches and sorcerers. "Who do you think you are?" Selena scornfully inquired of her son, before launching into a temperamental torrent directed at all her children, all of whom were still half-asleep:

> You are too arrogant, all of you! All you think about is how you look and how to get new clothes so you can strut around with your arms akimbo, looking important. Look at you, Willem. You do not even have pubic hair yet, but where are you spending your nights? If we are not taking care of ourselves, other people will certainly "take care" of us (*jaga it*) instead! You have to stop being so arrogant, for your own sake. Take care of yourselves ( *fajaga meu*), don't forget to be polite (*sopan re hormat*)!

I believe Selena's anger was not grounded in any moral condemnation of the clothes Willem was wearing, or in any moral indictment about where he was spending his nights. Rather, Selena was angry that Willem had failed to take the most basic kind of "care." If Willem did not "take care of himself" ( *fajaga*), sorcerers and witches would "take care" of him (*jaga*). The dangers of witchcraft and sorcery in this sense necessitate a constant ethics of "care" (*istiár*). This ethics of care entails a certain "technology of the self" (Foucault 1988b), particular ways of "conducting oneself" that are bodily inscribed and encapsulated in the precaution of "making oneself small." In a society where one's inside is essentially opaque, one's "they-self"—the self thrown into the world of others (Heidegger 1962:167)—is in a very real sense one's only truly available self, the self on which one can work, and for which one is obliged to care. It is the self-unto-others that Buli tradition seeks to regulate, not an interior self of free will and intentions. It is this public self that is the object of the care of *adat re atorang*. The same subject is also at stake in exchange.

## Exchange and the Tactics of Not-Having

Although they are part of *adat* and proper behavior, efforts "to make oneself small"—like the tacit incitement of generosity in *bolbolo*—are also a tactic to induce generosity. Such tactics are called *alemen*. *Alemen* is a form of circumspect behavior in which a motive for an action is not overtly stated, but nevertheless made clearly perceivable. By making oneself small, one tries to appeal to what usually makes people share and what engages them in exchange—namely, shame (*maimái*). Shame is the reason why the woman's side in a marriage ceremony always reciprocates (*sima*) the payments (*palpalas*) of the man's side, often surpassing in value the payment itself. It is said that the woman's side "reciprocates shamefully," out of shame (*sima maimái*). People are compelled by shame to give to the limit of their means. In a sense, therefore, it is shame that turns all participants in ceremonies, such as marriages or burials, into "suffering people" (*smat susa*). Shame (*maimái*) must be alleviated through gifts, yet it is also what makes one return gifts. Shame, one might say, is the *hau* of Buli reciprocity (Mauss 1970), the guiding sentiment of Buli exchange. Shame is incidentally also the only emotion that can prevent people from becoming witches, the only sentiment that will entice a *gua* to attempt a cure of its victim, and that may even make a person stop being a witch altogether. It is a lack of shame that makes a witch; that defines its inhumanity. Conversely, shame is the defining feature of human exchange and conviviality. As the proverb has it, "It is preferable to be dead than to be ashamed (*maimái, mancapá mat it*)."

By asking for things (*dor*) and by employing tactics of *alemen*, such as *bolbolo* and *fanenena it*, one seeks to inveigle a reluctant person into exchange, to shame them into sharing.[5] Nonetheless, there are equally important tactics by which one seeks to avoid sharing. The most straightforward method is simply to hide food (*gogan*). Selena, my adopted mother, was addicted to betel-nut chewing and always had a large stash hidden under her bed. Even so, she was forever lamenting the lack of betel nuts and would constantly send her children on errands to ask neighbors and relatives for betel nuts (*paliu*), lime (*yafi*), or betel pepper (*fawat*). Her subterfuge was so apparent that it became the topic of mild joking within her family, and after she died—suddenly and unexpectedly from witchcraft, in 1996— it was one of the characteristics for which her family would fondly remember her.

Hiding is also practiced in more circumspect ways. On returning from their gardens, women often pause before entering the village to rearrange (*fato*) the plaited baskets (*yan*) they carry on their backs. Desirable objects such as pineapple and sugarcane are placed at the bottom of the basket and covered by less easily digested crops like cassava and sweet potato. If desirable food items are left at the top of the basket, chances are that relatives will avail themselves of them as the woman walks through the village, and they will all be gone by the time she makes it home. People who return from fishing trips will similarly stop to stow their catch in bags and baskets before reaching the village so as to avoid the curious gaze of those waiting for them at the beach in order to "entice them to give" (*bolbolo*).

Instead of having to give (and causing oneself the kind of frustration that comes from being compelled to share something), or alternatively having to refuse (and risk the anger of the refused person), it is much easier to obviate the whole exchange situation by concealing the fruits of possible contention. Similarly, food (*an*) in the kitchen section of the house is habitually covered (*tabak*) to avoid accidental glances from visitors. While hiding (*gogan*) is an acceptable strategy among strangers (*smat[e] nesa*), it should not be exaggerated. For instance, it should not be practiced among people of the same bilateral group or "house" (comprising the patrilineal relatives of the "trunk-house" or *ebai pu* and the matrilineal relatives from "the house of relatives" or *ebai bangsá*). Consequently, hiding is inherently problematic. The problem is that hiding (*gogan*) and the deception (*darawa*) that it entails also are among the main characteristics of the *gua*. As an example of the problems involved in hiding food from people of the same "house," I was told the story of Kepiting and his wife, Doi. They had been fishing for some time on the islands off Buli when Kepiting found a packet of smoked fish wrapped in pandanus leaves (*sbólai*) hidden in Doi's clothes basket (*sabaénga*). Kepiting allegedly got so upset about this that he divorced Doi.

Given the delicacy that must pervade their application and their inherent danger, the tactics of demanding and strategic performances of not-having are concerns that occupy much of everyday life. The central dilemma of these tactical forms of behavior is that they straddle a fine line between right and wrong, between customary and witch-like behavior: One person's delicate enticement to share (*bolbolo*) is another person's greed; one person's careful tactics of not-sharing is another person's stinginess. As much as they are part of the game of exchange, these tactics are also potentially always an obviation of it. As a result, exchange, the mechanism for the creation of proper *adat* sociality, is also an intimation of witchcraft.

This aporia is inescapable. The reason is that one cannot just decide to dispense with tactical thinking. A man who never refuses to give, or a woman who never practices the art of hiding and not-sharing, for fear of becoming a witch would be either stupid or dangerous. Kenari pointed out to me that if your "inner core is too soft," as evidenced by an inability to refuse people's demands to share, this is not only a sign of hopeless social ineptitude. If your "inside gives too much" (*npo nauatú*), it either opens you to an attack by the *gua* or invites a dream visit by a *gua* spirit. People who are too generous are, therefore, likely witches and also likely witch-victims. Similarly, a total absence of demands to share is a sign not just of social ineptitude but also of a withdrawal into solitude that could be a forewarning of the *gua*. A person who never demands anything is extricating himself or herself from "the give and take of everyday life" (Schieffelin 1990), and that is something that is suspiciously close to exhibiting an aversion to good companionship (*farerér re faututi*).

Exchange, in short, entails a delicate balancing act between neither being completely taken in by all demands of reciprocity, nor entirely extricating oneself from them. Both stances, in their pure form, are dangerous. Instead, one must balance the tactics by which one elicits exchanges (*alemen, fanenena it,* and *bolbolo*) with the tactics by which one obviates them (*gogan*) in order to be able to negotiate ceremonial exchanges and everyday sharing. These tactics are simultaneously polite (part of *adat re atorang*) and necessary. But even though exchange is both polite and necessary, it entails, in its very practice, tactics that inevitably engender angry grumbling (*gurubu*) and feelings of greed (*magolojo*), stinginess (*matungtúng*), and unsociability (*farerér pa*). As such, the same tactics that go into the establishment of proper exchange also gesture dangerously in the direction of the *gua*.[6] Exchange, in essence, is both desirable and impossible. The contradiction inherent in exchange—the ideal morality of sharing and the practical ethics of hiding—is one with which Buli people live, and which implicates them in a social aporia where sharing is simultaneously highly desirable and highly volatile. It is within this aporia, as within other aporias of life in Buli, that the *gua* dwells. As Tali told me in 2004, "It all begins with that little pain, those little stings (*pirpir na*) that 'break your inner core' (*uló namgói*). You are angry about your share (*tolea lowat*), about other people's inheritance, food, or other people's houses. It is this small pain that creates a grudge (*singan*) that eventually leads to witchcraft (*nagua*)."

Indeed, as much as it is recognized as an everyday emotion, being "angry about one's share" (*tolea lowat*) is a frequent shorthand for the feelings that impel one toward becoming a witch. Worded differently, Buli sociality is simultaneously a human necessity and an "impossibility" (for a discussion of morality and impossibility, see Derrida 2001a). Proper subjectivity and sociality are premised on constant involvement with others in the knowledge that others cannot be known and may work to undo conviviality even while pretending to uphold it. In light of this, tradition (*adat re atorang*) is essentially cautious. Politeness, respect, and honesty are "precautions" (*istiár*) that seek to maintain a conviviality that these behaviors can never fully guarantee.

## Witchcraft and the Aporia of Alterity

Sociality is always magical. Magicality is built into intersubjectivity itself. Human life, as Bruce Kapferer puts it, "is magical in the sense that human beings span the space that may otherwise individuate them or separate them from others. Their magical conjunction with other human beings in the world—imaginative, creative, and destructive—is at the heart of human existence" (1997:2). The magic of the other is the magic of how one squares one's separation from other people with an "embodied passionate extension towards others" (2). A certain aporia is therefore always at the center of intersubjective existence—namely, the problem of overcoming the fundamental alterity of the other, the inaccessibility of other people, with one's desire for sociality. This aporia is heightened, I suggest, in societies such as Buli, where the intentions, desires, and "insides" of the other are fundamentally opaque (Robbins and Rumsey 2008).[7] In Buli, what I have called "an epistemology of guessing"—which characterizes people's relationship to witchcraft, and which is expressed in the assertion that when it comes to the *gua*, humans can only guess—extends basically to all other people: "One cannot measure the inside of other people." This chapter has suggested that the solution Buli tradition offers to this fundamental mystery of alterity is to advocate an ethics of "caution" (*istiár*) and "good companionship" (*farerér re faututi*). Tradition (*adat re atorang*) establishes a morality (and an epistemology) of "caution and "precaution" (*istiár*) coupled with an etiquette of exchange that seeks to produce "good companionship" (*farerér re faututi*) through the cultivation of honest speech (*budi bahasa*), respect (*ngaku se rasai*), and polite behavior (*sopan se hormat*).

In the end, however, the ethics of caution and the morality of exchange are, as every Buli person is acutely aware, only a partial solution. Indeed, companionship and exchange are being undermined by the very procedures that seek to reproduce them. A very similar aporia also characterized Christianity and state modernity, as I have described in chapters 3 and 6, respectively. And yet, I propose, the witchcraft-driven aporia at the heart of Buli custom (*adat re atorang*)—the impossibility of a morally good community of sociality and conviviality in the face of the persistence of the *gua*—is essentially different because it is an aporia about which tradition itself is fully, indeed painfully, cognizant. Take, for instance, this brief exchange between old lady Gambar and myself in 2011, so typical of the conversational exchanges that play themselves out every time I return to Buli and meet someone I know after a period of separation:

GAMBAR: Mister, you have arrived. I thought you wouldn't come down to visit us again. (*Mister, aum lafo to. Ku am lafo map pantó.*)

NILS: Yes, I have arrived again. To see how you are, you know. (*Ehh, ilafo fawé. Iningo meu pa ga.*)

GAMBAR: When you come back again, we shall surely all be dead. There are many witches here, so when you return they will have eaten us all. (*Osta au map fawé, amam mat ndumi. Gua nalale ga, aum map fawé si dan am ndumi.*)

"We shall surely all be dead"—using the first person plural form of "we," which excludes the person one speaks to (*amam*)—is a standardized expression about the future. It encapsulates a basic truth about the inescapability of witchcraft but wraps it in the polite humility of "making oneself small" (*fanenena it*) by emphasizing one's imminent mortality.[8] Somehow by making oneself small, by highlighting one's frailty and mortality vis-à-vis witchcraft, one may protect oneself against it: this is the basic insight of Buli moral norms. In other words, not only the ethics of "caution," humility, and "good companionship" but also the morality of exchange mandated by Buli tradition operate explicitly in the shadows of concerns and anxieties about witchcraft. Without a solution to the aporias of witchcraft, "caution" is the best and indeed the only approach.

Crucially, this ethics of caution is not only an effect of the opacity of other people's minds. It is also an effect of the opacity of one's own inside, the fundamental inaccessibility of one's own mind to oneself. It was this inaccessibility that Lolos struggled with in an acute form when he agonized over the possibility that he might really be a *gua*. But everyone in Buli—as illustrated by Frida's and Kenari's dreams—is faced with the possibility that they, too, might be witches. As a result, the concerns about witchcraft that suffuse sociality and exchange in Buli relate not only to fears of being attacked by a witch or of being accused of being a witch. They grow just as disconcertingly from the possibility of becoming a witch oneself, and even from the risk of being a witch without knowing it.

Alterity is, in this sense, not merely a feature of the social other. Radical alterity is a constituent part of who one might be, of identity itself. The presence of alterity at the heart of identity has, of course, been discussed in philosophy, especially by French thinkers, for some time (Bataille 1992; Derrida 2001b; Grosz 1994; Kristeva 1982; Lacan 1977), and recently it has also begun to be analyzed from a variety of vantage points within anthropology (Taussig 1993; Willerslev 2007). In a recent, and for my purposes very relevant, article that canvasses much of this discussion, Thomas Csordas suggests that alterity, a constituent part of embodied existence itself, "is the phenomenological kernel of religion" (2004:164). Csordas defines "religion" in the broadest sense, not as a particular kind of, say, world religion, but as a form of existential rumination or wonderment about being-in-the-world. In religion, defined in this broad sense, "the other" constitutes an inescapable source of puzzlement, an inaccessibility, in much the way I have talked about it in this chapter: "We are inevitably surprised by others, given the impossibility of perfectly coinciding with them in thought or feeling, mood or motivation. In this sense, the problem of subjectivity is that we are never completely ourselves, and the problem of intersubjectivity is that we are never completely in accord with others" (Csordas 2004:163). This "impossibility of perfectly coinciding" is radicalized in a society like Buli, where the minds of other people are opaque, and where even adequate access to one's own mind is impossible. Under such "epistemologically muddy" conditions of intersubjective existence, people are "never completely" themselves. Disturbingly, people are essentially always other to themselves. What Csordas refers to as "intimate alterity" (167), the way alterity is an embodied aspect of the self, very much characterizes Buli subjectivity: one is always other to oneself.

Csordas suggests that this "aporia of alterity" is religion's universal object (2004:167). Religion is the attempt to puzzle out humans' otherness to themselves and to each other. Now, what interests me here is that Csordas opens up the possibility that the human attempt to address this "aporia of alterity" may take a number of forms, and that religion and the notion of the divine are just one such form: "In the sense in which I am using it, alterity is an elementary constituent of subjectivity and intersubjectivity, and this is how it is part of the structure of being-in-the-world . . . [how] it [can] be elaborated into the monstrous as well as the divine" (164). Perhaps, in places where the aporia of alterity is particularly acute, it may sometimes also assume a monstrous form. Witchcraft is, in this way of phrasing the problem of intersubjectivity, a monstrous form that the aporia of alterity may take in some places and some situations. This, for me, is a helpful way of approaching, however warily, the inaccessibility of witchcraft in Buli: The *gua* is the embodiment of alterity, the monstrous shape of the foreignness of others to me and of me to myself. The inescapability of this radical alterity is the inescapability of witchcraft. It is the "immeasurability" of other people and the opacity of every person to themselves, I reason, that make the *gua* inaccessible in Buli. The *gua* is monstrous because it is unrecognizable, in that its existence and mode of action can be only "guessed at." The *gua* "can only be mis-known (*méconnue*)" (Derrida 1990:79). The truly monstrous dimension of the fact that the *gua* can only be "mis-known" is the possibility that someone, anyone, oneself, may be the embodiment of this monstrosity without knowing it. It is in this sense that witchcraft goes to the heart of an aporia that is profoundly and inextricably embedded in Buli ontology and sociality.

# 8

# TECHNOLOGY, MONEY, AND THE FUTURES OF WITCHCRAFT

> In the past when we only had oil lamps,
> witches could hide in the darkness.
> Now that we have 90-watt bulbs, let them try.
>
> *Popiseí kpake be poci egat rakrák*
> *gabe gua rcung amak kem si dgogan mali dororam ca.*
> *Gabe tane padamara 90 watt; coba.*
>
> MATEUS, 2011

## Soundscape 2004

The entry in my field notes for one evening in May 2004 reads as follows:

It is only half past eight, but I have gone to bed early. Partly I am a bit le-thargic, because all I have had today are two packets of *mie* (noodles). The rest of the household is equally hungry. Nobody has gone fishing because of the strong wind, and there is no fish. But the main reason that I have gone to bed early is that I am seeking refuge from the noise. It is almost un-bearable. The loudspeakers from yesterday's wedding reception (I. *resepsi*) next door are still piled up in the street behind the house, and a group of young guys are taking full advantage of this, blaring music into the night. It forces everyone else to turn up their already loud TVs, and the noise is, as people gleefully note, "dry" (*namáng*). The "dry" din from the stereos adds to the noise of the motorized trishaws, some of them without mufflers and all with mounted stereos, the 75cc motorbikes, the mining trucks that come here for sand, stones, and timber, and the distant sound of outboard motors and *ketinting* pipe motors out at sea. As I write this, a government loudspeaker car from the district office is announcing the results of the recent election for the district (I. *kecamatan*), but it can barely be heard above the general racket.

This entry is not unusual for my experience of Buli after 2000. Indeed, the decibel level has increased exponentially in the village in recent years. The sounds of the tropical forest that used to fill the night air have now given way to other, louder sounds. As night falls, a constantly increasing number of trucks, motorized trishaws (called *bentor*), and blaring music systems compete for auditory dominance. New sources of income and access to money have made these modern consumer items abundant, and people have a keen desire for them. This desire ties in well with their generally favorable view of the changes over recent years that have brought new people and new wealth to the region. When I began fieldwork in Buli in 1991, the most hotly desired goods and services were radios, bicycles, watches, cement houses, and household electricity. By the early years of the twenty-first century, the local wish-list had been upgraded to include refrigerators, roof tiles, prefabricated windows, motorbikes, satellite dishes, and mobile phones. In addition, and perhaps most important of all, were TVs, video CD players (VCDs), and stereo systems. These media technologies, icons of modernity throughout Indonesia, used to be restricted to the chosen few. By 2004, however, many people had acquired these machines of electronic noise-making. At all hours after dark, one is therefore likely to hear two or three stereos compete with each other at full volume. Before daybreak, stereos are turned on again, blasting out a mixture of Indonesian *dangdut*, Western soft rock, and Chinese pop music, as the young men who have secured themselves a position in the mining company get ready for the day shift. The soundscape in Buli has changed. Its volume has been turned up.

Anyone who has visited a fair-sized provincial town in Indonesia is likely to have noticed, and perhaps—like myself—at times felt overwhelmed by, its noise: the orchestra of honking cars, the melodic chimes of the *kaki lima* traders advertising their food items, and the blaring music from loudspeakers in stores and on public transport. In Ternate, Ambon, and Manado I often had to squeeze into the front seat of one of the public Suzuki minivans (*bemo*) that ply their routes through the cities, finding myself jackknifed into place on top of a full-sized loudspeaker that the young male driver has installed where the front-seat passenger's legs are supposed to go. The music inevitably is deafening. Or at least deafening to my ears. For whereas I had to make an effort not to mind, other passengers seemed unfazed. As Freek Colombijn has observed, what others might regard as intolerable noise is, in Indonesia, a "non-issue" (2007:257); it is a self-evident, doxic feature of urban Indonesian modernity.[1]

The new soundscape of Buli that I struggled so hard to accept that evening in 2004—admittedly because it clashed with my middle-class and Western sensibilities

**Figure 29.** A captivated crowd watches a South American soap opera. The public
TV set was made available by a mining exploration crew. 1996. Photo by author.

and romantic nostalgia for earlier periods of tropical fieldwork without amplified
sounds—was in this sense a joyous "performance of modernity," an emulation
of the soundscapes of regional urban centers like Tobelo, Ternate, Ambon, and
Manado, places that people had increasingly become familiar with, and that they
wanted Buli to one day resemble. These expectations of modernity formed a consensus with just a few exceptions. I fondly remember old Kuka, one of the rare
people who shared my aversion to the incessant clamor. In the early 1990s he had
ruined the public TV outside his house, dousing it with water because he was fed
up with the constant noise from the crowds that gathered to watch Latin American
soap operas till late at night (see fig. 29). Most people agreed, though, that now finally the sleepy village had become delightfully "bustling" (I. *ramai*).

## The Functions of Sound

Indonesian modernity is generally infused, as Karen Strassler has noted, with an
"aesthetic of *ramai*" (2010:88). On an Indonesian periphery that is eager to be part
of this modern aesthetic, bustling noise is a sign of, and even a vehicle for, modernity. This chapter will seek to substantiate the argument that in Buli there is a

double function to the appeal of this aesthetic of *ramai*: it seeks not only to bring about something, but also to "block out" something else.

*Ramai* is an index of modernity exactly *because* it drowns out sounds from the forest that cause people great concern, in particular the sounds of the bird forms that witches take. The "dry" noise of electronically amplified music is in fact widely regarded as a deterrent against witches, blocking them in much the same way as the ancestors and guardian spirits used to "block" (*tiban*) the *gua*. The *gua* is said to be afraid (*namcait*) of noise, just as it dislikes (*ulo loló pa*) bright lights and large groups of people. The *gua* therefore tends to attack people who are alone in dark and quiet places, while lights (*plangan*) and noise (*lio*) hold the *gua* at bay. For this reason, a powerful deterrent against witchcraft is said to be a magical spell that one buries under the entrance to the house to ensure that it will always look lively and bright to would-be guests passing by outside. The magic has the dual purpose of making one popular and therefore unlikely to become the object of a *gua*'s grudge, and of minimizing the risk of attacks, since the *gua* attacks only when one is alone. Witches frequent places that are deserted and quiet (I. *sunyi*), while they stay away from places that are bustling or *ramai*. The lights and noises that are so integral to the Indonesian modern aesthetic of *ramai* in this sense offer a refuge, an obstacle akin to that of magic and the ancestors, against the *gua*. While for me the sound-scape of modernity that electricity provided entailed "the dangers of an indiscriminate and imperialistic spread of more and larger sounds into every corner of man's life" (Schafer 1994:3), to Buli people it appeared to offer a safe haven. This, I believe, is a crucial dimension of the overall appeal of modern technology in Buli.

Objects that we desire always seem to make a certain promise to us: the promise to remake the world and to remake who we are (Berlant 2011). As this chapter will explore, technology and the socioeconomic changes that facilitated this technology seemed to hold the same implicit promise as Christianity and state modernism—namely, the promise that it might be used to counteract, scare off, or even eradicate the *gua*. I suggest that "techgnosis," the "mystical impulses" that fuel the contemporary obsession with technology on a global scale (Davis 2004:5), is overdetermined in Buli by the same concerns and expectations of modernity that also drove conversion to Christianity and loyalty to the New Order state. Technology exists, Bruno Latour (1996) argues, because of the love it instills in us for it, while lack of love and the end of its promise will kill it. Love relationships take a lot of work; promises have to be sustained within a large network of actors. Ninety-watt light bulbs, as the epigraph to this chapter indicates, harbor a promise that is not only built into Indonesian modernity, but also reverberates through Christian rhetoric: an ability to dispel darkness, to enlighten and to shape a bright future. In a "bustling," well-lit environment witches cannot hide. Such is the sublime promise of techno-modernity in Buli.

The sublime nature of technology, bent into a particular shape by the technocratic vision of Indonesian nationalism, has been transformed once more in Buli into an apparent answer to local people's concerns about witchcraft. In striking contrast to Africa, where modern technology is seen to be either empowered by or closely linked to witchcraft (Comaroff and Comaroff 2002; Shaw 1997; Smith 2001), technology in Buli comes with the promise to ward it off. This, the latest in a long series of promised solutions to witchcraft, came to Buli at a new historical juncture, which was also marked by the transition to democracy, the outbreak of ethnoreligious violence, and the abrupt shift to a monetized economy associated with large-scale mining. This chapter suggests that the fraught transition to democracy and monetization after 1997, like the desire for technology, continues to be driven by the problem of witchcraft. Like technology, money and democracy appear to hold out the promise of a radicalization of what magic and tradition sought—namely, conviviality without the *gua*. Crucially, however, this promise also remains unfulfilled. The bustling modernity of technology, money, and equality that the third millennium seemed to promise continues, against all hope, to also harbor the *gua*. The mixture of promise and disappointment that has characterized Buli history for a century therefore lingers—so far at least—in Buli relations to technology, democracy, and money.

## Minerals and the Promise of Venture Capitalism

The new Buli soundscape of the twenty-first century was driven by a social and economic revolution that began in the late 1990s, when the discovery of vast laterite nickel resources in Halmahera attracted commercial mining interests to the region. In 1997 the state-owned mining company, Aneka Tambang (or Antam), began operations on Gei, a small island off Buli. Antam's concession is centered on Buli and sits on an enormous nickel deposit, estimated to hold around 250 million tons of relatively high-grade nickel ore. A similar mining concession controlled by the now French-owned Weda Bay Minerals is located across the peninsula, on the south coast of Halmahera, and is said to have a similarly rich ore. Together these deposits on Halmahera appear to hold what Mark Evans, CEO of Weda Bay Minerals, has called "the largest undeveloped nickel resource in the world" (Perkins 2006). Estimates suggest that the central landmass of Halmahera may contain as much as 10 percent of the world's existing nickel resources, enough for several decades of intensive mining. Even with falling nickel prices on a world market caught up in a financial crisis, the estimated commercial value of these resources runs into many billions of dollars. Antam, the largest mining consortium in Indonesian hands, currently generates roughly 50 percent of its profits from the sale of ferronickel and nickel ore, a percentage the company hopes to expand. The company is consequently pursuing what it calls "an aggressive lateritic nickel exploration program" in Halmahera (ANTAM 2001:3). Through subcontractors, Antam now operates three open-pit mines in the vicinity of Buli. From here the nickel ore is transported on large cargo ships to the company's ferronickel smelter facilities in Pomalaa, on the island of Sulawesi, or exported directly to Australia, China, and Japan (see fig. 30). This encompassment of Buli within modernity is set to intensify dramatically in the near future with the construction of a large smelter to process the ore locally.[2] Commercial mining is projected to be feasible for at least a century, during which time Buli is expected to transform from a village into a major industrial hub of eastern Indonesia.

The arrival of commercial mining has already caused a demographic, economic, and social revolution in Buli. The population has mushroomed with the arrival of petty traders, mining staff, and government officials, more than quadrupling from some 2,000 mainly Buli-speaking people in the early 1990s to almost 10,000 in 2012. The seven subcontracting companies that operate the nickel mines and carry out exploration in the region's mountainous hinterland employ some

**Figure 30.** Arien Lero and Eric Guslaw returning from a fishing trip in their *ketinting* outrigger. The open pit nickel mine on the island of Gei and a cargo ship are visible in the background. 2004. Photo by author.

1,200 people either on permanent contracts or as casual laborers. A sealed airstrip was opened just north of Buli in 1997, and with the upgrading of the harbor to accommodate larger ships and the establishment of sealed roads connecting Buli to other coastal villages and transmigration sites in the regency, and also to the peninsula's north coast and the more populous areas of Halmahera around the main towns of Ternate and Tidore, the atmosphere in Buli has changed from that of a quiet fishing village to that of a bustling pioneer town. It now attracts a motley assortment of investment seekers, petty traders, prostitutes, and adventurous young men in search of "good fortune" (I. *rejeki*). The town has full mobile-phone coverage, a local branch of the government-owned bank BRI, and an armada of motorized trishaws that whisk government officials and mining staff from their houses to the mess area in Buli Karya, the mainly Muslim settlement that lies between the administrative capital of Buli Serani and the village of Waiflí.

Life in Waiflí has been dramatically affected by the presence of the mine. The first signs of change came in the late 1990s, when many families began receiving what by local standards were extravagant sums of money (on the order of 20 million to 40 million rupiah, or between 2,000 and 4,000 USD) in compensation for coconut trees, sago palms, and gardens plots that had to be bulldozed to make way for mining sites, access roads, or housing. The cash was almost invariably converted into consumer goods: bicycles, sheets of corrugated iron, cement, floor tiles, clothes, mobile phones, and stereo systems. In Waiflí around forty locals, mostly men, were as of 2012 employed by subcontractors. A few work alternative day and night shifts in permanent jobs with monthly wages and pension plans, while most are hired as casual laborers, porters, or security guards. A number of women work as cooks or maids in the camps and mess halls, and several young people with a secondary education have managed to secure jobs as government officials charged with quality or environmental control (see fig. 31).

Within a few years these changes radically reshaped the economy of the village, as the emphasis shifted away from subsistence farming and fishing to a cash economy that is heavily dependent on the mining company. To comply with good industrial practices, the mining company contributes to this monetization by channeling substantial amounts of money into its "community development fund" to build and upgrade infrastructure, provide scholarships for eligible students, and award microcredit loans. The local standard of living has visibly improved as a result. While electricity and corrugated iron roofs were rare in the early 1990s, most houses are now hooked up to the electric grid powered by the government PLN generator in the administrative capital. New Chinese-made jeans and shirts have replaced the tattered T-shirts, sandals, and shabby clothes that were standard dress in Buli only a few years ago. At the same time, prices for basic goods have risen steeply, land has been sharply commoditized with the influx of outside

**Figure 31.** A mining worker weighs and registers samples
of nickel ore for testing. 2012. Photo by author.

migrants, and the rivers in the area are becoming polluted as people settle farther inland—much farther inland than any sane person would have contemplated
only a few years before, since there one is much more exposed to witches. Food
consumption is turning away from sago and fish toward the sugar-, rice- and flour-
based products that the shops have on offer; fishing grounds are being overfished
by commercial fishermen; and the coral reefs along which people conventionally
fished and hunted for turtles are being destroyed by the muddy tailings that wash
into the sea from the open mining pits.

Even as I highlight these grimmer aspects of the changes brought about by
mining, it is equally important to stress that while people in Buli sometimes voice
concerns that overlap with my misgivings, their problem is not the shift away from

subsistence farming, or proletarization, or environmental degradation. Their complaint is, primarily, that these changes might, against all expectation, still allow witchcraft to thrive. Against this complaint, however, people also see in the opening of the nickel-mining operation and the attendant possibilities for wage labor and commoditization the possible fulfillment of the promise of modernity that the New Order regime had made but had proved unable to deliver. Now, with the mining company, the modern world appears to have finally come to Buli. With this has come the promise of social wealth (I. *kesejahteraan*), development, and progress (I. *kemajuan*); a modern world of good houses, friendly neighbors, wealth, and health. It is electricity, in particular, that appears to hold the capacity to reshape the social world by bringing light and sound to the village, creating a *ramai* world without *gua*.

## The Sounds of Witchcraft

Conventionally, the *gua* has three auditory manifestations: the calls of the *kokók*, the *cokaéko*, and the *ngangá*. These may appear to be birds to the outside observer, but people insist that while the calls may come from creatures that look like birds, they are in fact *gua* who use the birds as a cloak (*mef*) or as a canoe (*pelang*) (see fig. 32). On a silent night, the sudden call from one of these witch-birds will wake up most people in the village and send those still lingering outside to talk, flirt, or watch TV scuttling back into their houses. The sharp vocalizing of the *kokók*, the whistles of the *cokaéko,* and the nasal, seemingly mocking calls of the *ngangá* are all signs that a *gua* is on the prowl (*amngái*), and people expect that such calls will inevitably be followed the next day by news of illness or death in the village.[3]

Such calls will be the main topic of conversation the next morning as people wait in suspense to hear who has fallen ill during the night. Especially if someone is already ill from suspected witchcraft (*ungan*), the calling of witch-birds is likely to send the relatives into a panic. The dread that accompanies these sounds is extremely contagious, and it is impossible not to be caught up in the apprehensive atmosphere. Indeed, the calls of these birds have a truly eerie quality to them that even Western scientists cannot deny. An otherwise sober ornithological guidebook describes the warning calls of the Moluccan owlet-nightjar (Latin *Aegotheles crinifrons*)—probably the *ngangá* and the only one of the three witch-birds that can be approximately identified from the literature—as "a series of wild, maniacal blood-curdling screams" (Coates and Bishop 1997:364).[4] What makes these calls doubly disturbing in Buli is that, as is always the case with the *gua*, one cannot trust them. Convention has it that a loud call is an indication that the *gua* is far away, while a faint call means it is actually close at hand. This means that once

**Figure 32.** A witch-bird perched in the rafters of a house.
Drawing by Carolin Guslaw (nine years old).

people have been surprised by the call of a witch-bird, hearing it loud and clear in the night, they will need to spend a great deal of time afterward straining to catch the possible fainter calls that signal a much more imminent danger. The cessation of calls brings little comfort, because it ironically signifies the *presence* of the *gua*.

There are a number of ways to counter the vocalizing of the witch-bird by producing sounds of one's own. If one hears the *kokók*, one can, for instance, repeatedly chant the word *katekate* as a protective spell.[5] Nowadays, electronic media seem to offer a similar kind of protective spell. The prevalence of electronic media, which have come to play such an important part in Buli life in recent years, is thus not merely an indication of a different set of sensibilities toward sound than those cultivated by a middle-class, Western anthropologist, nor are TVs, video CD players, stereos, and motorbikes merely the standard luxury items on a wish list for people living in the Indonesian periphery. They are also a means of altering the soundscape of the village in an attempt to keep the sounds of the *gua* at bay. For people in Buli, the appeal of "the modern world" (I. *dunia modern*), as idealized and incorporated into the desire for technological consumer goods in Indonesia, is dependent upon an implicit promise to deliver them from the *gua*. Indeed, it is from this perspective that Buli expectations of, and engagement with, the modernity associated with mining need to be read. The new technologies afforded by the arrival of venture capitalism mean that the hope of an end to witchcraft has found a new form. Amplified sound constitutes one expression of this new hope; electric lights are another.

## The Sublime Nature of Technology

Back in 1993, Noah had been Sami's host on the night she went mad (as recounted in chapter 6). A few weeks after this disturbing incident, Noah installed electricity in his house. Noah's house is next to the stream where people go to bathe, also at night. It is a dark spot where the birdcalls of witches can often be heard, and so Noah suspended a light bulb outside his house to brighten up this area and keep the *gua* at bay. In the late afternoon, people often stop off at various bathing spots along the stream, and it is common to greet those bathing later than most with the sentence, "Hurry, it is getting dark" (*Mfatóal, bon dodórame to, ga*). Out of propriety, women tend to bathe somewhat later than men, and because it may already be dark, they never do so alone. After Noah's lamp went up, the women were careful to stay right on the outer edge of the light cone, just out of sight but within easy reach of the illuminated area (see fig. 33). For the same reason, most people—if they can afford to have electricity installed—keep their electric lights on all night. It took some time for me to get used to falling asleep under the glaring light of an electric bulb. During my first stint of fieldwork I insisted on using only a kerosene pressure lamp, rather than having electricity installed. I initially attributed the general muttering about my insistence on using the kerosene lamp to be merely a matter of status. A Westerner, I reasoned, was probably expected to want electric lights, an expectation I did not feel like honoring. Only very gradually did I come to realize that the issue of electricity was directly related to concerns for my personal well-being, and to the problem of witchcraft.

Electricity has been an index of modernity ever since the colonial period in Indonesia, and the technological ability of electricity to bring both light and sound was enrolled into the colonial civilizing project.[6] As Rudolph Mrázek (2002) has shown, the spread of electricity and the introduction of the wireless radio during the early decades of the twentieth century provided a means by which Dutch colonialists could seek refuge from the realities of the colony by isolating themselves in

**Figure 33.** An incandescent light bulb outside a bedroom window. 2011. Photo by author.

an enlightened and sound-filled indoor environment, imagining themselves to be part of an ideal modern colony and a community of fellow Dutchmen in the midst of the tropical Netherlands Indies. This idea of modernity as an escape from conditions associated with the darkness of native life also diffused into the Indonesian national consciousness. It came to Buli through New Order modernism, which understood technology—both in a literal sense and as the social technologies of political governance—as a tool of domestication.

David Nye (1994) has suggested that technology achieved a "sublime" quality in American modernity because of its ability to dominate nature, providing a kind of civil religion through which the United States came to see and understand itself. In New Order Indonesia the technological sublime was also associated with the ability to remake the nation. Taking his cue from Nye (1994), Joshua Barker has shown that a particular "technological sublime" has informed Indonesian modernity since independence. In this modernity new technologies, whether in the shape of radios or satellites, are ascribed the "capacity to mediate a culturally diverse, traditional, and underdeveloped past with a modern, nationally unified and developed future" (2005:710; Mrázek 2002). In the Indonesian political imagination, nationhood, development and statecraft are to be achieved through "technological fixes" (Barker 2005:715; Franke 1972; Heryanto 1988). Obviously, this kind of "techno-politics" is unique neither to Indonesia (see, e.g., Mitchell 2002) nor to the contemporary period. The human species has an evolution-based fascination with and propensity to remake itself through technology (Taylor 2010), a feature that has been turned into a driving force of modernity itself. As Bronislaw Szerszynski (2005) has shown, there is a close link between the sublime quality of technology to transform the human condition and notions of the sacred. Once it arose to prominence with the globalization of modernity, technology could become "the global sacred" (159). In my view, however, this globalization of the technological sublime is neither straightforward nor homogeneous. Technology as a sublime aspect of modernity was globalized throughout the regions formerly known as "the Third World" as a "cult of the modern" (Taussig 1987:278). In Indonesia this techno-political vision, which took on an iconic form in specific technologies, has been central to nation building. The vision came with an explicit desire to transcend the traditional, underdeveloped past. I suggest that it is upon this notion of modern technology as an instrument to alter social life that Buli people pin their hopes today. Technology's capacity to effect social change—to make society durable, as Latour (1991) puts it—endows it with a particular sublime quality (Davis 2004). In Buli, the sublime ability of technology to transform the past became closely linked to modernity's promise to dispel witchcraft, sorcery, and spirits. The technologically altered soundscapes and landscapes of modernity seemed to carry the potential to block out (*tiban*) the *gua* through electrically amplified sound and incandescent lights, in the same way that the ancestral and guardian spirits used to do.

This promise, I suggest, inspired Buli people to look to computers, stereos, and light bulbs as sublime means of warding off the *gua*. The promise of technology was already read into the invocation by the police chief in Buli of the imminent arrival of bulldozers, construction projects (I. *proyek*), and roads as the reasons why witchcraft trouble had to stop (see chapter 6). Recently, video cameras have been added to this list. Video cameras, like light bulbs, become artifacts where the logic of state notions and Buli notions of the technological sublime overlap, as the following example shows. In 2008, a woman was found dead in her coconut grove. She had gone to the garden alone but failed to return in the afternoon. The police came to the scene, and search parties were sent out. They eventually found the woman's lifeless body in the early hours of the morning. She was lying on her side at the foot of a coconut tree, but her physical condition was shocking. Her hair had completely fallen off, leaving her scalp bare, and her skin appeared to have peeled off entirely, leaving her with a white complexion "like the inner skin of the stingray (*fafagai*)." It looked, according to those who found her, "as if someone had soaked her in boiling water." Suspecting foul play, the police questioned her husband, but this failed to produce any evidence. The general consensus in Buli was that the woman had been attacked and her skin "peeled off" by a *gua*. In a move that seemed, in Buli eyes, to accept this interpretation, the police installed a video camera with movement sensors on a nearby coconut tree to catch any return of the culprit to the scene of the crime. In the village the camera was quickly dubbed "the demon tool" (I. *alat setan*), the implication being that it was of some special, possibly infrared, make that could also record spirit beings and roaming shadows. Confidence in the camera was short-lived, however, and when it failed to produce any revealing footage this confirmed the widespread sense that the *gua*'s tactics of concealment (*gogan*) and deceit (*darawa*) were too refined, even for advanced technology like the demon tool.

## The Auto-Immunity of Technology

The problem for hopes about the technological sublime in Buli is that witches are, themselves, technologically minded. *Gua* have their own "tools," their own *alat*. In 2007, an elderly woman died after falling off a hired motorbike. Her husband worked as a caretaker at one of the mining exploration sites near Buli, and she lived with him there. When a grandchild at home fell ill the woman had hailed a motorbike (I. *ojek*) and asked to be taken back to Buli. En route, however, she had fallen off without the *ojek* driver noticing. Discovering later that his passenger was missing, he doubled back and found her dead, the back of her head crushed. A fall from a motorbike, so people argued, could not possibly cause such damage. The woman had clearly been assaulted by a *gua*, and the witch had cleverly disguised the attack as an accident. This, one man explained, "is just how the *gua* tries to play with our minds (*totomói*). It can enter pigs, it can enter deer, it can sail a boat in the forest, it can enter a motorbike, it can enter all kinds of things. The *gua* has many tools (*alat*) available, but only one aim: to eat." In Buli, the sublime qualities of technology are undermined by the fact that the *gua* itself is "technological": it has its own appliances (*alat*). The *gua* is able to assume any form, human or nonhuman. It can take the shape of an animal or a plant, and it can become any object, mechanical or inanimate. The *gua* in that sense *can become* technology: a motorbike or a boat, for instance. It can even, some people told me, turn into a plastic water container. This ability of the *gua* to become technology means that the "technological sublime" in Buli is infected by what Derrida calls "auto-immunity": the new technology that people hope will ward off the *gua* may also be "producing, reproducing, and regenerating the very thing it seeks to disarm" (2003:99). The term "infected" is apt here, because when a *gua* spirit "enters" (*ncung*) a human being or a motorbike it literally "climbs aboard" (*saplo*) the person or the object in the same way a person climbs aboard a boat and a car, or indeed the way a disease "infects" a person's body. Technology in Buli is therefore potentially always "infected" or "boarded" by witchcraft—a potentiality that is, of course, problematic for the hopes people place in technology's ability to rid the village of witchcraft.

The auto-immunity of technology to witchcraft perpetuates a problematic issue that has always "infected" Buli protective measures against the *gua*. The animal guardian spirits (*suang*) that "blocked" Buli people from falling prey to witchcraft in animist times were vulnerable to the same auto-immunity. The *gua* could enter the same animal species that people honored as their spirit guardians. This meant that one's animal spirit (*suang*) might actually, without one's knowing it, be a witch (*gua*), so by honoring one's *suang* to protect oneself against witchcraft, one might inadvertently be turning oneself into a witch. This, some people claim, is exactly what happened to a family who honored as their *suang* a particular species of coral grouper. Perhaps because they fed the *suang* too much (*pei suang nauatú*), or perhaps because the coral grouper had been used as a disguise (*mef*) by a *gua*, several members of this family, so people say, became witches themselves. As people have "advanced" (I. *mahir*) their modes of protection against witchcraft by replacing their reliance on the animal spirits (*suang*) of a pre-Christian era with faith in the new technologies of a modern era, the *gua* has become more advanced, too, merely shifting its ability to enter animals toward a propensity to "infect" technology.

Indonesian modernity is, above all, technological. Therein lies a particular kind of promise, a recognizable kind of hope. And yet, the technological nature of the *gua* means that Buli hopes concerning technology are fraught with ambivalence. The background of the quotation as an epigraph to this chapter, that a witch could not possibly overcome a 90-watt bulb, a statement that appears so full of confidence in technology when taken out of context, illustrates this ambivalence well. The context for the quotation is as follows. It was the last day of my visit to Buli in July 2011, and I was chatting with a group of men, all in their twenties and thirties. We were talking about the West in general. The men felt that people "up in the West" (the world outside of North Maluku unilaterally being referred to as "up") were better off. Mateus specified one of the reasons for this: "Up in the West where you live there are no *gua*, so you have it good. Here in Buli there are *gua*, but we don't know (*ni gua ga amak to pa*)." I countered that surely with all of the changes in Buli in recent years things were getting better. This is a refrain that Buli people themselves often repeat. On this day, however, Mateus was less sure. "You know, the *gua* have their seasons (*gua tane ni musim*)," he replied. Attacks come in waves. Sometimes there are no attacks for long time; then suddenly there is a whole slew of attacks. Perhaps, a new "witchcraft season" might come soon. Then Mateus returned to the difference between Buli and the West: "You live in an 'advanced' (I. *mahir*) part of the world, so the *gua* are unable to do anything (*si dafena pa*). In the past when we only had oil lamps, the witches could hide in the darkness. Now that we have 90-watt bulbs, let them try."[7]

It is noteworthy that Mateus's confidence in technology is couched in a general uncertainty about the future of witchcraft. On the one hand, he confidently subscribes to the techno-political visions of the Indonesian national imagination, which attributes to technology the ability to effect a transformation from a backward past into an "advanced" future, a future that in many ways, on the periphery of the Indonesian nation, is like a foreign country (Lowenthal 1999)—namely, the Western world (Bubandt 2004b). On the other hand, Mateus also has a strong sense that Buli might never "get there," as it were. That "advancement" and "progress" (I. *kemajuan*) are somehow being dispersed by the "seasons" of witchcraft. The problem is that witches appear to be advancing, too. One woman, commenting on the apparent accident of the elderly woman who fell off a motorbike before being eaten by a *gua* in 2007, highlighted this ominous possibility. "The *gua*," she said, "was merely covering up (*tabak*) its own wound (*ungan*). This is what makes witchcraft so difficult to deal with these days. Against the *gua* even professors lose out. They are incredibly clever (I. *pintar*). These days all the *gua* are clever, and they are getting cleverer every day."

The tactics of concealment (*gogan*) that are a trademark of the witch appear to have become increasingly refined in recent years. The *gua*, it seems, is "modernizing" at least as quickly as Buli society, fine-tuning its technologies of concealment and its apparatus of deception to fit the new, modern age and its technologies.[8] Whereas witches in the 1930s were arguably among those most eager to convert to Christianity, and in the 1990s seemed more loyal to the New Order state than most, the *gua* in the beginning of the third millennium seemed to find new places of hiding in modern technology and tiled houses. In that sense, the relative prosperity and the acquisition of modern technology that the arrival of mining has enabled in Buli trap people in the same aporia of hope and disappointment that Christianity and New Order modernism did.

There is a common thread linking the electronic attempts to silence the sounds of the *gua* in 2004, Sami's loud accusations in 1993, and the soundscape of 1933, when angry animists tried to drown out the sermons of a Christian mission that had failed to produce a return of the ancestors and a world without *gua*. All three soundscapes are voices from particular historical moments when political power and existential anxieties have come together in a contentious relationship that invariably revolves around hopes and concerns about the *gua*. Techno-modernity entails the hope that it may banish the *gua*, even while the means by which this eradication is to be effected appears to enable the renewal of witchcraft. "Techgnosis"—the third transformation of the hope to rid Buli of witchcraft—is therefore, as Christianity and state modernism before it, thoroughly ambivalent. This ambivalence is nicely encapsulated in the ideas and concerns that people harbored about airplanes during the late 1990s as an airstrip was being built a few kilometers from the village.

## Of Planes and Shitting: Witchcraft and Expectations of Modernity

One afternoon, I was helping a group of men weed the area in front of the shrine of Íyan Toa, the cultural hero of Buli, in preparation for a ritual to request his protection, when a large commercial jet drew a white stripe across the sky high above our heads.

Airplanes occupy a central place in Indonesian national discourse and, like light bulbs, radios, and satellites, are powerful technological icons of modernity (Barker 2005; Bubandt 1998a; Mrázek 1997). There were rumors that Merpati, a subsidiary of the national airline, Garuda, would open an air route between Ternate and Buli, and airplanes were therefore at the time a favorite topic of conversation in Buli.

Wadone stopped weeding and asked me where the airplane might be going. Another man, without waiting for my answer, asked how many people such a plane might contain and what kept the passengers from falling overboard. Wadone found this question more interesting than his own, and he was eager to pursue its logic to the end: "Are you allowed to shit on board?" he asked. The image guiding this question was that of the open-air toilet pits of the wooden passenger ships that plow between Buli and the nearest major town, Tobelo. Using these toilets, with their clear view of the water underneath, is always accompanied by worries about falling overboard. Perhaps airplanes had toilets that were also merely holes onto the open air? Wadone, clearly pleased with his own question, turned to the other men to answer it himself: "If they are, then the shit will drop on our heads, and we will think it comes from a *gua*." This answer produced a gale of laughter from the other men. *Gua* can take the form of many things, including animals. It is said, however, that the excrement of *gua* is always human, even when the *gua* have assumed the shape of birds or other animals. The image of human excrement falling from the sky is therefore closely associated with flying witches. Placing the bizarre image of shitting witches in the context of an outside world that had its own strangeness—and the image of white people defecating in clean and tidy airplanes was strange indeed—had great humorous potential. Accompanied as Wadone's joke was by a small pantomime, in which he anxiously covered his head with one hand while he glanced furtively toward the sky—almost in mimicry of the ritual deference (*suba*) that people perform during marriage ceremonies—it had all the right ingredients for a particular brand of Buli humor, the self-deprecating joke. Ducking white people's turds that fall mysteriously from the sky as if they came from an invisible but superior marriage partner (*paing*), Buli people would make fools of themselves thinking the feces came from flying witches. Wadone's joke nicely encapsulated the entangled and ambivalent relationship between witchcraft and technology as a harbinger of modernity. The joke could be taken to mean at least two things. Perhaps it suggested that in the modern world, one had to get used to the changes that technology was bringing, and that in this brave new world the existence of witches was laughable. Or perhaps the joke implied the opposite: that modern technology proved what tradition had always claimed about being careful where one treads in unknown terrain. If excrement from Westerners falling from the sky became a problem as more airplanes began to traverse the sky above Buli, the conventional idea that birds sometimes shit human turds because witches use them as "canoes" might not be so stupid (I. *bodoh*) and backward (I. *terbelakang*) after all. In short, the technology of airplanes seemed to both dispel and confirm the reality of witchcraft.

## Democracy, Violence, and Falling Maggots

The same mixture of hope and anxiety that characterized people's expectations of technology also ran through their perception of the two other important changes to Buli society in the early twenty-first century: the politically arduous change to democracy, and the shift to a monetary economy.

The social and technological changes brought about by the arrival of mining in Buli coincided with a series of political changes that were set in train by the collapse of the New Order in May 1998. These political changes also had an impact on Buli society, in turn transforming the possibilities and impossibilities of witchcraft. The fall of Suharto was a direct result of persistent student protests in the main cities on Java that articulated an endemic political legitimacy crisis (Elson 2001). This crisis had been made palpable by the East Asian financial crisis after 1997, which seriously undermined the New Order regime's promise of development and meant that, as Mary Steedly has noted, it could "no longer even pretend to deliver modernity's material goods" (2000:813). In the lead-up to the first free general elections, the national parliament under the leadership of President Jusuf Habibie passed Laws No. 22 and 25, two far-reaching acts that entailed the devolution of administrative authority and allocation of a percentage of regional income to the regency (I. *kabupaten*) level (Aspinall and Fealey 2003). The laws, described by the World Bank as an administrative "Big Bang" (World Bank 2003), were initially hailed as a landmark change (Booth 1999). It soon became apparent, though, that—the new rhetoric of transparency and empowerment notwithstanding—decentralization did not necessarily mean democratization (Collins 2007). Corruption, patrimonialism, and "strong-man politics" were easily adapted to the new political landscape of democracy, and compounded by ethnic localism, these drove much of the process of *pemakaran* or "blossoming," the creation of new provinces and regencies (I. *kabupaten*), that accompanied decentralization. In what has been aptly described as a process of "administrative involution" (Schulte Nordholt and Klinken 2007:19), new administrative areas were established through sustained pressure from local elites, who spoke about the importance of empowering local "sons of the earth" (I. *putra bumi*) while collecting money to be paid as bribes to officials within the Ministry of the Interior in Jakarta. In return, the new administrative areas provided new opportunities for the same elites to gain lucrative government positions that ensured a steady source of payment for the licenses and approvals that private business needed.

As a result of this new alliance between the discourse of democracy, political localism, and the practices of patrimonialism, the number of regencies in Indonesia grew rapidly from 330 in 1999 to 440 in 2004, while seven new provinces were carved out. Especially in the resource-rich parts of Indonesia, the perceived stakes in the new dynamic of decentralization, direct elections, and patrimonialism were high, and violence frequently erupted (Bertrand 2003; Klinken 2007). North Maluku was a clear instance of this process (Bubandt 2006). Less than a month after it was inaugurated as a separate province in October 1999—one of the first provinces to be created after the decentralization laws had been passed— violent conflicts, framed mainly in religious terms, broke out in the administrative capitals on Tidore and Ternate, and soon clashes between Christians and Muslims spread to most parts of Halmahera, fueled by rumors of the ethnoreligious conflict in Ambon and an intense politics of suspicion that was part of the New Order legacy (Bertrand 2003; Hefner 2000; Klinken 2007; Sidel 2007). The causes and dynamics of the outbreaks were complex and have been analyzed in detail (Bubandt 2001, 2004b, 2008b; Duncan 2005, 2013; Wilson 2005), so here I will confine myself to describing the conflict and its aftermath from a Buli perspective.

As one of very few places on Halmahera, Buli did not become directly embroiled in the conflict—despite its mixed Christian and Muslim population. Waiflí is mainly Christian; Buli Karya, next to it, is Muslim; and Buli Serani, the administrative capital farthest north along the coast, is mixed. Because the area was still relatively isolated (the airstrip had only just opened, and the unsealed roads to other parts of Halmahera were still prone to being washed away by rain), had no sizable Makian population,[9] and maintained good cooperative relationships among the administrative and traditional leaders of the three villages, Buli managed to avoid communal violence. The conflicts elsewhere nevertheless affected the community deeply, as paranoia and fear of outside agitators (I. *provokator*) governed daily life between 1999 and 2001 (Bubandt 2004b). In late 1999, after conflict had erupted in the nearby town of Tobelo (Duncan 2013),[10] Muslim traders from southeast Sulawesi hurriedly fled Buli, while many Christian Chinese traders sought refuge in Manado. Local blacksmiths were inundated by requests for spears, machetes, and arrowheads for homemade spearguns, and many locals prepared for the expected confrontation by constructing small huts deep in the forest at the foot of Watileo Mountain for their women and children.

Although the violence never reached Buli, its impact was still strongly felt. Many people were visiting children who went to school in Tobelo, or had gone to the town to sell copra, and they were caught in Tobelo when violence erupted and all transport came to an abrupt halt. Markus, a Buli schoolboy boarding in Tobelo, remembers the smell of decomposition in particular: "The smell (*pupúi*) was terrible . . . bodies everywhere, on the side of the road and on the harbor front." Markus was not alone in associating the North Malukan conflict, and the Tobelo violence in particular, with the smell of decomposing corpses. While the conflict was euphemistically referred to as a "disturbance" (I. *kerusuhan*) in Indonesian, in Buli it was more straightforwardly known as "the killings" (*fapunpun ca*), "the explosion" (*pes ca*), or the "rottenness" (*jakam ca*). This emphasis on the violence as an olfactory event characterized by "rottenness" was significant because it forcefully linked the recent ethnoreligious violence to mythical forms of violence where the smell of decomposition (*pupúi*) and witchcraft play an important role (Bubandt 1998b). In the myth of Watowato, recounted in chapter 2, the world of Halmahera was created out of an act of witchcraft committed against the giant Watowato. The decomposition of his body gave off such a powerful smell that all other giants succumbed to it, and their bodies eventually formed the now nickel-bearing mountains in the region. According to another myth, Buli itself had to be moved after a battle with the Forest Tobelo, who were loyal to the sultan of Ternate, had left behind so many dead that the whole place reeked. The danger of rotten smells is that they attract the *gua*, and indeed, in the years following the violence in North Maluku, people insisted that the ongoing problem of *gua* attacks in Buli was caused by the smell of the many dead, which seemed to attract more *gua*, and—quite unfairly, so it seemed—led them to attack people in Buli.

On a visit to Buli in 2002, my first after the violence, Annie told me how there had been numerous cases of witchcraft after the conflict: "There are still witchcraft attacks now, but not so long ago, in 2000 and 2001 . . . weeeehhh . . . there was a lot of witchcraft illness (*ungan*). I'll tell you why, Nils. In Tobelo during the killing, they threw the bodies in the harbor. There were so many bodies that it was impossible to moor the boats to the pier. With all those deaths, the maggots (*uap*) began to fall on us." The image of "falling maggots" (*uap na marapawlo it*) makes a direct allusion to the problems associated with putrefaction. The conflict in Tobelo was "rotten" in the most literal of sense of the word, and it therefore carried the danger of spiritual contagion. The *gua* is always attracted to death and decomposition, perceiving the stench of decomposition (*pupúi*) as "fragrant" and "sweet" (*namná*). This goes for any death, but a death without burial fails to contain the smell and consequently holds a particular attraction for witches. As a result, witchcraft in Buli was seen to have been invigorated by political violence through olfactory means. The fact that the violent killings had happened elsewhere was counteracted by the sheer magnitude of the stench they caused. Annie was not alone in making this connection between political violence and witchcraft. Kenari also saw the violence in Tobelo as related to recent cases of witchcraft in Buli: "In my opinion it is like this: We didn't get any of the violence, so now we are hit in this way. This is God testing us. We were not involved in the war (I. *perang*), so now we have a war of being tried (I. *perang tantangan*). With all the dead bodies around, the ghosts of the unburied (*darári*) are hovering in the area, and now the illness is falling on us." The violent change from authoritarian rule to democracy in North Maluku rebounded on Buli in the form of witchcraft, as the village appeared to pay the price for its noninvolvement in the violence. The ghosts of the dead, it seemed, were defiant and were now unleashing a very familiar kind of war in Buli: a war of witchcraft. This notion of being at war with defiant spirits as a compensation for avoiding the conflict seemed to Kenari and Annie to accurately describe the new wave of witch attacks that appeared to accompany the aftermath of the violence. Both were still enthusiastic about the process of democratization and supportive of the political rhetoric of "giving power back to the sons of the region." But to Annie and to Kenari, democracy came at a price, and during 2001 and 2002 that price was a rash of witchcraft cases.

## Witchcraft, Mining, and Money

As we have already seen, during most of the 1990s Lolos had been one of the people most often accused of witchcraft. However, already before Lolos's illness and death in 1999, new *gua* suspects had emerged. These new suspected witches came from families that, only few years earlier, had been among those accusing Lolos of witchcraft, an irony that Lolos's family was quick to point out. This shift made the basic truth that anybody could be a *gua* painfully clear. Among those classified by many people in the early years of the twenty-first century as "terrible witches" (*gua na bahaya*) was Dina. Dina came from a family that had itself repeatedly fallen victim to witchcraft during the 1990s. Indeed, Dina's father, who had worked as a security guard for the mining company's drilling teams, had been "eaten" by a Buli coworker during an exploratory expedition to the interior of the island as late as 2001. The witch had "cut his throat" during the attack, preventing him from speaking during the illness that eventually killed him. Dina was married to Bawang, one of the few men who had obtained a permanent job with a mining contractor in the area. Bawang was related to Sami, another notorious victim of witchcraft during the 1990s (see chapter 6). Despite the fact that both Dina and Bawang came from families with long histories of falling victims to witchcraft, Dina now found herself accused. By 2010 she had been suspected of witchcraft in nine separate deaths, and some sarcastically called her "the king of all witches" (*gua ni kolano*). Pressure on Dina and her husband to leave the village had been mounting for several years, and when the mining contractor moved to Weda, Bawang managed to secure a job there, and the family moved. Since they had left, people agreed that the attacks had been fewer, and by 2011 people were again being cautiously optimistic about the future eradication of witchcraft in Buli.

Perhaps the influx of money, created by cash compensations and paid jobs in the mining industry, was finally making a dent in *gua* greed. Perhaps money was the technology that would once and for all bring an end to witchcraft. This scenario is one that many people hold out for themselves as a real possibility. It is a possibility, however, that was contradicted by Dina's witchcraft. Some people claimed that it was not Dina but her husband, Bawang, who was the real *gua*. But because he had a well-paying job in the mining company, they speculated, he had given up being a *gua* and had instead "infected" (*fasaplo*) his wife, loading the "seed of witchcraft" (*gua ni geo*) onto Dina in the manner that one loads baggage onto a canoe. Money and jobs, it seemed, did not mean the end of witchcraft, but merely its displacement into new places of hiding.

Early in the second decade of the twenty-first century, people in Buli were struggling with a new version of the same aporias of witchcraft that had entangled their grandparents a hundred years earlier: being caught between the promises of modernity and the irrepressible but inaccessible reality of witchcraft. Perhaps technology, democracy, and money could dispel the *gua*; perhaps they merely provided it with new places of hiding. The possibility that modernity, in this its third coming to Buli, could bring about an end to witchcraft appeared more likely than ever to many people, and yet it remained a tainted possibility, and therefore the object of a great deal of concern, speculation, and discussion. As a result people conducted, with themselves and each other, the same reflexive and self-conscious debate about witchcraft and modernity that people in Buli have been having for almost a century, hoping that a conversion to modernity will erase witchcraft from social life, and simultaneously fearing that it will not. Some feel that electricity, technology, money, and mining will mean the end of the *gua*, while others worry that the future will only create better opportunities for the *gua*, as people stop sharing and grudges grow. Yohan and Manus represent these two types of diagnosis.

## Yohan and Manus

In 2004, Yohan, the newly appointed village head, told me why he thought there would be no *gua* in the future:

> In the old days people hunted to get food. If I got a deer or wild pig and did not share it with you, you would be disappointed, and your "inside would break" (*uló namgói*). This is bad because it is the beginning of witchcraft. So in the past there were many *gua*. These days the mining company has arrived, and people have more money. If I buy a TV, you can buy one, too. If you build a nice house, I can build one, too. So there are fewer witches.
>
> In the past people drank dirty water, they ate sago and had no sugar, so they got worms. Then they would get sick and would say it was witchcraft (*ungan*). These days, people do not get sick as often. They have nice houses and TVs, so there will soon be no more *gua*. The *gua* will be "out of work" (I. *nganggur*).

Here Yohan holds out a vision for the future of the *gua* that is characteristic of what one might call "a Buli modern" (cf. Rabinow 1989). Yohan is not saying that the *gua* does not exist, for he is well acquainted with its reality from several angles. His grandfather had been regarded as a dangerous *gua* in the 1970s, and several members of his mother's family were later accused because of this connection. Inversely, when Yohan's brother had died of witchcraft in 1995 after only twelve hours of violent diarrhea, Yohan had been among those who had prepared to beat up the suspected *gua*, a distant in-law. It was therefore not the reality of the *gua* that was at stake in Yohan's scenario of its imminent demise. Instead, he made a sociological analysis of sorts of the job prospects of the *gua*. Yohan felt that the conditions of health, wealth, and welfare associated with modern consumer goods like cement, TVs, and sugar, which have become available to most people since the arrival of the mining company, would make witchcraft obsolete. As people got jobs in the mining industry, the *gua* would become unemployed (I. *nganggur*). Yohan's vision of witchcraft is about its demise with social and medical progress.

Contrast this optimistic view of modernity and the future of the *gua* with the statements made by Manus:

> Here in Buli we work hard, so the blood is always circulating and we do not get ill. In the cities they do not work much, and therefore they get

sick a lot. They have problems with the heart, paralysis, and high blood pressure. Here the air is clean, because there are no factories. However, the problem here is that there is a lot of witchcraft (*ungan*) and sorcery (*payao*). In the past people got along well. If someone got food, everybody would eat. These days, people are taken in by money, so they sell everything to get it. They sell the fish they catch and the game they kill. They even sell their gardens to the mining company. This has turned people's "insides sour" (*ulór na mayái*), and everybody is angry with everybody. Because of this, there is much more sorcery and witchcraft.

Manus was undertaking here an epidemiological analysis of the *gua*, as it were, portraying an alternative kind of Buli modern—namely, a pessimistic one.[11] For Manus, witchcraft and sorcery continued to reside in the social relations of Buli, and the new economic opportunities afforded by mining merely led to new opportunities for the *gua* to "flirt" with people as they became infatuated with money. Money allowed envious anger to brew anew. Here Manus holds out a nostalgic view of social relations. As he sees it, the contemporary obsession with money is destroying the "good companionship" (*farerér re faututi*) that Buli tradition mandates.

Manus's pessimism was hard-earned. In 2001, three years before I had this conversation with him, his daughter Tina had died of what appeared to be witchcraft (*ungan*). Tina had been a smiling thirteen-year-old, whom Manus had managed to get into junior high school (I. *SMP*), even though he had no job and made a living tapping and selling palm wine to mining personnel. One day, Tina's belly had begun to swell, and everyone had assumed that she was pregnant, despite her heated protests. As Tina's abdomen grew more and more distended, and she began to feel ill, her family had called in a local healer, who had diagnosed her illness as sorcery (*payao*). When the healer's cure did not seem to work, the family had taken Tina first to the local clinic in Buli and then to the hospital in Tobelo. The doctor had diagnosed her illness as the result of a tumor and recommended surgery. Tina, however, was frightened about the procedure and pleaded with her parents not to let the operation go ahead. Suspecting that sorcery was still the real cause (and unable to pay the cost of surgical intervention), Manus and his wife gave in to the girl's appeals. The family returned home, with the diagnosed tumor unremoved. Now, three years later, Manus regretted his decision. "If only she had been operated on," he said, looking away, "then she would be alive today." For Manus and his wife, who had only one other child, a severely handicapped boy, Tina's death was devastating. On one occasion Tina's mother, Maria, had approached me and quietly asked if I had any pills that could make her sorrow go away by helping her forget her dead daughter.

Manus's regrets grew from his recognition of the power of medical surgery, but they were also motivated by hindsight and by the knowledge about what had happened when the family returned to Buli. For as soon as they were back in the village, a *gua* had seized the opportunity of Tina's illness to attack her, "climb on board" (*saplo*) her body, and 'sit on top of'" (*totongo*) the tumor. Manus had witnessed the *gua* attack himself. One night, shortly after their return, Tina was in bed as usual, and Manus was asleep on his mat on the floor next to the bed when he suddenly felt like he was having difficulty breathing. Manus then experienced the condition called *babáif*, a state somewhere between being asleep and being awake. He looked up to find a *gua* crouching on top of his chest, getting ready to eat his liver:

> It was not like a dream (*mahngél*), Nils. I saw the *gua* as clearly as I see you now. I reached for my knife, but the *gua* disappeared. Then I got up. The door was blocked from the inside by a chair as always, so it must have gotten out somewhere else. It returned three times that night, each time disappearing before I could cut it down. Because I didn't fall asleep, it never succeeded in "taking my shadow" and eating me. So I never got ill. But I am sure this was the *gua* that ate my child. Soon afterward, Tina died.

Manus had recognized the *gua*. It was Dina, the current "king of all witches." Dina, ironically perhaps, was also a classificatory daughter of Yohan, the village head who optimistically said there would soon be no more *gua*. Manus was convinced of what he had seen, but he was unsure of what to make of it. There had been no grudges between his family and the family of Yohan and Dina. Perhaps, Manus speculated, the *gua* had merely used Dina's face as a mask to hide its true identity. He had therefore decided to keep his experience to himself and had never publicly accused Dina, not even when his daughter died a few days later. For him, the event did, however, point to something important: that the *gua* thrived among families with paid jobs. Indeed, it appeared that acquiring jobs, money, better houses, and TVs did not stop the gluttony of the *gua* for human liver. Quite the contrary, the desire for more food, more sex, more things, seemed only to be encouraged by the new comforts that mining afforded.

### The Futures of Witchcraft

Ultimately, both Manus and Yohan might be proven right. In the six years between 1991 and 1996, I recorded twenty-five instances of serious illness and death due to witchcraft. In the six years between 1999 and 2004, I recorded twenty-two cases. Perhaps, as Yohan felt, witchcraft really was decreasing as people prospered with mining. Or perhaps, as Manus sensed, witchcraft was continuing to thrive amid the new technologies and lives enabled by a monetary economy. For the moment the answer hangs in the balance.

There are no traditionalists in Buli today. Men like Dudu, who during the 1930s and 1940s fought to uphold Buli tradition as an alternative to Christianity, are long dead. Today's Buli people are modernists who hope that the changes associated with Christianity, the nation-state, and mining capitalism will bring about a rupture with the past, and hopefully a better world in the future. Still, time and again witchcraft intervenes to destroy this hope. That is why Manus and Yohan do not represent different "groups" in Buli: those against mining and modernity and those in favor of them. Instead, the two visions of witchcraft voiced by Manus and Yohan are views that most people I know in Buli hold at one time or another, hoping with Yohan and fearing with Manus. In that sense, Manus's and Yohan's accounts of the future of witchcraft complement rather than oppose each other. Taken together, they express the kind of ambivalence that continues to haunt Buli expectations of modernity and its promised capacity to reshape the world.

This ambivalence in Buli does not grow out of the internal dialectics of modernity, in some sort of Buli repetition of Western critical theory (Adorno and Horkheimer 1979). It is, I argue, neither modernity nor technology nor the monetization of society that is at issue, or lies at the heart of the problem. Rather, it is the articulation of the *gua* within these new social conditions that is at issue. It is witchcraft that calls for an explanation, and out of which ambivalence grows. It is the *gua* that undermines, time and again, the solution to witchcraft that technology, democracy, and money appear to offer. In order to come to an understanding of witchcraft's impossible undermining of money, technology, and social improvement, Manus and Yohan appeal to two visions of modernity, readily employed by everyone in Buli. Equally possible, equally plausible, these visions project witchcraft's multiple futures, its simultaneous disappearance and reinvigoration. The futures of the *gua*, it seems, are as multifarious and as uncertain as its origins (see chapter 2). Uncertainty is—as it always was—the last truth about witchcraft in Buli. Now, as in the past, the *gua* is there mainly through its absence—an inscrutable presence at best, and a "nonpresent remainder" in every possibility of its erasure.

# WITCHCRAFT BEYOND BELIEF

What is it like to live in a world where cannibal witches are undeniably real, and yet too ephemeral and contradictory to be an object of belief? What kind of history is enabled, and what kind of sociality is disabled, by the impossible reality of witchcraft? These are the central questions that this book has sought to answer, insisting in the process on taking people's doubts about witchcraft as seriously as their purported beliefs in it. Indeed, the general thrust of the book has been a critical engagement with the notion of "witchcraft beliefs." Witchcraft, I have sought to demonstrate, is not a cultural form of belief in Buli, but rather the historical elaboration of an aporia, a constant collapse of meaning into institutionalized doubt. Perhaps, I have advocated as a consequence, the time has come for the study of witchcraft to move beyond belief.

In light of this, I find it striking that witchcraft—for no apparent reason other than history[1]—is still treated as a subdiscipline of the study of religion (see, for instance, Bowen 2011; Bowie 2006; Stein and Stein 2008; Winzeler 2008). An upshot of this subsumption of witchcraft under religion—perhaps even, for some, its justification—has been a virtually unbroken tendency to treat witchcraft as a form of (proto)religion—that is, as a system of meaning, explanation, and belief. Let me give one example of this. In the influential undergraduate textbook *Cultural Anthropology: The Human Challenge*, currently in its thirteenth edition, the authors deal with witchcraft in a chapter devoted to religion, spirituality, and the supernatural. Here, they define witchcraft as "an explanation of events based on the belief that certain individuals possess an innate psychic power capable of causing harm, including sickness and death" (Havilland et al. 2011:547). Witchcraft, the textbook goes on to claim in its account of Ibibio witchcraft in Nigeria, "offers an explanation and, in so doing, also provides both the basis and the means for taking counteraction" (548). In the last paragraph on the topic, the authors conclude, "Anthropological research suggests that witchcraft, despite its often negative image, frequently functions in a very positive way to manage tensions within a society" (549). Witchcraft, in short, is presented as a set of beliefs that "offers an explanation," provides the means for action, and performs certain social functions. The result is a soothing view of witchcraft that treats it as a system of belief with a certain meaning and particular functions in relation to local and global worlds. The problem is the certainty that seems to accompany this notion of belief. As Malcolm Ruel has noted, witchcraft beliefs seem to come "with such unalterable firmness of conviction as would make a Calvinist jealous" (2003:111). The emphasis on witchcraft belief, the belief in the beliefs of the other, seemingly portrays a peculiarly Christian bias. Perhaps we ought to extend Talal Asad's (1993) critique of the Geertzian approach to religion, which according to Asad universalized a Christian notion of "belief," to also cover witchcraft studies?

In an attempt to pull free and distance myself from the gravitational force field that ties "belief" to witchcraft, I have argued that the study of witchcraft could usefully begin by focusing on its doubts. Witchcraft, from this alternative perspective, is not a system of belief, but a condition of doubt. It is a phenomenon that cannot be captured by merely following the conventional anthropological and inherently romantic injunction to "suspend disbelief." Instead, the study of witchcraft ought perhaps to begin with a suspension of "the belief in belief." Not until anthropology suspends its belief in witchcraft as a form of belief can an ignored, but in my view crucial, dimension of witchcraft—namely, its paradoxical grounding in doubt and aporia—come into focus.

Given that the association between witchcraft, belief, and meaning may be causally linked to the treatment of witchcraft as a subcategory of religion, it is encouraging that the anthropology of religion has begun in recent years to rebel against the predominant focus on meaning and belief (Asad 1993; Csordas 2004; Engelke and Tomlinson 2007; Ruel 2003).[2] Arthur Kleinman, for instance, laments that the Weberian tradition of seeing religion in terms of "how people make, negotiate, and unmake meaning" has been so hegemonic that "one wants to speak almost of a tyranny of meaning" at the expense of experience, smell, sound, moral sensibilities, bodily agency, social relations, and social memory, "fragmentary, contradictory, unexpressed and inexpressible, though they often are" (1997:317–318).

It is no doubt hyperbolic to speak of a "tyranny of meaning" in the contemporary anthropology of witchcraft. Indeed, recent studies of witchcraft strongly emphasize its experiential, ambivalent, and fragmentary aspects (Ashforth 2001; Geschiere 1998; West 2005). This book follows that new tradition by insisting on absence, the paradoxes of embodied experience, failed historical hopes, and ambivalent moral sensibilities as the starting points for its attempt to outline the impossibility of witchcraft in Buli. However, I also wish to question the continuing tendency also within contemporary studies of witchcraft to search for its meaning and function. For in spite of their emphasis on witchcraft as an experienced, ambivalent, and plastic phenomenon, recent witchcraft studies remain trapped in orbit around the "explanatory paradigm" that focuses on belief, meaning, and function. This focus on belief has been reinforced by the contemporary emphasis on witchcraft's "reality" in the eyes of its believers. Consequently, anthropologists wishing to convey how "real" witchcraft actually feels to the people they are studying are often led to assign to the contradictory and doubtful nature of witchcraft a new kind of meaning and explanation. Ambivalent and plastic witchcraft beliefs come to be mirrors of, or explanations for, the ambivalence and contradictions of the modern world itself. The problem with this is that the "explanatory paradigm" is thereby left intact. Doubt is emphasized—only to be redomesticated as meaning, and ambivalence is allowed to regress into being a temporary, but resolvable aspect of belief. Belief, as a result, comes away with its meaning-making functions intact. So, paradoxically, the tendency to study witchcraft in terms of "meaning" and "gauge" and "metaphor" and "belief" is actually promoted by the contemporary emphasis on witchcraft as a modern phenomenon rather than a form of exotic superstition. In order to "reassure ourselves that the pursuit of what seems to be esoteric ethnographic detail is really a form of high-minded public service" (Brown 1996:730), we are encouraged to give in to the impulse to make witchcraft into a system that, for all its internal contradictions and ambivalence, seems all the more suitable to serve the function of interpreting, critiquing, or even resisting the predicaments of modernity or the contradictions of global capitalism. I am not arguing that witchcraft is never a comment on, a gauge of, or a discourse about "the impact of global cultural and economic forces on local relations, on perceptions of money and markets, on the abstraction and alienation of 'indigenous' values and meanings" (Comaroff and Comaroff 1993:xxviii–xxix). But I am suggesting that what Siegel (2006:9) calls "a cheerful understanding of the witch," with a focus on witchcraft as an explanation that makes the world comprehensible, runs the risk of following "the anthropological tendency to avoid thinking about both the violence of witchcraft and the fear it inspires" (9). The focus on doubt has thus also been a way of approaching ethnographically the emotional dimensions of witchcraft. For fear of a new Orientalism that would repeat the Christian missionaries' emphasis on the fears associated with witchcraft in a pagan universe (see chapter 4), anthropologist have been reluctant to approach the fear and terror that dwells at the heart of witchcraft. I argue that the study of witchcraft should be less afraid of fear. Fear, anxiety, doubt, and horror, I have suggested, are in Buli constitutive of a life with witchcraft, but they are neither absolute nor incapacitating. Instead they are an impetus for action and a driving force for a particular kind of engagement with modernity. An analysis that opens itself to the emotions, fears, and doubts that constitute witchcraft may, I have sought to show, furnish a novel perspective on the causal relationship between witchcraft and modernity. In Buli, people strive continuously to seek meaning in witchcraft and relate this meaning to the changes they see around them, only to see that meaning collapse. As doubt fails to be domesticated, witchcraft fails as an explanation. Perhaps, I have been arguing, we are thinking the relationship between witchcraft and modernity the wrong way around. In Buli, at any rate, it is not modernity, kinship, or the global economy that is problematic and begs an explanation. It is witchcraft.

The analytical intervention into the witchcraft-modernity nexus that I am advocating can be phrased as follows: If the impulse conventionally driving most attempts—both academic and popular—to understand contemporary witchcraft has been to ask, "Why is there still belief in witchcraft in these modern times?" then the question that has driven this book is, instead, "Why do people in Buli believe in modernity in times of witchcraft?" The answer to this question, I have argued, is that people in Buli, like Western modernists (and academics), found in modernity the belief that witchcraft would end with modernity. Over the last hundred years of Buli history, the end of witchcraft has glimmered alluringly on the distant horizon of the future, a horizon established by modernity at different historical junctures in the guise of the church, the state, and modern technology. Take the state as an example. Whereas in East Java, according to James Siegel, it was popular worry about the absence of the state that appeared to trigger an explosion of sorcery, I have argued that people in Buli hoped that the presence of the state would, eventually, effect an absence of witchcraft. As this book has sought to demonstrate, it is this implicit promise that has historically ensured Buli people's loyalty to the Indonesian state, to the Christian Church, and to the mining companies in the face of witchcraft.

Extending Bruno Latour's provocation that it is modernity (rather than witchcraft) that entails a kind of belief, I propose that Buli may not be the only place where sociologically inclined witchcraft theories about the relationship between witchcraft and modernity ought to be turned upside down. I propose this not as an argument against what has been called the "modernity of witchcraft" hypothesis (Geschiere 1997). Rather, I am suggesting that the "modernity of witchcraft" approach could potentially be advanced by giving up the focus on witchcraft as belief or as "a means." As long as modernity is assigned the role of a phenomenon that calls for an explanation (or *explanandum*), witchcraft is forced to continue to play the role of that which explains something to its believers (*explanans*). I have suggested that such an approach, which sees witchcraft as a "magical interpretation" of "material realities" (Moore and Sanders 2001b), is blinkered by its hermeneutic ambition. The search for the meaning of witchcraft comes at the price of downplaying its aporetic dimensions, of forgoing an analysis of the way witchcraft stubbornly remains in experience and refuses to yield to interpretation. This tendency to see witchcraft as explanation, a tendency that I have suggested grew from the impact of E. E. Evans-Pritchard's analysis of Azande witchcraft, is unfortunate, because it was exactly Evans-Pritchard's great achievement to highlight how doubt, ambivalence, skepticism, and contradiction were at the very heart of the Azande experience of witchcraft. I have suggested the need to bring what Mathijs Pelkmans has called "the restlessness of doubt" (2011b:20) into analytical focus. I have tried to follow this restlessness empirically. Pelkmans has suggested that once "the dubious object is caught in the center of attention it needs to be acted upon, until it is tamed, sidelined, or transformed" (20) But, as I have argued, the *gua* in Buli is not an object. Rather, the witch is an abject, a "weight of meaninglessness about which there is nothing insignificant, and which crushes me" (Kristeva 1982:2). An abject "is-not." It cannot fully become the center of attention nor can it be tamed, because it cannot be grasped. An abject is beyond the control of hermeneutics. Witchcraft in Buli is therefore never domesticated into a system of beliefs or meaning that provides answers to social problems or a changing world. The witch is an existential abjection, a simultaneously corporeal and epistemological problem, to which answers must constantly be sought out in the world. It is this unendurable nature of the experience of witchcraft that has propelled people in Buli into a particular kind of historical action. But the abject nature of the *gua* also means that the doubts that cling to witchcraft cannot be "halted" (Pelkmans 2011b:20) through action, because the answers that people seek to the problem of witchcraft turn out to exacerbate rather than eradicate it. My argument is therefore not that people in Buli are completely mesmerized, rendered passive, by witchcraft. Quite to the contrary, I have suggested that a panoply of efforts, institutions, and actions—mythology, animism, ancestor worship, magic and divination, an "ethics of care" built into tradition, conversion to Christianity, political loyalty to the state, and "technognosis"—are part of Buli people's historically sustained but so far failing attempts to domesticate witchcraft. Witchcraft has in this book been a way to study the relationship between doubt and agency in a world where the restlessness of doubt cannot be domesticated into meaning. As such, witchcraft has for me been the starting point for an anthropology of doubt after hermeneutics.

This reorientation of our theoretical prejudice—in Gadamer's sense of a "fore-meaning" that anticipates a particular kind of knowledge (2013:282)—about witchcraft and doubt also entails a reorientation of the relationship of both doubt and witchcraft to modernity. If it is doubt and aporia that make up witchcraft, then witchcraft "has always been modern," to bend the catchphrase from Bruno Latour (1993). Witchcraft has always been modern in the sense that it is always already suffused with the kinds of doubts and aporias that we moderns tend to think are the monopoly of the modern condition. By attending to the restless doubts of witchcraft, rather than to its presumed beliefs and meaning-generating functions, the study of witchcraft may approach anew the curious symbiosis between the uncertainties of witchcraft and the uncertainties of the modern condition. This could be pursued in a comparative exploration of the commonalities of doubt and uncertainty that attend sociality and subjectivity in both witchcraft and other "modern" phenomena, such as nation building (see Geschiere 2013) or terrorism (see the preface to this book). An exploration of the doubts in witchcraft entails, in short, a fresh look at the belief in modernity. Taking the doubts of witchcraft seriously means suspending belief in the reality of modernity, and exploring comparatively the beliefs that people around the world have in modernity. Thus, the central undertaking of this book has not been to determine whether witchcraft is vanishing or increasing with modernization. Rather, it has been to trace ethnographically how modernity is experienced as succeeding and failing under the conditions of witchcraft.

I have attempted to detail the variety of ways in which doubt, horror, inaccessibility, unknowability, and uncertainty permeate witchcraft in Buli. The *gua* remains "an interminable experience" (Derrida 1993:16); an undecidability, troubling and destabilizing. Before the *gua* the limits of the senses, the fragility of corporeal existence, the opacity of the human mind, the impossibility of exchange and conviviality, the lies of Christian faith, the failures of state promises, and the witchcraft nature of technology are revealed. But this exposure in no way reflects back upon or sheds any light on the *gua*. Nor does the *gua* somehow explain or render more meaningful the human condition, Christianity, or modernity to the people in Buli. The *gua* is linked to the world through existential aporia, not through social causality. I have insisted that although it is a dimension in almost all aspects of sociality and subjectivity in Buli, the *gua* is not some kind of Maussian "total social fact" (Mauss 1990:78), simultaneously sensorial, corporeal, cognitive, and so forth. To claim that the *gua* is a "total social fact" would be to domesticate it by situating it in a social habitat it does not occupy, to assign to it a comfortable place in "the solid architecture of society" (Latour 2005:245) that it does not hold. The *gua* evades such easy assignment to society, or to social explanations: no lessons are ever learned from witchcraft in Buli, no stable knowledge gained. If anything, the *gua* is an aporia that precludes a social whole by preventing the emergence of stable social facts. Before the *gua*, only a troubling experience remains—always and invariably.

I have adopted Derrida's notion of aporia, not as an article of faith but as an *aide-mémoire,* to guard me against my own anthropological impulse to impute meaning and solid explanation to witchcraft when people in Buli kept trying to teach me that to the extent that the *gua* has an essence at all, it is that it has no meaning, no certainty, no explanation. It is this absence that is the horror of the *gua*. The basic impossibility of witchcraft makes it unbearable, and makes the promise of its eradication so appealing. This explains why, when people speak about the *gua* in Buli, they tend to use the conjectural or subjunctive mode: they are either guessing about certain conventions regarding the *gua* that keep being undermined by experience, or they are gesturing toward a barely perceivable but viscerally dangerous entity that they wish could be permanently banished. Tradition opted for the conjectural mode ("When it comes to the *gua* we can only guess"). Christianity, state ideology, and techno-modernity on the other hand introduced what, following Susan Whyte and Byron Good, one can reasonably subsume under the subjunctive mood: the promise or wishful possibility that the *gua* might vanish forever. In grammar, the "subjunctive mood" is a verbal form that indicates future possibilities. Whyte and Good have suggested, however, that the term also be used as a particular kind of attitude,[3] and I follow that suggestion here. "The subjunctive mode," as Good puts it, "is to be trafficking in human possibilities rather than settled certainties" (1994:153; quoted in Whyte 1997:24). The subjunctive, in other words, is about the uncertain hope harbored in possibility. As I sought to show in chapter 4, the hope of witchcraft's end introduced by Christianity was always undermined by witchcraft itself, consistently postponing this possibility. The subjunctive attitude did not vanquish the aporias of the *gua*; rather, subjunction exacerbated them and introduced new forms of absence within which the *gua* could thrive (as discussed in chapter 8).

One contemporary version of such a subjunctive presence-in-absence is the common denial that witchcraft even exists at all. On each of my trips to Buli since 1991, whenever the topic of the *gua* came up, people—including people I knew well, and whose agonizing trouble with witchcraft I had experienced firsthand—would begin by assuring me that in Buli there are no *gua* anymore. The *gua,* they would insist, is a thing of the past, something that their "backward" ancestors believed in. I always took this to be a simple form of mimicry of the Indonesian modernist rhetoric that outside ministers, police, army officers, and government bureaucrats struggled to implement and maintain. And frankly these statements annoyed me, for the performance of state modernism suggested false pretense to me. It was as if I did not know these people and their personal history and was being assigned the role of the ignorant outsider, while the *gua* was described as an unequivocal absence: there are no *gua* anymore, pure and simple. Upon reflection, however, I am inclined to think that Buli people are, in fact, speaking in the subjunctive mode when they assert that there are no *gua* anymore: there are no *gua* because there *should not be*; the *gua* is a thing of the past because it *ought to be*; the *gua* is merely an object of pagan belief because it *has to be*.

This subjunctive mode is closely related to the impossibility of truly believing in witchcraft, and the necessary displacement of belief onto others, that the preceding chapters have sought to outline. Throughout this book I have argued that belief implies a certainty that Buli people cannot afford, and which they therefore have to displace onto others. In developing this argument I have made repeated use of Latour's (2010) contention that modernity implies an almost faith-like ascription of belief to the nonmodern. I have also suggested that the "belief in the belief of others" as a way of assuring oneself of one's own modernity has therefore structured not only the academic study of witchcraft, but also Buli people's own pragmatic but vain attempts to "locate" the reality of the *gua*. Ironically, as I argued in chapter 6, the belief in witchcraft by iconic figures of modernity and authority in Buli seemed to ascribe to witchcraft a reality that Buli people themselves could only doubt. The common denial in Buli nowadays that any *gua* still exist today represents a similar, if more conventionally modernist, ascription of a belief in witchcraft to an "other." By assigning the *gua* to the beliefs of their nonmodern forebears, people are attempting to evict it, wishfully or subjunctively, from the modern present. This subjunction has always been at the core of the hope that made modernity attractive in the first place . . . and it has always already been a sign of its failure. The subjunctive mode/mood ("There are no/If only there were no *gua* today") is, in that sense, the imprint of a hundred years of historical engagement with modernity in Buli, in which the *gua* has consistently been on the cusp of vanishing and yet continued to be present under the very conditions that augured its end. As a result, the subjunctive speech act of claiming that "there-are-no-*gua*-anymore-because-there-should-not-be" ends up marking the possibility of a presence by insisting on its absence. Like all other institutional and discursive expressions of hope for its erasure, this speech act merely creates a new absence in which witchcraft is able to dwell.

Lauren Berlant has suggested that a "relation of cruel optimism exists when something you desire is actually an obstacle to your flourishing" (2011:1). In the face of witchcraft's persistence, Buli people are well aware of the cruel nature of their own modern optimism. I have tried to outline the cultural history of the impossible presence of witchcraft in Buli. The chapters have demonstrated that witchcraft—the bodily experiences, cultural narratives, and existential consequences of the *gua*—lies at the center of an aporetic mode of being-in-the-world that has evolved historically, and which has been at the core of Buli historical agency for well over a hundred years. The reality of the *gua*, continuously under erasure, throws itself into Buli existence as an insoluble problem, a "intolerable significance" (Kristeva 1982:11), that has motivated a series of constant but unsuccessful attempts to deal with its contradictory consequences in and for life. Heirs to a history of hope and disappointment, people in contemporary Buli live on—ambivalently—as faithful Christians, loyal state citizens, and compliant wage laborers, adopting in the early twenty-first century the same cautious attitude of "lying in wait" (*tantano*) that their grandparents adopted in the early years of the twentieth century, when Christianity first entered their world. They do so hoping that the reality of the *gua* might one day cease to be significant . . . and fearing that it will not. Around the time I was finishing up this manuscript, Verdianus Gueselaw, a Buli man who now functions as a minister to the congregation of the Christian Evangelical Church of Halmahera (GMIH) in Waiflí, e-mailed me a copy of his theological master's thesis. His work is an analysis of the *gua* or *suanggi*, based on interviews with accused *gua* in Buli and a review of the anthropological and theological literature. The work was accepted in 2010 at the Theological Seminary in Tobelo (Gueselaw 2010). Interestingly, the (translated) title of the thesis is "Halmahera Free from *Suanggi*—Is It Possible?" In 2012 when I asked Verdianus to answer the question posed in his own thesis title, he responded with one word: "Maybe!" (I. *Mungkin*)—a word that succinctly encapsulates the knotty conjectural and subjunctive relationship that people in Buli maintain with witchcraft, and which this book has tried to portray.

If the future of witchcraft is always in question, so too are its present and its past. This means that witchcraft is never entirely "there." The *gua* is constituted by its absence and never acquires the positivity of a presence. As such, the *gua* can never simply be the negation of a social positivity. This idea of witchcraft as a negation of "the social" is widespread in anthropology, and at first glance the claim of this book that witchcraft is an aporia, an existential impossibility, might appear to resemble, for instance, Michael Lambek's suggestion that witchcraft is "an imaginative inversion of dominant norms and values" (2003:258), or Mary Douglas's assertion that witches, like pollution, are "dangers from the crevices of the structure" of society (1995:169). However, there is an important difference between these two propositions and the one I have tried to advance here. Lambek and Douglas's wording suggests that society, structure, norms, and values "came first," as it were; that order is foundational to social life, and that witchcraft constitutes a secondary negation or danger. In Buli, however, witchcraft comes first, both chronologically and socially. As I demonstrated in chapter 2, the *gua* was there at the very beginning of life on Halmahera, the island's mountains being the petrified remains of victims of mythological witchcraft. Witchcraft, by another account, emerged before the dawn of mythical time itself, out of a world of *jin* spirits before the world "was turned around" ( *fulas i*) and the world of humans began. Order, it seems, is the momentary inversion of witchcraft—not the other way around. Social order is not the "original" condition. It came after witchcraft, with the fighting magic of Íyan Toa and the customs (*adat re atorang*) bestowed by the Tidore sultanate. Cosmologically speaking, then, witchcraft, not order and purity, came first—impossibly so, but first. But before even this troubling primary status can be turned into an explanation, it is itself destabilized by other myths that claim that witchcraft really, originally, came from Maba. Witchcraft is, in that sense, always a "non-present remainder" that is cut off from its own putative origin (Derrida 2000:53).

In the same way that witchcraft "comes first" in cosmological terms without attaining the status of a stable "origin," witchcraft also comes first socially speaking—but again, without being in any sense originary. Witchcraft "comes first" in social terms, because the very mechanisms by which one carries out the kind of exchanges demanded by tradition are themselves replications of *gua* behavior (such as hiding and cheating). Witchcraft is, impossibly, at the heart of the means by which one shapes "good companionship" and social conviviality through exchange (see chapter 7). In this disquieting way, it is witchcraft that "grants extension and durability to social ties" (Latour 2005:238)—making them necessary and impossible at the same time. Therefore the social does not constitute a "primary framework," an "outside" or a "beneath" that can be brought in to somehow explain the *gua*. Latour's critique of "the social" appears to me to be particularly apt in relation to the tendency within witchcraft studies to want to bring the witch into the secure orbits of "society," to make it submit to the laws of the social world by assigning to it a meaning, a function, a role. Describing witchcraft as a reversal of social values or as a structural exception, as Lambek and Douglas apparently do, seems to me to be examples of this approach that make "the social" primary. As Latour notes, this entails the danger of fetishizing the social: "The laws of the social world may exist, but they occupy a very different position from what the [sociological] tradition had first thought. They are not *behind* the scene, *above* our heads and *before* the action, but *after* the action, *below* the participants and smack in the *foreground*" (2005:246, italics in the original). Perhaps a "witchcraft theory" that does not deny the social but refrains from assigning to the social dimension a magical, explanatory power "behind" or "above" witchcraft might usefully begin with the concept of aporia.

Derrida's notion of aporia, as indeed his general framework, constitutes a critique of an "epistemology of presence" by emphasizing the impossibility of stable meaning and pure origin. This critique has been helpful for me in coming to terms with the way witchcraft in Buli never has the "positivity of a presence" (Derrida

1976:145), but is marked through and through by absence and inaccessibility. Witchcraft is fundamentally inaccessible—to the senses as well as to common sense. And yet it cannot be ignored. "The inaccessible," as Derrida asserts, always "incites from its place of hiding" (1992a:191). The dilemma of Buli witchcraft is that the *gua* is irrepressibly and corporeally present in all its absence, constituting a void of meaning about which there is nothing insignificant (see chapter 5).

People in Buli, in this sense, are faced with a paradox that strongly resembles the insoluble paradox posed by Meno, the interlocutor of the great Western philosopher Socrates (whom I introduced in chapter 1): they have no way of inquiring into or getting a handle on that which, by its very nature, is inaccessible.[4] In response to a life where certainty (of myth, of the senses, of sociality, of subjectivity) is being called into question at every turn by the aporias of witchcraft, people in Buli have fashioned an epistemology of guessing and an ethos of caution: conjecture is the best anyone can do when it comes to witchcraft. The *gua*, in short, is an aporia: an impossible experience that refuses to sediment into a meaningful phenomenon. And as with all aporias, every attempt to analytically domesticate it through reason, logic, or stable meaning entails its own trickery or autocolonization by witchcraft. From that perspective there is a common thread that runs from Socrates's attempt to circumvent Meno's paradox through an elenchic form of reasoning that ironically harbored its own witchcraft (chapter 1), and Anton Hueting's unmasking of the Halmaheran shamans only to find that Christian missionaries in the process came to be seen as shamans (chapter 3), to Evans-Pritchard's revelation of the trickery of the Azande witch doctor by using a trick of his own (see "The Shell of the Nautilus" in this book). Witchcraft has a way of reproducing itself in the means that seek to domesticate it, whether those means are philosophical, evangelical, or anthropological. This same ability of witchcraft to colonize the very processes that claim to domesticate or eradicate it has reverberated throughout a century of Buli history and Buli engagement with modernity.

This book has tried to take seriously Meno's paradox (which highlights the impossibility of knowledge about the unknowable) rather than relying, as witchcraft studies and anthropology have tended to do, on a Neoplatonic belief in Socrates's apparent solution to the paradox. The focus on function, rationality, meaning, and belief that has characterized the anthropological study of witchcraft is, I suggest, firmly located within the orbit of this Neoplatonic tradition by which the paradox of the unknowable is domesticated by something outside it (belief, meaning, social function, or *anamensis*). If there is an anthropological lesson to be learned from Buli witchcraft—a kind of ethnographic theory to be gleaned from the *gua*—for me, it is this: that the attempt to domesticate, provide meaning, or assign a function to that which, by its very nature, dissolves stable meaning and causality not only involves its own kind of witchcraft but also, and ultimately, fails to grasp what it so doggedly seeks to understand.

# NOTES

## Preface

1. Witchcraft, the topic of this book, is a precarious, embarrassing, and potentially libelous issue in Indonesia. I have therefore opted to use pseudonyms throughout, except when referring to historical figures, when acknowledging the authors of artwork or manuscripts, and when naming people depicted in photographs.

## The Shell of the Nautilus

1. The English terms "sorcery" and "witchcraft" are not used in the region. The English term "black magic," however, is known to some people in North Maluku with tertiary education and is used as a general gloss for all forms of malevolent magic.

2. Evans-Pritchard's distinction between sorcery and witchcraft has been roundly criticized for raising to analytical universality a culturally specific distinction (Middleton 1963; Stephen 1987). Recently, scholars have also advocated that the term "witchcraft" should be abandoned altogether as an analytical category because the term comes with heavy Western baggage and promotes an implicit exoticism (Crick 1978; Moore and Sanders 2001b), because as an English term it is now so globalized that it has lost all analytical value (Parés and Sansi 2011), and because it reflects a classificatory obsession to neatly delineate sorcery and witchcraft as distinct phenomena (Meyer and Pels 2003). Indeed, "sorcery," "magic," and "occult powers" have all been suggested as more neutral and encompassing terms (Comaroff and Comaroff 1999; Meyer and Pels 2003; Parés and Sansi 2011). But no concept will bring analytical clarity to an aporia. Indeed, it is my sense that the contemporary tendency to lump witchcraft, sorcery, and magic together, as if they were synonymous, into one analytical concept of the "occult" or "sorcery" presents as many problems as the obsession with classificatory distinction that characterized the anthropology of yesteryear. One problem is the assumption of a universal dichotomy between the realm of "nature," "fact," and "visibility" on the one hand, and a realm of the "supernatural" and the "occult" on the other—an assumption against which

Evans-Pritchard was the first to warn (1976:30–31). In a field where all concepts are "contaminated," I use the category of witchcraft heuristically and without implying it has "the force of an analytical category" (Ellen 1993b:8) that can speak for all other occult economies.

3. James Siegel's book *Naming the Witch* (2006), in spite of its title, analyzes the killing of sorcerers (*tukang santet*), not witches, in East Java (see Beatty 2012).

4. In a household survey conducted in 1992, I acquired information about 134 deaths over the last sixty years by asking the eldest couple of the household about the death of their parents. This procedure was, I now realize, full of problems. Firstly, the survey did not cover all deaths. Secondly and more importantly, the survey form itself is unsuitable to obtain information of this sort; it treats as easily ascertained what can barely be perceived and the apparent clarity of any answer glosses over all sorts of bias and retrospective revision. The fact that respondents can provide only one answer fails to reflect the fact that the cause of most deaths is surrounded by multiple interpretations. Indeed, several times my question evoked simultaneous but different responses from the people in the household who were present: "Oh, he died of malaria" and "Ah, someone ate him." A statistical will to knowledge of the kind that motivated my survey back in 1992 thus entails an assumption about what Anderson calls "bound seriality," which implies that identity or causes can be pinned down to one and just one position within a finite series (1998:29). In fact, however, illness and death are by their very nature "unbound." They are enigmatic and full of uncertainty, and rarely if ever is a death unilaterally ascribed to sorcery, witchcraft, "regular illness," or an accident. Still, for all its problems, the survey provides a general indication. Out of a total of 134 deaths, 81 (or 60 percent) were, in retrospect, attributed to "ordinary illness"; 31 deaths (23 percent) were, in retrospect, ascribed to witchcraft (*ungan*); and 22 cases (16 percent) were ascribed to sorcery (*payao*). The concept of "ordinary illness" (I. *penyakit biasa*) is Indonesian and has no Buli translation. Even so, it forms a conceptual counterpart to witchcraft and sorcery deaths, which are often referred to as "not easy" (*gampang pa*). Such witchcraft and sorcery deaths are "uneasy" in several ways: they are full of bodily suffering, they are hard to pin down or comprehend, and they bring lots of social trouble.

5. One may also become a *gua* by infection or contagion. Convention has it, for instance, that the *gua* will sometimes feed the seed of witchcraft to their spouse by placing it in the spouse's food; this convention is used to account for the general tendency that spouses remain loyal to accused *gua*, even when accusations originate from the spouse's own patriline (*ebai pu*) or extended bilateral kin (*ebai bangsá*).

6. Two concepts are important in Buli social organization: *fam* (patriline) and *ebai* (house). The "house" is a traditional concept and refers to a bilateral social unit of descendants and affines. The "house" consists of the "trunk-house" (*ebai pusa*), one"s patrilineal kin, and the "house-of-relatives" (*ebai bangsá*), bilateral kin outside of the immediate patriline. The *fam* is a recent introduction and overlaps with the "trunk-house." The Dutch instituted the *fam* at the beginning of the twentieth century and ordered, for schooling and administrative purposes, that each *fam* have a specific surname. Most *fam* in Buli now take their names from the personal name of a man in their patriline three or four generations back, which makes them easily identifiable. For more on Buli social organization, in particular on the importance of the "house" (*ebai*) as a social concept and unit, see chapter 5.

7. The close relationship between witches and spirits, where witchcraft is like a form of possession, is a defining feature of witchcraft not only in Buli, but also in other parts of eastern Indonesia, and this feature appears to set it apart from witchcraft in Africa and Melanesia.

8. Of the 91 witchcraft attacks that I recorded between 1991 and 2011, a specific *gua* was suspected in 67 cases. Of these 67 cases, roughly half (31 instances) were attacks on bilateral kin, and the other half (36 instances) were attacks on people in the village who were not kin. Anyone, it seemed, could be attacked.

9. See Laidlaw 2010 for an illuminating discussion of witchcraft as a form of moral agency.

10. The status of coherence in Azande witchcraft is itself full of contradiction it turns out. Rather than being an immanent feature of Azande beliefs themselves, coherence was thus really an academic artifact. As Evans-Pritchard writes in his conclusion, "Throughout I have emphasized the coherency of Zande beliefs [in witchcraft] *when they are considered together* and are interpreted in terms of situations and social relationships. . . . They are not indivisible ideational structures but loose associations of notions. *When a writer brings them together in a book and presents them as a conceptual system* their insufficiencies and contra-dictions are at once apparent. *In real life they do not function as a whole but in bits*" (1937:540, italics mine). This admission is in many ways both admirable and very contemporary in its emphasis on order as an academic artifact. Evans-Pritchard's point in this admission was furthermore to highlight the plasticity and contextual nature of these beliefs: "A man in one situation utilizes what in the beliefs are convenient to him and pays no attention to other el-ements which he might use in different situations" (540). But a particular irony nevertheless arises from this "admission." On the one hand, Evans-Pritchard emphasizes the coherence of witchcraft beliefs, which means that he leaves unexplored the existential consequences of the doubt and contradiction that characterized Azande witchcraft (other than to cite them as proof that their natural philosophy could never measure up to scientific reality). On the other hand, he takes this coherence away from Azande witchcraft in the conclusion when he admits that order and coherence were actually an effect of his academic inscription. This leaves me as a reader wishing that he had explored in greater detail the one thing that is now left in Azande witchcraft—namely, its context-dependent, contradictory, and doubtful nature.

11. It is worth noting here that the dominance of meaning and interpretation has begun to be criticized within the anthropology of Christianity (Bandak and Jørgensen 2012; Engelke 2002; Engelke and Tomlinson 2007).

12. Todd Sanders and I are not the first to criticize those who see witchcraft as an idiom for understanding or critiquing modernity. Others have already suggested that this analytical ap-proach reduces witchcraft to the level of discourse and representation (Ashforth 2000, 2005; Jackson 1989; Kapferer 1997; Pedersen 2011; Rutherford 1999; Stoller and Olkes 1989; West 2005), and that it shoehorns witchcraft into being a "specific argument about modernity" (Englund 1996:273; Englund and Leach 2000), or even a form of resistance to modernity (Brown 1996).

13. This kind of temporality is obviously not unique to modernity in Buli; it is a defining fea-ture of modernity that others have highlighted, too (Koselleck 1985). Modernity's "future-orientation," however—its premise and promise of anticipating the future by breaking with the present and the past—often acquires a specifically millenarian tone in Indonesian politics (Bubandt 1998a, 2004b).

14. See Richard Shweder, for instance, who makes a direct appeal to Evans-Pritchard's approach to witchcraft when he suggests that the "suspension of disbelief" is a prerequisite for good ethnography (Shweder 1997:152–153).

15. There is a long debate within philosophy about René Descartes's relation to previous kinds of doubt—for instance, that of the ancient Greek Skeptics. For an overview of these debates, see Fine 2000. In a fascinating history of the legal notion of "reasonable doubt," James Whitman (2008) suggests that the notion of reasonable doubt, which in today's American legal system is meant to protect the accused, grew out of a Christian concern for the juror. In a world of Christian morality, where it was considered a sin to sit in judgment of others unless one was certain of their guilt, the notion of "reasonable doubt" functioned between the Middle Ages and the nineteenth century as a theological method of ensuring that people would be willing to act as jurors in court cases. Whitman's analysis underscores not only that there is

no modern monopoly on doubt, but also that doubt needs to be contextualized morally and epistemologically.

16. According to the regional statistical office, the population of North Maluku in 2009 was just under one million. Eighty percent (753,000 people) were Muslims, and 20 percent (181,000 people) were Christians (BPSPMU 2010:142).

17. I have done fieldwork in Buli for over three years, and during the last two and a half years of fieldwork (conducted intermittently since mid-1992), the Buli language has been my main medium of communication. No recent linguistic analysis has been done on the Buli language, and the grammar and Dutch-Buli dictionary of the Dutch missionary G. Maan still provides the only, if not completely exhaustive, description of Buli language (Maan 1940, 1951). In rendering Buli words, I have followed Maan (1951) as closely as possible, have made changes where necessary. I have thus adapted the spelling to the orthography of Simplified Spelling (EYD) as applied to standard Indonesian after 1972. Pronunciation of vowels and consonants therefore generally follows standard Indonesian. The consonant /h/ is the exception, however. If it precedes one of the nasal consonants, /h/ is pronounced as a voiceless nasal (where the air is let out through the nose while the mouth is closed). Examples of this usage are [*mahngél*] meaning "dream," [*uhngo*] or [*usngo*], meaning "face," or [*hma*], meaning "father." Stress in Buli is generally on the penultimate syllable, but in a number of cases, stress is on the last syllable. In these cases I indicate word stress with an acute accent over the vowel on which the stress lies (/á/, /é/, /í/, /ó/, /ú/) to aid pronunciation. Buli has no diphthongs, and two consecutive vowels are both pronounced. Unless otherwise indicated, italicized words in parentheses are Buli words (or loan words from Tobelo, Ternate, Tidore, Indonesian, and North Malukan Malay that are treated as Buli words). Indonesian words are indicated by the abbreviation *I.*, while words in the Tobelo language are indicated by *T.* Dutch, Greek, and Azande words are indicated as such.

18. According to the 2010 census, Indonesia had a population of just over 237 million, 87 percent of which (a little over 207 million) were Muslim, 10 percent (or 23.5 million) were Christian, and 1.6 percent (4 million) were Hindu (see http://sp2010.bps.go.id/index.php/site/tabel?tid=321, accessed 8 January 2014).

19. As the name South Halmahera-West New Guinea (SHWNG) subgroup suggests, these Halmaheran languages have close ties with the Austronesian languages spoken in the coastal regions of Papua. In addition to Gebe, these include the languages spoken in the Raja Ampat group, and the Onin-related languages of Maccluer Bay on the south coast of the Bird's Head area, as well as a dozen or so languages along Cenderawasih Bay (Wurm and Hattori 1983) (see map 2). The SHWNG subgroup combines with the Austronesian languages farther along the north coast of New Guinea and the Oceanic subgroup in the Pacific to form the languages of the higher-level subgroup known as Eastern Malayo-Polynesian (Blust 1978:211). Although the Eastern Malayo-Polynesian subgroup contains extreme diversity and only much-disputed resemblances, Bellwood convincingly combines the linguistic resemblances between the south Halmaheran languages and the Austronesian languages of New Guinea with archaeological evidence to suggest that "soon after 2000 BC the Oceanic languages underwent their first expansion into Melanesia from an immediate homeland in the region of Halmahera and western New Guinea" (1985:125). Buli and the other Austronesian languages of eastern Halmahera are in that sense the most likely contemporary linguistic descendants of the groups that began the Austronesian colonization of the Pacific Ocean (Foley 2000:361; Pearce and Pearce 2010), one of the largest and most daring examples of global expansion in human history.

20. The linguistic online database "ethnologue" lists 706 individual languages in Indonesia, half of which are currently under threat or dying out (see http://www.ethnologue.com/country/ID, accessed 8 January 2014).

21. The witch spirit known in Buli as the *gua* can be traced through all seven Austronesian and nine Papuan languages spoken in the North Malukan area (Wurm and Hattori 1983). Concerns regarding this cognate figure can, in other words, be identified throughout the province of North Maluku, and it is endemic in the region across both linguistic and religious boundaries. Among the Austronesian-speaking Gimán of south Halmahera, "belief in witches (*go*)" is said to be "prevalent" (Teljeur 1985:21). In Weda, witches are referred to as *gwó*, while in the villages between Patani and Maba the same spirit-being is known by the similar-sounding word *guo*. Adding the Buli word (*gua*), we have, in south and central Halmahera, the following series of cognates: *go—gwó—guo—gua*. Among the Papuan-speaking groups of north Halmahera, a similar series of cognates can be found, ranging from *caka* (in Tidore), *coka* (in Ternate), *toka* (in Galela and Loloda), *tokata* (in Tobelo), and *ca'ata* (in Sahu) (see map 2).

22. The etymology of the term *suanggi* is unclear. As one of the only sources, Wilken ventures the conjecture that it is derived from *wangi* or *wengi* in Javanese, and *bangi* in Makassarese, all of which he translates as "night" or "at night" (1912:36). It is striking, however, that the term *suanggi* is almost exclusive to areas within the historical sphere of influence of the North Malukan sultanates of Ternate and Tidore (to which both Papua and the southern Philippines also belonged), where the term is documented in the earliest period of contact with European colonizers in the sixteenth century (compare maps 3 and 4). An example of the long archival trace of the *suanggi* in the colonial records is provided by the scribe of Antonio de Brito, the first Portuguese governor on Ternate (1522–25), who notes how the Ternate-Portuguese army was aided in one of its frequent bloody skirmishes with Tidore by inhabitants from Gam Konora on north Halmahera. Among these inhabitants were many who were known as "*suanggi* men" because of their ability to make themselves invisible (Tiele 1877:391). To test their claims, de Brito had one of them put in irons and guarded closely overnight. When the shackles were found empty the following morning, de Brito reportedly became very alarmed. He immediately dismissed all the "*suanggi* men" so that the sultan of Tidore could not accuse him of fighting Tidore with the help of "devilish tricks" (391). Tiele comments drily that de Brito did not show the same concern for fair play when, after the battle was over, he had three hundred captured Tidorese prisoners roasted on spits (391).

23. For an analysis of the variegated forms of holism in anthropology, see Otto and Bubandt 2010.

24. These changes include the recent fusion of the conventional figure of the *suanggi* with global figures of horror, such as Dracula; see Bubandt 2008a, 2012.

25. This is beginning to change. Since 2009, local media have begun reporting on the environmental effects of mining in the area, including the pollution of rivers and the destruction of coral reefs, mangroves, and lowland primary forest, as well as on violations of the geographical limits of mining licenses. There has also been a series of clashes between local residents and the police in connection with protests over wages and land disputes in several neighboring villages, such as Lolobata and Maba.

## 1. Witchcraft, Doubt, and Aporia

1. For an insightful review of Derrida's influence on anthropology, see Morris 2007.

2. The second book of Aristotle's *Metaphysics* thus starts with fifteen aporias or puzzles. Each aporia is pursued by two opposing answers, both of them to Aristotle equally unsatisfactory, as a way to begin Aristotle's own philosophical exposition (Aristotle 2004:51ff.).

3. I will occasionally use diagrams in this book as an aid to understanding the family relations between the victim of witchcraft and the accused witch—a relationship that is perversely undermined by the attack. I do so without wanting to imply that kinship somehow explains or motivates the attack. Rather, the relationship—if there is one between the victim and the

supposed witch, which often there is not—is one of the many impossibilities of witchcraft in Buli. The victim will bring up the kinship relation to point out why the attack *should* not have happened, while the accused witch will point to it as proof of why it *could* not have happened (I discuss this "subjunctive mode" in more detail in the final chapter of this book).

4. In chapter 6, I take up in more detail the issue of proof in light of James Siegel's (1998, 2002) insightful analyses.

5. In Greek philosophy the concept of *aporia* appears to have undergone a transformation of meaning over time (Liddell and Scott 1990:215). It shifted from being a logical embarrassment, an obstacle to be domesticated for philosophy to begin, in the works of Plato to being an Aristotelian problem of a second order that is inherent not in the conflicting opinions about the world, but in the world itself (Matthews 1999:30). With Aristotle, aporias became inherently impassable because they stuck to our knowledge of the world, impassable as much when we do not recognize them as when we do (Politis 2004:77). In Buli, the *gua* as aporia has shifted historically in the opposite direction: from epistemological and ontological impassability to embarrassment. From conventionally being an existential condition of knowledge and sociality for which a variety of partial solutions were established and sought, the *gua* has become a cultural embarrassment, a numbing reality that modern sensibilities try to domesticate, but which cannot be denied and which therefore is a constant source of humiliation and discomfort to people who see themselves as Christian and modern.

6. Siegel uses the word "witchcraft" even though *santet* in Java is closer to "sorcery" in Evans-Pritchard's sense. *Santet* is thus a learned technique rather than a physically inherited trait, and it is not associated with possession (Beatty 2012:178).

7. This analytical angle has provided a fertile field for a fascinating number of studies of how New Order fear of Communists and criminals was a stand-in for a generalized anxiety about society (Barker 2001; Florida 2008; Heryanto 1999; Strassler 2004).

8. In fact, in making this claim, fascinating as it is, Siegel is in danger of reproducing the kind of state-centric and functionalist argument that most of his book otherwise criticizes. In an interpretation that is not incompatible with that of Siegel, Nick Herriman (2010) claims it was local motives, set free by an emasculated state, that drove the sorcery killings. For an interesting, alternative explanation, see Beatty 2012.

9. Lucan's poem was probably written around AD 65, several centuries after Plato's time. Still, the Roman prejudice against Thessaly appeared not to be new, but rather to mirror an earlier Greek bias that dated back at least to Plato's contemporary Euripides (Ogden 2002:27).

10. Socrates was arrested (and eventually convicted) on the triple charge of not believing in the gods of Athens, of introducing other divinities, and of corrupting the youth (Brickhouse and Smith 1990:30). His crime was therefore not one of wizardry outright; rather, it was the crime of using his rhetorical skills, the elenchic method of inquiry and answer that he demonstrated in the *Meno* (Irwin 1979:315–316), to lead others astray. But there was a strong semantic link between the charge of religious heresy and philosophical rhetoric, a link that was provided by sorcery and magic. Sorcery and magic were thus in ancient Greece seen as forms of heresy (Morrow 1960:477), and rhetorical persuasion was in turn always tainted by accusations of sorcery. Rhetorical skills were interpreted as a kind of sorcery, because persuasion was perceived as a form of conjuring to affect the soul of others. Plato himself, for instance, associated sorcery and ghost-evocation with rhetorical persuasion (Ogden 2002:21), and he shared with other Greek philosophers a penchant for finding parallels to sorcery in the rhetoric of his philosophical opponents. Indeed, even Plato was not immune to this accusation. Pliny's *Natural History*—one of the world's first encyclopedias, written between AD 77 and 9—claims that sorcery originated with Zoroaster in Persia, and that Plato among others had journeyed there to learn these skills (Ogden 2002:42).

11. I would argue that Derrida does so by approaching aporia as it is understood by Aristotle rather than by Plato, as the beginning of philosophical engagement rather than as an embarrassment to be epistemologically circumvented. In his most explicit treatment of aporia, Derrida (1993) begins with Aristotle's and not with Plato's notion of aporia. For Derrida, aporia, in turn, became a way to philosophically deconstruct the metaphysics of philosophy itself (Lucy 2004). This philosophical lineage between Aristotle and Derrida was no doubt mediated by Derrida's intimate but ambivalent engagement with Heidegger (Protevi 1994; Rapaport 1989), and by what Vincent Descombes has called Derrida's "radicalisation of phenomenology" (Descombes 1994:136). While Derrida criticizes Aristotle for developing "the aporia in its own terms" (Derrida 1982:53), repeating the aporia of time and being "without deconstructing it" (50), Derrida's own deconstruction nevertheless proceeds through a critical engagement with the philosophical tradition that he traces all the way from Aristotle to Hegel and Heidegger.

## 2. The Origins of Witchcraft and the Doubts of Tradition

1. Buli ideas of the *jin*, which are known throughout Indonesia, derive to a large extent from Islamic thought (El-Zein 2009), as mediated, most likely, through the North Malukan sultanates.
2. The Buli concept of *gélat* is equivalent to the concept of *soa*, known throughout Maluku as the territorial groups that constitute the units of the sultanate's political organization. The four *gélat* were, in descending hierarchical order: Gélat Goimaslongan, Gélat Tatam, Gélat Gagáili, and Gélat Kabalál. The four *gélat* represented an image of wholeness replicated at a lower level in the four sultanates of North Maluku. At both levels, the number four indicated wholeness and completion, an ideal unity that could not be broken (Andaya 1993) (see also chapter 4).

## 3. Hope, Conversion, and Millennial Politics

1. The UZV was established in 1859 as one of the three main mission societies under the Dutch Reformed Church (Haire 1981:124). The mission's main target in Halmahera became the animist minorities, and until the Second World War it was the only mission society to operate in the predominantly Muslim domain of North Maluku. Establishing its first mission in Galela in 1866, the mission founded congregations in Tobelo, Ibu, Pagu, and Sahu in the northern part of Halmahera, as well as among the Buli, Weda, and Sawai peoples in the central and eastern parts of Halmahera (see map 2).
2. The *Berigten van de Utrechtsche Zendingsvereeniging* (hereafter *BUZ*) was the mission journal of the Utrecht Mission Union. Between 1865 and 1917 it constituted the main form of communication between missionaries in the field and the home congregations in Holland that supported them financially. After 1916 the *BUZ* was complemented by another mission journal, the *Zendingsblad voor de Classis Rotterdam der Nederlandsch Hervormde Kerk ten behoeve van de Zendingsposten Boeli, Weda, Kasigoentjoe en Mowewe* (hereafter *ZCR*).
3. While a historical perspective was often central to studies of witchcraft in the 1950s and 1960s, it is often absent from contemporary ethnographic studies of witchcraft. For examples of some of the few newer anthropological studies of witchcraft with a historical perspective, see, for instance, Apter 1993; Redding 2006; Shaw 2002; White 2000.
4. For recent critiques of the romanticism and exoticism of conventional writings on millenarianism in Melanesia, see Douglas 2001; Lindstrom 1993; Robbins 2003, 2007.
5. The word *Maluku* is itself said to be a reflection of the perceived importance of the four kingdoms. The Ternatan phrase *Moloko Kie Raha*, from which the Malay word *Maluku* is derived, can be translated as "The World of the Four Mountains" (Andaya 1993).

6. Andaya's book *The World of Maluku* received harsh criticism from Chris van Fraassen (1994) for its use of sources in particular. This criticism did little, however, as Anthony Reid (1995) pointed out in his spirited defense of Andaya, to undermine the basic argument of the book about the importance of the myth of the four realms for political history in North Maluku after 1780 (see also Van Fraassen 1995).

7. The United East India Company (*Vereenigde Oost-Indische Compagnie*, or VOC for short) was established in 1602 by Dutch merchant companies to protect and promote their common trade interests in the Indian Ocean region. Until 1800, when the Dutch state underwrote the huge deficits incurred by the VOC and a colonial government replaced it, the VOC was the institutional representative of Dutch colonialism in the Indonesian archipelago (Ricklefs 2008:29).

8. One event that illustrates central Halmahera's loyalty to Nuku occurred in 1783. The Dutch had assembled a fleet of thirty-four war boats (*juanga*), nine of which came from the Gamurange (see map 4). Their mission was to search for Nuku. But the Halmaheran crew staged a mutiny, killed the Dutch officers, and surrendered the entire fleet to Nuku (Andaya 1993:224).

9. The English interregnum (1801–3) was a consequence of war in Europe. In 1795, French troops under the command of Napoleon Bonaparte had invaded the Netherlands, and in the aftermath the English took over many of the Dutch colonies in the Indian Ocean (Tarling 1999:10). Mismanaged and bankrupt, the VOC had dissolved in 1800 (Ricklefs 2008:134). In the vacuum left by the Dutch, the English assumed control of several posts in Indonesia, including North Maluku. A second interregnum period, in which the English assumed more comprehensive control of the entire colony of the Dutch East Indies, followed in 1811–17 (137).

10. This brother was either Sahasoe or Niroe. A third brother, Soegoe, joined up with pirates in Mindanao. In 1819, this new Djelolo was reportedly attempting to bring "the Papuans" to revolt (Haga 1884b:3). This revolt induced about half of the population in Buli and Maba to leave their homes to support Asgar's struggle in Seram (Cambier 1872:251).

11. The name Adil was obviously a loan from the figure of Ratu Adil, a celebrated millenarian hero from the island of Java (Kartodirjo 1973, 1984). Hassan would have been familiar with this figure, having spent much of his life until the 1870s in Java during the exile of his father, Asgar. Sartono Kartodirjo reports at least five movements in Java in the late 1860s and early 1870s, all inspired by the Ratu Adil myth about "the Just King," Erucakra, whose reign would bring deliverance from evil, illness, and death (1973:77). The movements inspired by this myth begin in 1865 with the Mangkuwidjaja uprising, followed by the Bekasi movement in 1869. In the years 1870 and 1871, three movements occurred almost simultaneously: the Nurhakim revolt in Poerwakerta; the movement in the district of Priyangan inspired by the healer Nji Atjiah; and the revolt in Banyumas led by Amat Ngisa (74).

12. *Alifuru* is a Malukan Malay derogatory term used to refer to the inhabitants of Halmahera who retain their ancestral religion (Visser and Voorhoeve 1987:87). It derives from the north Halmaheran root *fufuru*, meaning "wild" or "undomesticated" (Baarda 1895:136; Fortgens 1917:23). Nowadays it is a common derisive term in North Maluku. It is used to refer to a backward, uneducated, and ignorant person.

13. Hassan's claims about the size of his following are most certainly exaggerated. Had they been true, he would have had the active support of the entire population of Halmahera, which in the early decades of the twentieth century was estimated at thirty to forty thousand (*ZCR* 1916 [7]:1).

14. Indeed, in Papua the mission work of the UZV centered on Masinam, where two German missionaries had begun work in 1855 (Rutherford 2003:31).

15. In 1883, for instance, a younger brother of Hassan named Haji Hias tried to revitalize the rebellion by inciting the population to revolt from a base in Maba. His efforts were in vain (Clerq 1890:187).

16. Haire spells the name "Andil," but I use "Adil" in the following in accordance with contemporary Indonesian spelling to avoid confusion.

17. The eschatological hope for the imminent return of Jesus was, in spite of the emphasis on moderation, far from foreign to the Dutch mission. Indeed, "the Great Awakening" (known in French as *le Réveil*) in the Dutch Reformed Church—the movement to which the Utrecht Mission Union belonged—had itself struggled to root out the influence of Calvinist eschatologists, such as Willem Bilderdijk, who during the nineteenth century felt that "the last pages of history were being written" (tenZynthoff 1987:97).

## 4. Christianity and Deception

1. A particular problem in Buli from the missionaries' point of view was the premarital sexual relations that young people traditionally have as the young man moves into the house of the girl's parents to perform "rowing service" for them. This "rowing service" (*kangelá re dao*) is an essential part of the prestations given to the girl's family, and like all other prestations it is meant to symbolically emphasize the asymmetrical relationship between wife-takers and wife-givers, in which the former are "subjects," and the latter are "rulers" or "sultans." Such asymmetry is a common feature of alliances throughout eastern Indonesia (Fox 1990; Fox and Sather 1996; Platenkamp 1988). The rowing service of the future groom ends only when the wife-givers, the woman's side, declare themselves ready to proceed to the phase of negotiating the payment of the bride price (*kaimulo*). Today this period is short (and sometimes dispensed with altogether), but in former times it could last for months, or even years, during which time the couple would often have produced one or more children before being officially married. The relations could even be broken off during this period. Such breaks were never taken lightly, and they always entailed the payment of compensation to "cover the shame" of the woman's side—and moreover, a break often permanently soured the relationship between the two families. Still, such breaks happened often enough to be a concern for missionaries in the area.

2. Obviously this link between Christianity and modernity is not universal. Even in Indonesia, Christianity does not always imply modernity (see, for instance, Rutherford 2006). See Cannell (2006:30–39) for a discussion of the relationship between Christianity and modernity.

3. In a very similar fashion, Michel de Certeau describes "the autonomy of the practice of reading underneath scriptural imperialism" as a form of "poaching" on the otherwise "private hunting terrain" of privileged meaning (1984:169). Living on the coast, Buli people are traditionally both hunters and fishermen. Both metaphors are therefore "ethnographically apt" ways of connoting how one may make a terrain of power and meaning one's own.

## 5. The Viscerality of Witchcraft and the Corporeality of the World

1. Pressure on the chest by a felt other is a component of "nightmares" throughout the world. For neurological accounts of this phenomenon, which I cite not as definitive explanations but as additional sources of insight, see Cheyne et al. 1999 and Solomonova et al. 2008.

2. The term *cokaéba* for these masks derives from *coka*, the Tidore word denoting a witch or *suanggi*. According to myth, these masks were first bestowed upon the *sangaji* of Maba by the sultan of Tidore as a gift in return for tribute (*cucatu*). The masks are used in many Muslim parts of North Maluku to celebrate Mawlid. One of the most important but also controversial of holy days in the Islamic calendar, Mawlid celebrates the birth of the prophet Muhammad

on 12 Rabi Awal (Woodward 2011:169ff.). The *cokaéba* masks, which are said to "mimic" (Tidore *éba*) the witch (Tidore *coka*), are anointed at dawn by the local imam, and during the entire day of Mawlid young men, wearing the masks and wielding small sticks and branches, chase children and young adults, who taunt them by crying, *Belo, belo, belo!* The masked figures do not speak, but they enter the houses and point to objects that people are then compelled to give them. Even though the official masks are restricted to Muslim villages, children in both Muslim and Christian villages make their own toy versions during the days around 12 Rabi Awal. The masks illustrate how across Halmahera the *suanggi* is an object of concern in both Christian and Muslim villages. For a description and analysis of the *cokaéba* masks, see Bubandt 1995:249–253.

3. This definition of the difference between significance and meaning partly follows Kristeva (1982) but also draws on Anthony Wilden (1980). Wilden characterizes the distinction between signification and meaning as follows: "Signification controls the creation of signs and signifiers; meaning is concerned with the survival of the whole in which it is involved" (1980:189). Witchcraft is full of significance because it is directed at the signs of the body and the world, but the *gua* does not aggregate into a meaningful whole, an ordered system of signs. Rather, in witchcraft, meaning collapses. For a theoretical overview and discussion of the tradition of meaning in anthropology, see Tomlinson and Engelke 2007 and Gardner 2010. For a nice analysis of meaninglessness in Telefolmin society in Papua New Guinea, see Jorgensen 1980.

4. The concepts of *nyawa* (as breath) and *semangat* (often translated as life-force) and their association with embodiment, ontogeny, healing, head-hunting, and animism have been discussed at length in Southeast Asian anthropology (Endicott 1970; Laderman 1993; Needham 1976; Skeat 2010).

5. While Buli custom prescribes that the intestines and tongue of game should be boiled (or roasted if the prey was caught while hunting with dogs), the liver (*momoan*) is always treated as meat (*wangto*) and is smoked on the *babala* shelf above the fire.

6. Jos Platenkamp, for one, relates how previously in North Halmaheran societies the slaying of an enemy was sometimes followed by the slayer's child drinking a little of the enemy's blood, or consuming a small piece of his liver (1988:144). See also *BUZ* 1877 (4):50 for a description of such an event on Morotai. Platenkamp sees in these acts an incorporation of the "image" (Tobelo *o gurumini*) of the slain victim through an analogy between the liver and the *gurumin*. In the Tobelo practice we see the same significance attributed to the liver (and blood) as the seat (and origin) of a person's human identity. Through the consumption of the liver, the *gurumin* is incorporated. In Buli, a bit of the blood of a slain enemy might have been drunk, but his liver is never eaten. This, Buli people have told me, would turn you into a *gua*. While in North Halmahera eating the enemy's liver is a triumphant incorporation, in Buli the same act when performed by the *gua* is a despicable and murderous violation.

7. Adults are always careful to turn sleeping children onto their sides (*fataslís*), for instance. Allowing them to sleep on their backs (*fatahlén*) would leave their livers exposed to a *gua* on the prowl.

8. The mangrove tree also has medicinal uses, its bark relieving fatigue and pain in the joints. The tree's bark is sometimes added to palm wine in North Halmahera for medicinal purposes, while elsewhere in Indonesia it is sometimes used to cure dysentery (Heyne 1950:888).

9. This phenomenon is one of the best-known details of the witch in North Maluku, where stories of witches (*suanggi* in North Malukan Malay) who "pull out" (I. *bercabut*) are legion.

10. See Geschiere 2013 for a brilliant exploration of the relationship between witchcraft and intimacy.

11. See Horridge 1978 for a description of the planked boats of Maluku.

12. On the analogy between the human body and the boat in Maluku, see also Barraud 1979:89; 1990.

13. *Long hapaluan*, the spine, also refers to the most powerful magical root (*aiwáo*) that a man owns, which is usually a root that endows the owner with magical fighting powers (*man de wela*). This "magical backbone" functions as the axis or foundation (*ifíf*) for the owner's body. Today, the traditional tight string waistband called *saópat* is worn only by certain older men, but formerly the *saópat* was where a man would keep his most powerful fighting magic, his (*aiwáo*) or "backbone." This piece of string, twisted to hold the magical roots and tied extremely tight around the waist, provided protection, especially during forays into the forest and on travels. The magical "backbone" protected the man throughout his adult life, and he should never part with it, as doing so would mean imminent death. Instead, as the time of his own death drew near he would pass the *saópat* on to a man within his lineage, usually to his *ntu man* (sons or brother's sons) or alternatively to his *fanó man* (sister's sons). I was told that some men swallowed their magical backbone and regurgitated it on their deathbed for the new owner to swallow. Alternatively, the magic would be exuded at the moment of death as seven drops of sweat (*sagigé sifít*). This would eagerly be licked from the deceased's forehead by his son, or in some anecdotal cases by a fortunate bystander.

14. See also Stanley Tambiah's (1983) analysis of flying canoes and flying witches in the Trobriands. Here, witches are usually female and attack at sea. In Tambiah's view, Trobriand witches make a mockery of the mythically derived, but perpetually unsuccessful, male magic that is said to make ordinary canoes fly. The female witches' ability to fly is a remnant of the mythical male ability to make canoes fly, now lost forever.

15. On the basis of a report from 1807, R. Leirissa (1986) estimates that almost half the male population of these appointed villages was required to serve on the sultanate fleet for a certain period every year.

16. In practice, the money from the extended family beyond the patrilineage is often not paid. It is said to remain "cold" (*maíring*) and is only paid if the man wishes to divorce the woman at a later stage.

17. The cooking pans are known as "the Gift That Wipes the Tears" and "the Gift for Cutting Wood and Fetching Water," respectively. *Oyang Safsafo*, "the Gift That Wipes the Tears," is a prestation directly from the groom's mother to the bride's mother to compensate for the emotional aspects of losing her daughter to the groom's side. After marriage, the couple will ritually move to the house of the groom's parents, and the bride will have "gone out of" the lineage or "Root-House" of her father. The gift consists of a pan (*ulan*) and is reciprocated from the bride's side with plates (*dodái*), a sarong (*obat*), a silver comb (*siséi*), and silver hairpins (*pugalebat*). *Kate Ai re Waya*, "the Gift for Cutting Wood and Fetching Water," is a pan presented by the groom's father to the bride's father to compensate for the loss of his daughter and the domestic work she performed in the home. It, too, is reciprocated with plates, hairpins, a comb, and a shirt.

18. The placenta (*dodomi*) is "same sex sibling" of the child (*tenó*) and maintains a spiritual connection with the infant after birth. This link has to be severed with a great deal of ritual care. If the birth is successful, the placenta is buried along with a small amount of money in the kitchen away from the fire. The money is "thrown as an offering" (*topa sadaka*) to entice the placenta not "to call its sibling" and cause it to die. Stillbirths are frequently seen as the result of a too powerful spiritual bond between the placenta and the fetus. In such cases, the stillborn infant is buried with the placenta.

## 6. New Order Modern

1. Pancasila, the political philosophy that undergirds the Indonesian state and since 1978 has been a mandatory part of political indoctrination, defines the five principles of a moral

society: belief in one God; justice and civility; the unity of Indonesian democracy; achieving this through deliberation and consultation; and social justice (Antlöv 2000; Morfit 1981; Stange 1986).

2. This expression is a variation on Murray Li's notion of "development deficit" (Li 2000:154).

3. The national electrical company (*Perusahaan Listrik Negara*, PLN) maintains a monopoly on the supply of electricity in the country. During the New Order, electricity supply was known for its unreliability and poor distribution, driven by underinvestment and mismanagement (Vial and Hanoteau 2010:697).

4. Of the ninety-one cases of witchcraft I have recorded between 1991 and 2011, a *gua* was identified in sixty-seven. Of these attacks, the suspected *gua* was unrelated to its victim in thirty-six cases (54 percent), while the suspected witch and its victim were related in thirty-one cases (46 percent). From this pool of thirty-one cases where a family relation existed, the majority of cases, precisely twenty-five in all (or 80 percent), involved a witch and a victim from the same "house of relatives" (*ebai bangsá*), the extended lineage beyond one's immediate patrilineage, including the relatives of one's mother as well as the maternal relatives of one's father. So while this confirmed the Buli saying that "witches do not recognize bilateral kin," such attacks still accounted for only 27 percent of the overall number of attacks.

5. Records in the regency court in Soa Sio on Tidore, which handled until 1999 all cases from the district of Central Halmahera (*Halmahera Tengah*), show that in the five-year period from 1988 to 1992, the regency court had heard 126 cases. Until 1991, none of these had been related to *suanggi*, which is the generic Malay term for "witches" in North Maluku. Then in 1991, one case of assault in Tidore arose out of suspicions of an attack by a *suanggi* (known in Tidore as *coka*), while in 1992 two cases, both from the district of Maba, were heard. One concerned an assault on a presumed *gua* in Mabapura, and the other was related to the attack on Lolos's house.

6. Missionary records reveal that people accused of witchcraft also in the past often chose to move temporarily either to a nearby village or to their garden hamlets (*ZCR* 1922 [71]:1). *Gua* attacks are highly local and always happen between covillagers. This in turn means that if one lives some distance away, one is unlikely to be accused of witchcraft, and after a period away, inhabitants formerly accused are often able to return to the village. Before the Dutch settled the Buli population in villages, the local semisedentary lifestyle of swidden farming, fishing, and hunting made it relatively easy for people to move to a new region along the coast for a while and set up new swidden gardens there. Today, however, settlement and property rights have made this a much harder proposition.

7. Essential to the New Order idea of Indonesia as a Pancasila state was a logic of "family-ness" (I. *kekeluargaan*), in which state and society formed an organic whole led by the father figure of the president (Berger 1997; Guinness 1994; Li 2007:52; Suryakusuma 1996).

8. This decision to annul the agreement of mutual accommodation that had been reached with the head of the army was related to a power struggle between the police and the army about whose jurisdiction the petition came under, and thus who could profit from it. The police resented that it was the army who, as part of their overall territorial commands during the election period, had been approached to handle the petition rather than the police—and had been paid the monetary enticements that always attend such dealings with the authorities. The police were, therefore, eager to reclaim their authority in this matter.

9. In pre-Christian times there were three kinds of ordeals, or tests, for suspected witches. *Sop Bebelas* (Diving by the Pole) was the most frequently used ordeal. Presided over by the village head (*oloán*) or in Muslim villages by the imam, the accused and an accuser—or representatives from their families—would submerge themselves underwater while holding onto a pole stuck into the seabed. The first one to surface would be in the wrong. *Sop Bebelas* was last

performed in the late 1960s when a man called Dolosi, who until recently still lived in Waiflí, was accused of witchcraft. Dolosi had emerged first, because, as he said, he felt as if his mouth had been filled by hundreds of tiny fish. Despite suspicions that the fish were a sign of magic used by his accusers, Dolosi moved away from the village "out of shame" (*mai*) and lived for years in his garden hut some distance from the village. A second ordeal was called *Lauwe Waya Sino* (To Reach into Hot Water). The two representatives would reach into a pot of boiling water to grab something on the bottom, and the hand of the person in the right would not be burnt. The third and most dangerous way of settling the veracity of an accusation, called *Sasi mali Íyan Toa* (Swearing before Íyan Toa), was an oath taken in front of Íyan Toa's shrine. This ordeal was also performed last in the 1960s, when a man called Sonny had been accused of witchcraft. Both he and a father's brother of the man he was accused of killing drank from the porcelain bowl (*guci*) in Íyan Toa's shrine. In this bowl, rust from Íyan Toa's sword and spear was mixed with water and *sulasi* and *takiwi* weeds. The *kapita* (the ritual leader in charge of Íyan Toa's shrine) had sworn an oath (*bobeto*) over the mixture, which was then drunk by the two men. Within a year, people remember, most members of Sonny's family had died, including his two siblings, his wife, and four of his six children.

## 7. Subjectivity, Exchange, Opacity

1. I borrow the distinction between morality and ethics from Michel Foucault. I take morality to refer to the "values and rules of action that are recommended to individuals through the intermediary of various prescriptive agencies such as the family" (Foucault 1988c:25). Ethics, meanwhile, can be described as the way in which we create ourselves as subjects (Foucault 1983:208). An ethics entails a set of practices by which one tries to establish one's self and attain a certain mode of being (Foucault 1988a:2).

2. A marvelous ethnographic example of the aporia built into any witchcraft accusation comes from Rupert Stasch's study of the Korowai area in Papua, the Indonesian half of the island of New Guinea. Among the Korowai until quite recently, people accused of being cannibal witches were often killed by the family of the victim, or they were captured and transported to a third-party group who would kill them and consume their body (Stasch 2001:38). As Stasch notes, the Korowai were acutely aware that this form of execution was a "close double" of the cannibalistic act of witchcraft itself, and this (along with state repression) played into the complex set of reasons why the Korowai abruptly gave up witch executions in the 1990s (41).

3. For an analysis of the relationship between an ethics of good companionship and sorcery in Melanesia, see Knauft 1985.

4. Dried anchovies (known in Indonesian as *ikan teri* or *ngafi*) are sold to local middlemen and provide a welcome source of cash income.

5. See Peterson (1993) for a discussion of the coexistence of reciprocity and hiding among hunter-gatherers, particularly in Australia. Miriam Kahn (1986) has a discussion similar to mine of the strategies of concealment among Wamira-speakers of Milne Bay, Papua New Guinea. For examples of strategies of humiliation by giving food, see Young 1972.

6. Nancy Munn's wonderful monograph *The Fame of Gawa* (1986) similarly posits exchange and witchcraft as two opposed but mutually linked forms of the social or intersubjective production of value. Exchange creates a positive evaluation of intersubjective relationships, while witchcraft subverts this process and threatens its realization. "Exchange" and "witch-craft," Munn argues, are analytical glosses for two opposed forms of value production that are linked closely to the intersubjective basis for sociality, which she takes from G. H. Mead (1962): "Social relationships can be seen as engaging the actor's perspective on an outside

other that implies a perception of the other's perspective on the self. . . . Indeed, what anthropologists sum up as 'exchange' and 'witchcraft' are among the fundamental kinds of practices formulated in ways that turn on this basic phenomenological structure" (Munn 1986:16).

7. Stasch (2009) similarly highlights the way otherness is an integral part of social intimacy in Korowai society in the southern part of Papua, in ways that also implicate witchcraft. The Korowai emphasis on spatial separation, social otherness, and the opacity of other people's minds is intimately related to a fear of male, cannibal witches known as *xaxua*, as well as to anxieties over the demons that humans turn into after death (Stasch 2009:6).

8. This humility is also inscribed through Buli deixis. When Gambar notes that she did not think I would come "down" to visit Buli again, she is making a reference to a spatial universe in which the world outside of the multidimensional region of North Maluku is placed in an "upward" direction (*puis*) (Bubandt 1997).

## 8. Technology, Money, and the Futures of Witchcraft

1. On sound and modernity in general, see also Schafer 1994; Thompson 2002.

2. In November 2011, the Indonesian minister for the economy, Hatta Rajasa, laid the first stone for the construction of the combined ferronickel factory and a 275-megawatt power plant a few kilometers from Waiflí. A so-called *mega proyek* estimated to cost 1.6 billion US dollars and funded by a consortium of Indonesian and international banks, the smelter is being constructed by Aneka Tambang and is a key node in the mining company's efforts to comply with a 2009 Indonesian law requiring all mining companies to process their commodities before export to raise the added-value of the country's natural resources. The smelter is planned to be operational in 2014 and is scheduled to produce 27,000 tons of nickel annually (Tempo 2011). The combined smelter and power plant will be built by three thousand construction workers and eventually employ around nine hundred factory workers, most of whom will be accommodated in housing complexes on the outskirts of Waiflí village.

3. *Cokaéko* is a compound word, the root of which, *coka,* is the Tidore equivalent of the Buli term *gua*. The names of both the *kokók* and the *nganga* are onomatopoeic of their calls. The *kokók* makes a rapid series of sharp, short calls: *koh-koh-koh*. The call of the *nganga* is coarser and more drawn out, emitted in a rapid decrescendo: *NGA-NGA-nga-nga*. This latter call is said to be the mocking laughter of the *gua*, trying to lure humans to answer it. Also, the call is said to cause death to any child who cries when the *nganga* calls out, and parents therefore sometimes refer to the *nganga* to silence children who are crying at night, usually with great effect.

4. I have been unable to identify the *cokaéko* and the *kokók*. Local informants in Buli who are fluent in both Buli and Tobelo have told me that the Tobelo equivalents of these are *o keka* and *o koko* (or *o kokoko*), respectively. Among the Forest Tobelo at Lili, who converted to charismatic Christianity during the 1980s, these two creatures were also previously thought to be witches (Chris Duncan, personal communication, 2012). In his study of ethnobiology among Tobelo people in Pasir Putih during the 1980s, Paul Taylor remarks on two unknown species of birds similarly thought to be witches (*o tokata*): the *o kigi-kigini* and the *o kou-kou*. Of the latter, probably identical to the Buli *kokók*, Taylor writes: "uncollected, and probably uncollectable! This is always considered to be a ghost in the form of an invisible bird that is heard at night flying around villages crying 'kou! kou!' to announce impending death" (1990:123–124).

5. This incantation has a mythical origin. Maan relates the myth of a woman who woke up one night to find the headless body of her husband next to her. In panic she waited till dawn for the return of the head, for it is well known that the *gua* often uses merely the head of its host (see chapter 5). Even as daylight returned, however, the head of her husband did not. The

head and entrails were later found entangled in the thorny branches of a *katekate* bush, where the *gua* had died (*ZCR* 1922 [71]:2).

6. For accounts of the relationship between electricity and modernity in general, see Delbourgo 2006; Morus 1998; Nye 1992; Rejali 2007:121–258. For analyses of electricity as a harbinger of modernity in Indonesia, see Maier 1997; Mrázek 1997. For more on witchcraft and electricity in Halmahera, see Bubandt 2008a.

7. In 2012, the Antam mining company unwittingly became a direct purveyor of such electronic protection against witchcraft when it distributed three high-lumen compact fluorescent light bulbs to each household as part of its community development program. In this way, the mining company's mediation of the Indonesian commitment to the global scheme to phase out high-energy bulbs with energy-friendly but poorly performing incandescent bulbs inadvertently provided Buli people with a new technology of witchcraft protection.

8. The ability of witches to employ advanced technology for their own purposes or to "mask" attacks as, say, traffic accidents or medical diseases has also been noted elsewhere (Ashforth 2005:46; Rödlach 2006; Shaw 1997).

9. The Makian are a Muslim ethnic group that had migrated to many parts of Halmahera since the 1970s. They had been involved in initial outbreaks of violence in August and October 1999, and also figured centrally as intended victims in a fake letter allegedly written by the Protestant church. The outbreak of violence in many localities on Halmahera after November 1999 revolved around the paranoia generated by this letter; see Bubandt 2009.

10. The violence in Tobelo, on the northern peninsula of Halmahera (see map 2), broke out suddenly and brutally soon after Christmas 1999, when Christians killed hundreds of Muslims in villages just outside of the town center in an anxiety-driven preventive strike. News of the massacre caused national outrage in the Muslim parts of Indonesia, and the onslaught was explicitly mentioned among the reasons for the formation of the Laskar Jihad, a militia that recruited volunteers from Java and Sumatra to defend their Muslim brethren in the conflict-torn areas of Indonesia. Their presence in Maluku and Poso, in particular, was an important factor in intensifying and prolonging these conflicts (Davis 2002; Hasan 2002; Hefner 2002).

11. Modernity, after all, is not singular but always plural. For a discussion of the multiple versions of, and splits within, Western modernity, see Cooper 2005; Knauft 2002; Lash 1999.

## Witchcraft beyond Belief

1. I owe this fortuitous phrase to Michael Lambek, who used it in a keynote lecture at Aarhus University in 2010 as part of the conference "Researching Religion: Methodological Debates in Anthropology and the Study of Religion."

2. This critique also has older roots, such as Smith 1978.

3. The *Cambridge Advanced Learner's Dictionary* defines "subjunctive" as "a set of forms of a verb, in some languages, that refer to actions which are possibilities rather than facts: In the sentence 'I wish I were rich,' the verb 'were' is in the subjunctive" (Gillard 2003:1274). The subjunctive mode, or mood (I. *bentuk pengandaian*), is not marked in the verb in Indonesian or Buli, but is rather expressed through conjunctions. Therefore, I am not referring to the subjunctive as a grammatical form here, but rather as a "mood." Following Susan Whyte (1997:24), I am suggesting the subjunctive as a kind of attitude informing one's attention to the future.

4. For an analysis of Meno's paradox, see Matthews 1999:53–65.

# BIBLIOGRAPHY

Abrams, M. H. 1958. Foreword to *Literature and Belief*, edited by M. H. Abrams, vii-xiii. New York: Columbia University Press.

Abu-Lughod, Lila. 1991. "Writing against Culture." In *Recapturing Anthropology: Working in the Present*, edited by R. Fox, 137–162. Santa Fe, NM: School of American Research Press.

Acciaioli, Greg. 1985. "Culture as Art: From Practice to Spectacle in Indonesia." *Canberra Anthropology* 8(1–2):148–172.

Adorno, Theodor, and Max Horkheimer. 1979. *Dialectic of Enlightenment*. London: Verso.

Andaya, Leonard. 1991. "Local Trade Networks in Maluku in the 16th, 17th and 18th Centuries." *Cakalele* 2(2):71–96.

———. 1993. *The World of Maluku: Eastern Indonesia in the Early Modern Period*. Honolulu: University of Hawai'i Press.

Anderson, Benedict. 1990. *Language and Power: Exploring Political Cultures in Indonesia*. Ithaca, NY: Cornell University Press.

———. 1998. *Spectres of Comparison: Nationalism, Southeast Asia, and the World*. London: Verso.

ANTAM. 2001. *Quarterly Report to Shareholders* [for the three months ending 30 June 2001]. Jakarta: PT Antam Tbk.

Antlöv, Hans. 1995. *Exemplary Centre, Administrative Periphery: Rural Leadership and the New Order in Java*. Asian Studies Monograph, no. 68. Richmond: Curzon Press.

———. 2000. "Demokrasi Pancasila and the Future Ideology in Indonesia." In *The Cultural Construction of Politics in Asia*, edited by H. Antlöv and T. Ngo, 203–222. Richmond: Curzon Press.

Apter, Andrew. 1993. "Atinga Revisited: Yoruba Witchcraft and the Cocoa Economy, 1950–1951." In *Modernity and Its Malcontents: Ritual and Power in Postcolonial Africa*, edited by J. Comaroff and J. Comaroff, 111–128. Chicago: University of Chicago Press.

Aragon, Lorraine. 2000. *Fields of the Lord: Animism, Christian Minorities, and State Development in Indonesia*. Honolulu: University of Hawai'i Press.

Argyrou, Vassos. 2000. "Reflexive Modernization and Other Mythical Realities." *Anthropological Theory* 3(1):27–41.

Aristotle. 2004. *Metaphysics*. Translated with an introduction by Hugh Lawson-Tangred. London: Penguin.

Asad, Talal. 1993. *Genealogies of Religion: Discipline and Reasons of Power in Christianity and Islam*. Baltimore: Johns Hopkins University Press.

Ashforth, Adam. 2000. *Madumo: A Man Bewitched*. Chicago: University of Chicago Press.

——. 2001. "On Living in a World with Witches." In *Magical Interpretations, Material Realities: Modernity, Witchcraft, and the Occult in Postcolonial Africa*, edited by H. Moore and T. Sanders, 206–225. London: Routledge.

——. 2005. *Witchcraft, Violence and Democracy in South Africa*. Chicago: University of Chicago Press.

Aspinall, Edward, and Greg Fealey, eds. 2003. *Local Power and Politics in Indonesia: Decentralisation and Democratisation*. Singapore: Institute of Southeast Asian Studies.

Atkinson, Jane Monnig. 1983. "Religions in Dialogue: The Construction of an Indonesian Minority Religion." *American Ethnologist* 10(4):684–696.

Baarda, M. van. 1895. *Woordenlijst: Galelareesch-Hollandsch met Ethnologische Aanteekeningen, op de Woorden, die daartoe Aanleiding Gaven* [Word list in Galela-Dutch with ethnological notes on relevant words]. The Hague: Martinus Nijhoff.

Bachelard, Gaston. 1969. *The Poetics of Space*. Boston: Beacon Press.

Badone, Ellen. 1995. "Suspending Disbelief: An Encounter with the Occult in Brittany." *Anthropology and Humanism* 20(1):9–14.

Baldwin, David. 1993. "Dispersal and the Dream of Integration: A Ritual Community on Taliabu, North Maluku, Indonesia." PhD diss., Cornell University.

Bandak, Andreas, and Jonas Adelin Jørgensen. 2012. "Foregrounds and Backgrounds: Ventures in the Anthropology of Christianity." *Ethnos* 77(4):477–458.

Barker, Joshua. 2001. "State of Fear: Controlling the Criminal Contagion in Suharto's New Order." In *Violence and the State in Suharto's Indonesia*, edited by B. Anderson, 20–53. Ithaca, NY: South East Asia Program, Cornell University.

——. 2005. "Engineers and Political Dreams: Indonesia in the Satellite Age." *Current Anthropology* 46(5):703–727.

Barnes, Robert. 1974. *Kedang: A Study of the Collective Thought of an Eastern Indonesian People*. Oxford: Clarendon Press.

Barraud, Cecile. 1979. *Tanebar-Evav: Une société de maisons tournée vers le large*. Cambridge: Cambridge University Press.

——. 1990. "Kei Society and the Person: An Approach through Childbirth and Funerary Rituals." *Ethnos* 55(3–4):214–231.

Bartels, Dieter. 1977. "Guarding the Invisible Mountain: Intervillage Alliances, Religious Syncretism and Ethnic Identity among Ambonese Christians and Moslems in the Moluccas." PhD diss., Cornell University.

Barton, Greg. 2002. *Gus Dur: The Authorized Biography of Abdurrahman Wahid*. London: Equinox Publishing.

Bataille, Georges. 1992. *Theory of Religion*. Cambridge, MA: MIT Press.

Batawi, Samadar. 1986. "Riwayat Hidup Singkatan Bapak Almarhum Mozes Mahulete" [A short biography of Mozes Mahulete]. Unpublished manuscript.

Baudrillard, Jean. 1993. *The Transparency of Evil*. London: Verso.

———. 2003. *The Spirit of Terrorism*. London: Verso.

Bauman, Zygmunt. 2000. *Liquid Modernity*. Oxford: Polity Press.

Beatty, Andrew. 2012. "Kala Defanged: Managing Power in Java away from the Centre." *Bijdragen to de Taal-, Land- en Volkenkunde* 168(2–3):173–194.

Beck, Ulrich. 2002. "The Terrorist Threat: World Risk Society Revisited." *Theory, Culture & Society* 19(4):39–55.

Behrend, Heike. 2011. *Resurrecting Cannibals: The Catholic Church, Witch-Hunts, and the Production of Pagans in Western Uganda*. Woodbridge, UK: James Currey.

Bellwood, Peter. 1985. *Prehistory of the Indo-Malaysian Archipelago*. Sydney: Academic Press.

Belo, Jane. 1949. *Rangda and Barong*. American Ethnological Society Monograph, no. 16. New York: J. J. Augustin.

Benda-Beckmann, F. von, K. von Benda-Beckmann, and A. Brouwer. 1995. "Changing 'Indigenous Environmental Law' in the Central Moluccas: Communal Regulation and Privatization of Sasi." *Ekonesia: A Journal of Indonesian Human Ecology* 2:1–38.

Benedict, Philip. 2002. *Christ's Churches Purely Reformed: A Social History of Calvinism*. New Haven, CT: Yale University Press.

Bennett, Jane. 2001. *The Enchantment of Modern Life: Attachments, Crossings, and Ethics*. Princeton, NJ: Princeton University Press.

Berger, Mark. 1997. "Old State and New Empire: Debating the Rise and Decline of Suharto's New Order." *Third World Quarterly* 18(2):321–361.

Bergh, Rudolph. 1964. "Soeangi in de Vogelkop van Nieuw-Guinea" [The *suanggi* in the Birdhead of New Guinea]. MA thesis, Christelijke Hogeschool, Oegstgeest.

Berlant, Lauren. 2011. *Cruel Optimism*. Durham, NC: Duke University Press.

Berman, Marshall. 1982. *All That Is Solid Melts into Air: The Experience of Modernity*. London: Verso.

Bertrand, Jacques. 1996. "False Starts, Succession Crises, and Regime Transition: Flirting with Openness in Indonesia." *Pacific Studies* 69(3):319–340.

———. 2003. *Nationalism and Ethnic Conflict in Indonesia*. Cambridge: Cambridge University Press.

Bloch, Maurice. 2013. "Types of Shared Doubt in the Flow of a Discussion." In *Ethnographies of Doubt: Faith and Uncertainty in Contemporary Societies*, edited by M. Pelkmans, 43–58. London: I. B. Tauris.

Bluck, R. S. 1961. *Plato's Meno*. Edited with introduction and commentary. Cambridge: Cambridge University Press.

Blust, Robert. 1978. "Eastern Malayo-Polynesian: A Subgrouping Argument." In *Proceedings of the Second International Conference on Austronesian Linguistics*, fascicle 1, edited by S. A. Wurm and L. Carrington, 181–234. Pacific Linguistics Series C, no. 61. Canberra: Australian National University.

Bond, George Clement, and Diane M. Ciekawy, eds. 2002. *Witchcraft Dialogues: Anthropological and Philosophical Exchanges*. Columbus: Ohio University Press.

Booth, Anne. 1999. "Survey of Recent Developments." *Bulletin of Indonesian Economic Studies* 35(3):3–38.

Bos, David. J. 2010. *Servants of the Kingdom: Professionalization among Ministers of the Nineteenth-Century Netherlands Reformed Church*. Leiden: Brill.

Bourdieu, Pierre. 1977. *Outline of a Theory of Practice*. Cambridge: Cambridge University Press.

———. 1990. *The Logic of Practice*. Stanford, CA: Stanford University Press.

Bowen, John. 2011. *Religions in Practice: An Approach to the Anthropology of Religion*. Boston: Prentice Hall.

Bowie, Fiona. 2006. *The Anthropology of Religion: An Introduction*. Malden, MA: Blackwell Publishing.

BPSPMU. 2010. *Maluku Utara Dalam Angka; North Maluku in Figures*. Ternate: Badan Pusat Statistik Provinsi Maluku Utara [Statistical Bureau of the Province of North Maluku].

Brenner, Suzanne. 1998. *The Domestication of Desire: Women, Wealth and Modernity in Java*. Princeton, NJ: Princeton University Press.

Brickhouse, Thomas C., and Nicholas D. Smith. 1990. *Socrates on Trial*. Oxford: Oxford University Press.

Broughton, Janet. 2002. *Descartes's Method of Doubt*. Princeton, NJ: Princeton University Press.

Brown, Michael. 1996. "On Resisting Resistance." *American Anthropologist* 98(4):729–735.

Bubandt, Nils. 1995. "Warriors of the Hornbill, Victims of the Mantis: History and Embodied Morality among the Buli of Central Halmahera." PhD diss., Australian National University.

———. 1997. "Speaking of Places: Spatial Poesis and Localized Identity in Buli." In *The Poetic Power of Place: Comparatove Perspectives on Austronesian Locality*, edited by J. J. Fox, 132–162. Canberra: Australian National University.

———. 1998a. "Imagined Globalities: Fetishism of the Global and the End of the World in Indonesia." *FOLK* 40:99–122.

———. 1998b. "The Odour of Things: Smell and the Cultural Elaboration of Disgust in Eastern Indonesia." *Ethnos* 63(1):48–80.

———. 2001. "Malukan Apocalypse: Themes in the Dynamics of Violence in Eastern Indonesia." In *Violence in Indonesia*, edited by I. Wessel and G. Wimhoefer, 228–253. Hamburg: Abera.

———. 2004a. "Genesis in Buli: Christianity, Blood, and Vernacular Modernity on an Indonesian Island." *Ethnology* 43(3):249–270.

———. 2004b. "Violence and Millenarian Modernity in Eastern Indonesia." In *Cargo, Cult and Culture Critique*, edited by H. Jebens, 92–116. Honolulu: University of Hawai'i Press.

———. 2005a. "On the Genealogy of Sasi: The Transformations of an Imagined Tradition in Eastern Indonesia." In *Tradition and Agency: Tracing Cultural Continuity and Invention*, edited by T. Otto and P. Pedersen, 193–232. Aarhus: Aarhus University Press.

———. 2005b. "Vernacular Security: The Politics of Feeling Safe in Global, National, and Local Worlds." *Security Dialogue* 36(3):275–296.

———. 2006. "Sorcery, Corruption, and the Dangers of Democracy in Indonesia." *Journal of the Royal Anthropological Institute* 12(2):413–431.

———. 2008a. "Ghosts with Trauma: Global Imaginaries and the Politics of Post-Conflict Memory." In *Conflict, Violence, and Displacement in Indonesia*, edited by E. Hedman, 275–301. Ithaca, NY: Southeast Asia Program, Cornell University.

———. 2008b. "Rumors, Pamphlets, and the Politics of Paranoia in Indonesia." *Journal of Asian Studies* 67(3):789–817.

———. 2009. "From the Enemy's Point of View: Violence, Empathy, and the Ethnography of Fakes." *Cultural Anthropology* 24(3):553–588.

———. 2011. "Shadows of Secularism: Money Politics, Spirit Politics and the Law in an Indonesian Election." In *Varieties of Secularism: Religion, Politics and the Spiritual in Asia*, edited by N. Bubandt and M. van Beek, 183–207. Honolulu: University of Hawai'i Press.

——. 2012. "A Psychology of Ghosts: The Regime of the Self and the Reinvention of Spirits in Indonesia and Beyond." *Anthropological Forum* 22(1):1–23.

——. 2014. *Democracy, Corruption and the Politics of Spirits in Contemporary Indonesia*. Modern Anthropology of Southeast Asia. London: Routledge.

Burke, Anthony. 2002. "Aporias of Security." *Alternatives* 27(1):1.

Burridge, Kenelm. 1960. *Mambu: A Melanesian Millennium*. London: Methuen.

——. 1969. *New Heaven, New Earth: A Study of Millenarian Activities*. Oxford: Basil Blackwell.

Cambier, J.P.C. 1872. "Rapport over Tidoreesch-Halmahera." *Bijdragen tot de Taal-, Land- en Volkenkunde* 19(7):240–266.

Campen, C. F. H. 1884. "Halémahera." *Tijdschrift voor Nederlandsch-Indie* 13(2):1–9.

Campion, Nicolas. 1994. *The Great Year: Astrology, Millenarianism and History in the Western Tradition*. Oxford: Basil Blackwell.

Cannell, Fenella. 1999. *Power and Intimacy in the Christian Philippines*. Cambridge: Cambridge University Press.

——. 2006. "Introduction: The Anthropology of Christianity." In *The Anthropology of Christianity*, edited by F. Cannell, 1–50. Durham, NC: Duke University Press.

Carsten, Janet, and Stephen Hugh-Jones, eds. 1995 *About the House: Lévi-Strauss and Beyond*. Cambridge: Cambridge University Press.

Certeau, Michel de. 1984. *The Practice of Everyday Life*. Berkeley: University of California Press.

——. 1988. *The Writing of History*. New York: Columbia University Press.

Cheyne, J. Allan, Steve D. Rueffer, and Ian R. Newby-Clark. 1999. "Hynagogic and Hypnopompic Hallucinations during Sleep Paralysis: Neurological and Cultural Construction of the Night-Mare." *Consciousness and Cognition* 8:319–337.

Clark, Stuart. 1997. *Thinking with Demons: The Idea of Witchcraft in Early Modern Europe*. Oxford: Oxford University Press.

Clerq, F. S. A. de. 1890. *Bijdragen tot de Kennis der Residentie Ternate* [A contribution to insight in the realm of Ternate]. Leiden: E. J. Brill.

Clifford, James. 1988. *The Predicament of Culture: Twentieth-Century Ethnography, Literature, and Art*. Cambridge, MA: Harvard University Press.

Clifford, James, and George Marcus, eds. 1986. *Writing Culture: The Poetics and Politics of Ethnography*. Berkeley: University of California Press.

Coates, Brian, and David Bishop. 1997. *A Guide to the Birds of Wallacea: Sulawesi, the Moluccas and Lesser Sunda Islands, Indonesia*. Alderley, AU: Dove Publications.

Collins, Derek. 2008. *Magic in the Ancient Greek World*. Oxford: Wiley-Blackwell.

Collins, Elizabeth Fuller. 2007. *Indonesia Betrayed: How Development Fails*. Honolulu: University of Hawai'i Press.

Colombijn, Freek. 2007. "Toooot! Vroooom! The Urban Soundscape in Indonesia." *Sojourn: Journal of Social Issues in Southeast Asia* 22(2):255–273.

Comaroff, Jean, and John Comaroff. 1993. Introduction to *Modernity and Its Malcontents: Ritual and Power in Postcolonial Africa*, edited by J. Comaroff and J. Comaroff, xi–xxxvii. Chicago: University of Chicago Press.

——. 1999. "Occult Economies and the Violence of Abstraction: Notes from the South African Postcolony." *American Ethnologist* 26(2):279–303.

——. 2000. "Millennial Capitalism: First Thoughts on a Second Coming." *Public Culture* 12(2):291–343.

——. 2002. "Alien-Nation: Zombies, Immigrants, and Millennial Capitalism." *South Atlantic Quarterly* 101(4):779–805.

Cooper, Frederick. 2005. *Colonialism in Question: Theory, Knowledge, History*. Berkeley: University of California Press.

Corbin, Alain. 1999. *Village Bells: Sound and Meaning in the 19th-Century French Countryside*. London: Papermac.

Covarrubias, Miguel. 1937. *Island of Bali*. New York: Knopf.

Craib, Ian. 1994. *The Importance of Disappointment*. London: Routledge.

Crapanzano, Vincent. 2003. "Reflections on Hope as Category of Social and Psychological Analysis." *Cultural Anthropology* 18(1):3–32.

———. 2004. *Imaginative Horizons: An Essay in Literary-Philosophical Anthropology*. Chicago: University of Chicago Press.

Cribb, Robert, and Colin Brown. 1995. *Modern Indonesia: A History since 1945*. London: Longman.

Crick, Malcolm. 1978. *Explorations in Language and Meaning: Towards a Semantic Anthropology*. London: Malaby Press.

Csordas, Thomas. 2004. "Asymptote of the Ineffable: Embodiment, Alterity, and the Theory of Religion." *Current Anthropology* 45(2):163–185.

Dalton, Bill. 1989. *Indonesia Handbook*. 4th ed. Chico, Ca: Moon Publications.

Davidson, Jamie, and David Henley, eds. 2007. *The Revival of Tradition in Indonesian Politics: The Deployment of Adat from Colonialism to Indigenism*. London: Routledge.

Davis, Erik. 2004. *Techgnosis: Myth, Magic, and Mysticism in the Age of Information*. London: Serpent's Tail.

Davis, Michael. 2002. "Laskar Jihad and the Political Position of Conservative Islam in Indonesia." *Contemporary Southeast Asia* 24(1):12–32.

Delbourgo, James. 2006. *A Most Amazing Scene of Wonders: Electricity and Enlightenment in Early America*. Cambridge, MA: Harvard University Press.

Derrida, Jacques. 1976. *Of Grammatology*. Baltimore: Johns Hopkins University Press.

———. 1982. *Margins of Philosophy*. Chicago: University of Chicago Press.

———. 1990. "Some Statements and Truisms about Neo-Logisms: Newisms, Postisms, Parasitisms, and Other Small Seismims." In *The State of 'Theory': History, Arts, and Critical Discourse*, edited by D. Carroll, 63–95. New York: Columbia University Press.

———. 1992a. *Acts of Literature*. New York: Routledge.

———. 1992b. *Given Time: I, Counterfeit Money*. Chicago: University of Chicago Press.

———. 1993. *Aporias*. Stanford, CA: Stanford University Press.

———. 1994. *Spectres of Marx: The State of the Debt, the Work of Mourning, and the New International*. New York: Routledge.

———. 1995. *The Gift of Death*. Chicago: University of Chicago Press.

———. 2000. *Limited Inc*. Evanston, IL: Northwestern University Press.

———. 2001a. *On Cosmopolitanism and Forgiveness*. New York: Routledge Press.

———. 2001b. *Writing and Difference*. London: Routledge.

———. 2002. *Acts of Religion*. New York: Routledge.

———. 2003. "Auto-Immunity: Real and Symbolic Suicides; A Dialogue with Jacques Derrida." In *Philosophy in a Time of Terror: A Dialogue with Jürgen Habermas and Jacques Derrida*, edited by G. Borradori, 85–136. Chicago: University of Chicago Press.

———. 2005. *The Politics of Friendship*. London: Verso.

———. 2008. *Dissemination*. London: Continuum.

Descombes, Vincent. 1994. *Modern French Philosophy*. Cambridge: Cambridge University Press.

Deutscher, Penelope. 2005. *How to Read Derrida*. London: Granta Books.

Douglas, Bronwen. 2001. "From Invisible Christian to Gothic Theatre: The Romance of the Millennial in Melanesian Anthropology." *Current Anthropology* 42(5):615–650.

Douglas, Mary, ed. 1970. *Witchcraft Confessions and Accusations*. London: Tavistock.

——. 1980. *Edward Evans-Pritchard*. New York: Viking Press.

——. 1995. *Purity and Danger: An Analysis of Concepts of Pollution and Danger*. 1966. London: Routledge.

Douglas, Mary, and Aaron Wildavsky. 1982. *Risk and Culture: An Essay on the Selection of Technological and Environmental Dangers*. Berkeley: University of California Press.

Dove, Michael, ed. 1988. *The Real and Imagined Role of Culture in Development: Case Studies in Indonesia*. Honolulu: University of Hawai'i Press.

Duncan, Christopher. 2005. "The Other Maluku: Chronologies of Conflict in North Maluku." *Indonesia* 79(2):53–80.

——. 2013. *Violence and Vengeance: Religious Conflict and Its Aftermath in Eastern Indonesia*. Ithaca, NY: Cornell University Press.

Dwyer, Kevin. 1977. "On the Dialogic of Fieldwork." *Dialectical Anthropology* 2(1–4):143–151.

Echols, John, and Hassan Shadily. 1989. *Kamus Indonesia-Inggris: An Indonesian-English Dictionary*. 3rd ed. Jakarta: PT Gramedia.

Ellen, Roy. 1993a. "Anger, Anxiety, and Sorcery: An Analysis of Some Nuaulu Case Material from Seram, Eastern Indonesia." In *Understanding Witchcraft and Sorcery in Southeast Asia*, edited by C. W. Watson and R. Ellen, 81–97. Honolulu: University of Hawaii Press.

——. 1993b. Introduction to *Understanding Witchcraft and Sorcery in Southeasia*, edited by C. W. Watson and R. Ellen, 1–25. Honolulu: University of Hawai'i Press.

Elson, R. E. 2001. *Suharto: A Political Biography*. Cambridge: Cambridge University Press.

El-Zein, Amira. 2009. *Islam, Arabs, and the Intelligent World of the Jinn*. New York: Syracuse University Press.

Endicott, Kirk. 1970. *An Analysis of Malay Magic*. Oxford: Clarendon Press.

Engelke, Matthew. 2002. "The Problem of Belief: Evans-Pritchard and Victor Turner on 'the Inner Life'." *Anthropology Today* 18(6):3–8.

Engelke, Matthew, and Matt Tomlinson, eds. 2007. *The Limits of Meaning: Case Studies in the Anthropology of Christianity*. New York: Berghahn Books.

Englund, Harri. 1996. "Witchcraft, Modernity, and the Person: The Morality of Accumulation in Central Malawi." *Critique of Anthropology* 16(3):257–279.

Englund, Harri, and James Leach. 2000. "Ethnography and the Meta-Narratives of Modernity." *Current Anthropology* 41(2):225–248.

Evans-Pritchard, E. E. 1935. "Witchcraft." *Africa* 8(4):417–422.

——. 1937. *Witchcraft, Oracles and Magic among the Azande*. Oxford: Clarendon Press.

——. 1976. *Witchcraft, Oracles and Magic among the Azande*. Abridged with an introduction by Eva Gillies. Oxford: Clarendon Press.

Evers, Pieter. 1995. "Preliminary Policy and Legal Questions about Recognizing Traditional Land in Indonesia." *Ekonesia: A Journal of Indonesian Human Ecology* 3:1–24.

Favret-Saada, Jeanne. 1980. *Deadly Words: Witchcraft in the Bocage*. Cambridge: Cambridge University Press.

Fenna, Donald. 2002. *A Dictionary of Weights, Measures, and Units (Oxford Reference Online)*. Edited by D. Fenna. Oxford: Oxford University Press.

Ferguson, James. 1990. *The Anti-Politics Machine: "Development," Depoliticization and Bureaucratic Power in Lesotho*. Cambridge: Cambridge University Press.

Ferme, Mariane. 2001. *The Underneath of Things: Violence, History, and the Everyday in Sierra Leone*. Berkeley: University of California Press.

Festinger, Leon, Henry Riecken, and Stanley Schachter. 1956. *When Prophecy Fails*. Minneapolis: University of Minnesota Press.

Figal, Gerald. 1999. *Civilization and Monsters: Spirits of Modernity in Meiji Japan*. Durham, NC: Duke University Press.

Fine, Gail. 1992. "Inquiry in the *Meno*." In *The Cambridge Companion to Plato*, edited by R. Kraut, 200–226. Cambridge: Cambridge University Press.

———. 2000. "Descartes and Ancient Skepticism: Reheated Cabbage?" *Philosophy Review* 109(2):195–234.

Flint, Valerie, et al. 1999. *The Athlone History of Witchcraft and Magic in Europe*. Vol. 2, *Ancient Greece and Rome*. London: Athlone Press.

Florida, Nancy. 2008. "A Proliferation of Pigs: Specters of Monstrosity in Reformation Indonesia." *Public Culture* 20(3):497–530.

Foley, William. 2000. "The Languages of New Guinea." *Annual Review of Anthropology* 29:357–404.

Fortgens, J. 1917. *Kitab Arti Logat Ternate: Woordenlijst van het Ternatesch (met Maleisch—Nederlandsch Verklaringen)* [Dictionary of the Ternatan dialect: Word list in Ternatan with a Malay-Dutch translation]. Semarang: Van Dorp.

Forth, Gregory. 1989. "Animals, Witches, and Wind: Eastern Indonesian Variations on the 'Thunder Complex'." *Anthropos* 84:89–106.

———. 1993. "Social and Symbolic Aspects of the Witch among the Nage of Eastern Indonesia." In *Understanding Sorcery and Witchcraft in Southeast Asia*, edited by C. W. Watson and R. Ellen, 99–122. Honolulu: University of Hawai'i Press.

Foucault, Michel. 1980. *Power/Knowledge: Selected Interviews and Other Writings, 1972–1977*. Brighton: Harvester.

———. 1981. "Is It Useless to Revolt?" Translated by James Bernauer. *Philosophy and Social Criticism* 8(1):8.

———. 1983. "The Subject and Power." In *Michel Foucault: Beyond Structuralism and Hermeneutics*, edited by P. Rabinow and H. Dreyfus, 208–226. Chicago: University of Chicago Press.

———. 1988a. "The Ethic of Care of the Self as a Practice of Freedom." In *The Final Foucault*, edited by J. Bernauer and D. Rasmussen, 1–20. Cambridge, MA: MIT Press.

———. 1988b. "Technologies of the Self." In *Technologies of the Self: A Seminar with Michel Foucault*, edited by M. Luther, H. Gutman, and P. Hutton, 16–49. Amherst: University of Massachusetts Press.

———. 1988c. *The Use of Pleasure*. Vol. 2 of *The History of Sexuality*. London: Penguin Books.

Fox, James. 1973. "On Bad Death and the Left Hand: A Study of Rotinese Symbolic Inversion." In *Right and Left: Essays on Dual Symbolic Classification*, edited by R. Needham, 342–368. Chicago: University of Chicago Press.

———. 1980. Introduction to *The Flow of Life: Essays on Eastern Indonesia*, edited by J. Fox, 1–18. Cambridge, MA: Harvard University Press.

———. 1988. *To Speak in Pairs: Essays on the Ritual Languages of Eastern Indonesia*. Cambridge: Cambridge University Press.

———. 1989. "F. A. E. van Wouden (1908–1987): A Tribute." *Bijdragen tot de Taal-, Land- en Volkenkunde* 145(4):425–429.

———, ed. 1990. *Flow of Life: Essays on Eastern Indonesia*. Cambridge, MA: Harvard University Press.

———, ed. 1993. *Inside Austronesian Houses: Perspectives on Domestic Designs for Living*. Canberra: Research School of Pacific Studies (ANU).

Fox, James, and Clifford Sather, eds. 1996. *Origins, Ancestry, and Alliance: Explorations in Austronesian Ethnography*. Canberra: Australian National University.

Franke, Richard. 1972. "Limited Good and Cargo Cult in Indonesian Economic Development." *Journal of Contemporary Asia* 2(4):366–381.

Gable, Eric. 2002. "Beyond Belief? Play, Scepticism, and Religion in a West African Village." *Social Anthropology* 10(1):41–56.

Gadamer, Hans-Georg. 2013. *Truth and Method*. London: Bloomsbury.

Gardner, Don. 2010. "The Scope of 'Meaning' and the Avoidance of Sylleptical Reason: A Plea for Some Modest Distinctions." *Ethnos* 75(3):346–375.

Geertz, Clifford. 1973. "Thick Description: Towards an Interpretive Theory of Culture." In *The Interpretation of Cultures*, edited by C. Geertz, 3–30. New York: Basic Books.

Geschiere, Peter. 1997. *The Modernity of Witchcraft: Politics and the Occult in Postcolonial Africa*. Charlottesville: University of Virginia Press.

———. 1998. "Globalization and the Power of Indeterminate Meaning: Witchcraft and Spirit Cults in Africa and East Asia." *Development and Change* 29(4):811–837.

———. 2003. "Witchcraft as the Dark Side of Kinship: Dilemmas of Social Security in New Contexts." *Etnofoor* 16(1):43–61.

———. 2011. "Witchcraft and Modernity: Perspectives from Africa and Beyond." In *Sorcery in the Black Atlantic*, edited by L. N. Parés and R. Sansi, 233–258. Chicago: University of Chicago Press.

———. 2013. *Witchcraft, Intimacy, and Trust: Africa in Comparison*. Chicago: University of Chicago Press.

Giddens, Anthony. 1991. *Modernity and Self-Identity: Self and Society in the Late Modern Age*. Cambridge: Polity Press.

Gillard, Patrick. 2003. *Cambridge Advanced Learner's Dictionary*. Cambridge: Cambridge University Press.

Good, Byron. 1994. *Medicine, Rationality, and Experience: An Anthropological Perspective*. Cambridge: Cambridge University Press.

Grosz, Elizabeth. 1994. *Volatile Bodies: Towards a Corporeal Feminism*. Sydney: Allen and Unwin.

Gueselaw, Verdianus. 2010. "Halmahera bebas dari 'suanggi', mungkinkah? Analisis sosial-antropologis dan refleksi teologi kontekstual" [Halmahera free from *suanggi*—Is it possible? Social anthropological analysis and contextual theological reflections]. Master's thesis, Universitas Kristen Indonesia, Tomohon.

Guinness, Patrick. 1994. "Local Society and Culture." In *Indonesia's New Order: The Dynamics of Socio-Economic Transformation*, edited by H. Hill, 267–304. Sydney: Allen & Unwin.

Haga, Anton. 1884a. *Nederlandsch Nieuw Guinea en de Papoesche Eilanden: Historische Bijdrage 1500–1883*. Vol. 1. Batavia: W. Buining & Co.

———. 1884b. *Nederlandsch Nieuw Guinea en de Papoesche Eilanden: Historische Bijdrage 1500–1883*. Vol. 2. Batavia: W. Buining & Co.

Haire, James. 1981. *The Character and Theological Struggle of the Church in Halmahera, Indonesia, 1941–1979*. Frankfurt am Main: Verlag Peter Lang.

Harrison, Jane. 1961. *Prolegomena to the Study of Greek Religion*. London: Merlin Press.

Hasan, Noorhaidi. 2002. "Faith and Politics: The Rise of the Laskar Jihad in the Era of Transition in Indonesia." *Indonesia* 73 (April):145–169.

Havilland, William A., et al. 2011. *Cultural Anthropology: The Human Challenge*. 13th ed. Belmont, CA: Wadsworth.

Hecht, Jennifer Michael. 2010. *Doubt: A History*. New York: HarperCollins.

Hefner, Robert, ed. 1993. *Conversion to Christianity: Historical and Anthropological Perspectives on a Great Transformation*. Berkeley: University of California Press.

——. 2000. "Suharto's Maluku Legacy." *Wall Street Journal Interactive Edition*, 16 August.

——. 2002. "Global Violence and Indonesian Muslim Politics." *American Anthropologist* 104(3):754–765.

Heidegger, Martin. 1962. *Being and Time*. Oxford: Blackwell.

Held, G. 1957. *The Papuas of Waropen* [The Papuan people on Waropen]. Koninklijk Instituut voor Taal-, Land- en Volkenkunde Translation Series 2. The Hague: Martinus Nijhoff.

Heller, Agnes. 1984. *Everyday Life*. London: Routledge and Keegan Paul.

Herriman, Nicholas. 2010. "The Great Rumor Mill: Gossip, Mass Media, and the Ninja Fear." *Journal of Asian Studies* 69(3):723–748.

Hertz, Robert. 1960. *Death and the Right Hand*. London: Cohen and West.

Heryanto, Ariel. 1988. "The Development of 'Development'." *Indonesia* 46:1–21.

——. 1999. "Where Communism Never Dies: Violence, Trauma, and Narration in the Last Cold War Capitalist Authoritarian State." *International Journal of Cultural Studies* 2(2):147–177.

——. 2006. *State Terrorism and Political Identity in Indonesia: Fatally Belonging*. Milton Park and New York: Routledge.

Herzfeld, Michael. 2004. "Intimating Culture: Local Contexts and International Power." In *Off Stage, On Display: Intimacy and Ethnography in the Age of Public Culture*, edited by A. Shryock, 317–335. Stanford, CA: Stanford University Press.

——. 2005. *Cultural Intimacy: Social Poetics in the Nation-State*. 2nd ed. New York: Routledge.

——. 2009. "Convictions: Embodied Rhetorics of Earnest Belief." In *Culture and Rhetorics*, edited by I. Strecker and S. A. Tyler, 182–206. New York: Berghahn.

Heyne, K. 1950. *De Nuttige Planten van Indonesië*. Vol. 2. The Hague: N.V. Uitgeverij W. van Hoeve.

Hill, Hal. 1992. "Survey of Recent Developments." *Bulletin of Indonesian Economic Studies* 28(2):3–41.

——, ed. 1994. *Indonesia's New Order: The Dynamics of Socio-Economic Transformation*. Sydney: Allen & Unwin.

Hollis, Martin, and Steven Lukes, eds. 1982. *Rationality and Relativism*. Oxford: Basil Blackwell.

Honna, Jun. 2001. "Military Ideology in Response to Democratic Pressure during the Late Suharto Era: Political and Institutional Contexts." In *Violence and the State in Suharto's Indonesia*, edited by B. Anderson, 54–89. Ithaca, NY: Southeast Asia Program, Cornell University.

Horridge, Adrian. 1978. *The Design of Planked Boats of the Moluccas*. Maritime Monograph and Report 38. London: National Maritime Museum.

Howell, Signe, ed. 1996. *For the Sake of Our Future: Sacrificing in Eastern Indonesia*. Leiden: Research School CNWS.

Hueting, Anton. 1925. "Djailolo, Sangadji's en Andil op Halmahera" [Jailolo, Sangadjis, and the Just King on Halmahera]. *Adatrechbundels* 24:49–51.

———. 1935. *Geschiedenis der Zending op het Eiland Halmahera. Utrechtse Zendings-Vereeininging* [The history of the mission on the island of Halmahera: The Utrecht Mission Union]. Oegstgeest: Zendingsbureau.

Ionescu, Christina. 2007. *Plato's Meno: An Interpretation*. Plymouth: Lexington Books.

Irwin, Terence. 1979. *Plato's Moral Theory: The Early and Middle Dialogues*. Oxford: Clarendon Press.

Jackson, Michael. 1989. *Paths towards a Clearing: Radical Empiricism and Ethnographic Inquiry*. Bloomington: Indiana University Press.

———. 2000. *At Home in the World*. Durham, NC: Duke University Press.

Johnson, Barbara. 2008. Introduction to *Dissemination*, edited by J. Derrida, vii-xxxv. London: Continuum.

Jorgensen, Dan. 1980. "What's in a Name: The Meaning of Meaninglessness in Telefolmin." *Ethos* 8(4):349–366.

Kahn, Miriam. 1986. *Always Hungry, Never Greedy: Food and the Expression of Gender in a Melanesian Society*. Cambridge: Cambridge University Press.

Kamma, Freerk. 1948–49. "De Verhouding tussen Tidore en de Papoese Eilanden in Legende en Historie, III-IV" [Relations between Tidore and the islands of Papua in myth and history]. *Indonesie* 2:177–188; 256–275.

———. 1972. *Koreri: Messianic Movements in the Biak-Numfor Culture Area*. Koninklijk Instituut voor Taal-, Land- en Volkenkunde Translations Series, no. 15. The Hague: Martinus Nijhoff.

Kapferer, Bruce. 1997. *The Feast of the Sorcerer: Practices of Consciousness and Power*. Chicago: University of Chicago Press.

———. 2001. "Anthropology: The Paradox of the Secular." *Social Anthropology* 9(3):341–344.

———, ed. 2003. *Beyond Rationalism: Rethinking Magic, Witchcraft and Sorcery*. New York: Berghahn Books.

Kartodirjo, S. 1973. *Protest Movements in Rural Java*. Kuala Lumpur: Oxford University Press.

———. 1984. *Ratu Adil*. Jakarta: Penerbit Sinar Harapan.

Katoppo, E. 1984. *Nuku: Riwayat Perjuangan Kemerdekaan di Maluku Utara, 1780–1805* [Nuku: An account of the struggle for independence in North Maluku, 1780–1805]. Jakarta: Penerbit Sinar Harapan.

Keane, Webb. 1997. "Knowing One's Place: National Language and the Idea of the Local in Eastern Indonesia." *Cultural Anthropology* 12(1):37–63.

———. 2007. *Christian Moderns: Freedom and Fetish in the Mission Encounter*. Berkeley: University of California Press.

Kendall, Laurel. 2010. *Shamans, Nostalgias, and the IMF: South Korean Popular Religion in Motion*. Honolulu: University of Hawai'i Press.

Kipp, Rita Smith. 1993. *Dissociated Identities: Ethnicity, Religion, and Class in an Indonesian Society*. Ann Arbor: University of Michigan Press.

Kleinman, Arthur. 1997. "'Everything That Really Matters': Social Suffering, Subjectivity, and the Remains of Human Experience in a Disordered World." *Harvard Theological Review* 90(3):315–335.

Klima, Alan. 2002. *The Funeral Casino: Meditation, Massacre, and Exchange with the Dead in Thailand*. Princeton, NJ: Princeton University Press.

Klinken, Gerry van. 2007. *Communal Violence and Democratization in Indonesia: Small Town Wars*. New York: Routledge.

Kluckhohn, Clyde. 1944. *Navaho Witchcraft*. Cambridge, MA: Peabody Museum of American Archaeology and Ethnology.

Knauft, Bruce. 1985. *Good Company and Violence: Sorcery and Social Action in a Lowland New Guinea Society*. Berkeley: University of California Press.

———, ed. 2002a. *Critically Modern: Alternatives, Alterities, Anthropologies*. Bloomington: Indiana University Press.

———. 2002b. *Exchanging the Past: A Rainforest World of Before and After*. Chicago: Chicago University Press.

Kniphorst, J. 1883. "Een Korte Terugblik op de Molukken en Noordwestelijk Nieuw-Guinea" [A brief retrospect on the Moluccas and Northwest New Guinea]. *De Indische Gids* 5(2):465–526.

Kofman, Sarah. 1988. "Beyond Aporia?" In *Post-Structuralist Classics*, edited by A. Benjamin, 7–44. London: Routledge.

Kordt Højbjerg, Christian. 2002a. "Inner Iconoclasm: Forms of Reflexivity in Loma Rituals of Sacrifice." *Social Anthropology* 10(1):57–75.

———. 2002b. "Religious Reflexivity: Essays on Attitudes to Religious Ideas and Practice." *Social Anthropology* 10(1):1–10.

Kors, Alan Charles, and Edward Peters, eds. 2001. *Witchcraft in Europe, 400–1700: A Documentary History*. Philadelphia: University of Pennsylvania Press.

Koselleck, Reinhart. 1985. *Futures Past: On the Semantics of Historical Time*. Cambridge, MA: MIT Press.

Krige, J. D. 1947. "The Social Function of Witchcraft." *Theoria* 1:8–21.

Kristeva, Julia. 1982. *Powers of Horror: An Essay on Abjection*. New York: Columbia University Press.

Kumar, Krishnan. 1995. *From Post-Industrial to Post-Modern Society: New Theories of the Contemporary World*. Oxford: Blackwell.

Kwon, Heonik. 2008. *Ghosts of War in Vietnam*. Cambridge: Cambridge University Press.

Lacan, Jacques. 1977. *The Mirror Stage as Formative of the Function of the I as Revealed in Psychoanalytic Experience*. In *Écrits: A Selection*, translated by Alan Sheridan, 8–29. New York: W. W. Norton.

Laderman, Carol. 1993. *Taming the Wind of Desire: Psychology, Medicine, and Aesthetics in Malay Shamanistic Performance*. Berkeley: University of California Press.

Laidlaw, James. 2010. "Agency and Responsibility: Perhpas You Can Have Too Much of a Good Thing." In *Ordinary Ethics: Anthropology, Language, and Action*, edited by M. Lambek, 143–184. New York: Fordham University Press.

Lambek, Michael. 2003. *A Reader in the Anthropology of Religion*. Oxford: Wiley-Blackwell.

Lash, Scott. 1999. *Another Modernity, a Different Rationality*. Oxford: Blackwell.

Latour, Bruno. 1991. "Technology Is Society Made Durable." In *A Sociology of Monsters: Essays on Power, Technology and Domination*, edited by J. Law, 103–131. London: Routledge.

———. 1993. *We Have Never Been Modern*. New York: Harvester/ Wheatsheaf.

———. 1996. *Aramis, or the Love of Technology*. Cambridge, MA: Harvard University Press.

———. 2005. *Reassembling the Social: An Introduction to Actor-Network-Theory*. Oxford: Oxford University Press.

———. 2010. *On the Modern Cult of the Factish Gods*. Durham, NC: Duke University Press.

Latourette, Kenneth Scott. 1959. *Christianity in a Revolutionary Age: A History of Christianity in the Nineteenth and Twentieth Centuries.* Vol. 2, *The Nineteenth Century in Europe: The Protestant and Eastern Churches.* New York: Harper & Brothers.

Lattas, Andrew. 1998. *Cultures of Secrecy: Reinventing Race in Bush Kaliai Cargo Cults.* Madison: University of Wisconsin Press.

Lawrence, Peter. 1964. *Road Belong Cargo.* Manchester: Manchester University Press.

Lear, Jonathan. 2006. *Radical Hope: Ethics in the Face of Cultural Devastation.* Cambridge, MA: Harvard University Press.

Leirissa, R. 1986. "Factors Conducive to the Raja Jailolo Movement in North Maluku (1790–1832)." In *Agrarian History,* vol. 1 *of Papers of the Fourth Indonesian-Dutch History Conference, Yogyakarta 1983,* edited by S. Kartodirdjo, 96–111. Yogyakarta: Gadjah Mada University Press.

———. 1990. "Masyarakat Halmahera dan Raja Jailolo: Studi Tentang Sejarah Masyarakat Maluku Utara" [The people of Halmahera and the ruler of Jailolo: A study of the history of North Maluku]. PhD diss., Universitas Indonesia.

Levinas, Emmanuel, and Richard Kearney. 1986. "Dialogue with Emmanuel Levinas." In *Face to Face with Levinas,* edited by R. Cohen, 13–34. New York: SUNY Press.

Lévi-Strauss, Claude. 1955. "The Structural Study of Myth." *Journal of American Folklore* 68(270):428–444.

———. 1963. "The Sorcerer and His Magic." In *Structural Anthropology,* edited by C. Lévi-Strauss, 161–180. New York: Basic Books.

———. 1987. *Anthropology and Myth: Lectures, 1951–1982.* Oxford: Blackwell.

Lévy-Bruhl, Lucien. 1966. *How Natives Think.* New York: Washington Square Press.

Li, Tania Murray. 2000. "Articulating Indigenous Identity in Indonesia: Resource Politics and the Tribal Slot." *Comparative Studies in Society and History* 42(1):149–179.

———. 2007. *The Will to Improve: Governmentality, Development, and the Practice of Politics.* Durham, NC: Duke University Press.

Liddell, Henry George, and Robert Scott. 1990. *A Greek-English Lexicon.* Oxford: Clarendon Press.

Lieban, Richard. 1967. *Cebuano Sorcery: Malign Magic in the Philippines.* Berkeley: University of California Press.

Lindstrom, Lamont. 1993. *Cargo Cult: Strange Stories of Desire from Melanesia and Beyond.* Honolulu: University of Hawai'i Press.

Lingis, Alphonso. 1985. "Phenomenology of the Face and Carnal Intimacy." In *Libido: The French Existential Theories,* edited by A. Lingis, 58–73. Bloomington: Indiana University Press.

———. 1994. *Foreign Bodies.* New York: Routledge.

LiPuma, Edward. 2001. *Encompassing Others: The Magic of Modernity in Melanesia.* Ann Arbor: University of Michigan Press.

Lowenthal, David. 1999. *The Past Is a Foreign Country.* Cambridge: Cambridge University Press.

Lucy, Niall. 2004. *A Derrida Dictionary.* Oxford: Blackwell Publishing.

Lukito, Ratno. 2012. *Legal Pluralism in Indonesia: Bridging the Unbridgeable.* London: Routledge.

Maan, G. 1912. "Hoe Bringen Wij Onzen Christenen eenig Begrip bij van het Heilsfeit der Verzoening?" [How do we teach our Christians the meaning of the salvation that comes from reconciliation?]. *Mededeelingen vanwege het Nederlandsche Zendelinggenootschap* 56:214–226.

——. 1920. "De Geestelijke Achtergrond van Ons Zendingswerk" [The spiritual background of our mission work]. *Mededeelingen: Tijdschrift voor Zendingswetenschap* 64:336–351.

——. 1940. *Boelisch-Nederlandsch Woordenlijst met Nederlandsch-Boelisch Register* [Buli-Dutch word list with a Dutch-Buli index]. Bandoeng: A. C. Nix & Co.

——. 1951. *Proeve van een Bulisch Spraakkunst* [A sample of the Buli language]. Verhandelingen van het Koninklijk Instituut voor Taal-, Land- en Volkenkunde, Deel 10. The Hague: 's-Gravenhage.

Magany, M. T. 1984. *Bahtera Injil di Halmahera* [The ark of the gospel in Halmahera]. Ambon: Gereja Masehi Injil di Halmahera (The Christian Evangelical Church in Halmahera).

Maier, Henk. 1997. "Maelstrom and Electricity: Modernity in the Indies." In *Outward Appearances: Dressing State and Society in Indonesia*, edited by H. Schulte Nordholt, 181–197. Leiden: Koninklijk Instituut voor Taal-, Land- en Volkenkunde.

Malinowski, Bronislaw. 1948. *Magic, Science and Religion, and Other Essays*. Boston: Beacon Press.

Martodirdjo, Haryo. 1991. "Orang Tugutil di Halmahera: Struktur dan Dinamika Sosial Masyarakat Penghuni Hutan" [The Tugutil of Halmahera, structure and social dynamics of a forest-dwelling community]. PhD diss., University of Padjadjaran, Bandung.

Marwick, Max. 1990. "Witchcraft as a Social Strain-Gauge" (1964). In *Witchcraft and Sorcery: Selected Readings*, edited by M. Marwick, 300–313. London: Penguin.

Matthews, Gareth. 1999. *Socratic Perplexity and the Nature of Philosophy*. Oxford: Oxford University Press.

Mauss, Marcel. 1970. *The Gift: Forms and Functions of Exchange in Archaic Societies*. London: Routledge.

——. 1990. *The Gift: The Form and Reason for Exchange in Archaic Societies*. 1924. London: Routledge.

McGrane, Bernard. 1992. *Beyond Anthropology: Society and the Other*. New York: Columbia University Press.

McNeill, John. 1954. *The History and Character of Calvinism*. New York: Oxford University Press.

Mead, George Herbert. 1962. *Mind, Self, and Society from the Standpoint of a Social Behaviourist*. Vol. 1 of *Works of George Herbert Mead*. Chicago: University of Chicago Press.

Meyer, Birgit. 1999. *Translating the Devil: Religion and Modernity among the Ewe in Ghana*. London: Edinburgh University Press.

Meyer, Birgit, and Peter Pels, eds. 2003. *Magic and Modernity: Interfaces of Revelation and Concealment*. Stanford, CA: Stanford University Press.

Middleton, J., and E. H. Winter. 1963. Introduction to *Witchcraft and Sorcery in East Africa*, edited by J. Middleton and E. H. Winter, 1–26. London: Routledge and Kegan Paul.

Miedema, Jelle, Cecilia Odé, and Rien A. C. Dam, eds. 1998. *Perspectives on the Bird's Head of Irian Jaya, Indonesia*. Amsterdam: Rodopi B.V. Editions.

Mitchell, Timothy. 2002. *Rule of Experts: Egypt, Techno-Politics, Modernity*. Berkeley: University of California Press.

Miyazaki, Hirokazu. 2007. *The Method of Hope: Anthropology, Philosophy, and Fijian Knowledge*. Stanford, CA: Stanford University Press.

Moltmann, Jürgen. 2002. *Theology of Hope*. London: SCM Press.

Moore, Henrietta, and Todd Sanders. 2001a. "Magical Interpretations and Material Realities: An Introduction." In *Magical Interpretations, Material Realities: Modernity, Witchcraft and the Occult in Postcolonial Africa*, edited by H. Moore and T. Sanders, 1–27. London: Routledge.

——, eds. 2001b. *Magical Interpretations, Material Realities: Modernity, Witchcraft and the Occult in Postcolonial Africa*. London: Routledge.

Morfit, Michael. 1981. "Pancasila: The Indonesian State Ideology according to the New Order Government." *Asian Survey* 21(8):838–851.

Morris, Rosalind. 2000a. *In the Place of Origins: Modernity and Its Mediums in Northern Thailand*. Durham, NC: Duke University Press.

——. 2000b. "Modernity's Media and the End of Mediumship? On the Aesthetic Economy of Transparency in Thailand." *Public Culture* 12(2):457–475.

——. 2007. "Legacies of Derrida: Anthropology." *Annual Review of Anthropology* 36: 355–389.

Morrow, Glenn R. 1960. *Plato's Cretan City: A Historical Interpretation of the Laws*. Princeton, NJ: Princeton University Press.

Morus, Iwan Rhys. 1998. *Frankenstein's Children: Electricity, Exhibition and Experiment in Early Nineteenth-Century London*. Princeton, NJ: Princeton University Press.

Mrázek, Rudolf. 1997. "'Let Us Become Radio Mechanics': Technology and National Identity in Late-Colonial Netherlands East Indies." *Comparative Studies in Society and History* 39(1):3–33.

——. 2002. *Engineers of Happy Land: Technology and Nationalism in a Colony*. Princeton, NJ: Princeton University Press.

Munn, Nancy. 1986. *The Fame of Gawa: A Symbolic Study of Value Transformation in a Massim (Papua New Guinea) Society*. Durham, NC: Duke University Press.

——. 1990. "Constructing Regional Worlds in Experience: Kula Exchange, Witchcraft and Gawan Local Events." *Man*, n.s. 25(1):1–17.

Needham, Rodney. 1976. "Skulls and Causality." *Man*, n.s. 11(1):71–88.

Nicholson, Trish. 1994. "Institution Building: Examining the Fit between Bureaucracies and Indigenous Systems." In *The Anthropology of Organizations*, edited by S. Wright, 68–84. London: Routledge.

Niehaus, Isak. 2001. *Witchcraft, Power and Politics: Exploring the Occult in the South African Lowveld*. London: Pluto Press.

——. 2012. *Witchcraft and a Life in the New South Africa*. Cambridge: Cambridge University Press.

——. 2013. "Confronting Uncertainty: Anthropology and Zones of the Extraordinary." *American Ethnologist* 40(4):651–660.

Nye, David. 1992. *Electrifying America: Social Meanings of a New Technology*. Cambridge, MA: MIT Press.

——. 1994. *American Technological Sublime*. Cambridge, MA: MIT Press.

Ogden, Daniel. 2002. *Magic, Witchcraft, and Ghosts in the Greek and Roman Worlds: A Sourcebook*. Oxford: Oxford University Press.

O'Neill, John. 2004. *Five Bodies: Refiguring Relationships*. 1985. Thousand Oaks, CA: Sage.

Ortner, Sherry. 1984. "Theory in Anthropology since the Sixties." *Comparative Study of Society and History* 26(1):126–166.

Otto, Ton, and Nils Bubandt, eds. 2010. *Experiments in Holism: Theory and Practice in Contemporary Anthropology*. Oxford: Wiley-Blackwell.

Parés, Luis Nicolau, and Roger Sansi, eds. 2011. *Sorcery in the Black Atlantic*. Chicago: University of Chicago Press.

Pearce, Charles E. M., and Frances M. Pearce. 2010. *Oceanic Migration: Paths, Sequences, Timing and Range of Prehistoric Migration in the Pacific and Indian Oceans*. Dordrecht and New York: Springer.

Pedersen, Morten Axel. 2011. *Not Quite Shamans: Spirit Worlds and Political Lives in Northern Mongolia*. Ithaca, NY: Cornell University Press.

Pelkmans, Mathijs, ed. 2011a. *Ethnographies of Doubt: Faith and Uncertainty in Contemporary Societies*. London: Tauris Academic Studies.

———. 2011b. "Outline for an Ethnography of Doubt." In *Ethnographies of Doubt: Faith and Uncertainty in Contemporary Societies*, edited by M. Pelkmans, 1–42. London: Tauris Academic Studies.

Pemberton, John. 1994. *On the Subject of "Java."* Ithaca, NY: Cornell University Press.

Perkins, Tara. 2006. "Eramet Bids for Weda Bay Minerals, Halmahera." ResourceInvestor.com, 15 March 2006, http://www.resourceinvestor.com/pebble.asp?relid = 17906.

Peterson, Nicolas. 1993. "Demand Sharing: Reciprocity and the Pressure for Generosity among Foragers." *American Anthropologist* 95(4):860–874.

Piot, Charles. 2010. *Nostalgia for the Future: West Africa after the Cold War*. Chicago: University of Chicago Press.

Platenkamp, Jos. 1988. "Tobelo: Ideas and Values of a North Moluccan Society." PhD diss., University of Leiden.

———. 1992. "Transforming Tobelo Ritual." In *Understanding Rituals*, edited by D. de Coppet, 74–96. London: Routledge.

Plato. 1964. *Plato's Meno*. With introduction and commentary by R. S. Bluck. Cambridge: Cambridge University Press.

Politis, Vasilis. 2004. *Routledge Philosophy Guidebook to Aristotle and Metaphysics*. London and New York: Routledge.

———. 2008. "Aporia and Searching for the Early Plato." In *Remembering Socrates: Philosophical Essays*, edited by L. Judson and V. Karamanes, 88–109. Oxford: Oxford University Press.

Pratt, Mary Louise. 1986. "Fieldwork in Common Places." In *Writing Culture: The Poetics and Politics of Ethnography*, edited by J. Clifford and G. E. Marcus, 27–50. Berkeley: University of California Press.

Protevi, John. 1994. *Time and Exteriority: Aristotle, Heidegger, Derrida*. Cranbury: Associated University Presses.

Rabinow, Paul. 1989. *French Modern: Norms and Forms of the Social Environment*. Cambridge, MA: MIT Press.

Rafael, Vicente. 1988. *Contracting Colonialism: Translation and Christian Conversion in Tagalog Society under Early Spanish Rule*. Durham, NC: Duke University Press.

Rapaport, Herman. 1989. *Heidegger and Derrida: Reflections on Time and Language*. Lincoln: University of Nebraska Press.

Redding, Sean. 2006. *Sorcery and Soverignty: Taxation, Power, and Rebellion in South Africa, 1880–1963*. Athens: Ohio University Press.

Reid, Anthony. 1995. "Maluku Revisited." *Bijdragen to de Taal-, Land- en Volkenkunde* 151(1):132–135.

Rejali, Darius. 2007. *Torture and Democracy*. Princeton, NJ: Princeton University Press.

Rescher, Nicolas. 2001. *Paradoxes: Their Roots, Range, and Resolution*. Chicago: Open Court.

Reynolds, Jack. 2005. *Merleau-Ponty and Derrida: Intertwining Embodiment and Alterity*. Athens: Ohio University Press.

Ricklefs, Merle. 2008. *A History of Modern Indonesia since c. 1200*. 4th ed. Houndsmills, UK: Palgrave Macmillan.

Robbins, Joel. 2003. "What Is a Christian? Notes toward an Anthropology of Christianity." *Religion* 33(3):191–199.

———. 2004. *Becoming Sinners: Christianity and Moral Torment in a Papua New Guinean Society*. Berkeley: University of California Press.

———. 2007. "Continuity Thinking and the Problem of Christian Culture: Belief, Time, and the Anthropology of Christianity." *Current Anthropology* 48(1):5–38.

Robbins, Joel, and Alan Rumsey. 2008. "Introduction: Cultural and Linguistic Anthropology and the Opacity of Other Minds." *Anthropological Quarterly* 81(2):407–420.

Rödlach, Alexander. 2006. *Witches, Westerners, and HIV: AIDS and Cultures of Blame in Africa*. Walnut Creek, CA: Left Coast Press.

Romberg, Raquel. 2003. *Witchcraft and Welfare: Spiritual Capital and the Business of Magic in Modern Puerto Rico*. Austin: University of Texas Press.

Ruel, Malcolm. 2003. "Christians as Believers." In *A Reader in the Anthropology of Religion*, edited by M. Lambek, 99–113. Oxford: Wiley-Blackwell.

Rutherford, Blair. 1999. "To Find an African Witch: Anthropology, Modernity and Witch-Finding in North-West Zambia." *Critique of Anthropology* 19(1):89–109.

Rutherford, Danilyn. 2000. "The White Edge of the Margin: Textuality and Authority in Biak." *American Ethnologist* 27(2):312–339.

———. 2003. *Raiding the Land of the Foreigners: The Limits of the Nation on a Indonesian Frontier*. Princeton, NJ: Princeton University Press.

———. 2006. "The Bible Meets the Idol: Writing and Conversion in Biak, Irian Jaya, Indonesia." In *The Anthropology of Christianity*, edited by F. Cannell, 240–272. Durham, NC: Duke University Press.

Sahlins, Marshall. 1987. *Islands of History*. London: Tavistock Publications.

Sanders, Todd. 2003. "Reconsidering Witchcraft: Postcolonial Africa and Analytic (Un)Certanties." *American Anthropologist* 105(2):338–352.

———. 2008. "Buses in Bongoland: Seductive Analytics and the Occult." *Anthropological Theory* 8(2):107–132.

Sansi, Roger, and Luis Nicolau Parés. 2011. "Introduction: Sorcery in the Black Atlantic." In *Sorcery in the Black Atlantic*, edited by L. N. Parés and R. Sansi, 1–18. Chicago: University of Chicago Press.

Sartre, Jean-Paul. 1948. *The Emotions: Outline of a Theory*. New York: Philosophical Library.

Schafer, Murray. 1994. *The Soundscape: Our Sonic Environment and the Tuning of the World*. Rochester: Destiny Books.

Schieffelin, Bambi. 1990. *The Give and Take of Everyday Life: Language Socialization of Kaluli Children*. Cambridge: Cambridge University Press.

Schielke, Samuli. 2012. "Being a Non-Believer in a Time of Islamic Revival: Trajectories of Doubt and Certainty in Contemporary Egypt." *International Journal of Middle East Studies* 44:301–320.

Schram, Ryan. 2010. "Witches' Wealth: Witchcraft, Confession, and Christianity in Auhelawa, Papua New Guinea." *Journal of the Royal Anthropological Institute* 16:726–742.

Schrauwers, Albert. 2003. "Through a Glass Darkly: Charity, Conspiracy, and Power in New Order Indonesia." In *Transparency and Conspiracy: Ethnographies in the New*

*World Order*, edited by H. West and T. Sanders, 125–147. Durham, NC: Duke University Press.

Schulte Nordholt, Henk, and Gerry van Klinken. 2007. Introduction to *Renegotiating Boundaries: Local Politics in Post-Suharto Indonesia*, edited by H. Schulte Nordholt and G. v. Klinken, 1–29. Leiden: KITLV Press.

Schulte Nordholt, Herman G. 1971. *The Political System of the Atoni of Timor.* The Hague: Martinus Nijhoff.

Schwarz, Adam. 1994. *A Nation In Waiting: Indonesia in the 1990s.* Sydney: Allen & Unwin.

Scott, James. 1985. *Weapons of the Weak: Everyday Forms of Resistance.* New Haven, CT: Yale University Press.

———. 1998. *Seeing Like a State: How Certain Schemes to Improve the Human Condition Have Failed.* New Haven, CT: Yale University Press.

Seale, Clive, and Sjaak van der Geest. 2004. "Good and Bad Death: Introduction." *Social Science and Medicine* 58(5):883–885.

Shaw, Rosalind. 1997. "The Production of Witchcraft/Witchcraft as Production: Memory, Modernity, and the Slave Trade in Sierra Leone." *American Ethnologist* 24(4):856–876.

———. 2002. *Memories of the Slave Trade: Ritual and Historical Imagination in Sierra Leone.* Chicago: University of Chicago Press.

Shweder, Richard. 1997. "The Surprise of Ethnography." *Ethos* 25(2):152–163.

Sidel, John. 2007. *Riots, Pogroms, Jihads: Religious Violence in Indonesia.* Singapore: NUS Press.

Siegel, James. 1986. *Solo in the New Order: Language and Hierarchy in an Indonesian City.* Princeton, NJ: Princeton University Press.

———. 1998. *A New Criminal Type in Jakarta: Counter-Revolution Today.* Durham, NC: Duke University Press.

———. 2001. "Suharto, Witches." *Indonesia* 71:27–78.

———. 2002. "Some Views of East Javanese Sorcery." *Archipel* 64:163–180.

———. 2006. *Naming the Witch.* Stanford, CA: Stanford University Press.

Skeat, Walter William. 2010. *Malay Magic: Being an Introduction to the Folklore and Popular Religion of the Malay Peninsula.* 1900. Avaliable at http://www.forgottenbooks.org.

Smith, Daniel Jordan. 2001. "Ritual Killing, 419, and Fast Wealth: Inequality and the Popular Imagination in Southeastern Nigeria." *American Ethnologist* 28(4):803–826.

Smith, James Howard. 2008. *Bewitching Development: Witchcraft and the Reinventions of Development in Neoliberal Kenya.* Chicago: University of Chicago Press.

Smith, Wilfred Cantwell. 1978. *The Meaning and End of Religion.* 1959. London: S.P.C.K.

Solomonova, E., et al. 2008. "Sensed Presence as a Correlate of Sleep Paralysis Distress, Social Anxiety and Waking State Social Imagery." *Consciousness and Cognition* 17(1):49–63.

Sonius, H. W. J. 1981. Introduction to *Van Vollenhoven on Indonesian Adat Law*, edited by J. F. Holleman, xxix–lxvii. The Hague: Martinus Nijhoff.

Sontag, Susan. 1988. *Aids and Its Metaphors.* New York: Farrar, Straus and Giroux.

Sperber, Dan. 1996. *On Anthropological Knowledge.* Cambridge: Cambridge University Press.

Spyer, Patricia. 1996. "Diversity with a Difference: *Adat* and the New Order in Aru (Eastern Indonesia)." *Cultural Anthropology* 11(1):25–50.

———. 2000. *The Memory of Trade: Modernity's Entanglements on an Eastern Indonesian Island.* Durham, NC: Duke University Press.

Stange, Paul. 1986. "Legitimate Mysticism in Indonesia." *RIMA* 20(2):76–117.

Stasch, Rupert. 2001. "Giving Up Homicide: Korowai Experience of Witches and Police (West Papua)." *Oceania* 72(1):33–52.

———. 2009. *Society of Others: Kinship and Mourning in a West Papuan Place*. Berkeley: University of California Press.

Steedly, Mary Margaret. 2000. "Modernity and the Memory Artist: The Work of Imagination in Highland Sumatra, 1947–1995." *Comparative Studies in Society and History* 42(4):811–846.

Stein, Rebecca, and Philip Stein. 2008. *The Anthropology of Religion, Magic, and Witchcraft*. Boston: Pearson.

Stephen, Michele. 1987. *Sorcerer and Witch in Melanesia*. Melbourne: Melbourne University Press.

Stephens, Walter. 2002. *Demon Lovers: Witchcraft, Sex and the Crisis of Belief*. Chicago: University of Chicago Press.

Stocker, Barry. 2006. *Routledge Philosophy Guidebook to Derrida on Deconstruction*. London: Routledge.

Stoller, Paul, and Cheryl Olkes. 1989. *In Sorcery's Shadow: Memoirs of Apprenticeship among the Songhay of Niger*. Chicago: University of Chicago Press.

Strassler, Karen. 2004. "Gendered Visibilities and the Dream of Transparency: The Chinese-Indonesian Rape Debate in Post-Suharto Indonesia." *Gender and History* 16(3):689–725.

———. 2010. *Refracted Visions: Popular Photography and National Modernity in Java*. Durham, NC: Duke University Press.

Suryakusuma, Julia. 1996. "The State and Sexuality in New Order Indonesia." In *Fantazising the Feminine in Indonesia*, edited by L. Sears, 92–119. Durham, NC: Duke University Press.

Szerszynski, Bronislaw. 2005. *Nature, Technology, and the Sacred*. Oxford: Blackwell Publishing.

Tambiah, Stanley. 1983. "On Flying Witches and Flying Canoes: The Coding of Male and Female Values." In *The Kula: New Perspectives on Massim Exchange*, edited by J. Leach and E. Leach, 171–200. Cambridge: Cambridge University Press.

———. 1990. *Magic, Science, Religion, and the Scope of Rationality*. The Lewis Henry Morgan Lectures 1984. Cambridge: Cambridge University Press.

Tan, Kenneth Paul. 2010. "Pontianaks, Ghosts and the Possessed: Female Monstrosity and National Anxiety in Singapore Cinema." *Asian Studies Review* 34(1):151–170.

Tarling, Nicholas. 1999. "The Establishment of the Colonial Regimes." In *The Cambridge History of Southeast Asia*, vol. 2, pt. 1, *From c. 1800 to the 1930s*, edited by N. Tarling, 1–74. Cambridge: Cambridge University Press.

Taussig, Michael. 1987. *Shamanism, Colonialism, and the Wild Man: A Study in Terror and Healing*. Chicago: University of Chicago Press.

———. 1993. *Mimesis and Alterity: A Particular History of the Senses*. New York: Routledge.

———. 1999. *Defacement: Public Secrecy and the Labor of the Negative*. Stanford, CA: Stanford University Press.

———. 2003. "Viscerality, Faith, and Skepticism: Another Theory of Magic." In *Magic and Modernity: Interfaces of Revelation and Concealment*, edited by B. Meyer and P. Pels, 272–306. Stanford, CA: Stanford University Press.

Taylor, Charles. 2007. *A Secular Age*. Cambridge, MA: The Belknap Press of Harvard University Press.

Taylor, Paul. 1990. *The Folk Biology of the Tobelo People: A Study in Folk Classification.* Smithsonian Contributions to Anthropology, no. 34. Washington, DC: Smithsonian Institution Press.

Taylor, Timothy. 2010. *The Artificial Ape: How Technology Changed the Course of Human Evolution.* New York: Palgrave Macmillan.

Teljeur, Dirk. 1985. "Het Symbolische Systeem van de Gimán van Zuid-Halmahera." PhD diss., Free University of Amsterdam.

———. 1990. *The Symbolic System of the Giman of South Halmahera.* Dortrecht: Foris Publications.

Tempo. 2011. "Indonesian Financial Review, Edisi 6, July 2011." *Tempo* 4–10 (July):1–18.

tenZynthoff, Gerrit. 1987. *Sources of Secession: The Netherlands Hervormde Kerk on the Eve of the Dutch Migration to the Midwest.* Grand Rapids, MI: Wm. B. Eerdmans.

Thomas, Keith. 1973. *Religion and the Decline of Magic.* London: Penguin.

Thompson, Damien. 1996. *The End of Time: Faith and Fear in the Shadow of the Millennium.* London: Minerva.

Thompson, Emily. 2002. *The Soundscape of Modernity: Architectural Acoustics and the Culture of Listening in America, 1900–1933.* Cambridge, MA: MIT Press.

Tiele, P. 1877. "De Europeërs in den Maleischen Archipel: Eerste Gedeelte 1509–1529." *Bijdragen to de Taal-, Land- en Volkenkunde* 25:321–420.

Tomko, Michael. 2007. "Politics, Performance, and Coleridge's 'Suspension of Disbelief'." *Victorian Studies* 49(2):241–249.

Tomlinson, Matt, and Matthew Engelke. 2007. "Meaning, Anthropology, Christianity." In *The Limits of Meaning: Case Studies in the Anthropology of Christianity*, edited by M. Engelke and M. Tomlinson, 1–37. New York: Berghahn.

Trevor-Roper, Hugh. 1969. *The European Witch-Craze of the Sixteenth and Seventeenth Centuries.* Harmondsworth, UK: Penguin.

Trouillot, Michel-Rolphe. 1991. "Anthropology and the Savage Slot: The Poetics and Politics of Otherness." In *Recapturing Anthropology*, edited by R. Fox, 17–44. Santa Fe, NM: School of American Research.

Tsing, Anna. 1993. *In the Realm of the Diamond Queen: Marginality in an Out-of-the-Way Place.* Princeton, NJ: Princeton University Press.

———. 2005. *Friction: An Ethnography of Global Connections.* Princeton, NJ: Princeton University Press.

———. 2010. "Worlding the Matsutake Diaspora: Or, Can Actor-Network Theory Experiment with Holism?" In *Experiments with Holism: Theory and Practice in Contemporary Anthropology*, edited by T. Otto and N. Bubandt, 47–66. Oxford: Wiley-Blackwell.

Valeri, Valerio. 2000. *The Forest of Taboos: Morality, Hunting, and Identity among the Huaulu of the Moluccas.* Madison: University of Wisconsin Press.

van der Veer, Peter, ed. 1996. *Conversions to Modernities: The Globalisation of Christianity.* London: Routledge.

van Fraassen, Chris. 1994. Review of *The World of Maluku*, by Leonard Andaya. *Bijdragen to de Taal-, Land- en Volkenkunde* 150(2):423–426.

———. 1995. "A Rejoinder to Reid." *Bijdragen to de Taal-, Land- en Volkenkunde* 151(2):289–291.

Vial, Virginie, and Julien Hanoteau. 2010. "Corruption, Manufacturing Plant Growth, and the Asian Paradox: Indonesian Evidence." *World Development* 38(5):693–705.

Visser, Leontine. 1989. *My Rice Field Is My Child: Social and Territorial Aspects of Swidden Cultivation in Sahu, Eastern Indonesia.* Verhandelingen van het Koninklijk Instituut voor Taal-, Land- en Volkenkunde, no. 136. Dordrecht: Foris Publications.

Visser, Leontine, and C. Voorhoeve. 1987. *Sahu-Indonesian-English Dictionary and Sahu Grammar Sketch*. Verhandelingen van het Koninklijk Instituut voor Taal-, Land- en Volkenkunde, no. 126. Dordrecht: Foris Publications.

Vivieros de Castro, Eduardo. 1998. "Cosmological Deixis and Amerindian Perspectivism." *Journal of the Royal Anthropological Institute*, n.s. 4(3):469–488.

von der Dunk, Hermann. 1978. "Conservatism in the Netherlands." *Journal of Contemporary History* 13(4):741–763.

Voorhoeve, C. 1983. "Some Observations on North-Moluccan Malay." In *Studies in Malay Dialects*, pt. 2, edited by J. Collins, 1–13. Jakarta: NUSA.

Ward, W. R. 2002. *The Protestant Evangelical Awakening*. Cambridge: Cambridge University Press.

Warneck, Johannes. 1908. *Die Lebenskräfte des Evangeliums: Missionserfahrungen innerhalb des animistischen Heidentums*. Berlin: M. Warneck.

Watson, C., and R. Ellen, eds. 1993. *Understanding Witchcraft and Sorcery in Southeast Asia*. Honolulu: University of Hawai'i Press.

West, Harry. 2005. *Kupilikula: Governance and the Invisible Realm in Mozambique*. Chicago: University of Chicago Press.

———. 2007. *Ethnographic Sorcery*. Chicago: University of Chicago Press.

White, Luise. 2000. *Speaking with Vampires: Rumor and History in Colonial Africa*. Berkeley: University of California Press.

Whitman, James Q. 2008. *The Origins of Reasonable Doubt: Theological Roots of the Criminal Trial*. New Haven, CT: Yale University Press.

Whyte, Susan Reynolds. 1997. *Questioning Misfortune: The Pragmatics of Uncertainty in Eastern Uganda*. Cambridge: Cambridge University Press.

Widjojo, Muridan S. 2008. *The Revolt of Prince Nuku: Cross-Cultural Alliance-Making in Maluku, c. 1780–1810*. Tanap Monographs on the History of Asian-European Interaction. Leiden: Brill.

Wilden, Anthony. 1980. *System and Structure: Essays in Communication and Exchange*. London: Tavistock Publications.

Wilken, G. A. 1912. *Verspreide Geschriften: Geschriften over Animisme en daarmede verband houdende Geloofsuitingen. Deel III*. The Hague: van Dorph and Co.

Willerslev, Rane. 2007. *Soul Hunters: Hunting, Animism, and Personhood among the Siberian Yukaghirs*. Berkeley: University of California Press.

Wilson, Bryan, ed. 1974. *Rationality*. Oxford: Basil Blackwell.

Wilson, Chris. 2005. "The Ethnic Origin of Religious Conflict in North Maluku, 1999–2000." *Indonesia* 79(1):69–91.

Winch, Peter. 1964. "Understanding a Primitive Culture." *American Philosophical Quarterly* 1:307–324.

Winzeler, Robert. 2008. *Anthropology and Religion: What We Know, Think, and Question*. Plymouth, UK: Altamira Press.

Wittgenstein, Ludwig. 1969. *On Certainty*. Oxford: Basil Blackwell.

Woodward, Mark. 2011. *Java, Indonesia, Islam*. Heidelberg: Springer.

The World Bank. 2003. *Decentralizing Indonesia: A Regional Public Expenditure Review; Overview Report*. Washington, DC: The World Bank.

Worsley, Peter. 1970. *The Trumpet Shall Sound: A Study of "Cargo" Cults in Melanesia*. 1957. London: Paladin.

Wouden, F. van. 1983. "Local Groups and Double Descent in Kodi, West Sumba." In *Structural Anthropology in the Netherlands: A Reader*, edited by P. E. de Josselin de Jong,

183–222. Koninklijk Instituut voor Taal-, Land- en Volkenkunde, Translation Series 17. Dordrecht: Foris Publications.

Wurm, S. A., and S. Hattori. 1983. *Language Atlas of the Pacific Area.* Part 2, *Japan Area, Taiwan (Formosa), Philippines, Mainland and Insular South-East Asia.* Canberra: Australian Academy of the Humanities.

Young, Michael. 1972. *Fighting with Food: Leadership, Values and Social Control in a Massim Society.* Cambridge: University of Cambridge Press.

# Index

- In Britain people didn't stop believing in w-
tery just tolerated inconsistent beliefs
about it

$$\boxed{\text{Malleable Malefice}}$$

- Aporia
- these were expressed at times in drama
  - eg. Late Lancashire Witches

- paper contains a series of illustrations
of doubt ① Tuzon Davies, multiple narratives (doubt about what really happened)
② Jeanne Favret-Saada Babine story
(doubt about who to blame, who is the
witch)
③ Wesley Kempe (ability to manipulate
the story of witchcraft - doubt again
about who to blame, and a journey
of role-playing)
  ↳ role-playing is key
    theatre can help us allow belief
    + doubt to exist in tension

Printed in Great Britain
by Amazon